Esquer Family Genealogy
A Journey through the Generations:

From the Basque Country of Spain to the

Northwestern Frontiers of Sinaloa, Sonora,

and Alta California,

New Spain and Mexico

1550~1850

Research Collaboration
Pamela Koppel
Ana Irene Peña Tamayo
José Antonio Rivera Fernández
Joaquín Blanco

Compilation
Stella Cardoza

Contents

Preface

The *Esquer Family Genealogy* is a companion volume to the book, *Esquer Family Chronicles, 1600–1800: From the Basque Country to the Northwestern Frontier of New Spain*, written and published by Stella Cardoza in 2014 (a new and revised edition is available). With the use of archival sources, the book documents episodes in the lives of the Esquer family as told within the context of historical events. The original book was written with contributions from the present team of online collaborators; as a team we embraced the idea of creating an eight-generation genealogy. Our goal has been to allow any interested persons to trace their own family back in time and to possibly connect with one or more ancestors we have identified in the genealogy.

As collaborators in the creation of the Esquer family genealogy we have spent years, and countless hours, hunting through records in search of the descendants of Blas Esquer and Catalina Landa, progenitors of the Esquer family tree. The search was a true labor of love as we sought nuggets of information hidden in various archives in Spain and Mexico (much of it online). The preponderance of what we found was contained in the parish sacramental records in what was then part of New Spain, present day Mexico. We wish to acknowledge the free genealogical service provided by the Church of Jesus Christ of Latter-Day Saints (LDS) at their Family History Centers and online at familysearch.org. Their online Mexico Catholic Church Records search was vital to the publication of the Esquer family genealogy.

As time went by with research, we were blessed with a wealth of information. So much so, that we finally set at date to cease research and prepare the genealogy for publication. When genealogical research came to a necessary conclusion, 1,006 direct descendants and their spouses had been discovered and included in the genealogy. It is by no means a complete picture of the Esquer family tree. As incomplete as it is, however, the genealogy offers a glimpse of family life through eight generations, with known children of the eighth generation annexed, covering a period of about 300 years.

Each record we consulted was read and interpreted by at least three members of our collaborative team. The records, written in seventeenth and eighteenth centuries Spanish cursive, were often very difficult to decipher and interpret because of the poor quality of the record. We were fortunate that two of our team members are native speakers of the Spanish language and have first-hand knowledge of Hispanic and Catholic Church customs and traditions. They were the ones whose opinion we relied most upon when making a final determination relating to any question of translation and interpretation. Although we have made every effort possible to ensure accuracy, we reserve credit to ourselves for any errors and oversights.

Every name that appears in the genealogy represents a once-living person whose stories, however sparse, we are attempting to tell. While engaged in reading what the archives have revealed to us, we have been witnesses to their lives. We have in a sense been present ourselves to share in happy family celebrations of baptisms and marriages, and the grieving times endured by the death and burial of loved ones. We now invite you to pull back the curtain of time and personally become acquainted with those ancestors whose lives have provided us with an unbroken chain to present times.

Stella Cardoza
Pamela Koppel
Ana Irene Peña Tamayo
José Antonio Rivera Fernández
Joaquín Blanco

Pam Koppel

I began my personal journey of discovery almost forty years ago. Family history research was something I undertook alone during stolen moments between work and family responsibilities. As passionate as I was about unearthing my ancestors, something was missing—I didn't have like-minded companions with whom to share my experiences. The invention of the internet changed all that. I met fellow researchers on genealogical online message boards and they injected new life to my research. Online communication made collaboration possible among the five of us named as authors of the Esquer genealogy. We became cyber associates who willingly shared data and argued the fine points of contents found in archival documents. Chief among us was the late Pam Koppel. It was she who named our team "the five amigos."

Our lives crossed paths in 2007 with an introductory email on my part. Pam and I began exchanging limited bits of information until we were each convinced of our mutual trust. Pam was a consummate genealogist who had over the years created an enviable database that she freely shared with those who had earned her confidence. She was a skeptic with a heart of gold.

Although we never personally met, our online relationship continued to grow. We became friends through almost daily emails that included not only genealogical subjects, but also personal and family news. The first thing I did on most mornings was to open my emails to see what Pam had to say about genealogical questions we had been debating. I could expect to receive tables, charts, and methodical explanations supporting her positions. And, much of the time we would later agree that she was right.

When Pam unexpectedly passed away two years ago it left a big void in my life. In the approximately ten years we had worked together we had formed a bond that energized us both to keep looking for elusive ancestors to add to our respective family trees. Pam had no familial ties to the families recorded in the Esquer genealogy. Yet, she so willingly spent countless hours over ten years searching for the benefit of others. I say without hesitation that most of the entries in the Esquer genealogy can be attributed to Pam's tireless efforts in searching the records.

Pam touched my life in ways she will never know. She was passionate about family history and resolute in her work, yet modest when given credit for her contributions. I am grateful for Pam's friendship and for the years we spent together while engaged in blissful family history pursuits. She is sorely missed.

Stella Cardoza

Reader's Guide

Genealogy Reporting Style

RootsMagic, a database genealogical software program, was used to enter all the family information gathered during years of research. For purposes of publication, RootsMagic was used to generate the written format used in this book. It is in the Register Style of the New England Historic Genealogical Society (NEHGS). The genealogy is grouped by generation through the eighth generation. The offspring of the eighth generation are listed, though often with limited information.

Numbering System

Children are listed in birth order. Each child's name is preceded with a lower-case Roman numeral. Children who later married were assigned Arabic numbers placed to the left of Roman numeral. For example:

First Generation
   1. Blas Esquer

    Blas Esquer and Catalina Landa had the following children:

       i. María Esquer was born about 1580 in Isaba.

  2   ii. Salvador Esquer (Landa), was born about 1588 in Isaba; he married María Delgada, about 1628 in Spain. [Expanded information is provided in the section "Second Generation."]

In the example, Blas Esquer, the progenitor of the Esquer family, was assigned the identification number "1." His daughter María was assigned the lower-case Roman numeral "i" and her younger brother Salvador Esquer (Landa) was assigned "ii." These Roman numerals enumerate the children in birth order. María is shown not to have been married or having had children, so she was not assigned an Arabic identification number. Juan Salvador is shown to have been married. For this reason, He was assigned identification number "2." His marriage information and a listing of his children are shown with expanded narrative under the section titled "Second Generation." This numbering system continues through the eighth generation. The offspring of the eighth generation were not assigned identification numbers because there is not a ninth generation in the genealogy for reference.

In the example below, Juan Salvador Esquer was assigned the identification number "6." Following his name is an upline in parenthesis. This indicates that Juan Salvador Esquer is in the fourth generation, Salvador his father is in the third generation, Salvador his grandfather is in the second generation and his great grandfather Blas is in the first generation. The uplines provide a road map through the generations that always end with the progenitor, Blas Esquer:

6. Juan Salvador Esquer (Salvador-3, Salvador-2, Blas-1).

Note: There are cases where the parents of an individual both descend from the progenitor, Blas Esquer. In those cases, the individual, even if lacking a spouse or children, is listed twice and assigned an identification number. Normally, unmarried descendants are not carried forward nor assigned Arabic numbers. This is an exception. In the case shown here, José Fernando Trinidad Martínez Mendívil (#144) was the son of Juan José Timoteo Martínez Mendívil (#123) and María Loreto González Barreda (#85). The uplines of each parent lead directly to Blas Esquer (#1):

123. Juan José Timoteo Martínez Mendívil (Petra María Gertrudis Féliz-7, Manuela Antonia Esquer-6, Joseph Cayetano-5, Juan Salvador-4, Salvador-3, Salvador-2, Blas-1), María Raphaela Esquer-6, Francisco Joseph-5, Juan Salvador-4, Salvador-3, Salvador-2, Blas-1).

85. María Loreto González Barreda (María Raphaela Esquer-6, Francisco Joseph-5, Juan Salvador-4, Salvador-3, Salvador-2, Blas-1).

Placement of Individuals in the Genealogy

The method used to place individuals in the genealogy involved civil and sacramental records. A person was added when a record provided clear proof of parentage that demonstrated a direct link to the genealogy's progenitor, Blas Esquer. When the parentage of an individual was not directly identified in the written records, that person was only placed in the genealogy if there was enough indirect evidence to justify inclusion. Indirect evidence might be through documented family connections by way of siblings, uncles, aunts, or cousins. When a person was placed in the genealogy with only indirect evidence of parentage, justification is provided. The Esquer genealogy is a reference document that should be used as a guide for readers to make their own decisions about family connections after consulting the records cited.

Social Class and Caste Designations

During the colonial period, Spanish America was governed by a caste system that determined a person's place in society. One was identified in official and church records as belonging to one caste or another, starting with a person's baptismal record. At the top of the social hierarchy were *españoles*: peninsular Spaniards (those born in Spain) followed by Creoles (persons born in Spanish America of ancestors who emigrated from Spain). The commonly used lower castes in the Northwestern frontier of Sinaloa and Sonora included Indians and black African slaves and the racial mixtures: mestizo (*español*/Indian), mulatto (*español*/African), *coyote* (Indian/mestizo). The caste system was fluid and situational. In some cases, persons within the same family could have distinct castes assigned to them. This situation might be attributed to facial and physical features by the official making the determination, or it might be self-identification of individuals themselves. The sacramental records of the provinces of Sinaloa and Sonora seldom use the term "mestizo." It might be that actual mestizos were recorded as *coyotes* and mulattos. One must keep in mind that social identification in civil and church records reflected policies of local authorities. They could differ between Mexico City and the northwestern provinces of Sonora, Sinaloa, and the Californias.

Most of the persons identified in the Esquer family genealogy were racially classified in the records as "*españoles*." This identifies them as born in New Spain of Spanish ancestors (Creoles). Peninsular Spaniards were sometimes identified in the records as "*españoles*" with a notation about their Spanish province of origin. Peninsular Spaniards, even on the frontier, maintained the highest status in the social hierarchy. In order to avoid repetition, the term "*español/la*" was not extracted from the documents. In cases where a person's race or caste differed it was recorded.

Honorifics and Titles

Unless otherwise noted, persons named in the Esquer genealogy were *hidalgos*, members of the lower, untitled nobility. This status allowed them to use the honorifics "*don*" and "*doña*." These honorifics are assumed but were not individually recorded to avoid repetition. Titles of honor or rank were used for persons who held government, military, and religious positions.

Spelling Practices

The Royal Spanish Academy in Madrid (Real Academia Española), Spain, was established in 1713 under King Philip V to establish rules for the Spanish language. The first orthography of the Spanish language was published in 1741, and the first dictionary of the Spanish Language—*Diccionario de la Real Academia Española*—was published in 1780.

Most of the records consulted in this genealogy were created prior to the rules established by the Royal Spanish Academy and thus reflect often confusing variations as to how individuals are identified. As an example, the spelling of "Joseph" became "José" when names where standardized. Many of the sacramental records of the Catholic Church contain archaic Roman spellings of personal names. The following letters were sometimes used interchangeably: "b" and "v;" "c" and "s," "s" and "z and "y" and "I," "x" and "j." Although proper genealogical practice is to spell names as shown on the record, the spelling of names found in the records consulted have sometimes been standardized to conform with current usage. Some examples of spelling variations where the given names were for the most part standardized include Bibiana to Viviana; Cefarina to Sefarina; Ynez to Ines; and Xavier to Javier. Exceptions occur when the original spelling for an individual's name was constant in the records.

Infants were given their full names at baptism. The names are often long compounds. They were sometimes named after the saint whose feast day happened to fall on the infant's birthdate. Children were also named after their parents and grandparents, and sometimes after their godparents. Many infants were given the first names "María" and "José," as their official names which always remained on the record. Those first names might later be dropped in everyday use. It would not be unusual for every daughter in a family unit to have "María" as a first name. In practice, individuals usually used only one given name in daily life, yet that name could change over the life-span of a person. The preferred practice seemed to be the adoption of the second given name in daily use, but that was not always the case. It was also common for parents to confer the same full name to an infant that was previously held by a deceased child. In situations where an infant was not expected to survive, the baptismal record in place of a given name would simply state that the infant was a *párvulo/la*, a small child.

Naming Practices, Surnames

During the Spanish colonial period legal and sacramental records used only paternal surnames when identifying a person. Maternal surnames were not affixed as they are today in Spanish-speaking countries. The exception in the Esquer genealogy is the surname "Ymaz y Esquer." In this case, the paternal and maternal surnames were combined and passed on to the succeeding generation. Compounded names were used during that time to enhance the status of the family.

The family surnames that appear in the Esquer genealogy provide examples as to how surname usage evolved over time. During the colonial period surnames were often compounded and joined by the Spanish nobiliary article "de." About the time that Mexico was seeking its independence from Spain in the early nineteenth century, compound names and the particle "de" fell out of favor. The name "Martínez de Mendívil," for example, was shortened to "Martínez Mendívil" or simply "Martínez." It was not unusual for members of the same family unit to identify themselves, or be identified by a scribe, with any variation of a surname. In some cases, the original surname might not be recognized by future generations. For example, "Gastélum" might be written as "Castélum" and "Castelo." The records show that full siblings sometimes carried variant spellings of their paternal surname.

Women, regardless of marital status, maintained their paternal surname. In cases where a child was born out of wedlock, and the father was not identified, the infant was recorded with only the mother's surname and classified as "*hijo/ja natural*" in the baptismal entry.

The System of Compadrazo

The system of *compadrazo* is about fictive kinships and social networks, and an extension of the definition of family. The selection of baptismal and matrimonial godparents (*padrinos*) is a great honor. Persons who serve as a *padrinos* or *madrinas* become "*compadres*" (literally, co-parents) within an extended family unit. As part of the extended family, all parties share a special symbiotic bond and a life-long commitment of loyalty. Those who act as *padrinos* in the genealogy are relatives, including parents, grandparents, aunts, uncles, and siblings. *Padrinos* also include business associates and close friends. The terms *"padrino and madrina"* are used in the Esquer family genealogy to emphasize the importance of this Hispanic tradition—being a godparent meant more than simply standing witness to the sacraments of baptism and marriage.

Examining a Family's Social and Economic Status

The contents of sacramental church records provide insight into the social and economic status of family members. Over the course of time the fortunes of the Esquer and related families rose and fell, depending on the condition of mining and ranching activities. War, droughts, and disease all took their toll. Some branches of the family were able to recover while others fell into poverty. The Esquer family genealogy provides a road map of the family's fortunes. While reading through the genealogy, one can discern social networks by examining who the *padrinos* and witnesses were in baptisms and marriages. The genealogy contains information from burial records that often tell of the deceased person, and his or her family's, economic condition. Burials, the final chapter in a person's life, paint a picture of both wealth and poverty. All this is evident in the price and location of the burial site and the purchase of funeral services that denote wealth and status.

Conclusion

Although every effort was made to maintain accuracy in translation, transcription, and interpretation, errors and omissions remain. The Esquer family genealogy is only the introduction to the family's past. It now rests on others to enhance the work that is here presented.

Source Abbreviations

AGI	Archivo General de Indias (Seville, Spain)
AGN	Archivo General de la Nación (Mexico City, Mexico)
AHAD	Los Archivos Históricos del Arzobispado de Durango
AHP	Archivo de Hidalgo del Parral (Parral, Mexico)
AHPS	Archivo Histórico Provincial de Sevilla
ARGN	Archivo General de Navarra (Pamplona, Spain)
ECPP	Early California Population Project Database, Huntington Library (http://missions.huntington.org/SimpleQuery)
EIFA	Esquer Ibarra Family Archives (Tijuana, Baja California, Mexico)
PARES	Portal de Archivos Españoles (online archive)

Contents of the Mexican Catholic Church Records

Most of the information for the Esquer genealogy was taken from sacramental records of the Catholic Church. Records at the local parish level constitute most of the cited references, but some are from the diocese or archdiocese where the local parish was then located. The church records cited were baptisms, marriage information, marriages, and burials. Sacraments of the Catholic Church are governed by canon law so some of the types of information gathered by parish priests remains unchanged to this day. Over time, however, the sacramental records display the traditions of the period in which they were written. Information taken from church records in this book reflect the traditions of the Spanish colonial period in New Spain and the early years of the Mexican Republic.

Baptismal Records

It was the custom to baptize children soon after they were born. If it appeared that the infant might not survive, the waters of baptism were poured on the child immediately after birth by a parent or godparent. If the infant survived, he or she would later be administered the holy oils at a formal baptismal ceremony at the church. It was customary to sometimes not name the infant at baptism if he or she was near death. The infant was simply identified as "*párvulo/la*," a small child.

Baptismal records provided the following information:

Location and date of baptism

Name of the child

Racial identification (social identity, *casta*)

Declaration of legitimacy (the parents were legally married in the Catholic Church)

Birthdate of the child, in some cases

Family's place of residence

Names, honorifics, titles, and racial and social identification of parents and *padrinos* (godparents). In some cases grandparents were named. Racial information ceased to be gathered after Mexico gained its independence in 1821.

Marriage information records are also known as pre-marriage investigations. They often contain a wealth of information of interest to family historians. Couples who planned to marry were required to petition their intentions. They had to prove that they were in good standing in the Catholic Church and that they did not have impediments to marriage. Impediments would include family relationships of blood and affinity to the fourth degree, third cousins (see marriage dispensations below), a declaration of a criminal record, and evidence that either petitioner had a living spouse that would result in an act of bigamy. Bigamy was not uncommon in the Spanish colonies. Groom candidates who were not known in the parish had to provide witnesses to attest to their eligibility to marriage. This was especially the case if the groom was from Europe and new in the area.

Marriage information records provided the following information:

Names, honorifics, titles and racial and social identification of the petitioners for marriage, their marital status (single or widowed), and place of residence. Racial information ceased to be gathered after Mexico gained its independence in 1821.

Names, honorifics, titles, and racial and social identification of parents and other named family members.

Dates of banns of marriage where anyone could come forward and provide any reason the couple should not be married. The marriage banns were announced on three separate occasions.

If this is a second marriage for either candidate, the document provides the name of the deceased spouse.

If either the bride or groom was from another parish there were documents attached that the person was in good standing in that parish. The document might also include baptismal records and dates of the banns of marriage in the other parish.

Marriage dispensations were required if the couple were related up to the fourth degree of consanguinity (blood relationship) or affinity (related through marriage). In order to demonstrate the relationships, parties provided genealogical graphs showing generational relationships up to the common ancestors. Dispensations were required when one of the candidates for marriage was from Europe. These were called "*ultramarino*," overseas dispensations. Another form of marriage dispensation was granted to wealthy and influential persons who requested that the banns of marriage be dispensed in order to expedite marriage.

After the marriage information was gathered, two to four witnesses were called to testify on behalf of the bride and groom. Information sometimes included personal information about the witness, such as residency, age, marital status and occupation. They also testified as to how long they had known the bride or groom, and if they are related to either of them.

Marriage dispensations were issued by the bishop of the diocese. A note at the end of the marriage information record provided the date of the dispensation, if it was issued, and in some cases the date of marriage. Copies of marriage dispensations were held at the parish level, sometimes found in the archives of the diocese.

Marriage Records

Marriage records provided the following information:

❖ Names of the bride and groom, parents, godparents, and witnesses; honorifics, titles, and racial and social identification of everyone named. Racial information ceased to be gathered after Mexico gained its independence in 1821.

❖ The place and date of the marriage. Sometimes ages were provided. Girls generally married between the ages of fourteen and twenty, while men married in their twenties. Some girls married as young as twelve years of age.

❖ If it was a first marriage, parental information was generally provided. If either the bride or groom were widowed it was noted.

❖ If the bride or groom were minors, it was sometimes noted that a parent gave permission.

❖ Parents proved their place of residence and it was noted if they were living or deceased.

❖ Marriage records sometimes gave the dates on which the marriage banns were announced.

❖ Couples were traditionally married at the home parish of the bride.

Burial Records

Burial records provided the following information:

❖ The deceased person's name, and date and place of burial.

❖ Racial identification (social identity, *casta*).

❖ Information about the deceased having received the last sacraments before death. Mention is sometimes made about wealthy deceased persons having special prayers (*honras*) said for the repose of his or her soul.

❖ In some cases, the person's age, place of residence and, marital status.

❖ Sometimes the cause of death and names of the surviving spouse and children are provided.

❖ At times it was noted if the deceased left a will.

❖ If the deceased was unmarried, names of parents might be provided

❖ The ceremonial items used during the funeral, the person's place of burial, and the cost.

Glossary

abogado. Lawyer, attorney.

alcalde mayor. Chief executive officer in a town or district composed of several towns.

andas. Bier with shafts to be carried on men's shoulders that were used in funeral processions.

ataúd. Casket used for burials.

bachiller. The honorific title of a parish priest. Bachelor's degree in the sciences and liberal arts.

balanzario. Official who weighed silver bars and determined the royal tax levied by the Spanish treasury on mining production.

cadaver. Corpse (see *cuerpo*).

caja, cajón. Casket used for burials (see *ataúd*).

campanas. Bells tolled during a procession or funeral service.

capa. Cape worn by prelates during a funeral procession and service.

capilla. Chapel.

capitán. In Northern New Spain, it was generally the rank bestowed on an individual who maintained a private militia.

colegio. School, seminary, or society of men of the same profession.

contador. Accountant.

copula ilicita. Illicit carnal union.

copula licita. Licit carnal union.

coro. Choir loft. Children were often buried in the church beneath the choir loft.

coyote/ta. A Spanish colonial social caste designation assigned to a person having a mixture of Spanish, Indian, and Black parentage.

cruz alta. Processional cross (possibly made of silver) mounted on a high pole that accompanied the body of the deceased in procession. This was a symbol of high social status.

cruz baja. Processional cross mounted on a low pole accompanied the body of the deceased. Mostly used by people of lower economic status.

cuerpo. Cadaver, corpse. In burial records, "*misa con cuerpo presente*," means the the body of the deceased was present during the funeral Mass. Floor or story of a structure. "*Túmulo de tres cuerpos*," signifies a three-paneled funerary structure shaped like a four-sided pyramid constructed with horizontal wooden panels and painted with religious themes. The number of panels depended on the social caliber and wealth of the deceased (see *túmulo*).

cura. Parish priest, member of the secular clergy.

doble. The toll of a passing bell in funeral processions.

dolor. Pain. In burial records, cause of death was sometimes attributed to pain in some part of the body.

doncella. Maiden, unmarried woman. The term was used in marriage information records to describe the virtues of the bride.

ensayador. Assayer who recorded, assayed, and stamped refined silver bars with an identity number and a symbol specifying quality of the ore.

escribano. Secretary or notary expert in executing documents in correct legal format.

español. In New Spain the term was used to socially identify peninsular Spaniards (Spaniards born in Spain), Creoles (Spaniards born in New Spain), and those passing as whites (*como español*).

firma. Signature.

gobernador. Governor of a region or province who was subordinate to the viceroy.

hidalgo/ga. A member of the untitled lower nobility. In theory, a "son of somebody."

honras. A set of funerary honors for the deceased in the form of ceremonies and prayers.

huérfana. Female orphan. Term used to justify a marriage dispensation when the prospective bride was poor and without parents to provide support.

incensario. The vessel in which incense is burned. It was sometimes used in funerary services as a sign of social status.

ligitimo/ma. Legitimate. Term used to identify a child born of a legal union (*hijo legitimo, hija legitima, legtitimo matrimonio*).

limosna. Charity, alms. Term used in burial records to signify the deceased required charitable donations for funeral services provided.

madrina. Godmother at baptism, matron or maid of honor at marriage. The honor is usually given to a close relative or friend.

mesa. Table. A funeral procession might contain several stops for sung responses. The deceased would be placed on a table covered in mourning cloth and surrounded by candelabras holding lit candles. The number of these stops depended on the social caliber and wealth of the deceased.

mestizo/za. A Spanish colonial social caste designation assigned to a person having a mixture of white and Indian parentage.

misa. Mass, a Catholic celebration of the Holy Eucharist.

mozo/za. A young person.

mulato/ta. A Spanish colonial social caste designation assigned to a person of mixed Spanish and Black parentage. The terms, "*esclavo/va*" or "*libre*" were often added in civil and church records to further identify the person as a slave or free person. (The sacramental books consulted to create the Esquer genealogy the term "*mulato*" was sometimes used to identify a person who is a mixture of Spanish and Indian parentage.)

natural. A person born out of wedlock, but not of an adulterous union; native, pertaining to a person's place of birth (see *original*).

notario. Secretary or scribe, attorney.

original. Native, pertaining to a person's place of origin (see *natural*).

padrino. Godfather at the sacrament of baptism and as best man at a wedding. The honor is usually given to a close relative, friend, or business associate.

padrinos. Godparents at the sacrament of baptism and marriage. Godparents become part of the extended family and assumed special roles throughout the lives of those they sponsored. The godparents named in the sacramental records can be an indicator of social status and wealth.

párvulo/la. A small child. The term was often used in burial records when a small unnamed child was buried.

presidio. A military post established for the defense of a defined area.

provincia. A large political area in the Spanish colonies under the jurisdiction of a governor.

reyno. Kingdom.

sacristán. Sacristan in a church who would in some cases function as a witness to baptisms and marriages. He was the person who is at the church to help the priest and to make sure that everything was in order. The sacristan was always present and sometimes appears as a witness to a sacramental document because that was one of his duties if called upon.

tapa. A cover. In funerary terms, the cover placed over a casket.

teniente. Lieutenant or deputy who reported to the ranking officer within a jurisdiction.

testamento. A testament (will) that was commonly dictated to a scribe when death was eminent. The testament arranged for the disposition of personal property and left instructions for funerary prayers and services.

túmulo. A paneled funerary structure shaped like a four-sided pyramid made of horizontal wooden panels painted with religious themes. The number of panels depended on the social caliber and wealth of the deceased. The structure could be disassembled and reused. (see *cuerpos*).

ultramarino. Overseas. The term was used in marriage records of New Spain to identify one of the marriage candidates (usually the groom) as a person from abroad. This would automatically require a marriage investigation as to the candidate's eligibility to marry. Following a positive investigation, a marriage dispensation would be granted by the bishop.

vecino/na. Citizen or resident of a locality, usually a property owner of a particular location. A person might be identified as "*originario*" (place of birth) and "*vecino*" (place of residency).

velación. A nuptial blessing Mass. The blessing generally took place on the same day the bridal couple exchanged marriage vows, but it was not always used. During the blessing, a veil would be placed over the shoulders of the groom and over the head of the bride and the officiating priest would celebrate Mass and recite prayers appropriate for the occasion. Nuptial blessings were prohibited during the Lenten period before Easter. This is why the matrimonial record might indicate that the couple did not received a nuptial blessing because it was prohibited.

vigilia. A funerary vigil of song and prayer held in the church for the repose of the soul of a deceased person.

Sources: Thomas C. Barnes, Thomas H. Naylor, and Charles W. Polzer, *Northern New Spain: A Research Guide* (Tucson, Arizona: the University of Arizona Press, 2016); Thomas H. Naylor, and Charles W. Polzer, *The Presidio and Militia on the Northern Frontier of New Spain: A Documentary History* (Tucson, Arizona: University of Arizona Press, 1986); Lillian Ramos Wold and Ophelia Marquez, *Compilation of colonial Spanish terms and document related phrases* (Midway City, California: SHAAR Press, 1998); María de los Ángeles Rodríguez Álvarez, *Usos y costumbres funerarias en la Nueva España* (Zamora, Mexico: El Colegio de Michoacán, 2001); Mariano Velázquez de la Cadena, Edward Gray, Juan L. Iribas, Ida Hinojosa Navarro, and Manual Blanco-González, *New Revised Velázquez Spanish and English Dictionary* (Chicago: Follett Publishing, 1964).

The Esquer Name

The name Esquer (also Ezquer) is the Castilian form of the Basque name, Ezker, a name that may have once been given to a person who was left-handed. The name derives from the Basque word "*esker*," meaning "*izquierda*" (left) in Spanish. Although the Basque language of Vasconavarro was the spoken language of the Roncal Valley until recent times, official transactions as early as the sixteenth century were written in Castilian Spanish. This explains why the signature of Blas Esquer, dated 1605 is not spelled "Ezker," but rather "Ezquer."

In order to differentiate between the generations of family members with the given name "Salvador," scribes and notaries in Seville identify the son of Blas Esquer, the family progenitor, as "Salvador Esquer Landa." His son, in turn, is identified as "Salvador Esquer Ortíz." The identifier "Landa" is Salvador Esquer's maternal surname. However, Salvador Esquer Ortiz is not identified with his maternal surname, "Delgada." It is not known where the name "Ortíz" fits into the family tree.

All the documents consulted for this family history use the spelling "Ezquer." A double "r" was added to the end of the name in the seventeenth century by Salvador Esquer Landa. This practice continued throughout the eighteenth century in New Spain. Thus, the signatures of Esquer family members from that time are written as "Ezquerr." In present-day Isaba, Spain, the name is written "Ezquer," while in Álamos, Mexico, it is "Esquer."

In order to avoid ambiguity, the Mexican spelling of the name, "Esquer" is used to tell the family's story. The maternal surname is sometimes inserted by the author to differentiate between generations of persons with the given name, "Salvador."

Source: Patrick Hanks, *Dictionary of American Family Names* (Oxford: Oxford University Press, 2003).

Map of Spain

Map of Spain displaying place names associated with persons identified in the sacramental records (prepared by Michael Malone).

Map of New Spain (partial)

Partial Map of New Spain displaying place names associated with persons identified in the sacramental records (prepared by Michael Malone).

First Generation

1. **Blas Esquer** was born about 1555 in Isaba, Navarra, Spain.

Blas Esquer and Catalina Landa were married about 1575, in Isaba.[1] The cited document stated that Blas Esquer, Escribano Real, and Catalina Landa were legally married and were the parents of Salvador Esquer Landa.

Blas died in 1605 in Isaba.[2] He left instructions for his funeral, prayers, and burial, stating that he wished to be buried in the family crypt in San Cipriano, the parish church of Isaba. He named his wife, Catalina Landa, as his *heredera universal* (universal heir) in his will, meaning she would inherit any remaining possessions after the settlement of his debts. His son Salvador and daughter María were disinherited with a variant of the legal clause in their father's will, saying they were to receive *cinco sueldos y una robada de tierra en monte común*. This is a legal rhetorical statement meaning that those so named in the will would inherit medieval coins of no value and land held in common in the community that by law cannot be given away. The only exception to the disinheritance of his children was that Salvador would receive his father's weapons, consisting of a flintlock gun, a sword, powder horn, and other related apparatus.

Blas Esquer provided for his daughter through an outright gift unrelated to his will. In a covenant dated June 14, 1605, Blas Esquer specified that out of respect and consideration for the good and laudable services that his daughter María Esquer provided him, he was giving her title to a house he owned in the town of Ansó, located in the Kingdom of Aragon. This house had at one time been gifted to Esquer by his cousin María Surio, daughter of his uncle Pedro Surio, both deceased. The gift of the house in Ansó was given to María with no restrictions. She could use the property for her sustenance in any manner she desired. María Esquer was present at the signing of the covenant, and duly accepted the gift as offered by her father.

At the time of his death in 1605, Blas Esquer was young enough to have been actively engaged in official duties as a royal scribe and notary, and in commercial transactions. He was a person who would have been highly respected in the Roncal Valley, yet he was not a wealthy man.

---

1. Petition before the Junta General del Valle de Roncal made by Salvador Esquer Ortiz for certification of nobility (hereafter Petition before the Junta General), Roncal Valley, Spain, May 12,1654–December 8, 1654, pp. 10–52, Esquer Ibarra Family Archive, Tijuana, Baja California, Mexico (hereafter EIFA).
2. Testamento de Blas Esquer, escribano real, vecino de la villa de Isaba, Roncal, March 23, 1605, escribanía de Hernando George (menor), Sección Protocolos Notariales de Roncal, 1563–1709, caja 22742/1, Archivo General de Navarra, Pamplona, Spain (hereafter ARGN).

Catalina Landa, daughter of Sancho Landa and Catalina Pérez, was born about 1557 in Isaba.

Blas Esquer and Catalina Landa had the following children:

     i.   **María Esquer** was born about 1580 in Isaba.

2   ii.   **Salvador Esquer (Landa)** was born about 1588 in Isaba and married María Delgada about 1628 in Spain.

Second Generation

2. Salvador Esquer (Landa) (Blas-1) was born about 1588 in Isaba. He is identified as Salvador Esquer Landa in legal documents to avoid confusion between himself and his son, also named Salvador Esquer. Salvador Esquer (Landa) and María Delgada were married about 1628 in Spain.[3] The cited baptismal record for their son Salvador Esquer notes that Salvador Esquer (Landa) and María Delgada were legally married.

María Delgada was born about 1592 in Spain.

Salvador Esquer (Landa) and María Delgada had one known child:

3   i.   **Salvador Esquer (Ortiz) was** born in 1630, Seville, Andalusia, Spain. He married María Enríquez de Aponte on November 16, 1664, in Seville, and died on February 1, 1697, in Mexico City, New Spain.

---

3. Petition before the Junta General, Roncal, Spain, May 12, 1654–December 8, 1654, pp. 10–52, EIFA. Laurenzo Ezquerr, abad, *vecino* of Isaba, provided marriage verification in sworn testimony.

Third Generation

3. **Salvador Esquer (Ortiz)** (Salvador-2, Blas-1) was born in 1630 in Seville, Andalusia, Spain. He was baptized on December 10, 1630, at the church of San Marcos in Seville.[4] The baptismal record for Salvador Esquer named Christóbal Galindo, *vecino* of San Gil, as his *padrino*. Salvador Esquer is sometimes identified in legal records as Salvador Esquer Ortiz in order to avoid confusion between himself and his father, Salvador Esquer (Landa).

Salvador Esquer (Ortiz) and María Enríquez de Aponte were married on November 16, 1664, at the parish church of Santa María la Mayor (also known as the Iglesia Mayor and, the Sagrario) in Seville.[5] The marriage record named Francisco Antonio de Santa Ana, Juan de Carrascosa, and Gerónimo de Bayas as witnesses to the marriage. Parents of the bridal couple were named. They received a nuptial blessing on February 5, 1665.

Salvador Esquer emigrated on July 14, 1695.[6] He set sail together with his surviving children and one servant on the *Santísimo Sacramento,* a ship in the Flota de Nueva España of 1695. (His wife, María Enríquez de Aponte died the previous year.) The fleet set sail on July 14 from the port of Cádiz and entered the port of Veracruz in New Spain on September 28 and 29, 1695.

Salvador died on February 1, 1697, at the age of sixty-seven in Mexico City. His funeral was held on February 2, 1697, at the parish church of San Miguel Arcángel in Mexico City.[7] The burial record stated that he died on February 1, and that he was the widowed husband of María Enríquez de Aponte. Salvador Esquer's date of burial was not stated, rather it is assumed based on the record's placement in the burial registry. He dictated his last will and testament on January 17, 1697, to notary Antonio de Avilés, naming his executors as Capitán Diego García Cano, and his sons Miguel and Juan Salvador Esquer. Esquer's assets were willed to all his children; he left nothing to the church for pious works. Salvador received the last sacraments of the Catholic Church before his death. He was said to have resided in a house adjacent to the Convento de San Gerónimo and was buried at the monastery of San Augustín in Mexico City.

---

4. Libro de bautismos, December 10, 1630, Registro Parroquial, Iglesia de San Marcos, Seville, p. 213, EIFA.

5. Registros de matrimonios, November 16, 1664, libro 17, folio 17, Registros Parroquiales, Iglesia del Sagrario, Seville, Spain.

6. List of passengers for the *Santísimo Sacramento*, of which Antonio de Arana was the maestre, destined for New Spain, Cádiz, July 9,1695, Contratación, 5455, N.3, R.91, Archivo General de Indias, Seville (hereafter AGI), (Portal de Archivos Españoles; hereafter PARES, http://pares.mcu.es/). July 14 was given as the date of embarkation, which may not have been the actual day of departure.

7. Defunciones de españoles 1690–1730, February 1, 1697, film 206251, images 97–98, Registros Parroquíales, Iglesia San Miguel Arcángel, Mexico City, Mexico, (FamilySearch, https://familysearch.org).

María Enríquez de Aponte, daughter of Juan Enríquez de Aponte and Francisca de Paula, was born about 1650. She died on July 6, 1694, in Seville. She was buried on July 7, 1694, at the parish church of Santa María Magdalena in Seville.[8] The burial record stated that she gave power to her husband Salvador Esquer Ortiz to create her last will and testament. María Enríquez de Aponte named her husband and Jacinto Asencio as executors. At the time of her death María lived on the Calle del Sacramento in Seville. Her funeral was very well appointed as a public show of affection and social status.

Salvador Esquer (Ortiz) and María Enríquez de Aponte had the following children:

4   i.   **María Salvadora Esquer** was born about 1665 in Seville; she married Domingo Romero y Fuentes in Spain and died on March 15, 1695, in Seville.

5   ii.   **Baltazar Joseph Esquer** was born in 1667 in Seville; he married María de Aguilar y Cueto about 1690 in Spain.

6   iii.   **Juan Salvador Esquer** was born in 1668 in Seville; he married twice: to Mathiana de Valdez in about 1688 in Mexico City and to Michaela de Amarillas in about 1696 in New Spain. He died before October 25, 1714, in Álamos, Sonora, New Spain.

7   iv.   **Agustina Salvadora Esquer** was born in 1669 in Seville. She married Francisco Antonio Florencio Mallén de Navarrete in about 1699 in New Spain and died April 9, 1722, in Álamos.

8   v.   **Miguel Salvador Esquer** was born in 1670 in Seville. He married Gertrudis de Ibarra y Valenzuela in about 1698 in New Spain and died October 28, 1758 in Culiacán, Sinaloa, New Spain.

9   vi.   **Blas Salvador Esquer** was born in 1672 in Seville. He married Josepha González de Rodero in about 1699 in New Spain and died before October 28, 1759.

10   vii.   **Teresa María Esquer** was born in 1675 in Seville. She married Francisco de la Cerda y Espíndola before 1695 in Spain.

        viii.   **Juan Manuel Esquer** was born in 1677 in Seville. He was baptized on July 8, 1677, at the church of the Sagrario in Seville.[9] The baptismal record named Juan López de Gamarra, customs collector for the Real Casa de la Contratación, as his *padrino*. Juan Manuel must not have survived childhood because his name never again was mentioned in family records.

11   ix.   **Salvadora Manuela Silvestra Esquer** was born about 1679 in Seville. She married Sebastián de Ymaz y Arbilaga on September 3, 1697, in Mexico City and died on November 10, 1708, in Mexico City.

12   x.   **Miguel Fernando Simón Esquer** was born on October 28, 1684, in Seville. He married Augustina Guillerma Romero y Fuentes in about 1712 in New Spain.

---

8. Registros de defunciones, July 7, 1694, libro 3 (1667–1701), folio 242v–243r, Registros Parroquiales, Iglesia de Santa María Magdalena, Seville, Spain.

9. Registros de bautismos, July 8, 1677 (libro 46, folio 198), Registros Parroquiales, Iglesia del Sagrario, Seville, Spain.

Fourth Generation

4. **María Salvadora Esquer** (Salvador-3, Salvador-2, Blas-1) was born about 1665 in Seville. She married Domingo Romero y Fuentes in Spain.[10] The marriage document has not been located.

María Salvadora Esquer died on March 15, 1695, in Seville.[11] At the time of her death she resided on the Calle de San Roque, located in the district of Magdalena. María Salvadora's will, dated March 3, 1695, named her father Salvador Esquer Ortiz as heir of her personal possessions. In her will she affirmed that, although she was ill, she was of sound mind to express her last testament. María Salvadora wished to be buried at her parish church and her burial should be accompanied with a sung requiem Mass and other accompaniments as convenient to the executors of her will. She left her husband a third of her holdings, debts, claims, and actions that pertained at the time of her death. This she claimed was because of the good will she held for her husband and the good company that he provided her. María Salvadora gave power to her father and husband to receive and sell her holdings and conduct financial transactions upon her death. María Salvadora claimed that she had no children and named her father as her universal heir. She also revoked all previous wills. The will was signed at the home of her father and witnessed by Lázaro Muñoz de Ayllón and Benito de Cuéllar Hidalgo. The witnesses were from the districts of Magdalena and San Vicente, respectively. She was buried on March 16, 1695, at the parish church of Santa María Magdalena in Seville.[12]

Domingo Romero y Fuentes was born about 1664 in Spain.

5. **Baltazar Joseph Esquer** (Salvador-3, Salvador-2, Blas-1) was born in 1667 in Seville. He was baptized on February 18, 1667, at the church of the Sagrario in Seville.[13]

Baltazar Joseph Esquer and María de Aguilar y Cueto were married about 1690, in Spain.[14] The cited notarial record provided proof of their marriage.

---

10. Testament of María Salvadora Esquer, Seville, March 3, 1695, escribanía de Tomás de Agredano, Sección Protocolos, libro 1, legajo 17961, folio 154r–154v; Salvador Esquer provided an inventory of the assets belonging to María [Salvadora] Esquer, Seville, March 17, 1695, escribanía de Sebastián de Santa María Ibarra, Protocolos, legajo 13052, folio 650r–652v, Archivo Histórico Provincial de Sevilla, Seville (hereafter AHPS).

11. Registros de defunciones, March 16, 1695, libro 3 (1667–1701), folio 250v, Registros Parroquiales, Iglesia de Santa María Magdalena, Seville, Spain.

12. Ibid.

13. Registros de bautismos, February 18, 1667, libro 44, folio 166, Registros Parroquiales, Iglesia del Sagrario, Seville, Spain.

14. Power given by María Enríquez de Aponte to her husband, Salvador Esquer, to dictate her last will and testament, Seville, June 13, 1694, escribanía de Sebastián de Santa María Ibarra, Protocolos, legajo 13051, folio 266, AHPS.

María de Aguilar y Cueto was born about 1669 in Spain.

Baltazar Joseph Esquer and María de Aguilar y Cueto had the following known children:

    i.   **Salvador Antonio Esquer** was born about 1693 in Seville. He professed in the Franciscan order in 1711 at the monastery of San Francisco de Mexico in Mexico City. His life as a missionary is not known.[15] His parents were named in the cited reference.

    ii.   **Pedro Antonio Esquer** was born about 1694 in Seville. He, along with his brother, professed his vows in the Franciscan Order in 1711 at the monastery of San Francisco de Mexico in Mexico City.[16] Pedro Antonio was seventeen years of age when he professed. He served as a missionary in the Spanish frontier province of New Mexico from 1724 until 1749, a total of twenty-five years.

6. **Juan Salvador Esquer** (Salvador-3, Salvador-2, Blas-1) was born in 1668 in Seville. He was baptized on February 12, 1668, at the parish church of the Sagrario in Seville.[17] His baptismal record named Andrés de León as his *padrino*.

Juan Salvador Esquer emigrated in July 1688 to New Spain, seven years before his father and siblings.[18] He was listed as the cook's helper on the Armada de Azogues. The new viceroy of New Spain, the Conde de Galve, Gaspar de la Cerda Sandoval Silva y Mendoza, was the king's representtative on the armada. It is this viceroy, who during his short reign, provided Juan Salvador Esquer official favors and granted him the order to establish the Real Casa de Ensaye (Royal Assay House) in Álamos, Sinaloa, New Spain. Although Álamos is currently in the Mexican state of Sonora, in colonial times it was in Sinaloa.

Juan Salvador Esquer and Mathiana de Valdez were married about 1688 in Mexico City.[19] The sources cited named Mathiana de Valdez as the wife of Juan Salvador Esquer. The sources reveal a petition to the authorities in Guadalajara for him to be reunited with his wife who was living in Mexico City. He was living in Guadalajara as the *teniente ensayador* (deputy assayer). Juan <u>Salvador Esquer</u> provided testimony in 1691 that he had been married to Mathiana de Valdez

15. Jim Norris, *After "the Year Eighty": The Demise of Franciscan Power in Spanish New Mexico* (Albuquerque: University of New Mexico Press, 2000), p. 168.

16. Ibid.

17. Registros de bautismos, February 12, 1668, libro 44, folio 223, Registros Parroquiales, Iglesia del Sagrario, Seville, Spain.

18. Don Gaspar de la Cerda Sandoval Silva y Mendoza, July 1, 1688, Pasajeros, L.13, E.2634, AGI (PARES, http://pares.mcu.es/); Gaspar de la Cerda Sandoval Silva y Mendoza, informational documents and passenger license to travel to New Spain, for himself, his wife and servants, Seville, July 1,1688, Contratación, 5450, N47, AGI (PARES, http://pares.mcu.es/).

19. María de la Luz Montejano Hilton, *Sagrada Mitra de Guadalajara, Antiguo Obispado de la Nueva Galicia: Expedientes de la serie de matrimonios extractos siglos XVII–XVIII*, p.4 (Mexico: Montejano Hilton, 1999); Reunión matrimonial, petition made by Juan Salvador Esquer to be reunited with his wife, as he performs the duties of *teniente ensayador* in Guadalajara, Jalisco, Mexico, August 1, 1691, film 167971, Archivo de la Sagrada Mitra en Guadalajara (FamilySearch, https:// familysearch.org).

for a period of three and one-half years. There were no known children from this marriage. Mathiana died in 1693.

Juan Salvador Esquer and Michaela de Amarillas were married about 1696, in New Spain.[20] Their matrimonial record has not been located. The cited document provided personal testimony by Juan Salvador Esquer regarding his marriage to Michaela de Amarillas.

Juan Salvador became the head of the Esquer family when his father died in 1697. Juan Salvador died before October 25, 1714, in Álamos.[21] Included in the cited letter written by Nicolás de Salas to the tithing administrators of the Archdiocese of Durango was a statement that Miguel Esquer (brother of Juan Salvador) was in default of his obligatory tithes on the production of his hacienda. The letter claimed that Juan Salvador was deceased, and that he died in Álamos. Prior to his death, he had lost most of the dowry his wife brought into the marriage. Also, the hacienda in Topia (Los Molinos) that Miguel managed was for the most part also lost. The hacienda in Topia had been used to secure Miguel's debts. Upon his death, Juan Salvador Esquer left very little to satisfy the terms of his wife's dowry, and he left nothing for his children. The author of the letter figuratively stated that the children of Juan Salvador Esquer were in a state of nakedness (poverty): *"se hallan sus hijos en cueros."*

Mathiana de Valdez was born about 1670 in New Spain. She died on January 2, 1693, in Guadalajara, Nueva Galicia, New Spain. She was buried on January 3, 1693, at the church of San Francisco in Guadalajara.[22] According to her burial record, Mathiana de Valdez was a Creole, born in Mexico City. She received the sacrament of penance before death and did not leave a will or power of attorney for a will. A vigil was held prior to her sung funeral Mass. The funeral service took place at the church of the Sagrario Metropolitano.

Michaela de Amarillas, daughter of Diego de Amarillas and Leonor López de Siqueiros, was born about 1676.

Juan Salvador Esquer and Michaela de Amarillas had the following known children:

13 i. **Juana Esquer** was born in 1698 in Culiacán; she married Joaquín Alcayde Pérez de la Puente in about 1717 in Culiacán.

14 ii. **Salvador Esquer (Amarillas)** was born in 1699 in Culiacán. He married twice: first to Andrea Mallén de Navarrete on December 2, 1725, in Álamos and then to María Rosa Nicolasa Anguís on September 8, 1736, in Álamos. He died before January 1,

20. Copies of documents relating to the passenger license to travel to New Spain for the Esquer family and claim of nobility (hereafter Copies of documents in Alcaldía de San Ildefonso), Mexico City, September 1697. These documents were presented by Juan Salvador Esquer as evidence while defending the case against Blas Esquer, McCaa reference year (hereafter year) 1705, fr. 83–131. See "Guide to the Archivo Municipal del Hidalgo de Parral, Chihuahua, México, 1631–1821" by Robert McCaa, et al. This is a guide to the microfilm of the Parral Archive held at various university libraries: El Archivo de Hidalgo del Parral, México, 1631–1821 (Parral, Mexico: Archivo) (hereafter AHP). See also the Hispanic Heritage Project website: http://hhp.org/links.html where the McCaa guide and other updated guides are available, and where digital images of documents are available online.
21. Diezmos, Nicolás de Salas, Culiacán, October 25, 1714, AHAD-04, frames 576–577, Los Archivos Históricos del Arzobispado de Durango, 1606–1899 (microfilm) (hereafter AHAD), New Mexico State University, Las Cruces.
22. Defunciones 1641–1730, January 2, 1693, film 38418, image 269, Registros parroquiales, Iglesia del Sagrario Metropolitano, Guadalajara, Jalisco, Mexico (FamilySearch, https://familysearch.org).

1762.

15   iii.   **Joseph Cayetano Esquer** was born in 1700 in Culiacán. He married María [Nicolasa]
             de Valenzuela in March 1720 Álamos and died on September 6, 1739, in Álamos.

16   iv.   **Francisco Joseph Esquer** was born about 1710. He married María Nicolasa Murillo
             on January 6, 1729, in Culiacán and died on April 16, 1752, in Álamos.

7. **Agustina Salvadora Esquer** (Salvador-3, Salvador-2, Blas-1) was born in 1669 in Seville. She
was baptized on September 7, 1669, at the church of the Sagrario in Seville.[23] The baptismal
record named Capitán Pedro Asperiqueta as her *padrino*. She emigrated on July 14, 1695.[24]
Agustina Esquer left Spain with her father and siblings on the *Santísimo Sacramento*, a ship in the
Flota de Nueva España of 1695. The fleet set sail on July 14 from the port of Cádiz and entered
the port of Veracruz in New Spain on September 28 and 29, 1695.

Agustina Salvadora Esquer and Francisco Antonio Florencio Mallén de Navarrete were
married about 1699 in New Spain.[25] Although the matrimonial record has not been located,
testimony provided by Juan Salvador Esquer in the document cited stated that Francisco Mallén
de Navarrete and Agustina Salvadora Esquer were lawfully married.

The following is evidence used to determine the paternity of those listed as children of Francisco
Mallén de Navarrete and Agustina Esquer. The marriage documents, dated November 8, 1750,
for María Theresa Mallén de Navarrete and Miguel Alexandro Rivera are notarized statements
made by the priest Bachiller Juan Antonio de Anguís claiming that María Theresa, daughter of
Vicente Mallén de Navarrete, was the granddaughter of Francisco Mallén de Navarrete.[26] Within
the matrimonial record, dated September 14, 1721, for Gaspar de los Reyes and Josefa Mendívil,
the officiating priest stated that the godparents were Vicente Joachín Mallén de Navarrete and
María Mallén de Navarrete, siblings.[27] A third piece of evidence is the December 28, 1771,
marriage document of Gabriel Antonio Mallén de Navarrete and Rita Gil Samaniego which
stated that the groom's parents were Vicente Mallén de Navarrete and María Francisca de
Amarillas.[28] These three pieces of evidence provided a high level of confidence that María Mallén
de Navarrete was the sister of Vicente and the daughter of Francisco Mallén de Navarrete and

23. Registros de bautismos, September 7, 1669 (libro 45, folio 14) Registros Parroquiales, Iglesia del Sagrario,
Seville, Spain.
24. Salvador de Ezquer, June 13, 1695, Pasajeros, L.14, E.698; Salvador Ezquer, Seville, June 24, 1695,
Contratación, 5455, N.3, R.73, AGI, (PARES, http://pares.mcu.es/). Also in, Copies of documents, in Alcaldía
de San Ildefonso, Mexico City, September 1697, reel 1705, fr. 83–131, AHP.
25. Copies of documents, in Alcaldía de San Ildefonso, Mexico City, September 1697, reel 1705, frames 94–192,
AHP.
26. Información matrimonial 1731–1757, November 8, 1750, film 667001, images 165–166, Registros
Parroquiales, Iglesia de La Purísima Concepción, Álamos, Sonora, Mexico (FamilySearch, https://familysearch.
org).
27. Matrimonios 1716–1757, September 14, 1721, [no film number], image 33, Registros Parroquiales, Iglesia
de La Purísima Concepción, Álamos, Sonora, Mexico (FamilySearch, https://familysearch.org).
28. Matrimonios 1758–1779, December 28, 1761, film 666564, image 42, Registros Parroquiales, Iglesia de La
Purísima Concepción, Álamos, Sonora, Mexico (FamilySearch, https://familysearch.org).

Augustina Salvadora Esquer.

Agustina died on April 9, 1722, at the age of fifty-three in Álamos. She was buried on April 10, 1722, in Álamos.[29] Agustina Salvadora was laid to rest in a tomb by the altar of San Antonio in the church of La Purisima Concepción in Álamos at a cost of fifty-two pesos.

Francisco Antonio Florencio Mallén de Navarrete, son of Gabriel Mallén de Navarrete and Inés María Pacheco, was born on February 21, 1672, in the Villa de Palma (present day Palma del Río), Córdoba, Andalusia, Spain. The cited baptismal record provided his date of birth. He was baptized on March 5, 1672, at the parish church of San Francisco in Villa de Palma.[30] The baptismal record named Licenciado Diego Castillo y Carrillo as his *padrino*. Licenciado Sebastián Bravo de la Peña, Juan Verdugo de Noria Porto Carrozo, and Gregorio de Torres were named as witnesses. All of them were *vecinos* of the Villa de Palma. He emigrated on July 16, 1692, to New Spain.[31] The cited license stated that Francisco was an employee of Cristóbal de Agramont, Alcalde Mayor de Culiacán. They were listed as passengers on the Flota de Nueva España of 1692, which took sail on July 16, and arrived at the port of Veracruz on October 15, 1692. Extensive research in the Archivo de Protocolos Notariales de Palma del Río (located in Posadas) traced Francisco's paternal and maternal family lines to the early sixteenth century. The Mallén de Navarrete and related families were *hidalgos* who held positions of power within the Catholic Church hierarchy and in service to the Crown.

Francisco Antonio Florencio Mallén de Navarrete and Agustina Salvadora Esquer had the following known children:

17 i. **María Mallén de Navarrete** was born about 1700; she married Joseph Cayetano Anguís on March 30, 1723, in Álamos.

18 ii. **Vicente Mallén de Navarrete** was, born about 1706. He married María Francisca de Amarillas on October 24, 1728, in Álamos and died on February 24, 1779, in Álamos.

19 iii. **Micaela Salvadora Mallén de Navarrete** was born about 1710; she married Fernando González Barreda on July 8, 1731, in Álamos.

20 iv. **Andrea Mallén de Navarrete**, born about 1710; she married Salvador Esquer (Amarillas) on December 2, 1725, in Álamos and died on October 17, 1730, in Álamos.

21 v. **Manuela Mallén de Navarrete** was born about 1714. She married Joseph de Acedo on May 26, 1734, in Álamos and died in September 29, 1734, in Álamos.

22 vi. **Augustina Mallén de Navarrete** was born about 1718. She married Joseph Francisco

29. Defunciones 1717–1751, 1764–1792, April 10, 1722, film 666995, image 28, Registros Parroquiales, Iglesia de La Purísima Concepción, Álamos, Sonora, Mexico (FamilySearch, https://familysearch.org).

30. Cristóbal de Agramont, information and passenger license to travel to New Spain, Seville, June 19, 1692, Contratación, 5454, N.3, R.31, AGI (PARES, http://pares.mcu.es/). The baptismal record is located on page 13 of this document.

31. Cristóbal de Agramont, information and passenger license to travel to New Spain, Seville, June 19, 1692, AGI, Contratación, 5454, N.3, R.31, (PARES, http://pares.mcu.es/).

Avilés on September 20, 1737, in Álamos and died before January 1, 1762.

8. **Miguel Salvador Esquer** (Salvador-3, Salvador-2, Blas-1) was born in 1670 in Seville. He was baptized on December 7, 1670, at the church of the Sagrario in Seville.[32] The baptismal record named Agustín de Urquijo as his *padrino*. He emigrated in July 1688 to New Spain.[33] Although Miguel Esquer was not listed as a passenger along with his brother Juan Salvador on the voyage of 1688, the argument can be made that they traveled to New Spain together. Miguel was listed in the census of Spanish persons living in Mexico City in 1689.[34] The census was taken between September 16 and October 10 of that year, and in it he was listed as a "*mozo,*" a young man. He was living with his brother Juan Salvador at the time of the census.

Miguel Salvador Esquer and Gertrudis de Ibarra y Valenzuela were married about 1698, in New Spain.[35] Their matrimonial record has not been located. The source cited stated that Miguel Salvador Esquer and Gertrudis de Ibarra y Valenzuela were married. The couple had no known children.

Miguel died on October 28, 1758, at the age of eighty-eight in Culiacán. He was buried on October 29, 1759, at the church of the Sagrario de San Miguel in Culiacán.[36] His funeral service was held with a *cruz alta*. According to the burial record, he died suddenly at an advanced age. It is likely that Miguel Esquer outlived all his siblings, and that his death brought the end of an era in the family's history.

Gertrudis de Ibarra y Valenzuela, daughter of Juan de Ibarra and Josefa de Valenzuela, was born about 1675 in Culiacán. In the cited book, *Tres Alcaldes Mayores de la Provincia de Culiacán, 1681-1700,* in the chapter titled "Titulo de Alcalde Mayor y de la Santa Hermandad de la Provincia de San Miguel de Culiacán por tiempo de un año en el Capitán don Miguel de Esquer," the wife of Miguel Esquer was named as "Ibarra y Valenzuela." All other documents state her name as only "Valenzuela." It was also noted in this cited source that she was a native of Culiacán, a person of known nobility, the daughter and descendant, both paternally and maternally, of conquistadores, and colonizers of the provinces of Sinaloa and Sonora.

9. **Blas Salvador Esquer** (Salvador-3, Salvador-2, Blas-1) was born in 1672 in Seville. He was baptized on February 28, 1672, at the church of the Sagrario in Seville.[37] The baptismal record

32. Registros de bautismos, December 7, 1670, libro 45, folio 82, Registros Parroquiales, Iglesia del Sagrario, Seville, Spain.
33. Gaspar de la Cerda Sandoval Silva y Mendoza, informational documents and passenger license to travel to New Spain, for himself, his wife, and servants, Seville, July 1, 1688, Contratación, 5450, N.47, AGI (PARES, http://pares.mcu.es/). For related information see Don Gaspar de la Cerda Sandoval Silva y Mendoza, July1, 1688, Pasajeros, L.13, E.2634, AGI (PARES, http://pares.mcu.es/).
34. J. Ignacio Rubio Mañé, *Gente de España en la Ciudad de México, año de 1689* (Mexico: Archivo General de la Nación, 1966), p. 165.
35. Rina Cuéllar Zazueta and Benita Escárcega Rios, *Tres Alcaldes Mayores de la Provincia de Culiacán, 1681–1700* (Sinaloa: Archivo Histórico General del Estado de Sinaloa, 2000).
36. Defunciones 1746–1833, October 29, 1758, film 674051, image 124, Registros Parroquiales, Iglesia Sagrario de San Miguel, Culiacán, Sinaloa, Mexico (FamilySearch, https://familysearch.org).
37. Registros de bautismos, February 28, 1672, libro 45, folio 16, Registros Parroquiales, Iglesia del Sagrario,

named Seprian Serbi *vecino* of Santa Cruz as his *padrino*.

He emigrated on July 14, 1695[38] Blas Esquer left Spain with his father and siblings on the *Santísimo Sacramento*, a ship in the Flota de Nueva España of 1695. The fleet set sail on July 14 from the port of Cádiz and entered the port of Veracruz in New Spain on September 28 and 29, 1695.

Blas Salvador Esquer and Josepha González de Rodero were married about 1699.[39] The document cited provided testimony by his brother, Juan Salvador Esquer, that Blas and Josefa González Rodero were married.

Blas died before October 28, 1759.[40] The cited matrimonial record for his son, Joaquín Esquer, described Blas Esquer as deceased on October 28, 1759, the day the marriage took place.

Josepha González de Rodero, daughter of Andrés González de Rodero and Gertrudis López de Siqueiros, was born about 1680 in Culiacán. She died before October 28, 1759.[41] The cited matrimonial record for her son, Joaquín Esquer, described Josefa González Rodero as deceased on the day the marriage took place.

Blas Salvador Esquer and Josepha González de Rodero had the following known children:

    i.   **Juan Esquer** was born in 1700 in Culiacán. He was baptized on April 5, 1700, at the church of the Sagrario de San Miguel in Culiacán.[42] The baptismal record named Capitán Pasqual de Bolado and his wife María de Siqueiros, as the child's *padrinos*.

    ii.   **Juan Antonio Esquer** was born in 1707 in Culiacán. He was baptized on August 19, 1707, at the church of the Sagrario de San Miguel in Culiacán.[43] The baptismal record named Juan Esquer as his *padrino*.

23   iii.   **Joaquín Esquer** was born in 1711 in Culiacán. He married Antonia Rita Beltrán Alberstrain on October 28, 1759, in Culiacán and died in 1783 in Culiacán.

Seville, Spain.

38. Salvador de Ezquer, June 13, 1695, Pasajeros, L.14, E.698; Salvador Ezquer, Seville, June 24, 1695, Contratación, 5455, N.3, R.73, AGI (PARES, http://pares.mcu.es/). Also in Copies of documents, in Alcaldía de San Ildefonso, Mexico City, September 1697, year 1705, fr. 83–131, AHP.

39. Copies of documents, in Alcaldía de San Ildefonso, Mexico City, September 1697, year 1705, frames 94–192, AHP.

40. Matrimonios 1755–1784, October 28, 1759, film 673389, image 35, Registros Parroquiales, Iglesia Sagrario de San Miguel, Culiacán, Sinaloa, Mexico (FamilySearch, https://familysearch.org).

41. Matrimonios 1755–1784, film 673389, image 35, Registros Parroquiales, Iglesia Sagrario de San Miguel, Culiacán, Sinaloa, Mexico (FamilySearch, https://familysearch.org). This matrimonial record for her son Joaquin Esquer stated that Josefa González de Rodero was deceased on the day the marriage took place, October 28, 1759.

42. Bautismos 1690–1746, 1731–1769, April 5, 1700, film 665425, image, image 15, Registros Parroquiales, Iglesia Sagrario de San Miguel, Culiacán, Sinaloa, Mexico (FamilySearch, https://familysearch.org).

43. Bautismos 1690–1746, 1731–1769, August 19, 1707, film 665425, image 103, Registros Parroquiales, Iglesia Sagrario de San Miguel, Culiacán, Sinaloa, Mexico (FamilySearch, https://familysearch.org).

10. **Teresa María Esquer** (Salvador-3, Salvador-2, Blas-1) was born in 1675 in Seville. She was baptized on January 1, 1676, at the church of the Sagrario in Seville.[44] The baptismal record named Juan de Gamarra as her *padrino*. She emigrated on July 14, 1695.[45] Teresa María Esquer left Spain with her father and siblings on the *Santísimo Sacramento*, a ship in the Flota de Nueva España of 1695. The fleet set sail on July 14 from the port of Cádiz and entered the port of Veracruz in New Spain on September 28 and 29, 1695.

Teresa María Esquer and Francisco de la Cerda y Espíndola were married before 1695 in Spain.[46] Their matrimonial record has not been located. Evidence of marriage is provided in the cited last will and testament for Teresa María's mother, María Enríquez de Aponte. It stated that Teresa María was the legal wife of Francisco de la Cerda y Espíndola.

Francisco de la Cerda y Espíndola was born about 1676.

Francisco de la Cerda y Espíndola and Teresa María Esquer had the following known children:

i. **Augustín Joseph Marcelo de la Cerda y Espíndola** was born in 1695 in Mexico City. His birth occurred only weeks after his parents arrived in New Spain at the end of September 1695. This supports the notion that his mother must have made the arduous journey from Spain while pregnant. He was baptized on November 13, 1695, at the parish church of San Miguel Arcángel in Mexico City.[47] The baptismal record named Augustín de Mesa as his *padrino*.

24 ii. **María Josepha de la Cerda y Espíndola** was born in 1697, Mexico City; she married Bartolomé Abaroaon June 14, 1716, in Álamos.

iii. **Pedro Joseph de la Cerda y Espíndola** was born in 1698 in Mexico City. He was baptized on July 8, 1698, at the parish church of the Asunción Sagrario Metropolitano in Mexico City.[48] The baptismal record named Sebastián Ymaz as his *padrino*.

iv. **Manuela Josepha Dominga de la Cerda y Espíndola** was born in 1699 in Mexico City. She was baptized on August 17, 1699, at the parish church of San Miguel Arcángel in Mexico City.[49] The baptismal record named Sebastián Ymaz Arbilaga as

---

44. Registros de bautismos, January 1, 1676, libro 46, folio 104, Registros Parroquiales, Iglesia del Sagrario, Seville, Spain.

45. Salvador de Ezquer, June 13, 1695, Pasajeros, L.14, E.698; Salvador Ezquer, Seville, June 24, 1695, Contratación, 5455, N.3, R.73, AGI (PARES, http://pares.mcu.es/). Also in Copies of Documents, in Alcaldía de San Ildefonso, Mexico City, September 1697, year 1705, fr. 83–131, AHP.

46. Power of Attorney given by María Enríquez de Aponte to her husband, Salvador Esquer, to dictate her last will and testament, Seville, June 13, 1694, escribanía de Sebastián de Santa María Ibarra, Protocolos, legajo 13051, folio 266, AHPS.

47. Bautismos de españoles 1690–1716, November 13, 1695, film 205938, image 132, Registros Parroquiales, Iglesia San Miguel Arcángel, Mexico City, Mexico (FamilySearch, https://familysearch.org).

48. Bautismos de españoles 1691–1705, July 8, 1698, film 35176, image 271, Registros Parroquiales, Iglesia Asunción Sagrario Metropolitano, Mexico City, Mexico (FamilySearch, https://familysearch.org).

49. Bautismos de españoles 1690–1716, August 17, 1699, film 205938, image 216, Registros Parroquiales, Iglesia San Miguel Arcángel, Mexico City, Mexico (FamilySearch, https://familysearch.org).

her *padrino.*

11. **Salvadora Manuela Silvestra Esquer** (Salvador-3, Salvador-2, Blas-1) was born about 1679 in Seville.[50] The cited document stated that she was sixteen years of age at the time of her departure. She left for New Spain on July 14, 1695.[51] Salvadora Manuela Silvestra Esquer left Spain with her father and siblings on the *Santísimo Sacramento*, a ship in the Flota de Nueva España of 1695. The fleet set sail on July 14 from the port of Cádiz and entered the port of Veracruz in New Spain on September 28 and 29, 1695.

Salvadora Manuela Silvestra Esquer and Sebastián de Ymaz y Arbilaga were married on September 3, 1697, at the parish church of the Asunción Sagrario Metropolitano in Mexico City.[52] The marriage record named Pedro Varela and Miguel de la Gala as witnesses to the marriage. The couple received a dispensation from the archbishop of Mexico City, likely because both bride and groom were born in Spain and their eligibility for marriage had to be investigated. The couple received a nuptial blessing, *velación*, on January 27, 1698.

The marriage information record, dated September 1, 1697, provided the place of birth and named parents of the candidates for marriage. The record stated that Sebastián de Ymaz Arbilaga had been a resident of both Mexico City and the province of Sonora for seventeen years, and that Manuela Esquer had been a resident of Mexico City for a period of two years.

Salvadora Manuela Silvestra Esquer died on November 10, 1708, in Mexico City. She was buried on November 11, 1708, at the church of San José de Carmelitas Descalzos in Mexico City.[53] Her burial record stated that she had been married to the *contador* (accountant) Sebastián de Ymaz Arbilaga, and that she dictated her last will and testament to Escribano Real Mathias de Herrero Gutiérrez. She named her husband as executor and her children as her only heirs. Salvadora Manuela did not provide for Masses to be said for the repose of her soul, and she received the last sacraments of the Catholic Church before her death. Her place of residence was said to have been a house facing the church of Santa Inés in Mexico City.

Sebastián de Ymaz y Arbilaga, son of Sebastián de Ymaz and Francisca de Arbilaga, was born about 1660 in Oñate, Guipúzcoa, País Vasco, Spain. The cited marriage information record provided his place of birth. According to the cited records, Sebastián de Ymaz y Arbilaga held the position of *contador* (accountant). He married for a second time on April 21, 1709, in Mexico City to Manuela Francisca Ossorio.

---

50. Salvador Ezquer, Seville, June 24, 1695, Contratación, 5455, N.3, R.73, AGI (PARES, http://pares.mcu.es/).

51. Salvador de Ezquer, June 13, 1695, Pasajeros, L.14, E.698; Salvador Ezquer, Seville, June 24, 1695, Contratación, 5455, N.3, R.73, AGI (PARES, http://pares.mcu.es/). Also in Copies of documents, in Alcaldía de San Ildefonso, Mexico City, September 1697, AHP, year 1705, fr. 83–131.

52. Matrimonios 1688–1701, September 3, 1697, film 035270, image 445, Registros Parroquiales, Iglesia Asunción Sagrario Metropolitano, Mexico City, Mexico (FamilySearch, https://familysearch.org); Información matrimonial de españoles 1694–1734, September 1, 1697, film 35256, image 68, Registros Parroquiales, Iglesia Asunción Sagrario Metropolitano, Mexico City, Mexico (FamilySearch, https://familysearch.org).

53. Defunciones de españoles 1693–1714, November 11, 1708, film 35750, image 776, Registros Parroquiales, Iglesia Asunción Sagrario Metropolitano, Mexico City, Mexico (FamilySearch, https://familysearch.org).

Sebastián de Ymaz y Arbilaga and Salvadora Manuela Silvestra Esquer had the following known children:

25   i.   **Juan Miguel Gordiano Ymaz y Esquer** was born in 1698 in Mexico City, New Spain. He married María Gertrudis Luyando Gutierres on December 28, 1727, in Mexico City. Juan Miguel died on May 1, 1761, in Mexico City.

    ii.   **Joseph Juan Simón Ymaz y Esquer** was born in 1700 in Mexico City. He was baptized on February 23, 1700, at the parish church of the Asunción Sagrario Metropolitano in Mexico City.[54] The baptismal record named Capitán Felipe de la Peña and Catalina de Borja as his *padrinos*.

    iii.   **Patricio Joseph Ymaz y Esquer** was born on March 17, 1701, in Mexico City.[55] He was baptized on March 28, 1701, at the parish church of the Asunción Sagrario Metropolitano in Mexico City.[56] The baptismal record named Capitán Lucas de Careaga as his *padrino*. Patricio Ymaz (also spelled Imaz) y Esquer entered the Society of Jesus (Jesuit Order) on April 10, 1718. He was ordained on August 20, 1725, and made his Solemn Profession on May 16, 1735, in Mexico City.[57] Father Ymaz y Esquer served at Mission San Ignacio, Sinaloa, from 1730 to 1737, and Mission Conicari, Sinaloa, from 1744 to 1755. He was the superior at Conicari in 1744 and 1748. In 1744 his superiors gave him good grades for intelligence and learning. In the opinion of his superiors, Father Ymaz y Esquer had a sanguine complexion and possessed the talent for his ministries, but he was mediocre in judgment and prudence, and in his ability to govern. Father Ymaz y Esquer died on March 28, 1764, at the age of sixty-three. He lived his life in the service of the Sinaloan missions. Those missions are currently located in the Mexican state of Sonora.[58]

    iv   **Pedro Joseph Amador Ymaz y Esquer** was born in 1703 in Mexico City. He was baptized on May 13, 1703, at the parish church of the Asunción Sagrario Metropolitano in Mexico City.[59] The baptismal record named Capitán Nicolás López de Landa as his *padrino*. He died on October 21, 1761, at the age of fifty-eight in Mexico City.[60]

---

54. Bautismos de españoles 1691–1705, February 23, 1700, film 35176, image 477, Registros Parroquiales, Iglesia Asunción Sagrario Metropolitano, Mexico City, Mexico (FamilySearch, https://familysearch.org).

55. Francisco Zambrano, *Diccionario Bio-bibliográfico de la Compañía de Jesús*, vol. 15, pp. 772–73 (Mexico: Editorial Tradición, S.A., 1977).

56. Bautismos de españoles 1691–1705, March 28, 1701, film 35176, image 591, Registros Parroquiales, Iglesia Asunción Sagrario Metropolitano, Mexico City, Mexico (FamilySearch, https://familysearch.org).

57. Francisco Zambrano, *Diccionario Bio-bibliográfico de la Compañía de Jesús*, vol. 15, pp. 772–73 (Mexico: Editorial Tradición, S.A., 1977).

58. Ibid.

59. Bautismos de españoles 1691–1705, May 13, 1703, film 35176, image, 844, Registros Parroquiales, Iglesia Asunción Sagrario Metropolitano, Mexico City, Mexico (FamilySearch, https://familysearch.org).

60. Juzgado de Bienes de Distrito, expediente sobre el intestado de Joseph Imaz y Esquer. Averiguación de bienes, Mexico, 1761–1762, Instituciones Coloniales/Indiferente Virreinal/Expediente18 (intestados Caja 0779), fojas 1r–23v, AGN (http://www.agn.gob.mx/).

Pedro Joseph Ymaz y Esquer died without leaving a will. The document cited listed all his personal belongings and presented arguments from those claiming to be his heirs. Pedro made his religious profession and served as a priest in the Archdiocese of Mexico City.[61] The cited death-related document relates to the death of "Joseph Ymaz y Esquer." The assumption is made that he and Pedro Joseph Amador Ymaz y Esquer were one and the same person.

26   v.   **Raymundo Joseph Ymaz y Esquer** was born on April 26, 1705, in Mexico City. He married Francisca Lugarda Tomasa de Rosales on October 17, 1727, in Mexico City.

27   vi.   **María Josepha Francisca Ymaz y Esquer** was born on October 4, 1706, in Mexico City. She married Francisco Manuel Antonio Chirlín on September 26, 1723, in Mexico City.

    vii.   **Sebastián Frutos Joseph Xavier Ymaz y Esquer** was born on October 24, 1707, in Mexico City, according to the cited baptismal record. He was baptized on November 13, 1707, at the parish church of the Asunción Sagrario Metropolitano in Mexico City.[62] The baptismal record named Manuel de Aretio y Inda as his *padrino*.

    viii.   **Feliziana Manuela Josepha Xaviera Ymaz y Esquer** was born on October 20, 1708, in Mexico City, according to the cited baptismal record. She was baptized on October 25, 1708, at the parish church of the Asunción Sagrario Metropolitano in Mexico City.[63] The baptismal record named Joseph de Galisteo as her *padrino*.

12. **Miguel Fernando Simón Esquer** (Salvador-3, Salvador-2, Blas-1) was born on October 28, 1684, in Seville, according to the cited baptismal record. He was baptized on November 14, 1684, at the church of Santa María Magdalena in Seville.[64] He emigrated on July 14, 1695.[65] Miguel Fernando Esquer left Spain with his father and siblings on the *Santísimo Sacramento*, a ship in the Flota de Nueva España of 1695. The fleet set sail on July 14 from the port of Cádiz and entered the port of Veracruz in New Spain on September 28 and 29, 1695.

Miguel Fernando Simón Esquer and Augustina Guillerma Romero y Fuentes were married about 1712 in New Spain. Their marriage record has not been located. Of note is that Domingo Romero y Fuentes, father of the bride, may have once been married to María Salvadora Esquer. She was the oldest child of Salvador Esquer and María Enríquez de Aponte. María Salvadora died in Seville before the family emigrated to New Spain. Thus, his once brother-in-law with this marriage may have become his father-in-law.

---

61. Ibid.

62. Bautismos de españoles 1705–1713, November 13, 1707, film 35177, image 235, Registros Parroquiales, Iglesia Asunción Sagrario Metropolitano, Mexico City, Mexico (FamilySearch, https://familysearch.org).

63. Bautismos de españoles 1705–1713, October 25, 1708, film 35177, image 340, Registros Parroquiales, Iglesia Asunción Sagrario Metropolitano, Mexico City, Mexico (FamilySearch, https://familysearch.org).

64. Registros de bautismos, November 14, 1684, libro 24, folio 304, Registros Parroquiales, Iglesia de Santa María Magdalena, Seville.

65. Salvador de Ezquer, June 13, 1695, Pasajeros, L.14, E.698; Salvador Ezquer, Seville, June 24, 1695, Contratación, 5455, N.3, R.73, AGI, (PARES, http://pares.mcu.es/). Also in Copies of Documents, in Alcaldía de San Ildefonso, Mexico City, September 1697, vol. 15, pp. 772–73, year 1705, fr. 83–131, AHP.

Augustina Guillerma Romero y Fuentes, daughter of Domingo Romero y Fuentes and Juana Valenzuela, was born about 1697.

Miguel Fernando Simón Esquer and Augustina Guillerma Romero y Fuentes had the following known children:

i.   **Basilio Miguel Fernando Esquer** was born in 1713 in Culiacán. He was baptized on June 24, 1713, at the church of the Sagrario de San Miguel in Culiacán.[66] The baptismal record for Basilio Miguel Fernando Esquer named Gertrudis Valenzuela as his *madrina*.

ii.   **Basilio Esquer** was born in 1715 in Culiacán. He was baptized on June 7, 1715, at the church of the Sagrario de San Miguel in Culiacán.[67] The baptismal record named Gertrudis Valenzuela as his *madrina*.

iii.   **Hermenegilda Esquer** was born in 1716 in Culiacán. She was baptized on May 5, 1716, at the church of the Sagrario de San Miguel in Culiacán.[68] The baptismal record named María Rosa Valenzuela as her *madrina*.

28   iv.   **Pedro Fernando Esquer** was born about 1720. He married María Loreto Encinas about 1740.

v.   **María Manuela Esquer** was born in 1739.[69] The cited marriage investigation for Pablo Esquer and María Dolores Valenzuela stated that María Manuela was forty years of age at the time of Pablo and Maria Dolores's marriage.

29   vi.   **Nicolás Esquer** was born about 1740. He married Ygnacia Petrona de Cortabarria Sarmiento on September 8, 1767, in Mexico City. He died before May 10, 1777, in Mexico City.

---

66. Bautismos 1690–1746, 1731–1769, June 24, 1713, film 665425, image 107, Registros Parroquiales, Iglesia Sagrario de San Miguel, Culiacán, Sinaloa, Mexico (FamilySearch, https://familysearch.org).
67. Bautismos 1690–1746, 1731–1769, June 7, 1715, film 665425, image 109, Registros Parroquiales, Iglesia Sagrario de San Miguel, Culiacán, Sinaloa, Mexico (FamilySearch, https://familysearch.org).
68. Bautismos 1690–1746, 1731–1769, May 5, 1716, film 665425, image 109, Registros Parroquiales, Iglesia Sagrario de San Miguel, Culiacán, Sinaloa, Mexico (FamilySearch, https://familysearch.org).
69. Diligencias matrimoniales, Pablo de Esquerr y María Dolores de Valenzuela, Real de Río Chico, 1779, AHAD-30, frames 101–110, AHAD; Pablo Esquerr y María Dolores Valenzuela, Pueblo de Movas, 1779 AHAD-31, frames 429–443, AHAD.

Fifth Generation

13. **Juana Esquer** (Juan Salvador-4, Salvador-3, Salvador-2, Blas-1) was born in 1698 in Culiacán. Sinaloa. She was baptized on June 10, 1698, at the parish church of the Sagrario de San Miguel in Culiacán.[70] The baptismal record named Miguel Esquer and Gertrudis de Valenzuela as her *padrinos*. Juana Esquer was referred to as "Juana María Esquer" in the cited baptismal record for her daughter, Josefa María Perfecta.

Juana Esquer and Joaquín Alcayde Pérez de la Puente were married about 1717 in Culiacán. Although their matrimonial record has not been located, it is safe to assume that the couple married in Culiacán where they resided, and where their children were born.

Joaquín Alcayde Pérez de la Puente was born about 1696.

Joaquín Alcayde Pérez de la Puente and Juana Esquer had the following known children:

30   i.   **Francisco Xavier Alcayde Pérez de la Puente** was born in 1720 in Culiacán. He married Ana Antonia del Castillo y Cabanillas, about 1741 in New Spain. Francisco Xavier died on September 4, 1754, in Culiacán.

     ii.   **Josefa María Perfecta Alcayde Pérez de la Puente** was born in 1722 in Culiacán. She was baptized on May 3, 1722, at the church of the Sagrario de San Miguel in Culiacán.[71] The baptismal record named Capitán Francisco Xavier Alvarez de la Bandera as her *padrino*. On April 18, 1722, Capitán Alvarez de la Bandera administered the waters of baptism on the child, in case of necessity (fearing she might die). The priest baptized the child conditionally on the third of May. Josefa María Perfecta died on May 9, 1722, in Culiacán. She was buried on May 10, 1722, at the church of the Sagrario de San Miguel in Culiacán.[72] The burial record stated that she was buried in the parish church. She was said to have been the child of Joaquín Alcayde and Juana Esquer. Her funeral service was held with a *cruz alta*.

---

70. Bautismos 1690–1746, 1731–1769, June 10, 1698, film 665425, image 14, Registros Parroquiales, Iglesia Sagrario de San Miguel, Culiacán, Sinaloa, Mexico (FamilySearch, https://familysearch.org).
71. Defunciones 1690–1746 (incluye bautismos), May 3, 1722, film 665425, image 130, Registros Parroquiales, Iglesia Sagrario de San Miguel, Culiacán, Sinaloa, Mexico (FamilySearch, https://familysearch.org).
72. Defunciones 1690–1746, film 665425, May 10, 1722, image 187, Registros Parroquiales, Iglesia Sagrario de San Miguel, Culiacán, Sinaloa, Mexico (FamilySearch, https://familysearch.org).

14. **Salvador Esquer (Amarillas)** (Juan Salvador-4, Salvador-3, Salvador-2, Blas-1) was born in 1699 in Culiacán. He was baptized on April 13, 1699, at the church of the Sagrario de San Miguel in Culiacán.[73] The baptismal record named Miguel Esquer and Gertrudis de Valenzuela as his *padrinos.*

Salvador Esquer served as *Teniente General de Gobernador en la politica de este Reino de la Nueva Andalucía, Provincia de Sinaloa y* Sonora (Lieutenant General of [the] Governor in the politics of this Kingdom of the New Andalusia, Province of Sinaloa and Sonora). He was very involved in the political and military campaigns in response to the Yaqui, Seri, and Pima rebellions that took place in Sonora during the mid-eighteenth century.

Salvador Esquer (Amarillas) and Andrea Mallén de Navarrete, his first wife, were married on December 2, 1725, at the church of the Purísima Concepción in Álamos.[74] The matrimonial record named Miguel de Amarillas and his wife, Gracia de Luzenilla, as *padrinos.* Phelipe de León and Cristóbal Góngora were named as witnesses to the marriage.

Salvador Esquer (Amarillas) and María Rosa Nicolasa Anguís, his second wife, were married on September 8, 1736, in Álamos.[75] The matrimonial record named Capitán Joseph Quintano, Joseph Ignacio de Peralta, and Juan Francisco de Gómez y Parras as witnesses to the marriage. Parents of the bride and groom were not named. There is no absolute evidence that the same Salvador Esquer married both Andrea Mallén de Navarrete and María Nicolasa Anguís, but the time frame of events seems to strongly suggest that this was the case.

Salvador Esquer (Amarillas) died before January 1, 1762.[76] The cited January 1, 1762, matrimonial record for his son, Joseph Gabriel Esquer, stated that Salvador Esquer was deceased at the time of Joseph Gabriel's wedding.

Andrea Mallén de Navarrete, daughter of Francisco Antonio Florencio Mallén de Navarrete and Agustina Salvadora Esquer, was born about 1710. Her parentage was not documented. It was assumed based on her estimated year of birth and marriage date. Francisco Mallén de Navarrete and Agustina Esquer were the progenitors of the Mallén de Navarrete family in Álamos, in about 1700. She died on October 17, 1730, in Álamos. She was buried on October 18, 1730, at the church of the Purísima Concepción in Álamos.[77] Andréa Mallén de Navarrete was buried at the foot of the altar of San Antonio, *con las honras y cruz alta.*

María Rosa Nicolasa Anguís was born about 1715. She died before January 1, 1762. The cited January 1, 1762, matrimonial record for her son Joseph Gabriel Esquer stated that María Rosa Nicolasa was deceased at the time of the wedding.

---

73. Bautismos 1690–1746, 1731–1769, film 665425, image 14, Registros Parroquiales, Iglesia Sagrario de San Miguel, Culiacán, Sinaloa, Mexico (FamilySearch, https://familysearch.org).
74. Matrimonios 1716–1767, [no film number], image 49, Registros Parroquiales, Iglesia de La Purísima Concepción, Álamos, Sonora, Mexico (FamilySearch, https://familysearch.org).
75. Matrimonios 1716–1767, [no film number], image 105, Registros Parroquiales, Iglesia de La Purísima Concepción, Álamos, Sonora, Mexico (FamilySearch, https://familysearch.org).
76. Matrimonios 1758–1779, film 666564, image 43, Registros Parroquiales, Iglesia de La Purísima Concepción, Álamos, Sonora, Mexico (FamilySearch, https://familysearch.org).
77. Defunciones 1717–1751, 1764–1792, film 666995, image 63, Registros Parroquiales, Iglesia de La Purísima Concepción, Álamos, Sonora, Mexico (FamilySearch, https://familysearch.org).

Salvador Esquer (Amarillas) and María Rosa Nicolasa Anguís had the following known children:

i. **Isabel Esquer** was born about 1737.[78] The parentage of Isabel Esquer has not been directly established. The cited baptismal record for Joseph Joaquín María Murietta dated September 18, 1757, named Isabel Esquer y Anguís as his *madrina*. That evidence was used to place her as the daughter of Salvador Esquer and María Rosa Nicolasa Anguís. She died on January 4, 1801, in Álamos. She was buried on January 5, 1801, at the church of the Purísima Concepción in Álamos.[79] Her burial record stated that she was an adult at time of death and that she was buried in the church beneath the choir loft. Her funeral service was held with a *cruz baja*.

31 ii. **Juan Salvador Esquer**, was born in 1739. He married María Manuela Campoy in November 22, 1764, in Álamos. He died before July 27, 1797.

iii. **[*párvulo*] Esquer** was born between 1735 and 1745. He died in 1745 as a child in Álamos. He was buried on September 15, 1745, at the church of the Purísima Concepción in Álamos.[80] The unnamed child was interred in a burial site valued at five pesos, located at the altar of San Antonio inside the church. His funeral service was held with *cruz alta y capa campanas y túmulo, ataúd y incensario*.

32 iv. **Joseph Gabriel Esquer** was born in 1742 He married Francisca Augustina Avilés on January 1, 1762, in Álamos. He died on February 10, 1793, in Álamos.

v. **María Jesús Esquer** was born about 1743.[81] The cited marriage (1743) and nuptial blessing record (1761) for Manuel de Anaya and María Justa Esquer named Juan Salvador Esquer and María Jesús as siblings. María Justa Esquer was the daughter of Miguel Antonio Esquer and María Ygnacia Carrasco. Their place on the family tree has not been determined. The cited baptismal record dated May 25, 1762, for María Balvanera Gertrudis, daughter of Miguel Millán and Catarina Molina, named Joseph Cayetano Esquer and María Jesús as *padrino*s who were said to be first cousins.

33 vi. **Ana María Esquer** was born about 1746. She married Miguel Martínez on December 25, 1764, in Álamos.

34 vii. **María Loreto Esquer** was born about 1750. She married Juan Pablo Fox on December 8, 1769, in Álamos. She died on August 2, 1801, in Álamos.

---

78. Bautismos 1751–1794, matrimonios 1848, defunciones 1735–1752, September 18, 1757, film 666999, image 152, Registros Parroquiales, Iglesia de La Purísima Concepción, Álamos, Sonora, Mexico (FamilySearch, https:// familysearch.org).
79. Defunciones 1786–1819, January 5, 1801, film 666996, image 107, Registros Parroquiales, Iglesia de La Purísima Concepción, Álamos, Sonora, Mexico (FamilySearch, https://familysearch.org).
80. Defunciones 1717–1751,1764–1792, September 15, 1745, film 666995, image 125, Registros Parroquiales, Iglesia de La Purísima Concepción, Álamos, Sonora, Mexico (FamilySearch, https://familysearch.org).
81. Matrimonios 1716–1757, 1743, film 663806, image 135, Registros Parroquiales, Iglesia de La Purísima Concepción, Álamos, Sonora, Mexico (FamilySearch, https://familysearch.org); Bautismos 1751–1794, matrimonios 1848, defunciones 1735–1752, May 25, 1762, film 666999, images 228–229, Registros Parroquiales, Iglesia de La Purísima Concepción, Álamos, Sonora, Mexico (FamilySearch, https://familysearch. org).

15. **Joseph Cayetano Esquer** (Juan Salvador-4, Salvador-3, Salvador-2, Blas-1) was born in 1700 in Culiacán, Sinaloa. He was baptized on February 9, 1700, at the parish church of the Sagrario de San Miguel in Culiacán.[82] The baptismal record named Capitán Pasqual de Bolado and María de Siqueiros as his *padrinos*.

Joseph Cayetano Esquer and María [Nicolasa] de Valenzuela were married in March 1720 at the parish church of the Purísima Concepción in Álamos.[83] The matrimonial record did not name *padrinos*, nor did it name parents of the bride and groom. Although the parents of Joseph Cayetano Esquer and María de Valenzuela were not named in the marriage document, it is highly probable, if not verified, that he was the son of Juan Salvador Esquer and Micaela de Amarillas.

Joseph Cayetano Esquer died on September 6, 1739, at the age of thirty-nine in Álamos. He was buried on September 7, 1739, at the parish church of the Purísima Concepción in Álamos.[84] Cayetano Esquer was laid to rest in a burial site valued at twenty-five pesos. His funeral services were held with the use of *tres mesas, ataúd, capa, incensario, campanas, y cruz alta.*

María [Nicolasa] de Valenzuela was born about 1700. She died on August 8, 1748, in Álamos. She was buried on August 9, 1748, at the parish church of the Purísima Concepción in Álamos.[85] The body of María de Valenzuela was carried on a bier and she was buried beneath the choir. She was also known as "Nicolasa Valenzuela."

Joseph Cayetano Esquer and María [Nicolasa] de Valenzuela had the following known children:

35   i.   **Manuela Antonia Esquer** was born about 1719. She married Joseph Saterino Féliz on November 12, 1731, in Álamos. She died on October 29, 1774, in Álamos.

      ii.   **[*párvulo*] Esquer** was born between 1720 and 1722 in Álamos. He died on November 29, 1722, before the age of seven in Álamos. He was buried on November 30, 1722, at the church of the Purísima Concepción in Álamos.[86] The unnamed child was buried beneath the choir at the church. Cloth and thread were ordered from the church to make the child a garment for burial.

36 iii. **Joseph Cayetano Esquer** was born about 1721. He married Juliana Astorga on November 1, 1749, in Álamos.

16. **Francisco Joseph Esquer** (Juan Salvador-4, Salvador-3, Salvador-2, Blas-1) was born about 1710. There is no direct evidence that Francisco Joseph Esquer was the son of Juan Salvador Esquer and Micaela de Amarillas. The following is an analysis provided by José Antonio Rivera

82. Bautismos 1690–1746, 1731–1769, February 9, 1700, film 665425, image 15, Registros Parroquiales, Iglesia Sagrario de San Miguel, Culiacán, Sinaloa, Mexico (FamilySearch, https://familysearch.org).
83. Matrimonios 1716–1757, March 1720, film 663806, image 26, Registros Parroquiales, Iglesia de La Purísima Concepción, Álamos, Sonora, Mexico (FamilySearch, https://familysearch.org).
84. Defunciones 1717–1751, 1764–1792, September 7, 1739, film 666995, image 106, Registros Parroquiales, Iglesia de La Purísima Concepción, Álamos, Sonora, Mexico (FamilySearch, https://familysearch.org).
85. Defunciones 1717–1751, 1764–1792, August 9, 1748, film 666995, image 137, Registros Parroquiales, Iglesia de La Purísima Concepción, Álamos, Sonora, Mexico (FamilySearch, https://familysearch.org).
86. Defunciones 1717–1751, 1764–1792, November 30, 1722, film 666995, image 30, Registros Parroquiales, Iglesia de La Purísima Concepción, Álamos, Sonora, Mexico (FamilySearch, https://familysearch.org).

Fernández that explains the relationship: "In the marriage information of Andrés Quirós y Mora and Micaela Esquer Murillo (daughter of Francisco Esquer and Nicolasa Murillo), dated January 18, 1751, Andrés Amarillas declared he was the cousin of Micaela's father. If Andrés was the son of Nicolás Amarillas López de Siqueiros and Rosa Beltrán, then, Francisco Esquer must be a son from an Esquer and Amarillas marriage."[87] For Francisco and Andrés to be first cousins they must have shared a grandfather. In this case, the grandfather was Diego Amarillas.

Francisco Joseph Esquer and María Nicolasa Murillo were married on January 6, 1729, in Culiacán.[88] The matrimonial record named Juan de Boveda and Toribio Gonzáles, among others present, as witnesses to the marriage. Parents of the bride and groom were not named in the record.

Francisco Joseph Esquer died on April 16, 1752, in Álamos. He was buried on April 17, 1752, at the church of the Purísima Concepción in Álamos.[89] The burial record for Francisco Joseph Esquer stated that he had been a *vecino* of Culiacán, and husband of Nicolasa Murillo. He was said to have received the last sacraments of the Catholic Church and left a last testament.

María Nicolasa Murillo was born about 1710.

Francisco Joseph Esquer and María Nicolasa Murillo had the following known children:

37 i.   **María Raphaela Esquer** was born in 1729 in Culiacán. She married Fernando Antonio González Barreda on April 1, 1750, in Culiacán and died on May 7, 1785, in Álamos.

38 ii. **Micaela Matilde Esquer** was born in 1732 in Culiacán. She married Andrés Quirós y Mora on February 9, 1751, in Culiacán.

39 iii. **Francisco Gabriel Esquer** was born in 1734 in Culiacán. He married Anna Antonia Páez de Guzmán about 1764 in Culiacán.

40 iv. **Luis Antonio Esquer** was born in 1736 in Culiacán. He married Juana Paula Barraza about 1756. Luis Antonio married María Serafina Verdugo after November 29, 1772, in Culiacán. He married Cayetana Medina on August 9, 1794, in Culiacán and died on March 3, 1809, in Culiacán.

    v.   **Juan Joseph Esquer** was born in 1738 in Culiacán. He was baptized on July 30, 1738, at the church of the Sagrario de San Miguel in Culiacán.[90] The baptismal record

---

87. Información matrimonial 1733–1757, January 18, 1751, film 673538, images 110–112, Registros Parroquiales, Iglesia Sagrario de San Miguel, Culiacán, Sinaloa, Mexico (FamilySearch, https://familysearch.org); José Antonio Rivera Fernández, Mexico City, Mexico, email message from P G Koppel to Stella Cardoza, February 27, 2012.

88. Bautismos 1690–1746, 1731–1769, January 6, 1729, film 665425, image 161, Registros Parroquiales, Iglesia Sagrario de San Miguel, Culiacán, Sinaloa, Mexico (FamilySearch, https://familysearch.org).

89. Bautismos 1751–1794, matrimonios 1848, defunciones 1735–1752, April 17, 1752, film 666999, image 36, Registros Parroquiales, Iglesia de La Purísima Concepción, Álamos, Sonora, Mexico (FamilySearch, https://familysearch.org).

90. Matrimonios 1731–1755, July 30, 1738, film 665426, image 19, Registros Parroquiales, Iglesia Sagrario de San Miguel, Culiacán, Sinaloa, Mexico (FamilySearch, https://familysearch.org).

named Francisco Ramos and Antonia Murrillo as his *padrinos*. Francisco Ramos was said to have previously poured the water of baptism on the child, likely because his survival was in doubt. The priest then performed the formal ceremony of baptism at the church.

41 vi. **Pedro Sebastián Esquer** was born in 1741 in Culiacán. He married Anna María Murrieta about 1767.

vii. **Miguel Joaquín Esquer** was born in 1743 in Culiacán. He was baptized on June 24, 1743, at the church of the Sagrario de San Miguel in Culiacán.[91] The baptismal record named José Avilés and Josefa Chavarría as his *padrinos*. The recorded date and year are uncertain because the entry is included with baptisms recorded in 1744; the priest only referenced "*dicho dia veinte y cuatro*." There is a baptismal record above that is clearly dated October 13, 1743. This 1743 record is inserted among baptismal records dated June 1744. The composite June 24, 1743, baptismal date was used because there was another child with the same parents who was named "Joaquín Miguel." He was clearly baptized on March 1, 1744. The June 24, 1743, date is the only one that works, given the proximity of the next child born after Miguel Joaquín Esquer. It is likely that the child here baptized died as an infant, and that his brother, born in 1744, was given the same names, only inverted.

viii. **Joaquín Miguel Esquer** was born in 1744 in Culiacán. He was baptized on March 1, 1744, at the church of the Sagrario de San Miguel in Culiacán.[92] The baptismal record did not name *padrinos*.

42 ix. **María Nicolasa Esquer** was born in 1746 in Culiacán. She married Juan Manuel Rojo on May 5, 1764, in Culiacán and died on August 5, 1827, in Culiacán.

43 x. **María Gertrudis Anacleta Esquer** was born in 1748 in Culiacán. She married Ygnacio Francisco López de Siqueiros on July 28, 1764, in Culiacán. María Gertrudis later married José Onofre Páez on September 23, 1782, in Culiacán.

17. **María Mallén de Navarrete** (Agustina Salvadora Esquer-4, Salvador-3, Salvador-2, Blas-1) was born about 1700. María Mallén de Navarrete and Joseph Cayetano Anguís were married on March 30, 1723, in Álamos.[93] The matrimonial record named Juan Goytratigue (possibly, Goyategui) and Ysabel Tello de Méndez as *padrinos*. The couple received a nuptial blessing on June 6, 1723. Parents of the bridal couple were not named in the record.

Joseph Cayetano Anguís was born about 1700. He died on November 4, 1742, in Álamos. He was buried on November 5, 1742, at the church of the Purísima Concepción in Álamos.[94] His burial service was held with *cruz alta y capa campanas*.

---

91. Matrimonios 1731–1755 (incluye bautismos y defunciones), June 24, 1743, film 665426, image 34, Registros Parroquiales, Iglesia Sagrario de San Miguel, Culiacán, Sinaloa, Mexico (FamilySearch, https://familysearch.org).
92. Bautismos 1690–1746, bautismos 1731–1769, March 1, 1744, film 665425, image 217, Registros Parroquiales, Iglesia Sagrario de San Miguel, Culiacán, Sinaloa, Mexico (FamilySearch, https://familysearch.org).
93. Matrimonios 1716–1757, March 30, 1723, [no film number], image 39, Registros Parroquiales, Iglesia de La Purísima Concepción, Álamos, Sonora, Mexico (FamilySearch, https://familysearch.org).
94. Defunciones 1717–1751, 1764–1792, November 5, 1742, film 666995, image 115, Registros Parroquiales, Iglesia de La Purísima Concepción, Álamos, Sonora, Mexico (FamilySearch, https://familysearch.org).

Joseph Cayetano Anguís and María Mallén de Navarrete had the following known children:

      i.   **Juan Antonio Anguís** was born after 1723 in Álamos. The cited burial record provided his place of birth. Juan Antonio died on April 10, 1770, in Álamos. He was buried on April 11, 1770, at the church of the Purísima Concepción in Álamos.[95] The record named his parents and stated that he was interred in burial site valued at five pesos.

44 ii.   **Augustina Anguís** was born about 1725. She married Thadeo Iturríos on August 25, 1740, in Álamos.

    iii.   **Joseph Cayetano Anguís** was born after 1723. His parentage was determined by evidence contained in the cited baptismal record.[96] The record named Joseph Cayetano Anguís and Francisca Mallén de Navarrete as *padrinos* in the baptism of María Cayetana Anduaga, daughter of Ysidro Anduaga and María Lorenza Urbalejo. Joseph Cayetano was identified in the record as the first cousin of Francisca Mallén de Navarrete (daughter of Vicente Mallén de Navarrete and María Francisca de Amarillas). He was thus the son of Joseph Cayetano Anguís and María Mallén de Navarrete.

    iv.   **Gertrudis Anguís** was born about 1728. Her parentage was determined by evidence contained in the cited baptismal record.[97] The record named Gertrudis Anguís as the sister of Juan Antonio Anguís in the baptismal entry for Juan Manuel Anguís, May 5, 1762. Gertrudis and Juan Antonio were *padrinos* for their nephew, son of Francisco Antonio Baptista Anguís.

45 v.   **Thomas Antonio Anguís** was born about 1740. He married Juana de Dios María Gil Samaniego on November 22, 1763, in Álamos and died on June 5, 1775, in Álamos.

46 vi.   **Francisco Antonio Baptista Anguís** was born about 1734. He married Rosa Martínez Mendívil on August 16, 1754, in Álamos and died in 1775 in Álamos.

18. Vicente Mallén de Navarrete (Agustina Salvadora Esquer-4, Salvador-3, Salvador-2, Blas-1) was born about 1706.[98] He was a witness at the marriage investigation of Gabriel Campoy and Gertrudis Velarde, dated November 16, 1763, where his age was given as fifty-seven.

---

95. Defunciones 1717–1751, 1764–1792, April 11, 1770, film 666995, image 220, Registros Parroquiales, Iglesia de La Purísima Concepción, Álamos, Sonora, Mexico (FamilySearch, https://familysearch.org).
96. Bautismos 1751–1794, matrimonios 1848, defunciones 1735–1752, August 22, 1770, film 666999, images 217–218, Registros Parroquiales, Iglesia de La Purísima Concepción, Álamos, Sonora, Mexico (FamilySearch, https://familysearch.org).
97. Bautismos 1751–1794, matrimonios 1848, defunciones 1735–1752, May 5, 1762 film 666999, images 242–243, Registros Parroquiales, Iglesia de La Purísima Concepción, Álamos, Sonora, Mexico (FamilySearch, https://familysearch.org).
98. Diezmos, Pregón de los diezmos del Real de los Álamos, 1758–1766, Álamos, 1758–1766, AHAD-114, frames 22–35, AHAD.

Vicente Mallén de Navarrete and María Francisca de Amarillas were married on October 24, 1728, at the church of the Purísima Concepción in Álamos.[99] The matrimonial record named Capitán Miguel de Lucenilla and General Luis Aranda as witnesses to the act of matrimony. The bride and groom received a nuptial blessing on the day they were married. Parents of the couple were not named in the record.

Vicente Mallén de Navarrete died on February 24, 1779, in Álamos. He was buried on February 25, 1779, at the church of the Purísima Concepción in Álamos.[100] His funeral service was held with *cruz alta, misa vigilia, túmulo de tres cuerpos y caja*. He was interred in a burial site valued at twenty-five pesos. Vicente Mallén de Navarrete received the last sacraments of the Catholic Church before he died. He was absolved of his sins through a papal bull that granted plenary indulgences. He left a power of attorney for his last will and testament. The cited burial record noted that like his father he was an *ensayado*r (assayer) by profession. The cited record from the Archdiocese of Durango archives provided his parentage. It stated that he was the brother of Michaela Salvadora Mallén de Navarrete.

María Francisca de Amarillas was born about 1701. She died before December 28, 1761.[101] The cited marriage record for her son Gabriel Mallén de Navarrete noted that María Francisca was deceased on the day the marriage took place on December 28, 1761.

Vicente Mallén de Navarrete and María Francisca de Amarillas had the following known children:

47   i.   **María Theresa Mallén de Navarrete** was born about 1730. She married Miguel Alexandro Rivera after November 8, 1750, in Álamos She died on May 18, 1775, in Álamos.

     ii.   **Francisca Mallén de Navarrete** was born about 1732. She died on July 26, 1764, in Álamos. She was buried on July 27, 1764, at the church of the Purísima Concepción in Álamos.[102] She received the last sacraments of the Catholic Church before her death.

48   iii.   **Gabriel Mallén de Navarrete** was born about 1741. He married Rita Antonia Gil Samaniego on December 28, 1761, in Álamos and died on July 30, 1777, in Álamos.

     iv.   **[*párvula*] Mallén de Navarrete** was born in 1742 in Álamos. She died on May 4, 1742, in Álamos. She was buried on May 5, 1742, at the church of the Purísima Concepción in Álamos.[103] Her funeral service was held with *cruz alta y capa campanas*. The cost of the burial was five pesos, which were placed on the account of Francisco Mallén de Navarrete, the child's grandfather.

---

99. Matrimonios 1716–1757, October 24,1728, [no film number], image 61, Registros Parroquiales, Iglesia de La Purísima Concepción, Álamos, Sonora, Mexico (FamilySearch, https://familysearch.org).
100. Defunciones 1717–1751, 1764–1792, February 25, 1779, film 666995, image 316, Registros Parroquiales, Iglesia de La Purísima Concepción, Álamos, Sonora, Mexico (FamilySearch, https://familysearch.org).
101. Matrimonios 1758–1779, December 28, 1761, film 666564, image 42, Registros Parroquiales, Iglesia de La Purísima Concepción, Álamos, Sonora, Mexico (FamilySearch, https://familysearch.org).
102. Defunciones 1717–1751, 1764–1792, July 27, 1764, film 666995, image 162, Registros Parroquiales, Iglesia de La Purísima Concepción, Álamos, Sonora, Mexico (FamilySearch, https://familysearch.org).
103. Defunciones 1717–1751,1764–1792, May 5, 1742, film 666995, image 114, Registros Parroquiales, Iglesia de La Purísima Concepción, Álamos, Sonora, Mexico (FamilySearch, https://familysearch.org).

49   v.   **Rita Antonia Mallén de Navarrete** was born about 1742. She married Lorenzo
          Antonio Noriega on February 16, 1766, in Álamos.

Vicente Mallén de Navarrete and an unnamed woman had the following child:

   i.   **María Antonia Mallén de Navarrete** was born before 1728.[104] The birth record
        has not been located. María Antonia Mallén de Navarrete was said to have been the
        illegitimate daughter of Vicente Mallén de Navarrete and an unnamed mother in the
        cited marriage information record dated 1779 for his nephew, Pablo Esquer.

19. Micaela Salvadora Mallén de Navarrete (Agustina Salvadora Esquer-4, Salvador-3,
Salvador-2, Blas-1) was born about 1710.

Micaela Salvadora Mallén de Navarrete and Fernando González Barreda were married on July
8, 1731, at the church of the Purísima Concepción in Álamos.[105] The matrimonial record named
Bartolomé Abaroa, Domingo [?] de Ymas and the Alférez Juan de Huidobro as witnesses to the
marriage. Parents of the bride and groom were named.

Fernando González Barreda, son of Domingo González Barreda and Theresa de Carballo,
was born about 1700 in Cádiz, Andalusia, Spain.[106] Proof of Fernando's parentage was provided
in the cited marriage document for his son Fernando Antonio. He died on March 19, 1749,
in Álamos. He was buried on March 20, 1749, at the church of the Purísima Concepción in
Álamos, at the steps of the church sanctuary at a cost of fifty pesos (silver reales). His burial
service was held with *cruz alta, capa campanas, túmulo, ataúd, mesa y un porta todo*. On March
29 a service of *honras* for the repose of his soul was held with *túmulo de tres cuerpos, cruz alta,
capa campanas y incensario.*[107]

Fernando González Barreda and Micaela Salvadora Mallén de Navarrete had the following
known children:

50   i.   **Fernando Antonio González Barreda** was born about 1733. He married María
          Raphaela Esquer on April 1, 1750, in Culiacán and died before May 8, 1785.

51   ii. **Ana María González Barreda** was born about 1732 in Álamos. She married Juan
          Augustín de Yriarte on April 11, 1751, in Álamos.

---

104. Diligencias matrimoniales, Pablo de Esquerr y María Dolores de Valenzuela, Real de Río Chico, 1779,
AHAD-30, frames 101–110, AHAD; Pablo Esquerr y María Dolores Valenzuela, Pueblo de Movas, 1779 AHAD-
31, frames 429–443, AHAD.
105. Matrimonios 1716–1757, July 8,1731, film 663806, image 75, Registros Parroquiales, Iglesia de La
Purísima Concepción, Álamos, Sonora, Mexico (FamilySearch, https://familysearch.org).
106. Matrimonios 1731–1755, April 1, 1750, film 665426, images 104–105, Registros Parroquiales, Iglesia
Sagrario de San Miguel, Culiacán, Sinaloa, Mexico (FamilySearch, https://familysearch.org).
107. Defunciones 1717–1751, 1764–1792, March 20, 1749, film 666995, image 142, Registros Parroquiales,
Iglesia de La Purísima Concepción, Álamos, Sonora, Mexico (FamilySearch, https://familysearch.org).

20. **Andrea Mallén de Navarrete** (Agustina Salvadora Esquer-4, Salvador-3, Salvador-2, Blas-1) was born about 1710. Her parentage was not documented. It was assumed based on her estimated year of birth and marriage date. Francisco Mallén de Navarrete and Agustina Esquer were the progenitors of the Mallén de Navarrete family in Álamos in about 1700.

Andrea Mallén de Navarrete and Salvador Esquer (Amarillas) were married on December 2, 1725, at the church of the Purísima Concepción in Álamos.[108] The matrimonial record named Miguel de Amarillas and his wife Gracia de Luzenilla as *padrinos*. Phelipe de León and Cristóbal Góngora were named as witnesses to the marriage.

Andrea Mallén de Navarrete died on October 17, 1730, in Álamos. She was buried on October 18, 1730, at the church of the Purísima Concepción in Álamos.[109] Andréa Mallén de Navarrete was buried at the foot of the altar of San Antonio, *con las honras y cruz alta*.

Salvador Esquer (Amarillas), son of Juan Salvador Esquer and Michaela de Amarillas, was born in 1699 in Culiacán. He was baptized on April 13, 1699, at the church of the Sagrario de San Miguel in Culiacán.[110] The baptismal record named Miguel Esquer and Gertrudis de Valenzuela as his *padrinos*. Salvador Esquer served as *Teniente General de Gobernador en la politica de este Reino de la Nueva Andalucía, Provincia de Sinaloa y Sonora* (Lieutenant General of [the] Governor in the politics of this Kingdom of the New Andalusia, Province of Sinaloa and Sonora). He was very involved in the political and military campaigns in response to the Yaqui, Seri, and Pima Indian rebellions that took place in Sonora during the mid-eighteenth century.

He died before January 1, 1762.[111] The cited January 1, 1762, matrimonial record for his son, Joseph Gabriel Esquer, stated that Salvador Esquer was deceased at the time of Joseph Gabriel's wedding.

21. **Manuela Mallén de Navarrete** (Agustina Salvadora Esquer-4, Salvador-3, Salvador-2, Blas-1) was born about 1714.

Manuela Mallén de Navarrete and Joseph de Acedo were married on May 26, 1734, at the church of the Purísima Concepción in Álamos.[112] The matrimonial record named Bachiller Juan Antonio Anguís and Salvador Esquer as witnesses to the marriage. The groom was said to have been the widowed husband of Isabel Roxas. Parents of the bride and groom were named, and the marriage was said to have taken place at the home of the bride's father, Capitán Francisco Mallén de Navarrete, *ensayador y balanzario* (assayer and balancer) of Álamos.

---

108. Matrimonios 1716–1767, [no film number], image 49, Registros Parroquiales, Iglesia de La Purísima Concepción, Álamos, Sonora, Mexico (FamilySearch, https://familysearch.org).
109. Defunciones 1717–1751, 1764–1792, film 666995, image 63, Registros Parroquiales, Iglesia de La Purísima Concepción, Álamos, Sonora, Mexico (FamilySearch, https://familysearch.org).
110. Bautismos 1690–1746, 1731–1769, film 665425, image 14, Registros Parroquiales, Iglesia Sagrario de San Miguel, Culiacán, Sinaloa, Mexico (FamilySearch, https://familysearch.org).
111. Matrimonios 1758–1779, film 666564, image 43, Registros Parroquiales, Iglesia de La Purísima Concepción, Álamos, Sonora, Mexico (FamilySearch, https://familysearch.org).
112. Matrimonios 1716–1757, May 26, 1734, film [no film number], image 89, Registros Parroquiales, Iglesia de La Purísima Concepción, Álamos, Sonora, Mexico (FamilySearch, https://familysearch.org).

Manuela Mallén de Navarrete died on September 29, 1734, in Álamos. She was buried on September 30, 1734, at the church of the Purísima Concepción in Álamos.[113] She was interred in a burial site valued at twenty-five pesos. Her funeral service was held with *cruz alta, caja, incensario, and túmulo de dos cuerpos.*

Joseph de Acedo, son of Joseph de Acedo and Juana de Amarillas, was born about 1704.

22. **Augustina Mallén de Navarrete** (Agustina Salvadora Esquer-4, Salvador-3, Salvador-2, Blas-1) was born about 1718. Augustina Mallén de Navarrete and Joseph Francisco Avilés were married on September 20, 1737, in Álamos.[114] The matrimonial record named Salvador Esquer, Fernando González Barreda and Vicente Mallén de Navarrete as witnesses to the marriage. The couple received a nuptial blessing on their wedding day. Parents of the bride and groom were not named in the record.

Augustina Mallén de Navarrete died before January 1, 1762. She was said to have been deceased at the time of her daughter Francisca Augustina's marriage. In the document cited for the marriage of Joseph Gabriel Esquer and Francisca Augustina Avilés, Micaela Salvadora Mallén de Navarrete was said to have been the widowed aunt of both the bride and groom. This would make her a sibling of Augustina Mallén de Navarrete. Micaela Mallén de Navarrete was a witness at the marriage of her niece, Francisca Augustina Avilés.[115]

Joseph Francisco Avilés was born about 1717. He died before January 1, 1762. Joseph Francisco Avilés was said to have been deceased at the time of his daughter Francisca's marriage on January 1, 1762.

Joseph Francisco Avilés and Augustina Mallén de Navarrete had one known child:

52   i.   **Francisca Augustina Avilés** was born about 1740. She married Joseph Gabriel Esquer on January 1, 1762, in Álamos.

23. **Joaquín Esquer** (Blas Salvador-4, Salvador-3, Salvador-2, Blas-1) was born in 1711 in Culiacán. He was baptized on October 19, 1711, at the parish church of the Sagrario de San Miguel in Culiacán.[116] The baptismal record named Licenciado Juan de Equirrola as his *padrino.*

Joaquín Esquer and Antonia Rita Beltrán Alberstrain were married on October 28, 1759, at the church of the Sagrario de San Miguel in Culiacán.[117] The matrimonial record identified Manuel Volado, Manuel Ygnacio de Castañeda, among many others, as witnesses to the marriage. The

---

113. Defunciones 1717–1751, 1764–1792, September 30, 1734, film 666995, image 81, Registros Parroquiales, Iglesia de La Purísima Concepción, Álamos, Sonora, Mexico (FamilySearch, https://familysearch.org).
114. Matrimonios 1716–1757, September 20, 1737, [no film number], image 110, Registros Parroquiales, Iglesia de La Purísima Concepción, Álamos, Sonora, Mexico (FamilySearch, https://familysearch.org).
115. Matrimonios 1758–1779, January 1, 1762, film 666564, image 43, Registros Parroquiales, Iglesia de La Purísima Concepción, Álamos, Sonora, Mexico (FamilySearch, https://familysearch.org).
116. Bautismos 1690–1746, 1731–1769, October 19, 1711, film 665425, image 105, Registros Parroquiales, Iglesia Sagrario de San Miguel, Culiacán, Sinaloa, Mexico (FamilySearch, https://familysearch.org).
117. Matrimonios 1755–1784, October 28, 1759, film 673389, image 35, Registros Parroquiales, Iglesia Sagrario de San Miguel, Culiacán, Sinaloa, Mexico (FamilySearch, https://familysearch.org).

bride was said to have been widowed for three years. Her previous husband had been Nicolás Quirós y Mora. Parents of the bride and groom were named, and all were said to be deceased.

Joaquín Esquer died in 1783 at the age of seventy-two in Culiacán. He was buried at the church of the Sagrario de San Miguel in Culiacán.[118] The burial record for Joaquín Esquer is badly faded and difficult to decipher so the month and day of burial are unknown. The record stated that Joaquín Esquer had been married to Antonia Beltrán. Justicia Mayor Francisco Velásquez recorded Joaquín's last will and testament in which he named as executor in first place, Miguel de la O. His wife was named executor in second place. Joaquín Esquer named his legitimate sons, Blas, Claudio, and Albino as his survivors. Joaquín's wife and three sons were named in the will.

Antonia Rita Beltrán Alberstrain, daughter of Joseph Beltrán and Gerónima Isabel Albestrain, was born about 1728.

Joaquín Esquer and Antonia Rita Beltrán Alberstrain had the following known children:

    i.   **Blas Manuel Esquer** was born on August 6, 1760, in Culiacán. The baptismal record stated that the child had been born nine days before his day of baptism. He was baptized on August 15, 1760, at the church of the Sagrario de San Miguel in Culiacán.[119] The baptismal record named Bachiller Diego Yturríos and Leonor Yturríos as his *padrinos*. He died on March 5, 1788, at age of twenty-seven in Culiacán. Blas was buried on March 6, 1788, at the church of the Sagrario de San Miguel in Culiacán.[120] His funeral service was held with *cruz alta, capa y incensario*. He was interred in a burial site valued at five pesos. Blas Manuel received the last sacraments of the Catholic Church before death. He died in Tepuche of a renal condition *dolor de costado*. The record stated that Blas Manuel did not leave a will, although he had possessions for which to do so.

    ii.   [*párvulo*] **Esquer** was born between 1761 and 1769 in Culiacán. He died on June 1, 1769, in Culiacán. He was buried on June 2, 1769, at the church of the Sagrario de San Miguel in Culiacán.[121] The child's burial service was held with a *cruz alta*.

53   iii.   **José Claudio Esquer** was born about 1761. He married María Ignacia Mejia sometime after July 6, 1794, in Culiacán.

    iv.   **María Nicolasa Esquer** was born on September 30, 1764, in Culiacán, according to the baptismal record. She was baptized on October 8, 1764, at the church of the Sagrario de San Miguel in Culiacán.[122] The baptismal record named Miguel Amarillas

---

118. Defunciones 1746–1833, 1783, film 674051, images 213–214, Registros Parroquiales, Iglesia Sagrario de San Miguel, Culiacán, Sinaloa, Mexico (FamilySearch, https://familysearch.org).

119. Bautismos 1755–1789, August 15, 1760, film 665427, image 58, Registros Parroquiales, Iglesia Sagrario de San Miguel, Culiacán, Sinaloa, Mexico (FamilySearch, https://familysearch.org).

120. Defunciones 1746–1833, March 6, 1788 film 674051, image 241, Registros Parroquiales, Iglesia Sagrario de San Miguel, Culiacán, Sinaloa, Mexico (FamilySearch, https://familysearch.org).

121. Defunciones 1746–1833, June 2, 1769, film 674051, image 172, Registros Parroquiales, Iglesia Sagrario de San Miguel, Culiacán, Sinaloa, Mexico (FamilySearch, https://familysearch.org).

122. Matrimonios 1731–1755 (incluye bautismos y defunciones), October 8, 1764, film 665426, image 222, Registros Parroquiales, Iglesia Sagrario de San Miguel, Culiacán, Sinaloa, Mexico (FamilySearch, https://familysearch.org).

and Theresa Verdugo as her *padrinos*. María Nicolasa died on August 29, 1782, at the age of seventeen in Culiacán. She was buried on August 30, 1782, at the church of the Sagrario de San Miguel in Culiacán.[123] Her funeral service was held with *cruz alta y misa de cuerpo presente*.

   v.   **Albino Esquer** was born about 1766. The cited burial record for Joaquín Esquer listed Albino Esquer, along with his mother and siblings, as a surviving family member.[124]

24. **María Josepha de la Cerda y Espíndola** (Teresa María Esquer-4, Salvador-3, Salvador-2, Blas-1) was born in 1697 in Mexico City. She was baptized on January 19, 1697, at the parish church of San Miguel Arcángel in Mexico City.[125] The baptismal record named Joseph de Vera as her *padrino*.

María Josepha de la Cerda y Espíndola and Bartolomé Abaroa were married on June 14, 1716, at the church of the Purísima Concepción in Álamos.[126] The matrimonial record named Capitán Francisco Mallén de Navarrete, *ensayador* (assayer), and his wife Agustina Esquer as *padrinos*. All the *vecinos* of Álamos were said to have been witnesses to the marriage.

Bartolomé Abaroa was born about 1696 in Villa de Cestona, País Vasco, Spain, according to the cited matrimonial record.

25. **Juan Miguel Gordiano Ymaz y Esquer** (Salvadora Manuela Silvestra Esquer-4, Salvador-3, Salvador-2, Blas-1) was born in 1698 in Mexico City, New Spain. He was baptized on May 15, 1698, at the parish church of the Asunción Sagrario Metropolitano in Mexico City.[127] The baptismal record named Capitán Joaquín de Zavaleta as his *padrino*. The cited matrimonial record for Juan Ymaz Esquer noted his name as "Juan de Ymaz Arbilaga," yet throughout his life he uses "Ymaz Esquer."

Juan Miguel Gordiano Ymaz y Esquer and María Gertrudis Luyando Gutierres were married on December 28, 1727, at the parish church of the Asunción Sagrario Metropolitano in Mexico City.[128] The matrimonial record named Licenciado Joseph Arias Villafañe and Melchora Gutierres as witnesses. The marriage took place at the home of the priest, Doctor Manuel Antonio de

---

123. Defunciones 1746–1833, August 30, 1782, film 674051, image 211, Registros Parroquiales, Iglesia Sagrario de San Miguel, Culiacán, Sinaloa, Mexico (FamilySearch, https://familysearch.org).
124. Defunciones 1746–1833, 1783, film 674051, images 213–214, Registros Parroquiales, Iglesia Sagrario de San Miguel, Culiacán, Sinaloa, Mexico (FamilySearch, https://familysearch.org).
125. Bautismos de españoles 1690–1716, January 19, 1697, film 205938, image 164, Registros Parroquíales, Iglesia San Miguel Arcángel, Mexico City, Mexico (FamilySearch, https://familysearch.org).
126. Matrimonios 1716–1757, June 14, 1716, [no film number] images 4–5, Registros Parroquiales, Iglesia de La Purísima Concepción, Álamos, Sonora, Mexico (FamilySearch, https://familysearch.org).
127. Bautismos de españoles 1691–1705, May 15, 1698, film 35176, image 256, Registros Parroquiales, Iglesia Asunción Sagrario Metropolitano, Mexico City, Mexico (FamilySearch, https://familysearch.org).
128. Matrimonios de españoles 1702–1708, December 28, 1727, film 35271, image 1006, Registros Parroquiales, Iglesia Asunción Sagrario Metropolitano, Mexico City, Mexico (FamilySearch, https://familysearch.org).

Luyando y Bermeo, located on Monte Alegre street. The record stated that the groom was an attorney at the Real Audiencia.

Juan Miguel Gordiano Ymaz y Esquer died on May 1, 1761, at the age of sixty-three in Mexico City. He was buried on May 2, 1761, at the parish church of the Asunción Sagrario Metropolitano in Mexico City.[129] The burial record noted that he had been married to María Gertrudis de Luyando, and that he had received the last sacraments of the Catholic Church. He lived at the Real Universidad in Mexico City, and was buried at the church of Jesús María, where his body lay with the permission of the archbishop. At the time of his death, Juan Ymaz Esquer held the dual positions of Abogado de la Real Audiencia, and Secretario de la Real Universidad.

A medallion placed within the memorial painting of Juan Ymaz Esquer illustrates his life's accomplishments, and the esteem in which he was held at the time of his death. He was an attorney in the Colegio de Abogados who provided endowments in literature, business and subjects related to ethics and integrity. He was a judge, fiscal agent, corrector, and purger of books of the Holy Office of the Inquisition, and Secretary of the Real Universidad for thirty-three years. Before his death he bequeathed his archive to his successors in order to preserve his legacy. The portrait painted by Miguel Cabrera was copied as a gesture of gratitude to Juan Ymaz Esquer and hung in an unnamed cloister on May 2, 1761. In 1762, the painting was moved to the chapel of the Convent of San Francisco, where the confraternity of the Santísimo Cristo de Burgos hung paintings of their members. The painting is currently at the Museo Nacional de Historia in Mexico City.

María Gertrudis Luyando Gutierres was born about 1709. She appeared in some records using the singular surnames Luyando or Gutierres.

Juan Miguel Gordiano Ymaz y Esquer and María Gertrudis Luyando Gutierres had the following known children:

54   i.   **Joseph Mateo Miguel Ymaz Esquer y Luyando** was born on September 21, 1728, in Mexico City. He married María Gertrudis de Olavarría Caballero de los Olivos in May 1, 1757, in Mexico City. He later married Ygnacia Josefa Bustamante on February 26, 1785, in Mexico City; died April 29, 1785, Mexico City.

    ii.   **María Manuela Josefa Ymaz Esquer y Luyando** was born on April 23, 1730, in Mexico City. The cited baptismal record provided her date of birth. She was baptized on April 27, 1730, at the parish church of the Asunción Sagrario Metropolitano in Mexico City.[130] The baptismal record named Luis Miguel de Luyando y Bermeo as her *padrino*. She made her religious profession at an unspecified place and time.[131] María Manuela Josefa assumed the name "María Manuela de San Luís Gonzaga" at

129. Defunciones de españoles 1757–1766, May 2, 1761, film 35754, image 416, Registros Parroquiales, Iglesia Asunción Sagrario Metropolitano, Mexico City, Mexico (FamilySearch, https://familysearch.org); Abelardo Carrillo y Gariel, *El pintor Miguel Cabrera*, illustration 17, p. 65 (Mexico: Instituto Nacional de Antropología e Historia, 1966).

130. Bautismos de españoles 1724–1730, April 27, 1730, film 35180, image 1099, Registros Parroquiales, Iglesia Asunción Sagrario Metropolitano, Mexico City, Mexico (FamilySearch, https://familysearch.org).

131. Juzgao de Bienes de Distrito, expediente sobre el intestado de Joseph Imaz y Esquer. Averiguación de bienes, Mexico, 1761–1762, Instituciones Coloniales/Indiferente Virreinal/Expediente 18 (intestados Caja 0779), fojas 1r–23v, AGN (http://www.agn.gob.mx/).

the time of her religious profession. She carried the distinction of *profesa de coro y velo negro*. This means she entered the convent with a dowry, which gave her high status. She lived at the Real Convento de Jesús María.

iii. **Mariano Patricio Joseph Francisco Ymaz Esquer y Luyando** was born on March 16, 1731, in Mexico City, according to the cited baptismal record. He was baptized on March 19, 1731, at the parish church of the Asunción Sagrario Metropolitano in Mexico City.[132] The baptismal record named Bachiller Juan Roldán, priest of the archdiocese, as his *padrino*. He died on May 19, 1784, at the age of fifty-three.[133] The cited summary of the last testament for Mariano Patricio Joseph Francisco Ymaz Esquer y Luyando provided his date of death and named his brother José Ymaz Esquer as his executor and heir. The entry stated that the deceased had held the title of bachiller and served as a parish priest, *teniente de cura que fue de Teotihuacan, Puebla* (lieutenant curate who was from Teotihuacan, Puebla). The date and location of Father Mariano's religious profession are unknown.

iv. **Juana María Josepha Ymaz Esquer y Luyando** was born on May 6, 1732, in Mexico City, according to the cited baptismal record. She was baptized on May 12, 1732, at the parish church of the Asunción Sagrario Metropolitano in Mexico City.[134] The baptismal record named Juan Joseph Echeverría as her *padrino*. She made her religious profession at an unspecified time and place.[135] Juana María Josepha Ymaz Esquer assumed the name "María Josepha de San Ignacio" at the time of her religious profession. She carried the distinction of *profesa de coro y velo negro*, This means she entered the convent with a dowry, which gave her high status. She lived at the Real Convento de Jesús María.

v. **Antonio María León Ymaz Esquer y Luyando** was born on April 11, 1734, in Mexico City, according to the cited baptismal record. He was baptized on April 17, 1734, at the parish church of the Asunción Sagrario Metropolitano in Mexico City.[136] The baptismal record named Doctor Manuel Luyando, member of the clergy, as his *padrino*.

---

132. Bautismos de españoles 1730–1735, March 19, 1731, film 35181, image 94, Registros Parroquiales, Iglesia Asunción Sagrario Metropolitano, Mexico City, Mexico (FamilySearch, https://familysearch.org).
133. Fernando Muñoz Altea, *Documentos Notariales, siglos XVII al XIX* (Mexico, D.F. n.d.: Francisco Muñoz Altea), Tomás Quintero (548) folio 67 vto., Testó 21–VIII–1784.
134. Bautismos de españoles 1730–1735, May 12, 1732, film 35181, image 303, Registros Parroquiales, Iglesia Asunción Sagrario Metropolitano, Mexico City, Mexico (FamilySearch, https://familysearch.org).
135. Juzgado de Bienes de Distrito, expediente sobre el intestado de Joseph Imaz y Esquer. Averiguaciónde bienes, Mexico, 1761–1762, Instituciones Coloniales/Indiferente Virreinal/Expediente18 (intestados Caja 0779), fojas 1r–23v, AGN (http://www.agn.gob.mx/).
136. Bautismos de españoles 1730–1735, April 17, 1734, film 35181, image 673, Registros Parroquiales, Iglesia Asunción Sagrario Metropolitano, Mexico City, Mexico (FamilySearch, https://familysearch.org).

vi. **María Theresa de Jesús Ymaz Esquer y Luyando** was born on October 14, 1735, in Mexico City, according to the cited baptismal record. She was baptized on October 20, 1735, at the parish church of the Asunción Sagrario Metropolitano in Mexico City.[137] The baptismal record named Francisco Manuel Chirlín and María Francisca Ymaz as her *padrinos.*

vii. **Juan Francisco Regis Joseph Antonio Ymaz Esquer y Luyando** was born on November 14, 1741, in Mexico City, according to the baptismal record. He was baptized on November 18, 1741, at the parish church of the Asunción Sagrario Metropolitano in Mexico City.[138] The baptismal record named Father Juan Manuel Careaga, priest of the parish of Santa Catarina Mártir in Mexico City, as his *padrino.*

55 viii. **Pedro Martín Joseph Manuel Ymaz Esquer y Luyando** was born about 1743. He married María Josepha Regina Hidalgo Cabanillas on December 8, 1766, in Mexico City.

26. Raymundo Joseph Ymaz y Esquer (Salvadora Manuela Silvestra Esquer-4, Salvador-3, Salvador-2, Blas-1) was born on April 26, 1705, in Mexico City, according to the cited baptismal record. He was baptized on May 10, 1705, at the parish church of the Asunción Sagrario Metropolitano in Mexico City.[139] The baptismal record named Joseph de Madina as his *padrino.*

Raymundo Joseph Ymaz y Esquer and Francisca Lugarda Tomasa de Rosales were married on October 17, 1727, at the parish church of the Asunción Sagrario Metropolitano in Mexico City.[140] The matrimonial record named Francisco Chirlín, and Juan Romo de Vera as witnesses. The following day, October 18, the couple received a nuptial blessing at the church of San Gregorio, in the chapel of Loreto, Mexico City. Parents were not named in the record. The cited marriage information record, dated September 5, 1727, named the parents of the bride and groom.[141]

In 1744 Francisca Lugarda de Rosales filed two complaints against her husband, claiming that he was not providing for her maintenance. She stated that she lacked money for food, and that her mother was assisting her. Francisca solicited the authorities in Mexico City to make her husband pay the expenses for her support with great penalties imposed.[142]

---

137. Bautismos de españoles 1730–1735, October 20, 1735, film 35181, image 979, Registros Parroquiales, Iglesia Asunción Sagrario Metropolitano, Mexico City, Mexico (FamilySearch, https://familysearch.org).
138. Bautismos de españoles 1741–1745, November 18, 1741, film 35183, image, 160, Registros Parroquiales, Iglesia Asunción Sagrario Metropolitano, Mexico City, Mexico (FamilySearch, https://familysearch.org).
139. Bautismos de españoles 1691–1705, May 10, 1705, film 35176, image 1059, Registros Parroquiales, Iglesia Asunción Sagrario Metropolitano, Mexico City, Mexico (FamilySearch, https://familysearch.org).
140. Matrimonios de españoles 1728–1751, October 17, 1727, film 35272, image 23, Registros Parroquiales, Iglesia Asunción Sagrario Metropolitano, Mexico City, Mexico (FamilySearch, https://familysearch.org).
141. Información matrimonial de españoles 1694–1734, September 5, 1727, film 35256, image 901, Registros Parroquiales, Iglesia Asunción Sagrario Metropolitano, Mexico City, Mexico (FamilySearch, https:// familysearch.org).
142. Francisca Rosales solicita se notifique a Raymundo de Ymaz, su esposo que bajo grandes penas de apercibimiento debe acudirla con lo necesario para su mantenimiento, México, 1744, Instituciones Coloniales/ IndiferenteVirreinal/ Expediente, 53, Cajas 5000–5999/ Caja 5981, AGN (http://www.agn.gob.mx/); Francisca Rosales, en autos con Raymundo de Ymaz, su esposo y vecino de Texcoco, solicitase le carguen a él las costas derivadas de ellos, puesto que ella no tiene ni para alimentos y está siendo ayudada por su madre, Mexico,

Francisca Lugarda Tomasa de Rosales, daughter of Francisco Antonio Rosales and Michaela González Cortez, was born on September 18, 1712, in Mexico City. She was baptized on September 29, 1712, at the parish church of the Asunción Sagrario Metropolitano in Mexico City.[143] The baptismal record named Thomas Ximenes and Nicolasa Torres as her *padrinos*.

Raymundo Joseph Ymaz y Esquer and Francisca Lugarda Tomasa de Rosales had one known child:

    i.   **Rosa María Ymaz y Esquer** was born on August 29, 1729, in Mexico City, according to the baptismal record. She was baptized on September 9, 1729, at the parish church of the Asunción Sagrario Metropolitano in Mexico City.[144] The baptismal record named Michaela Gonzáles as her *madrina*.

27. **María Josepha Francisca Ymaz y Esquer** (Salvadora Manuela Silvestra Esquer-4, Salvador-3, Salvador-2, Blas-1) was born on October 4, 1706, in Mexico City, according to the baptismal record. She was baptized on October 17, 1706, at the parish church of the Asunción Sagrario Metropolitano in Mexico City.[145] The baptismal record named Pantaleón de Palazuelos y Peña y Bolado and Josepha de la Gradilla, his wife, as her *padrinos*.

María Josepha Francisca Ymaz y Esquer and Francisco Manuel Antonio Chirlín were married on September 26, 1723, at the parish church of the Asunción Sagrario Metropolitano in Mexico City.[146] The matrimonial record named Bachiller Joseph de Soria and Antonio Tamariz as witnesses, but did not name parents. On the day following their marriage the couple received a nuptial blessing at the church of Amor de Dios. The cited marriage information record, dated September 1723, named the parents of the bride and groom.

Francisco Manuel Antonio Chirlín, son of Pedro León Chirlín and María Theresa Tamariz y Salcedo, was born in 1692 in Mexico City. He was baptized on December 13, 1692, at the parish church of the Asunción Sagrario Metropolitano in Mexico City.[147] The baptismal record named Antonio Francisco de Salas as his *padrino*. He died in 1737 at the age of forty-five in Mexico City.[148] The cited reference to the last testament of Francisco Manuel Antonio Chirlín is 1737.

1744, Instituciones Coloniales/Indiferente Virreinal/ Expediente 52, Cajas 5000–5999/ Caja 5981, AGN (http://www.agn.gob.mx/).

143. Bautismos de españoles 1705–1713, September 29, 1712, film 35177, image 878, Registros Parroquiales, Iglesia Asunción Sagrario Metropolitano, Mexico City, Mexico (FamilySearch, https://familysearch.org).

144. Bautismos de españoles 1724–1730, September 9, 1729, film 35180, image 985, Registros Parroquiales, Iglesia Asunción Sagrario Metropolitano, Mexico City, Mexico (FamilySearch, https://familysearch.org).

145. Bautismos de españoles 1705–1713, October 17, 1706, film 35177, image 115, Registros Parroquiales, Iglesia Asunción Sagrario Metropolitano, Mexico City, Mexico (FamilySearch, https://familysearch.org).

146. Matrimonios de españoles 1702–1728, September 26, 1723, film 35271, image 844, Registros Parroquiales, Iglesia Asunción Sagrario Metropolitano, Mexico City, Mexico (FamilySearch, https:// familysearch.org); Información matrimonial de españoles 1694–1734, September 1723, film 35256, image 745, Registros Parroquiales, Iglesia Asunción Sagrario Metropolitano, Mexico City, Mexico (FamilySearch, https:// familysearch.org).

147. Bautismos de españoles 1690–1716, December 13, 1692, film 205938, image 60, Registros Parroquiales, Iglesia Asunción Sagrario Metropolitano, Mexico City, Mexico (FamilySearch, https://familysearch.org).

148. Fernando Muñoz Altea, *Documentos Notariales, siglos XVII al XIX* (Mexico, D.F. n.d.: Francisco Muñoz Altea), Juan Antonio de Arroyo, notario, (19) folio 499 vto. Testó-VIII-1737.

His named children were María Antonia and Juan Ángel Chirlín. No mention was made of his other children. Chirlín held the title of Procurador Propietario de Número de la Real Audiencia y Chancilleria at the time of his death. The notary who recorded the last testament was identified as Juan Antonio de Arroyo. The cited matrimonial and marriage information records identified Francisco Manuel Antonio Chirlín as "Francisco Xavier Chirlin" in what appears to have been in error.

Francisco Manuel Antonio Chirlín and María Josepha Francisca Ymaz y Esquer had the following known children:

i. **María Antonia Matilde Chirlín** was born on March 14, 1725, in Mexico City, according to the baptismal record. She was baptized on March 19, 1725, at the parish church of the Asunción Sagrario Metropolitano in Mexico City, New Spain.[149] The baptismal record named Antonio Tamariz y Carmona as her *padrino*.

56 ii. **Juan Antonio Joseph Chirlín** was born on June 23, 1726, in Mexico City. He married Anna María de Tamariz y Gradillas on February 2, 1756, in Mexico City.

iii. **Ygnacio Fausto Joseph Chirlín** was born on September 6, 1728, in Mexico City, according to the baptismal record. He was baptized on September 13, 1728, at the parish church of the Asunción Sagrario Metropolitano in Mexico City.[150] The baptismal record named Bachiller Juan Pedro Villa de Moros as his *padrino*.

iv. **Manuel Joseph Antonio Chirlín** was born on August 5, 1730, in Mexico City, according to the baptismal record. He was baptized on August 10, 1730, at the parish church of the Asunción Sagrario Metropolitano in Mexico City.[151] The baptismal record named Pedro López and Manuela de Quirós as his *padrinos*.

v. **Juan Ángel Chirlín** was born about 1732 in Mexico City.[152] The cited last testament for Francisco Manuel Antonio Chirlín named Juan Angel Chirlín as his son. No other documents have been located to confirm his birth and parentage.

28. **Pedro Fernando Esquer** (Miguel Fernando Simón-4, Salvador-3, Salvador-2, Blas-1) was born about 1720.[153] The cited marriage investigation for Pedro's son, Pablo Esquer, and María Dolores Valenzuela named Miguel Fernando Esquer and Augustina Guillerma Romero y Fuentes as parents of Pedro Esquer.

---

149. Bautismos de españoles 1724–1730, March19, 1725, film 35180, image 152, Registros Parroquiales, Iglesia Asunción Sagrario Metropolitano, Mexico City, Mexico (FamilySearch, https://familysearch.org).
150. Bautismos de españoles 1724–1730, September 13, 1728, film 35180, image 752, Registros Parroquiales, Iglesia Asunción Sagrario Metropolitano, Mexico City, Mexico (FamilySearch, https://familysearch.org).
151. Bautismos de españoles 1724–1730, August 10, 1730, film 35180, image 1149, Registros Parroquiales, Iglesia Asunción Sagrario Metropolitano, Mexico City, Mexico (FamilySearch, https://familysearch.org).
152. Fernando Muñoz Altea, *Documentos Notariales, siglos XVII al XIX* (Mexico, D.F. n.d.: Francisco Muñoz Altea), Juan Antonio de Arroyo, notario, (19) folio 499 vto. Testó-VIII-1737.
153. Diligencias matrimoniales, Pablo Esquerr y María Dolores Valenzuela, Pueblo de Movas, 1779, AHAD-31, frames 429–443, AHAD.

Pedro Fernando Esquer and María Loreto Encinas were married about 1740. Their matrimonial record has not been located.

María Loreto Encinas was born about 1722. The cited marriage investigation for Pablo Esquer and María Dolores Valenzuela named Pedro Esquer and María Loreto Encinas as Pablo's parents.

Pedro Fernando Esquer and María Loreto Encinas had the following known children:

57   i.   **Pablo Esquer** was born about 1755 and married María Dolores Valenzuela sometime after November 13, 1779.

58   ii.   **María Manuela Esquer** was born about 1760 and married Juan Francisco Campoy about 1776.

29. **Nicolás Esquer** (Miguel Fernando Simón-4, Salvador-3, Salvador-2, Blas-1) was born about 1740. Nicolás Esquer and Ygnacia Petrona de Cortabarria Sarmiento were married on September 8, 1767, at the parish of the Asunción Sagrario Metropolitano in Mexico City.[154] The marriage record named Licenciado Joseph Laguna, attorney; Joseph Tobio, Profesor de Medicina; and Francisco Madrigal as witnesses to the marriage. The wedding took place at the home of the groom, which was located on the Calle del Parque del Palacio, Casa del Hospital del Amor de Dios.

Nicolás Esquer held the title of Abogado de la Real Audiencia. He died before May 10, 1777, in Mexico City.[155] Upon his death his mother Augustina Romero y Fuentes was named his heir. He left her a sum of 4,887 pesos.

---

154. Matrimonios de españoles 1765–1766, September 8, 1767, film 35275, image 149, Registros Parroquiales, Iglesia Asunción Sagrario Metropolitano, Mexico City, Mexico (FamilySearch, https://familysearch.org).
155. Nicolás Esquer, Agustina Romero y Fuentes, heredera, Mexico, 1777, Instituciones Coloniales/ RealAudiencia/Bienes de Difuntos (013)/Contenedor 06/Volumen 12/Expediente 4, hojas 91r–91v, AGN (http://www.agn.gob.mx/).

Sixth Generation

30. Francisco Xavier Alcayde Pérez de la Puente (Juana Esquer-5, Juan Salvador-4, Salvador-3, Salvador-2, Blas-1) was born in 1720 in Culiacán. He was baptized on December 12, 1720, at the church of the Sagrario de San Miguel in Culiacán.[156] The baptismal record named María López de Siqueiros as his *madrina*.

Francisco Xavier Alcayde Pérez de la Puente and Ana Antonia del Castillo y Cabanillas were married about 1741 in New Spain. Their marriage document has not been located.

Francisco Xavier died on September 4, 1754, at the age of thirty-four in Culiacán. He was buried on September 5, 1754, at the church of the Sagrario de San Miguel in Culiacán.[157] The burial record stated that he had been married to Ana Antonia Cabanillas. He died having received the last sacraments of the Catholic Church. His burial services included the honors of *cruz alta y misa de cuerpo presente*.

Ana Antonia del Castillo y Cabanillas, daughter of Tomás del Castillo y Cabanillas and Nicolasa Verdugo Cebreros, was born in 1720 in Culiacán. She was baptized on April 25, 1720, at the church of the Sagrario de San Miguel in Culiacán.[158] Her baptismal record named Alférez Nicolás Verdugo and Josefa del Castillo y Cabanillas as her *padrinos*.

Francisco Xavier Alcayde Pérez de la Puente and Ana Antonia del Castillo y Cabanillas had the following known children:

59   i.   **María Matilde de la Luz Alcayde Pérez de la Puente** was born in 1742 in Culiacán. She married Bruno Joseph de Liceaga on February 26, 1758, in Culiacán.

60   ii.   **Joaquín Andrés Alcayde** was born about 1745 in Culiacán. He married María Ysidora Rivera on April 22, 1772, in Álamos and died on October 10, 1781, in Álamos.

61   iii.   **Miguel Alcayde Pérez de la Puente** was born about 1744 in Culiacán. He married María Balvanera de Yriarte on December 6, 1775, in Álamos and died on November 15, 1797, in Álamos.

---

156. Bautismos 1690–1746, 1731–1769, December 12, 1720, film 665425, image 113, Registros Parroquiales, Iglesia Sagrario de San Miguel, Culiacán, Sinaloa, Mexico (FamilySearch, https://familysearch.org).
157. Defunciones 1746–1833, September 5, 1754, film 674051, image 16, Registros Parroquiales, Iglesia Sagrario de San Miguel, Culiacán, Sinaloa, Mexico (FamilySearch, https://familysearch.org).
158. Bautismos 1690–1746, 1731–1769, April 25, 1720, film 665425, image 113, Registros Parroquiales, Iglesia Sagrario de San Miguel, Culiacán, Sinaloa, Mexico (FamilySearch, https://familysearch.org).

31. **Juan Salvador Esquer** (Salvador-5, Juan Salvador-4, Salvador-3, Salvador-2, Blas-1) was born in 1739.[159] His year of birth was based on information he provided as a witness in the cited marriage investigation record for Gabriel Mallén de Navarrete dated December 1761. In that record, he stated that he was twenty-two years of age at the time.

Juan Salvador Esquer and María Manuela Campoy were married on November 22, 1764, at the parish of the Purísima Concepción in Álamos.[160] The matrimonial record named Capitán Juan Augustín de Yriarte and Anna María González Barreda as *padrinos*. Bachiller Juan Antonio de Anguís, Bachiller Pedro Joaquín Campoy and Bachiller Joaquín Antonio Esquer, among many others present, were identified as witnesses to the marriage. Parents of the bride and groom were named in the record. The marriage ceremony took place at the home of the newly married couple, which was located in the mining town of La Aduana, jurisdiction of Álamos.

Juan Salvador Esquer died before July 27, 1797.[161] The cited marriage record for his son, José Rafael Esquer, stated that Juan Salvador was deceased on the date of the marriage, July 27, 1797.

María Manuela Campoy, daughter of Raymundo Antonio Campoy and Ana María González de Zayas, was born about 1740. She died on September 7, 1780, in Álamos. She was buried on September 8, 1780, at the church of the Purísima Concepción in Álamos.[162] María Manuela Campoy was laid to rest in a burial site valued at twenty-five pesos. Her funeral service was held with a *cruz alta*. The record stated that because of her poverty, she did not leave a will. She was survived by five legitimate children: Anna, Gertrudis, Rafaela, Ygnacia, and Rafael.

Juan Salvador Esquer and María Manuela Campoy had the following children:

62   i.   **Anna María Esquer** was born before 1780. She married Juan Joseph Pantaleón Morales on July 4, 1808, in Álamos.

      ii.   **Rafaela Esquer** was born before 1780.[163] The cited 1780 burial record for her mother listed Rafaela Esquer as a surviving child.

      iii. **María Balvanera Gertrudis Esquer** was born in 1769 in Álamos.[164] The cited 1780 burial record for her mother listed Gertrudis as a surviving child. She was baptized on March 26, 1769, at the church of the Purísima Concepción in Álamos.[165] Her

---

159. Información matrimonial 1760–1799, December 1761, film 667002, image 67, Registros Parroquiales, Iglesia de La Purísima Concepción, Álamos, Sonora, Mexico (FamilySearch, https://familysearch.org).

160. Matrimonios 1758–1779, November 22, 1764, film 666564, image 76, Registros Parroquiales, Iglesia de La Purísima Concepción, Álamos, Sonora, Mexico (FamilySearch, https://familysearch.org).

161. Matrimonios 1779–1817, July 27, 1797, film 666565, images 334–335, Registros Parroquiales, Iglesia de La Purísima Concepción, Álamos, Sonora, Mexico (FamilySearch, https://familysearch.org).

162. Defunciones 1717–1751, 1764–1792, September 8, 1780, film 666995, image 337, Registros Parroquiales, Iglesia de La Purísima Concepción, Alamos, Sonora, Mexico (FamilySearch, https://familysearch.org).

163. Defunciones 1717–1751, 1764–1792, September 8, 1780, film 666995, image 337, Registros Parroquiales, Iglesia de La Purísima Concepción, Álamos, Sonora, Mexico (FamilySearch, https://familysearch.org).

164. Defunciones 1717–1751, 1764–1792, September 8, 1780, film 666995, image 337, Registros Parroquiales, Iglesia de La Purísima Concepción, Alamos, Sonora, Mexico (FamilySearch, https://familysearch.org).

165. Bautismos, matrimonios y defunciones 1696–1699, bautismos 1768–1781, March 26, 1769, film 663487, image 129, Registros Parroquiales, Iglesia de La Purísima Concepción, Álamos, Sonora, Mexico (FamilySearch, https://familysearch.org).

baptismal record named Raymundo Antonio Campoy and María Lucía Gastélum as her *padrinos*. Vicario Superintendente Pedro Gabriel de Aragón, and Bachiller Pedro Joaquín Elías González de Zayas, among various *vecinos*, were named as witnesses to the baptism. She died on April 15, 1781, at the age of twelve in Álamos. María Balvarena was buried on April 16, 1781, at the church of the Purísima Concepción in Álamos.[166] She was interred in a burial site valued at five pesos. Her funeral service was held with *cruz alta, capa, y una mesa.*

63   iv.   **José Rafael Esquer** was born in 1775, Álamos. He married María Rita Cano de los Ríos on July 27, 1797, in Álamos.

64   v.   **María Gertrudis Esquer** was born about 1777; she married Luis Juan Joseph Raphael Fox on March 28, 1797, in Álamos.

65   vi.   **María Ignacia de la Trinidad Esquer** was born in 1779 in Álamos. She married Ignacio María Gonzáles de Zayas on February 24, 1800, in Álamos.

32. Joseph Gabriel Esquer (Salvador-5, Juan Salvador-4, Salvador-3, Salvador-2, Blas-1) was born in 1742.[167] Joseph Gabriel's year of birth is based on information he provided as a witness in the marriage investigation record of his second cousin, Gabriel Mallén de Navarrete, dated December 1761. In the record, he stated that he was nineteen years of age.

Joseph Gabriel Esquer and Francisca Augustina Avilés were married on January 1, 1762, at the church of the Purísima Concepción in Álamos.[168] The matrimonial record named Joseph Francisco de Avilés and Michaela Salvadora Mallén de Navarrete as *padrinos*. Michaela Salvadora Mallén de Navarrete was said to have been a widow and the aunt of both the bride and groom. Bachillers Juan Antonio de Anguís, Ygnacio Fernández Valdez, and Joaquín Antonio Esquer, among others present were identified as witnesses to the sacrament of marriage. The couple received a dispensation to marry because they were related in the third degree of consanguinity, meaning they were second cousins. Parents of the bride and groom were named in the record. Parents of the groom were said to have been deceased, as was the mother of the bride.

Joseph Gabriel died on February 10, 1793, at the age of fifty-one in Álamos. He was buried on February 11, 1793, at the church of the Purísima Concepción in Álamos.[169] He was interred in a grave valued at four pesos, with *cruz alta y tres dobles.* The record stated that he had been married to Francisca Avilés and that there was a debt remaining for the funeral services.

---

166. Defunciones 1717–1751,1764–1792, April 16, 1781, film 666995, images 359–360, Registros Parroquiales, Iglesia de La Purísima Concepción, Álamos, Sonora, Mexico (FamilySearch, https://familysearch.org).

167. Información matrimonial 1760–1799, December 1761, film 667002, image 67, Registros Parroquiales, Iglesia de La Purísima Concepción, Álamos, Sonora, Mexico (FamilySearch, https://familysearch.org).

168. Matrimonios 1758–1779, January 1, 1762, film 666564, image 43, Registros Parroquiales, Iglesia de La Purísima Concepción, Álamos, Sonora, Mexico (FamilySearch, https://familysearch.org).

169. Defunciones 1786–1819, February 11, 1793, film 666996, image 58, Registros Parroquiales, Iglesia de La Purísima Concepción, Álamos, Sonora, Mexico (FamilySearch, https://familysearch.org).

Francisca Augustina Avilés, daughter of Joseph Francisco Avilés and Augustina Mallén de Navarrete, was born about 1740.

Joseph Gabriel Esquer and Francisca Augustina Avilés had one known child:

    i.   **María del Carmen Esquer** died on December 1, 1781, in Álamos. She was buried on December 2, 1781, at the church of the Purísima Concepción in Álamos.[170] Her funeral service was held with *cruz alta, capa y una mesa y caja*. She was interred in a grave site valued at ten pesos. The record appeared to indicate that she was the adopted daughter of Joseph Gabriel Esquer and Francisca Augustina Avilés.

33. **Ana María Esquer** (Salvador-5, Juan Salvador-4, Salvador-3, Salvador-2, Blas-1) was born about 1746.

Ana María Esquer and Miguel Martínez were married on December 25, 1764, at the parish of the Purísima Concepción in Álamos.[171] The matrimonial record named Capitán Juan Augustín de Yriarte and Ana María González Barreda as *padrinos*. Bachiller Manuel Gil Samaniego, Joseph Francisco de Avilés, and Vicente Mallén de Navarrete were named as witnesses to the marriage. The marriage required an *ultramarino* (across the sea) dispensation because the groom was a native of Spain and not locally known to be eligible for marriage. Parents of the bride and groom were named in the record. The marriage ceremony took place at the home of Bachiller Juan Antonio de Anguís.

Miguel Martínez, son of Miguel Martínez and Cipriana de Salazar, was born about 1740 in Castile, Spain. The cited baptism record for his son, Joseph Ygnacio Sebastián, stated that Miguel Martínez held the position of *notario publico* (public notary) in the mining town of La Aduana.

Miguel Martínez and Ana María Esquer had the following known children:

    i.   **María Luisa Josefa Martínez** was born in 1765 in Álamos. She was baptized on August 27, 1765, at the church of the Purísima Concepción in Álamos.[172] The baptismal record named Bachiller Pedro Gabriel de Aragón and Ana María Aragón as her *padrinos*. Bachiller Juan Joseph de Avilés, Juan Augustín de Yriarte, and Francisco Julián de Alvarado, among others, were named as witnesses. María Luisa Josefa died on July 20, 1776, at the age of eleven in Álamos. She was buried on July 21, 1776, at the church of the Purísima Concepción in Álamos.[173] She was laid to rest in burial site valued at fifty pesos, and her funeral service was held with a *cruz alta*.

---

170. Defunciones 1717–1751, 1764–1792, December 2, 1781, film 666995, image 386, Registros Parroquiales, Iglesia de La Purísima Concepción, Álamos, Sonora, Mexico (FamilySearch, https://familysearch.org).
171. Matrimonios 1758–1779, December 25, 1764, film 666564, images 77–78, Registros Parroquiales, Iglesia de La Purísima Concepción, Álamos, Sonora, Mexico (FamilySearch, https://familysearch.org).
172. Bautismos 1751–1794, matrimonios 1848, defunciones 1735–1752, August 27, 1765, film 666999, image 312, Registros Parroquiales, Iglesia de La Purísima Concepción, Álamos, Sonora, Mexico (FamilySearch, https://familysearch.org).
173. Defunciones 1717–1751, 1764–1792, July21, 1776, film 666995, image 181, Registros Parroquiales, Iglesia de La Purísima Concepción, Álamos, Sonora, Mexico (FamilySearch, https://familysearch.org).

ii. **Joseph Francisco Xavier Vicente Martínez** was born in 1767 in Álamos. He was baptized on August 23, 1767, at the church of the Purísima Concepción in Álamos.[174] The baptismal record named Vicente Sagada and Petra de Goycochea as his *padrinos*. Teniente General Juan Augustín Yriarte, Bachiller Juan Antonio de Anguís, and Bachiller Luis de Padilla were named as witnesses.

iii. **María Josefa Balvanera Martínez** was born in 1769 in Álamos. She was baptized on March 12, 1769, at the church of the Purísima Concepción in Álamos.[175] The baptismal record named Juan Augustín Yriarte and Ana María González Barreda as his *padrinos*. Fernando Barreda and Joseph Gabriel Esquer were named as witnesses.

iv. **Joseph Ygnacio Sebastián Martínez** was born on February 11, 1770, in Álamos. The cited baptismal record stated that he was eleven days old when baptized. He was baptized on February 21, 1770, at the parish of the Purísima Concepción in Álamos.[176] The baptismal record named Bachiller Joseph Joaquín Elías Zayas, parish priest of the pueblo of Navojoa, and Lorenza Goycochea as his *padrinos*. The record also stated that his father was the *notario publico* (public notary) in La Aduana, jurisdiction of Álamos, where the baptism took place. Both parents were said to be *vecinos* of La Aduana.

v. **Francisco Xavier Rafael Martínez** was born in 1771 in Álamos. He was baptized on December 17, 1771, at the parish church of the Purísima Concepción in Álamos.[177] The baptismal record named Francisco Julián de Alvarado and Antonia González de Zayas as his *padrinos*.

34. María Loreto Esquer (Salvador-5, Juan Salvador-4, Salvador-3, Salvador-2, Blas-1) was born about 1750. She was also known as "María Loreto de Anguís." The cited marriage record for her son Luis Juan Francisco identified her as such.

María Loreto Esquer and Juan Pablo Fox were married on December 8, 1769, at the parish of the Purísima Concepción in Álamos.[178] The matrimonial record did not name *padrinos* or witnesses. Parents of the bride were named. The groom was said to be from Castile, Spain, and a *vecino* of Álamos. The marriage took place at the home of Bachiller Juan Antonio Anguís.

---

174. Bautismos 1751–1794, matrimonios 1848, defunciones 1735–1752, August 23, 1767, film 666999, image 331, Registros Parroquiales, Iglesia de La Purísima Concepción, Álamos, Sonora, Mexico (FamilySearch, https://familysearch.org).
175. Bautismos, matrimonios y defunciones 1696–1699, bautismos 1768–1781, March 12, 1769, film 663487, image 128, Registros Parroquiales, Iglesia de La Purísima Concepción, Álamos, Sonora, Mexico (FamilySearch, https://familysearch.org).
176. Bautismos, matrimonios y defunciones 1696–1699, bautismos 1768–1781, February 21, 1770, film 663487, image 144, Registros Parroquiales, Iglesia de La Purísima Concepción, Álamos, Sonora, Mexico (FamilySearch, https://familysearch.org).
177. Bautismos, matrimonios y defunciones 1696–1699, bautismos 1768–1781, December 17, 1771, film 663487, image 199, Registros Parroquiales, Iglesia de La Purísima Concepción, Álamos, Sonora, Mexico (FamilySearch, https:// familysearch.org).
178. Matrimonios 1758–1779, December 8, 1769, film 666564, image 128, Registros Parroquiales, Iglesia de La Purísima Concepción, Álamos, Sonora, Mexico (FamilySearch, https://familysearch.org).

She died on August 2, 1801, in Álamos. María Loreto was buried on August 3, 1801, at the parish church of the Purísima Concepción in Álamos.[179] María Loreto Esquer was interred in a burial a site valued at five pesos. Her funeral service was held with *cruz alta, capa, y caja*. The record stated that she had been the wife of Juan Fox.

Juan Pablo Fox was born about 1743 in Castile, Spain. He died before January 27, 1823. The cited matrimonial record for his daughter María del Carmen Gertrudis Fox claimed that he was deceased on the day her marriage took place, January 27, 1823.

Juan Pablo Fox and María Loreto Esquer had the following known children:

      i.   **Ygnacio Fox** was born about 1771. He died on May 24, 1781, likely before the age of ten in Álamos. He was buried on May 25, 1781, at the church of the Purísima Concepción in Álamos.[180] The burial record stated that Ygnacio Fox was a child [*párvulo*] who was laid to rest in burial site valued at five pesos. His funeral service was held with *cruz alta y ataúd*. His parents were named in in record.

66   ii.   **Luis Juan Joseph Raphael Fox** was born in 1772 in Álamos. He married María Gertrudis Esquer on March 28, 1797, in Álamos. He died before May 7, 1823.

67   iii.   **Luis Juan Francisco Telmo Fox** was born in 1772 in Álamos. He married María Petra Acuña on February 12, 1795, in Álamos.

      iv.   **María Balvanera Francisca Xaviera Fox** was born in 1777 in Álamos. She was baptized on December 20, 1777, at the church of the Purísima Concepción in Álamos.[181] The baptismal record named Lucas de la Serna and Tomasa Rivera as her *padrinos*.

68   v.   **María del Pilar Fox** was born about 1779.

69   vi.   **María del Carmen Gertrudis Fox** was born on January 4, 1782, in Álamos. She married Francisco Moreno y Ladosa, January 27, 1823, in Álamos.

35. Manuela Antonia Esquer (Joseph Cayetano-5, Juan Salvador-4, Salvador-3, Salvador-2, Blas-1) was born about 1719. Evidence of parentage was provided by Joseph Cayetano Esquer, who testified under oath in the cited marriage information document, dated October 9, 1760, for his niece María Gertrudis Feliz. This document stated that Joseph Cayetano Esquer was the uncle of the bride. Manuela Antonia Esquer was then his sister.[182]

---

179. Defunciones 1786–1819, August 3, 1801, film 666996, image 111, Registros Parroquiales, Iglesia de La Purísima Concepción, Álamos, Sonora, Mexico (FamilySearch, https://familysearch.org).
180. Defunciones 1717–1751, 1764–1792, May 25, 1781, film 666995, image 379, Registros Parroquiales, Iglesia de La Purísima Concepción, Álamos, Sonora, Mexico (FamilySearch, https://familysearch.org).
181. Bautismos, matrimonios y defunciones 1696–1699, bautismos 1768–1781, December 20, 1777, film 663487, image 363, Registros Parroquiales, Iglesia de La Purísima Concepción, Álamos, Sonora, Mexico (FamilySearch, https://familysearch.org).
182. Información matrimonial 1760–1799, October 9, 1760, film 667002, images 29–33, Registros Parroquiales, Iglesia de La Purísima Concepción, Álamos, Sonora, Mexico (FamilySearch, https://familysearch.org).

Manuela Antonia Esquer and Joseph Saterino Féliz were married on November 12, 1731, at the parish of the Purísima Concepción in Álamos.[183] The wedding ceremony was held at the hacienda of the groom's father, Nicolás Féliz, located one league from Álamos. Francisco Mallén de Navarrete, Fernando Barreda, and Licenciado Antonio Díaz were named as witnesses to the marriage. The couple received a nuptial blessing on the day of their marriage. Parents were not named in the record. Manuela Antonia Esquer must have been about twelve years old at marriage. This was the youngest marriageable age permitted for girls at the time. The groom's middle name appeared on the margin of the matrimonial record, but what was written is very difficult to read. It is possible the name in the margin was intended to be "Saturnino."

Manuela Antonia died on October 29, 1774. Her date of death was provided in the burial record. Manuela Antonia was buried on October 30, 1774, at the church of the Purísima Concepción in Álamos.[184] She was said to have been the widow of Joseph Féliz at the time of her death. Her burial was provided through an act of charity, *fue de limosna*.

Joseph Saterino Féliz, son of Nicolás Féliz and María Margarita de León, was born about 1712. He died on September 19, 1764, in Álamos. He was buried on September 20, 1764, at the church of the Purísima Concepción in Álamos.[185] His burial service was held with a *cruz alta* and he was laid to rest in a burial site valued at five pesos. Joseph Féliz served as a military officer who held the title of Capitán de Guerra during his career.

Joseph Saterino Féliz and Manuela Antonia Esquer had the following children:

    i.   **Féliz** was born about 1738. He died in 1738 in Álamos. He was buried on August 23, 1738, in Álamos.[186] The burial record provided no given name, only that the deceased was a small child.

70   ii.   **Petra María Gertrudis Féliz** was born about 1739 in Álamos. She married Francisco Antonio Martínez Mendívil on October 26, 1760, in Álamos.

71   iii.   **Joseph Vicente Féliz** was born about 1741 in Álamos. He married Manuela Ygnacia López Peñuelas on July 13, 1760 in Álamos. He died on January 29, 1809, in Santa Bárbara, Alta California.

72   iv.   **María Guadalupe Féliz** was born about 1746 in Álamos. She married Manuel Cornelio Maldonado on May 11, 1766, in Álamos. He died on June 21, 1769, in Álamos.

73   v.   **Joseph Salvador Féliz** was born in 1752 in Álamos. He married María Loreto Jacinta del Carmen Muñoz on July 5, 1791, in Álamos.

---

183. Matrimonios 1716–1757, November 12, 1731, [no film number], image 77, Registros Parroquiales, Iglesia de La PurísimaConcepción, Álamos, Sonora, Mexico (FamilySearch, https://familysearch.org).

184. Defunciones 1717–1751,1764–1792, film 666995, image 266, Registros Parroquiales, Iglesia de La Purísima Concepción, Álamos, Sonora, Mexico (FamilySearch, https://familysearch.org).

185. Defunciones 1717–1751,1764–1792, film 666995, image 162, Registros Parroquiales, Iglesia de La Purísima Concepción, Álamos, Sonora, Mexico (FamilySearch, https://familysearch.org).

186. Bautismos 1751–1794, matrimonios 1848, defunciones 1735–1752, film 666999, image 30, Registros Parroquiales, Iglesia de La Purísima Concepción, Álamos, Sonora, Mexico, (FamilySearch, https://familysearch.org).

74 vi. **Ana María Yrene Féliz** was born in 1757 in Álamos. She married José Ygnacio Ybarra on December 27, 1772, in Álamos.

75 vii. **Manuel Féliz** was born about 1760. He married María Ygnacia Pardo in about 1784. He married María Francisca Padilla on May 15, 1822, in Álamos.

36. Joseph Cayetano Esquer (Joseph Cayetano-5, Juan Salvador-4, Salvador-3, Salvador-2, Blas-1) was born about 1721. His baptismal record has not been located to prove that he was the son of Joseph Cayetano Esquer and María [Nicolasa] Valenzuela. There was, however, compelling evidence to establish his parentage.

The cited October 1777 marriage investigation for Juan Pedro Armenta and María Ynocencia Esquer named Nicolasa Valenzuela. as the mother of Joseph Cayetano Esquer.[187] His mother's full name was likely "Maria Nicolasa Valenzuela." Joseph Cayetano Esquer testified under oath in the cited marriage information document, dated October 9, 1760, for his niece María Gertrudis Féliz. He claimed that he was forty-four or forty-five years of age in 1760. This document stated that Joseph Cayetano Esquer was the uncle of the bride. Presumably, their common ancestors were grandparents Juan Salvador Esquer and Michaela de Amarillas.[188]

The cited baptismal record dated May 25, 1762, for María Balvarena Gertrudis, daughter of Miguel Millán and Catarina Molina, named Joseph Cayetano Esquer and María Jesús Esquer as godparents. They were said to be first cousins.[189] This lends further evidence that the common ancestors were Juan Salvador Esquer and Michaela de Amarillas.

The cited marriage record dated October 9, 1743 and nuptial blessing recorded in the margin of the entry, dated April 14, 1761, for Manuel de Anaya and María Justa Esquer named Juan Salvador Esquer and María Jesús as siblings, making the common ancestors Juan Salvador Esquer and Michaela de Amarillas.[190] Joseph Cayetano Esquer did not have the ability to sign his name on documents where he gave testimony.

Joseph Cayetano Esquer and Juliana Astorga were married on November 1, 1749, at the church of the Purísima Concepción in Álamos.[191] The matrimonial record lists Sebastián López Bravo and Joseph Féliz as witnesses. Parents of the bride and groom were not named.

---

187. Información matrimonial 1760–1799, October 1777, film 667002, images 310–313, Registros Parroquiales, Iglesia de La Purísima Concepción, Álamos, Sonora, Mexico (FamilySearch, https://familysearch.org).
188. Información matrimonial 1760–1799, October 9, 1760, film 667002, images 29–33, Registros Parroquiales, Iglesia de La Purísima Concepción, Álamos, Sonora, Mexico (FamilySearch, https://familysearch.org).
189. Bautismos 1751–1794, matrimonios 1848, defunciones 1735–1752, May 25, 1762, film 666999, images 228–229, Registros Parroquiales, Iglesia de La Purísima Concepción, Álamos, Sonora, Mexico (FamilySearch, https://familysearch.org).
190. Matrimonios 1716–1757, October 9, 1743, film 663806, image 135, Registros Parroquiales, Iglesia de La Purísima Concepción, Álamos, Sonora, Mexico (FamilySearch, https://familysearch.org).
191. Matrimonios 1716–1757, November 1, 1749, [no film number], image 159, Registros Parroquiales, Iglesia de La Purísima Concepción, Álamos, Sonora, Mexico (FamilySearch, https://familysearch.org).

Juliana Astorga, daughter of Ygnacio Astorga and Efigenia García, was born about 1730. Juliana Astorga was recorded as "Juliana García" (her mother's surname) in the baptismal entries for two of her children, María Balvanera Antonia and María Dolores Margarita.

Joseph Cayetano Esquer and Juliana Astorga had the following known children:

76 i.   **María Ynocencia Esquer** was born in 1752 in Álamos and married Juan Pedro Segundo Armenta on June 7, 1778, in Álamos.

    ii.   **Manuela Antonia Margarita Esquer** was born in 1754 in Álamos. She was baptized on September 16, 1754, at the church of the Purísima Concepción in Álamos.[192] The baptismal record named Manuel Velarde and Manuela Antonia Féliz as her *padrinos*.

    iii.   **Pedro Manuel Alexandro Esquer** was born in 1755 in Álamos. He was baptized on December 8, 1755, at the church of the Purísima Concepción in Álamos.[193] The baptismal record named Manuel Velarde and Gertrudis Velarde as his *padrinos*.

    iv.   **Joaquín Antonio Esquer** was born in 1757 in Álamos. He was baptized on September 1, 1757, at the church of the Purísima Concepción in Álamos.[194] The baptismal record for Joaquín Antonio Esquer named Joseph Gabriel Esquer and Micaela Salvadora Esquer as his *padrinos*.

77 v.   **María Balvanera Antonia Esquer** was born in 1759 in Álamos and married Salvador Manuel Víctor Corral on June 24, 1782, in Álamos.

78 vi.   **María de la Merced Dolores Esquer** was born in 1761 in Álamos and married Guillermo Antonio Armenta on July 4, 1788, in Álamos.

    vii.   **María del Carmen Rosalía Esquer** was born in 1763 in Álamos. She was baptized on January 3, 1763, at the church of the Purísima Concepción in Álamos.[195] The baptismal record named Juan Agustín Yriarte and his wife Ana María González Barreda as her *padrinos*.

    viii. **María Dolores Margarita Esquer** was born in 1765 in Álamos. She was baptized on June 19, 1765, at the church of the Purísima Concepción in Álamos.[196] The baptismal record named Manuel Velarde and Manuela Féliz as her *padrinos*.

---

192. Bautismos 1751–1794, matrimonios 1848, defunciones 1735–1752, September 16, 1754, film 666999, image 100, Registros Parroquiales, Iglesia de La Purísima Concepción, Álamos, Sonora, Mexico (FamilySearch, https://familysearch.org).

193. Bautismos 1751–1794, matrimonios 1848, defunciones 1735–1752, December 8, 1755, film 666999, image 119, Registros Parroquiales, Iglesia de La Purísima Concepción, Álamos, Sonora, Mexico (FamilySearch, https://familysearch.org).

194. Bautismos 1751–1794, matrimonios 1848, defunciones 1735–1752, September 1, 1757, film 666999, image 150, Registros Parroquiales, Iglesia de La Purísima Concepción, Álamos, Sonora, Mexico (FamilySearch, https://familysearch.org).

195. Bautismos 1751–1794, matrimonios 1848, defunciones 1735–1752, January 3, 1763, film 666999, image 255, Registros Parroquiales, Iglesia de La Purísima Concepción, Álamos, Sonora, Mexico (FamilySearch, https://familysearch.org).

196. Bautismos 1751–1794, matrimonios 1848, defunciones 1735–1752, June 19, 1765, film 666999, image 311, Registros Parroquiales, Iglesia de La Purísima Concepción, Álamos, Sonora, Mexico (FamilySearch, https://familysearch.org).

79 ix.   **María Gertrudis Esquer** was born on 1768 in Álamos. She married Agustín Castro on June 18, 1798 in Álamos and died on June 2, 1811, in Álamos.

80 x.   **José Joaquín Esquer** was born about 1768. He married María Manuela del Carmen Hurtado on June 18, 1787, in Álamos and died on December 15, 1796, in Álamos.

81 xi.   **Joseph Julián Esquer** was born on February 15, 1770, in Álamos. He married María Juliana García on November 13, 1795, in Álamos.

37. María Raphaela Esquer (Francisco Joseph-5, Juan Salvador-4, Salvador-3, Salvador-2, Blas-1) was born in 1729 in Culiacán. She was baptized on November 8, 1729, at the church of the Sagrario de San Miguel in Culiacán.[197] Her baptismal record named Santiago Páez and María Rosa Páez as her *padrino*s.

María Raphaela Esquer and Fernando Antonio González Barreda were married on April 1, 1750, at the parish of the Sagrario de San Miguel in Culiacán and they received their nuptial blessing in Álamos on August 30, 1750.[198] The matrimonial record named Francisco Ramos, and his wife Antonia Murillo as *padrinos*. Francisco Alcayde, Miguel Yturríos, and Ildefonso Verdugo were named as witnesses to the marriage. The marriage ceremony took place in Culiacán at the home of Francisco Esquer. The cited record for their nuptial blessing named Manuel Sobarzo and Vicente Mallén de Navarrete as witnesses.

María Raphaela Esquer died on May 7, 1785, at the age of fifty-six in Álamos. She was buried on May 8, 1785, at the church of the Purísima Concepción in Álamos.[199] She was interred in a burial site valued at five pesos. Her funeral service was held with *capa y cruz alta*. The record stated that she had been the widow of Fernando Barreda. María Rafaela received the last sacraments of the Catholic Church before death.

Fernando Antonio González Barreda, son of Fernando González Barreda and Micaela Salvadora Mallén de Navarrete, was born about 1733. He died before May 8, 1785. The cited burial record, dated May 8, 1785, for his wife María Raphaela Esquer stated that she was the widow of Fernando González Barreda. The cited baptismal records for his sons Joseph Fernando Antonio and Joseph Francisco noted that their father's name was "Fernando Antonio Barreda." Also, the cited record for his nuptial blessing noted his name as "Fernando Martín Antonio González Barreda."

---

197. Bautismos 1690–1746, bautismos 1731–1769, film 665425, image 143, Registros Parroquiales, Iglesia Sagrario de San Miguel, Culiacán, Sinaloa, Mexico (FamilySearch, https://familysearch.org).
198. Matrimonios 1731–1755, April 1, 1750, film 665426, images 104–105, Registros Parroquiales, Iglesia Sagrario de San Miguel, Culiacán, Sinaloa, Mexico (FamilySearch, https://familysearch.org); Matrimonios 1716–1757, August 30, 1750, [no film number], image 164, Registros Parroquiales, Iglesia de La Purísima Concepción, Álamos, Sonora, Mexico (FamilySearch, https://familysearch.org).
199. Defunciones 1717–1751, 1764–1792, May 8, 1785, film 666995, image 459, Registros Parroquiales, Iglesia de La Purísima Concepción, Álamos, Sonora, Mexico (FamilySearch, https://familysearch.org).

Fernando Antonio González Barreda and María Raphaela Esquer had the following known children:

82   i.   **Joseph Fernando Antonio González Barreda** was born in 1752 in Álamos; he married Maria Lucía Gastélum about 1778.

83   ii.   **Joseph Patricio Benito González Barreda** was born in 1754 in Álamos. He married María Guadalupe Amarillas on December 25, 1775, in Álamos and died on April 13, 1791, in Álamos.

      iii. **Joseph Francisco González Barreda** was born in 1756 in Álamos. He was baptized on June 7, 1756, at the church of the Purísima Concepción in Álamos.[200] The baptismal record named Juan Agustín de Yriarte and Anna Esquer as his *padrinos.*

84   iv.   **María de la Luz González Barreda** was born in 1758 in Álamos; she married José Pérez Contreras on July 21, 1772, in Álamos.

      v.   **María Phelipa Matilde González Barreda** was born in 1760 in Álamos. She was baptized on September 3, 1760, in Álamos.[201] The baptismal record named María Juana de Aragón as her *madrina.*

      vi.   **Joseph Luis Sepherino González Barreda** was born on August 25, 1762, in Álamos. The cited baptismal record stated that the child had been born eighteen days prior to his date of baptism. He was baptized on September 12, 1762, at the church of the Purísima Concepción in Álamos.[202] The baptismal record named Francisco Xavier Aragón and his sister Anna María Aragón as his *padrinos.* The *padrinos* were said to have been *vecinos* of La Aduana. Bachiller Juan Antonio de Anguís; Teniente General Juan Agustín de Yriarte; and Teniente de Cura, Bachiller Joaquín Antonio Esquer, were named as witnesses to the sacrament of baptism.

85   vii. **María Loreto González Barreda** was born about 1766; she married Juan José Timoteo Martínez Mendívil in June 11, 1787, in Álamos.

      viii. **Josefa Antonia Demetria González Barreda** was born in 1768 in Álamos. It is assumed that she was born during the final days of 1768. The baptismal record did not indicate that the child was in danger of death, a situation that would have required baptism on the day of her birth. Josefa Antonia Demetria was baptized on January 1, 1769, at the church of the Purísima Concepción in Álamos.[203] The baptismal record

---

200. Bautismos 1751–1794, matrimonios 1848, defunciones 1735–1752, June 7, 1756, film 666999, image 130, Registros Parroquiales, Iglesia de La Purísima Concepción, Álamos, Sonora, Mexico (FamilySearch, https://familysearch.org).

201. Bautismos 1751–1794, matrimonios 1848, defunciones 1735–1752, September 3, 1760, film 666999, image 201, Registros Parroquiales, Iglesia de La Purísima Concepción, Álamos, Sonora, Mexico (FamilySearch, https://familysearch.org).

202. Bautismos 1751–1794, matrimonios 1848, defunciones 1735–1752, September 12, 1762, film 666999, image 248, Registros Parroquiales, Iglesia de La Purísima Concepción, Álamos, Sonora, Mexico (FamilySearch, https://familysearch.org).

203. Bautismos, matrimonios y defunciones 1696–1699, bautismos 1768–1781, January 1, 1769, film 663487, images 120–121, Registros Parroquiales, Iglesia de La Purísima Concepción, Álamos, Sonora, Mexico (FamilySearch, https://familysearch.org).

named Vicente Mallén de Navarrete as her *padrino*. Lorenzo Noriega and Miguel Martínez were named as witnesses to the sacrament of baptism.

86   ix.   **Serafina González Barreda** was born in 1768 in Álamos; she married Juan Manuel Anguís on December 30, 1794, in Álamos.

38. Micaela Matilde Esquer (Francisco Joseph-5, Juan Salvador-4, Salvador-3, Salvador-2, Blas-1) was born in 1732 in Culiacán. She was baptized on November 10, 1732, at the church of the Sagrario de San Miguel in Culiacán.[204] The baptismal record is of very poor quality, making it difficult to read the date. November 10 is an estimate based on the dates of the records preceding and following Micaela's baptism. The record named Pedro Barraza and Antonia Rangel as her *padrinos*.

Micaela Matilde Esquer and Andrés Quirós y Mora were married on February 9, 1751, at the church of the Sagrario de San Miguel in Culiacán.[205] The matrimonial record named Francisco Esquer, Miguel Rojo, and Cristóbal de la Virgen, among others present at the ceremony as witnesses to the marriage. The couple received a nuptial blessing the day of their marriage.

The cited marriage information record dated January 18–28, 1751, claimed there were no impediments to the marriage. [206] It gave the age of the groom as twenty-three years, more or less. The record contained a statement dated February 10 and March 16, 1751, to the effect that the marriage had taken place.

Andrés Quirós y Mora, son of Andrés Quirós y Mora and Mariana Féliz, was born about 1728.

Andrés Quirós y Mora and Micaela Matilde Esquer had the following known children:

87   i.   **María Guadalupe de la Merced de Quirós y Mora** was born in 1753 in Culiacán; she married Francisco Ochoa, June 24, 1782, in Culiacán.

      ii.   **Joaquín Andrés Quirós y Mora** was born on February 15, 1761, in Culiacán. He was said to have been eleven days old on the day of his baptism. Joaquín was baptized on February 26, 1761, at the church of the Sagrario de San Miguel in Culiacán.[207] The baptismal record named Bachiller Diego de Yturríos Amarillas and his sister, Leonor Yturríos Amarillas as his *padrinos*.

      iii.   **María Petra Quirós y Mora** was born on October 12, 1765, in Culiacán. The cited baptismal record stated that she was born nine days before her day of baptism. María Petra was baptized on October 21, 1765, at the church of the Sagrario de San Miguel

---

204. Matrimonios 1731–1755 (incluye bautismos y defunciones), November 10, 1732, film 665426, image 8, Registros Parroquiales, Iglesia Sagrario de San Miguel, Culiacán, Sinaloa, Mexico (FamilySearch, https://familysearch.org).
205. Matrimonios 1731–1755, February 9, 1751, film 665426, images 111–112, Registros Parroquiales, Iglesia Sagrario de San Miguel, Culiacán, Sinaloa, Mexico (FamilySearch, https://familysearch.org).
206. Información matrimonial 1733–1757, January 18–28, 1751, film 673538, images 110–112, Registros Parroquiales, Iglesia Sagrario de San Miguel, Culiacán, Sinaloa, Mexico (FamilySearch, https://familysearch.org).
207. Bautismos 1755–1789, February 26, 1761, film 665427, image 66, Registros Parroquiales, Iglesia Sagrario de San Miguel, Culiacán, Sinaloa, Mexico (FamilySearch, https://familysearch.org).

in Culiacán.[208] The baptismal record named José Joaquín Bolado y Bustamente as her *padrino*.

iv. **Luis Antonio Quirós y Mora** was born on November 22, 1767, in Culiacán. The cited baptismal record stated that he was born ten days before his baptismal day. He was baptized on December 2, 1767, at the church of the Sagrario de San Miguel in Culiacán.[209] The baptismal record named Antonia Quirós y Mora as his *madrina*.

v. **José Francisco Quirós y Mora** was born on June 8, 1770, in Culiacán. The cited baptismal record stated that he was born ten days prior to his day of baptism. José Francisco was baptized on June 18, 1770, at the church of the Sagrario de San Miguel in Culiacán.[210] The baptismal record named Josefa Verdugo as his *madrina*.

88 vi. **José Miguel Quirós y Mora** was born about 1773 in Culiacán; he married Juana Rosa Millán on September 28, 1793, in Cosalá, Sinaloa.

39. Francisco Gabriel Esquer (Francisco Joseph-5, Juan Salvador-4, Salvador-3, Salvador-2, Blas-1) was born in 1734 in Culiacán. He was baptized on April 30, 1734, at the church of the Sagrario de San Miguel in Culiacán.[211] The baptismal record named Manuel Fernández de Castañeda as his *padrino*.

Francisco Gabriel Esquer and Anna Antonia Páez de Guzmán were married about 1764 in Culiacán. Their matrimonial record has not been located. The family resided in Culiacán and it is assumed thatis where they were married.

Anna Antonia Páez de Guzmán, daughter of Santiago Páez de Guzmán and Ana Irene de Cárdenas, was born in 1740 in Culiacán. She was baptized on April 11, 1740, in Culiacán.[212] The baptismal record named Juan Alcayde and Juana Avilés as her *padrinos*.

---

208. Matrimonios 1731–1755 (incluye bautismos y defunciones), October 21, 1765, film 665426, image 239, Registros Parroquiales, Iglesia Sagrario de San Miguel, Culiacán, Sinaloa, Mexico (FamilySearch, https://familysearch.org).

209. Matrimonios 1731–1755 (incluye bautismos y defunciones), December 2, 1767, film 665426, image 289, Registros Parroquiales, Iglesia Sagrario de San Miguel, Culiacán, Sinaloa, Mexico (FamilySearch, https://familysearch.org).

210. Bautismos 1755–1789, June 18, 1770, film 665427, image 298, Registros Parroquiales, Iglesia Sagrario de San Miguel, Culiacán, Sinaloa, Mexico (FamilySearch, https://familysearch.org).

211. Defunciones 1731–1756 (incluye matrimonios y defunciones), matrimonios 1731–1755 (incluye bautismos y defunciones), April 30, 1734, film 665426, image 9, Registros Parroquiales, Iglesia Sagrario de San Miguel, Culiacán, Sinaloa, Mexico (FamilySearch, https://familysearch.org).

212. Matrimonios 1731–1755 (incluye bautismos y defunciones), April 11, 1740, film 665426, image 23, Registros Parroquiales, Iglesia Sagrario de San Miguel, Culiacán, Sinaloa, Mexico (FamilySearch, https://familysearch.org).

Francisco Gabriel Esquer and Anna Antonia Páez de Guzmán had the following known children:

i. **Francisco Javier Esquer** was born in 1765 in Culiacán. He was baptized on April 3, 1765, at the church of the Sagrario de San Miguel in Culiacán.[213] The baptismal record named Luis Antonio Esquer as his *padrino*.

89 ii. **María Irene Esquer** was born about 1768. She married Francisco Xavier Sambade on April 24, 1786, in Culiacán and died on September 9, 1787, in Culiacán.

90 iii. **María Manuela Esquer** was born about 1771 in Culiacán. She married Felipe Timoteo Verdugo on December 29, 1786, in Culiacán and married Pedro Zazueta on November 8, 1793, in Culiacán. She died on June 20, 1831, in Culiacán.

91 iv. **María Josefa Esquer** was born in 1772 in Culiacán. She married Francisco Rodríguez de la Rodriguera on September 13, 1790, in Culiacán.

v. **Francisco Gabriel Esquer** was born before 1773. He died on July 21, 1773 in Culiacán. He was buried on July 22, 1773, at the church of the Sagrario de San Miguel in Culiacán.[214] The burial service was held with a *cruz alta*. Francisco Gabriel received the last sacraments of the Catholic Church. His parents were named in the record.

vi. **José Joaquín Esquer** was born before 1781 in Culiacán. The burial record stated that the deceased was a small child, *párvulo*. He died on January 21, 1781, in Culiacán. He was buried on January 22, 1781, in Culiacán.[215] The burial service was held with a *cruz baja* and the child was laid to rest in a burial site valued at three pesos. Parents of the deceased were named in the record.

vii. **María Nicolasa Faustina Esquer** was born on December 13, 1774, in Culiacán. The cited baptismal record stated that she was born eight days prior to her day of baptism. María Nicolasa Faustina was baptized on December 21, 1774, at the church of the Sagrario de San Miguel in Culiacán.[216] The baptismal record named José Manuel Cárdenas and María Faustina Páez as her *padrinos*.

viii. **María Raphaela Esquer** was born on December 14, 1782, in Culiacán. The cited baptismal record provided her date of birth. María Raphaela was baptized on January 3, 1783, at the church of the Sagrario de San Miguel in Culiacán.[217] The baptismal record named María Faustina Páez as her *madrina*.

---

213. Matrimonios 1731–1755 (incluye bautismos y defunciones), April 3, 1765, film 665426, image 229, Registros Parroquiales, Iglesia Sagrario de San Miguel, Culiacán, Sinaloa, Mexico (FamilySearch, https://familysearch.org).

214. Defunciones 1746–1833, July 22, 1773, film 674051, image 53, Registros Parroquiales, Iglesia Sagrario de San Miguel, Culiacán, Sinaloa, Mexico (FamilySearch, https://familysearch.org).

215. Defunciones 1746–1833, January 22, 1781, film 674051, image 79, Registros Parroquiales, Iglesia Sagrario de San Miguel, Culiacán, Sinaloa, Mexico (FamilySearch, https://familysearch.org).

216. Bautismos 1755–1789, December 21, 1774, film 665427, image 346, Registros Parroquiales, Iglesia Sagrario de San Miguel, Culiacán, Sinaloa, Mexico (FamilySearch, https://familysearch.org).

217. Bautismos 1755–1789, January 3, 1783, film 665427, image 112, Registros Parroquiales, Iglesia Sagrario de San Miguel, Culiacán, Sinaloa, Mexico (FamilySearch, https://familysearch.org).

40. **Luis Antonio Esquer** (Francisco Joseph-5, Juan Salvador-4, Salvador-3, Salvador-2, Blas-1) was born in 1736 in Culiacán. He was baptized on April 15, 1736, in Culiacán.[218] The baptismal record named Juan Alcayde and Juana Esquer Amarillas as his *padrinos.*

Luis Antonio Esquer and Juana Paula Barraza were married about 1756. She died on July 5, 1759. They apparently did not have any children.

Luis Antonio Esquer and María Serafina Verdugo were married after November 29, 1772, in Culiacán.[219] The matrimonial record for Luis Antonio Esquer and María Serafina Verdugo has not been located. The cited marriage investigation, dated November 1772, stated that the two were related in the second degree, with a third degree of affinity. The relationship of affinity is indicated because María Serafina, and the first wife of Luis Antonio, Juana Paula Barraza, were second cousins once removed. In his testimony, Luis Antonio claimed that he was the widowed husband of Juana Paula Barraza, and that she was buried in the parish church in Culiacán. In her testimony, María Serafina claimed to be a *pobre huérfana* (poor orphan) and that she was twenty-two years of age (this contradicts the age provided in her cited burial record). She described depending upon charity for her livelihood. María Serafina did not sign her name after providing testimony because she could not: "*que no sabe firmar.*" The dispensation for marriage was issued on November 29, 1772, by the bishop in Durango. Much of what is contained in the marriage investigation record is very difficult to read. María Serafina Verdugo died on March 26, 1788, in Culiacán. Luis and María Serafina had seven known children.

Luis Antonio Esquer and Cayetana Medina were married on August 9, 1794, at the church of the Sagrario de San Miguel in Culiacán.[220] The matrimonial record named Manuel Romero, Manuel Roxo, and Francisco Xavier, assistant sacristan, as witnesses to the marriage.

The marriage information record was dated July 28, 1794.[221] It stated that the groom was the widower of Serafina Verdugo. The bride's ethnicity was said to have been *mulata libre.* There were no marriage impediments found, and the parents of the bride were named.

Luis Antonio Esquer died on March 3, 1809, at the age of seventy-three in Culiacán. He was buried on March 4, 1809, at the church of the Sagrario de San Miguel in Culiacán.[222] His funeral service was held with a *cruz alta* and he was interred in a burial site valued at ten pesos. The record stated that he had been married to Cayetana Medina at the time of his death and that he had received the last sacraments of the Catholic Church.

---

218. Matrimonios 1731–1755, April 15, 1736, film 665426, image 15, Registros Parroquiales, Iglesia Sagrario de San Miguel, Culiacán, Sinaloa, Mexico (FamilySearch, https://familysearch.org).
219. Diligencias matrimoniales (Legajo No. 43), Luis Antonio Vásquez [sic.], viudo de Paula Barraza, y Serafina Verdugo, Villa de Culiacán, 1772, AHAD-24, frames 609–615, AHAD.
220. Matrimonios 1755–1784, August 9, 1794, film 673389, image 358, Registros Parroquiales, Iglesia Sagrario de San Miguel, Culiacán, Sinaloa, Mexico (FamilySearch, https://familysearch.org).
221. Información matrimonial 1790–1794, 1820–1822, 1825–1827, July 28, 1794, film 673391, images 243–245, Registros Parroquiales, Iglesia Sagrario de San Miguel, Culiacán, Sinaloa, Mexico (FamilySearch, https://familysearch.org).
222. Defunciones 1746–1833, March 4, 1809, film 674051, image 433, Registros Parroquiales, Iglesia Sagrario de San Miguel, Culiacán, Sinaloa, Mexico (FamilySearch, https://familysearch.org).

Juana Paula Barraza, daughter of Pedro Barraza and Juana Paula Verdugo, died on July 5, 1759, in Culiacán. She was buried on July 6, 1759, at the church of the Sagrario de San Miguel in Culiacán.[223] Juana Paula Barraza received the last sacraments of the Catholic Church. Her burial services were held with *cruz alta y misa de cuerpo presente*. Juana Paula did not provide a will because she had nothing to leave behind. The burial record stated she had been married to Luis Antonio Esquer.

María Serafina Verdugo, daughter of Cayetano Verdugo and Ana Brígida de Ybarra, was born about 1753 in Culiacán. She died on March 26, 1788, in Culiacán. She was buried on March 27, 1788, at the church of the Sagrario de San Miguel in Culiacán.[224] María Serafina was interred in a burial site valued at ten pesos. Her burial service was held with *cruz alta, misa, y vigilia*. She was said to have been the wife of Luis Antonio Esquer, and that during their marriage they bore three children [who survived]. She received the last sacraments of the Catholic Church before her death, which was caused by an ulcer. She did not leave a will, having no reason to do so.

Luis Antonio Esquer and María Serafina Verdugo had the following known children:

i.   [*párvulo*] **Esquer** was born between 1772 and 1774 in Culiacán. He died on November 21, 1774, in Culiacán. He was buried on November 22, 1774, at the church of the Sagrario de San Miguel in Culiacán.[225] The burial service for the unnamed child was held with a *cruz alta*. He was laid to rest in a burial site valued at five pesos. This burial might be for the couple's first known son, José Vicente Esquer, who was baptized on November 8, 1773. In 1775 the parents named their second son "José Vicente," lending support to the notion that their first son was deceased.

ii.   [*párvulo*] **Esquer** was born between 1772 and 1775 in Culiacán. He died on July 27, 1775, in Culiacán. He was buried on July 28, 1775, at the church of the Sagrario de San Miguel in Culiacán.[226] The burial service for the unnamed child was held with a *cruz alta*.

iii.   **José Vicente Esquer** was born in 1773 in Culiacán. He was baptized on November 8, 1773, at the church of the Sagrario de San Miguel in Culiacán.[227] The baptismal record named María Dionisia de Sobarzo as his *madrina*. He died before 1775 at the age of two. The of death of José Vicente Esquer is assumed because there was another child born in 1775 who was baptized using the name "José Vicente Esquer."

92   iv.   **José Vicente Esquer** was born in 1775 in Culiacán. He married Juana María Cayetana Fernández Rojo on November 4, 1795, in Culiacán; he died in about 1798.

---

223. Defunciones 1746–1833, July 6, 1759, film 674051, image 2, Registros Parroquiales, Iglesia Sagrario de San Miguel, Culiacán, Sinaloa, Mexico (FamilySearch, https://familysearch.org).

224. Defunciones 1746–1833, March 27, 1788, film 674051, image 242, Registros Parroquiales, Iglesia Sagrario de San Miguel, Culiacán, Sinaloa, Mexico (FamilySearch, https://familysearch.org).

225. Defunciones 1746–1833, November 22, 1774, film 674051, image 58, Registros Parroquiales, Iglesia Sagrario de San Miguel, Culiacán, Sinaloa, Mexico (FamilySearch, https://familysearch.org).

226. Defunciones 1746–1833, November 22, 1774, film 674051, image 59, Registros Parroquiales, Iglesia Sagrario de San Miguel, Culiacán, Sinaloa, Mexico (FamilySearch, https://familysearch.org).

227. Bautismos 1755–1789, November 8, 1773, film 665427, image 322, Registros Parroquiales, Iglesia Sagrario de San Miguel, Culiacán, Sinaloa, Mexico (FamilySearch, https://familysearch.org).

v.   **María Phelipa Benigna Esquer** was born in 1777 in Culiacán. She was baptized on June 7, 1777, at the church of the Sagrario de San Miguel in Culiacán.[228] The baptismal record named María Ana de Quirós as her *madrina*.

vi.   **Juan Joseph Esquer** was born about 1780 in Culiacán. He died on January 17, 1782, in Culiacán. He was buried on January 18, 1782, at the church of the Sagrario de San Miguel in Culiacán.[229] Juan Joseph died as a child. His funeral service was held with a *cruz alta*.

vii.   **José Miguel Ciriaco Esquer** was born on January 2, 1783, in Culiacán, according to his baptismal record. He was baptized on January 13, 1783, at the church of the Sagrario de San Miguel in Culiacán.[230] The baptismal record named Ygnacio Burgos and Brígida Ybarra as his *padrinos*.

41. Pedro Sebastián Esquer (Francisco Joseph-5, Juan Salvador-4, Salvador-3, Salvador-2, Blas-1) was born in 1741 in Culiacán. He was baptized on January 1, 1742, at the church of the Sagrario de San Miguel in Culiacán.[231] The baptismal record named Felipe de Zataráin and Sebastiana Verdugo as his *padrinos*.

Pedro Sebastián Esquer and Anna María Murrieta were married about 1767.[232] Their matrimonial record has not been located. After many years of marriage, however, according to the record cited, they received their nuptial benediction on February 12, 1793. Manuel Anguís and Juan Gil Samaniego were named as *padrinos*.

Anna María Murrieta was born about 1742.

Pedro Sebastián Esquer and Anna María Murrieta had the following known children:

93   i.   **José Joaquín Esquer** was born about 1768; he married María Loreto Anguís on June 19, 1787, in Álamos.

ii.   **María Josepha Esquer** was born during or before 1770. She died on October 12, 1770. She was buried on October 13, 1770, at the church of the Purísima Concepción in Álamos.[233] The burial record noted she died as a child. She was buried beneath the choir of the church, and her service was held with a *cruz alta*.

228. Bautismos 1755–1789, June 7, 1777, film 665427, image 387, Registros Parroquiales, Iglesia Sagrario de San Miguel, Culiacán, Sinaloa, Mexico (FamilySearch, https://familysearch.org).
229. Defunciones 1746–1833, January 18,1782 film 674051, image 85, Registros Parroquiales, Iglesia Sagrario de San Miguel, Culiacán, Sinaloa, Mexico (FamilySearch, https://familysearch.org).
230. Bautismos 1755–1789, January 13, 1783, film 665427, image 114, Registros Parroquiales, Iglesia Sagrario de San Miguel, Culiacán, Sinaloa, Mexico (FamilySearch, https://familysearch.org).
231. Matrimonios 1731–1755 (incluye bautismos y defunciones), January 1, 1742, film 665426, image 29, Registros Parroquiales, Iglesia Sagrario de San Miguel, Culiacán, Sinaloa, Mexico (FamilySearch, https://familysearch.org).
232. Matrimonios 1779–1817, about 1767, film 666565, image 237, Registros Parroquiales, Iglesia de La Purísima Concepción, Álamos, Sonora, Mexico (FamilySearch, https://familysearch.org).
233. Defunciones 1717–1751,1764–1792, October 13, 1770, film 666995, image 224, Registros Parroquiales, Iglesia de La Purísima Concepción, Álamos, Sonora, Mexico (FamilySearch, https://familysearch.org).

42. **María Nicolasa Esquer** (Francisco Joseph-5, Juan Salvador-4, Salvador-3, Salvador-2, Blas-1) was born in 1746 in Culiacán. She was baptized on September 11, 1746, at the church of the Sagrario de San Miguel in Culiacán.[234] The baptismal record named Juan de Vitorica and Micaela de Agramont as her *padrinos.*

María Nicolasa Esquer and Juan Manuel Rojo were married on May 5, 1764, at the church of the Sagrario de San Miguel in Culiacán.[235] The matrimonial record named Joseph Antonio Rojo and Bárbara Verdugo as *padrinos.* Francisco de la Vega, Esteban Vega, among others present, were named as witnesses. Parents of the bride and groom were named in the record. The father of the bride was said to have been deceased. The couple received a nuptial blessing on the day of their marriage. The cited marriage information record is very heavily damaged; most is illegible.

María Nicolasa died on August 5, 1827, at the age of eighty-one in Culiacán. She was buried on August 6, 1827, at the church of the Sagrario de San Miguel in Culiacán.[236] She was interred in a burial site valued at three pesos. María Nicolasa's funeral service was held with *cruz alta y ataúd.* The burial record claimed that she had been the widow of Manuel Rojo. María Nicolasa received the last sacraments of the Catholic Church before her death. Her age given at death was said to have been eighty-five (this does not agree with her given year of birth in the baptismal record). She left no worldly goods to distribute.

Juan Manuel Rojo, son of Diego Rojo and Micaela López de Siqueiros, was born about 1744. He died on January 19, 1819, in Culiacán. He was buried on January 20, 1819, at the church of the Sagrario de San Miguel in Culiacán.[237] He was interred in a burial site valued at five pesos. Juan Manuel died of natural causes and received the last sacraments of the Catholic Church before his death. The record stated that he was married to María Nicolasa Esquer and that he left a last will and testament.

Juan Manuel Rojo and María Nicolasa Esquer had the following children:

94   i.   **José Miguel Rojo** was born on February 19, 1765, in Culiacán. He married Josefa Amarillas on July 9, 1788 in Culiacán, and later married Gertrudis Medina on April 26, 1824, in Culiacán. José died before July 8, 1830.

95   ii.   **María Juana Rafaela Rojo** was born about 1767 in Culiacán; she married José Manuel Palazuelos on May 16, 1788, in Culiacán.

---

234. Matrimonios 1731–1755 (incluye bautismos y defunciones), September 11, 1746, film 665426, image 37, Registros Parroquiales, Iglesia Sagrario de San Miguel, Culiacán, Sinaloa, Mexico (FamilySearch, https://familysearch.org).

235. Matrimonios 1755–1784, May 5, 1764, film 673389, image 89, Registros Parroquiales, Iglesia Sagrario de San Miguel, Culiacán, Sinaloa, Mexico (FamilySearch, https://familysearch.org); Información matrimonial 1760–1767, May 1764, film 673539, images 183–185, Registros Parroquiales, Iglesia Sagrario de San Miguel, Culiacán, Sinaloa, Mexico (FamilySearch, https://familysearch.org).

236. Defunciones 1746–1833, August 6, 1827, film 674051, image 637, Registros Parroquiales, Iglesia Sagrario de San Miguel, Culiacán, Sinaloa, Mexico (FamilySearch, https://familysearch.org).

237. Defunciones 1746–1833, January 20, 1819, film 674051, image 545, Registros Parroquiales, Iglesia Sagrario de San Miguel, Culiacán, Sinaloa, Mexico (FamilySearch, https://familysearch.org).

96 iii.   **José Manuel Rojo** was born in 1771 in Culiacán; he married Rafaela Palazuelos Cárdenas, about 1791.

43. María Gertrudis Anacleta Esquer (Francisco Joseph-5, Juan Salvador-4, Salvador-3, Salvador-2, Blas-1) was born in 1748 in Culiacán. She was baptized on July 23, 1748, at the church of the Sagrario de San Miguel in Culiacán.[238] The baptismal record named Bachiller Marcos de Vargas and María Manuela Esquer as her *padrinos.*

María Gertrudis Anacleta Esquer and Ygnacio Francisco López de Siqueiros were married on July 28, 1764, at the church of the Sagrario de San Miguel in Culiacán.[239] The matrimonial record named Antonio Verdugo and Anna Brígida Ybarra as *padrinos.* Juan Alcayde, Joseph Bueno, and Manuel Ramos were named as witnesses to the marriage. Parents of the bride and groom were named, and the father of the groom was said to be deceased. The couple received a nuptial blessing on the day of their marriage. The record stated that Ygnacio Francisco was first married to Gregoria Astorga.

The cited marriage information record related to a situation where the mother of María Gertrudis Anacleta voiced her objection to the marriage. Although no reason was stated, the most likely explanation was due to the age difference between the marriage candidates. She was only sixteen years of age, and he presumably was over the age of forty, based on the year that his first marriage took place. Because of her mother's objection, María Gertrudis Anacleta took refuge at the home of Josefa de Urrea. It is there that the parish priest recorded that she was entering into marriage under her own free will. The consent to marry was issued on July 21, 1764.[240] Ygnacio Francisco died in 1775.

María Gertrudis Anacleta Esquer and José Onofre Páez were married on September 23, 1782, at the church of the Sagrario de San Miguel in Culiacán.[241] The matrimonial record named Xavier Verdugo and Anna María Pizarro as *padrinos.* José Ygnacio Castaños and José Bobadilla were named as witnesses to the marriage. The record stated that the groom was a *mulato libre,* who was the widowed husband of María Gertrudis Cázares. The bride was said to be the widow of Ygnacio López.

Ygnacio Francisco López de Siqueiros, son of Domingo López de Siqueiros and Nicolasa Rabelo, was born about 1720 in Culiacán. He died on October 17, 1775, in Culiacán.He was buried on October 18, 1775, at the church of the Sagrario de San Miguel in Culiacán.[242] The cited burial record named the deceased as "Ygnacio López." It is here assumed that the deceased

---

238. Matrimonios 1731–1755 (incluye bautismos y defunciones), July 23, 1748, film 665426, image 48, Registros Parroquiales, Iglesia Sagrario de San Miguel, Culiacán, Sinaloa, Mexico (FamilySearch, https:// familysearch.org).
239. Matrimonios 1755–1829, July 28, 1764, film 673378, image 44, Registros Parroquiales, Iglesia Sagrario de San Miguel, Culiacán, Sinaloa, Mexico (FamilySearch, https://familysearch.org).
240. Información matrimonial 1760–1767, July 21, 1764, film 673539, images 203–205, Registros Parroquiales, Iglesia Sagrario de San Miguel, Culiacán, Sinaloa, Mexico (FamilySearch, https://familysearch.org).
241. Matrimonios 1755–1829, September 23, 1782, film 673378, image 130, Registros Parroquiales, Iglesia Sagrario de San Miguel, Culiacán, Sinaloa, Mexico (FamilySearch, https://familysearch.org).
242. Defunciones 1746–1833, October 8, 1775, film 674051, image 185, Registros Parroquiales, Iglesia Sagrario de San Miguel, Culiacán, Sinaloa, Mexico (FamilySearch, https://familysearch.org).

was actually Ygnacio Francisco López de Siqueiros. This is because his last child, María Manuela Máxima, was baptized on February 6, 1776, and her baptismal record stated that the father of the child was deceased.

Ygnacio Francisco López de Siqueiros and María Gertrudis Anacleta Esquer had the following known children:

i. **María Ignacia Tomasa López de Siqueiros** was born in 1771 in Culiacán. She was baptized on April 2, 1771, at the church of the Sagrario de San Miguel in Culiacán.[243] The baptismal record named Joseph Verdugo and Rita Cueva as her *padrinos*.

ii. **María Josefa López de Siqueiros** was born in 1772 in Culiacán. She was baptized on August 7, 1772, at the church of the Sagrario de San Miguel in Culiacán.[244] The baptismal record named María Josepha Roxo as her *madrina*.

iii. **María Ignacia López de Siqueiros** was born in 1773 in Culiacán. She was baptized on November 23, 1773, at the church of the Sagrario de San Miguel in Culiacán.[245] The baptismal record named Antonio Francisco García de Ávila as her *padrino*.

iv. **María Manuela Máxima López de Siqueiros** was born in 1776 in Culiacán. She was baptized on February 6, 1776, at the church of the Sagrario de San Miguel in Culiacán.[246] The baptismal record named Ana Theresa Cárdenas as her *madrina*. The record stated that Ana Theresa was the daughter of Rodrigo Cárdenas and Rosa Páez. Ygnacio Francisco, father of María Manuela Máxima, was said to have been deceased.

44. Augustina Anguís (María Mallén de Navarrete-5, Agustina Salvadora Esquer-4, Salvador-3, Salvador-2, Blas-1) was born about 1725.

Augustina Anguís and Thadeo Iturríos were married on August 25, 1740, at the church of the Purísima Concepción in Álamos.[247] The matrimonial record named Capitán Pablo Joseph Calvillo y Guerra (*Teniente de Gobernador de este Real*), Francisco Mallén de Navarrete, and Salvador Esquer as witnesses to the marriage. Only the parents of the bride were named in the record.

Thadeo Iturríos was born about 1720. He died on April 4, 1791, in Culiacán. He was buried on April 5, 1791, at the church of the Sagrario de San Miguel in Culiacán.[248] His funeral

---

243. Bautismos 1755–1789, April 2, 1771, film 665427, image 250, Registros Parroquiales, Iglesia Sagrario de San Miguel, Culiacán, Sinaloa, Mexico (FamilySearch, https://familysearch.org).
244. Bautismos 1755–1789, August 7, 1772, film 665427, image 292, Registros Parroquiales, Iglesia Sagrario de San Miguel, Culiacán, Sinaloa, Mexico (FamilySearch, https://familysearch.org).
245. Bautismos 1755–1789, November 23, 1773, film 665427, image 323, Registros Parroquiales, Iglesia Sagrario de San Miguel, Culiacán, Sinaloa, Mexico (FamilySearch, https://familysearch.org).
246. Bautismos 1755–1789, February 6, 1776, film 665427, image 361, Registros Parroquiales, Iglesia Sagrario de San Miguel, Culiacán, Sinaloa, Mexico (FamilySearch, https://familysearch.org).
247. Matrimonios 1716–1757, August 25, 1740, [no film number] image 124, Registros Parroquiales, Iglesia de La Purísima Concepción, Álamos, Sonora, Mexico (FamilySearch, https://familysearch.org).
248. Defunciones 1746–1833, April 5, 1791, film 674051, image 102, Registros Parroquiales, Iglesia Sagrario de San Miguel, Culiacán, Sinaloa, Mexico (FamilySearch, https://familysearch.org).

service was held with *cruz alta, y misa de cuerpo presente*. He received the last sacraments of the Catholic Church before death. Thadeo Iturríos left a will that named three surviving children: José Quinto, Vicente Antonio, and María Manuela. The burial record stated that he left four surviving children, but the fourth was not named.

Thadeo Iturríos and Augustina Anguís had the following known children:

i.   **Joseph Ignacio Cleto Iturríos** was born in 1744 in Culiacán. He was baptized on May 8, 1744, at the church of the Sagrario de San Miguel in Culiacán.[249] The baptismal record named Manuel Ignacio Fernández de Castañeda as his *padrino*.

ii.   **Ana María Bárbara Iturríos** was born in 1749 in Culiacán. She was baptized on November 15, 1749, at the church of the Sagrario de San Miguel in Culiacán.[250] The baptismal record named Ana Leonor de Avilés as her *madrina*.

iii. **María Gertrudis Bárbara Iturríos** was born in 1752 in Álamos. She was baptized on October 25, 1752, at the church of the Purísima Concepción in Álamos.[251] The baptismal record named Juan Augustín Yriarte and Micaela Mallén de Navarette as her *padrinos*.

iv.   **Joseph Miguel María Iturríos** was born in 1755 in Culiacán. He was baptized on August 15, 1755, at the church of the Sagrario de San Miguel in Culiacán.[252] The baptismal record named Francisco Xavier Banderas as his *padrino*.

v.   **María Rita Catharina Iturríos** was born in 1757 in Culiacán. She was baptized on December 5, 1757, at the church of the Sagrario de San Miguel in Culiacán.[253] The baptismal record named Panteleón de Urrea and Josefa de Urrea as her *padrinos*.

vi.   **María Josefa Iturríos** was born on May 25, 1767, in Culiacán. The cited baptismal record for María Josefa Iturríos stated that she was born twenty-one days prior to her date of baptism. She was baptized on June 15, 1767, at the church of the Sagrario de San Miguel in Culiacán.[254] The baptismal record named Eugenia del Castillo y Cabanillas as her *madrina*.

---

249. Bautismos 1690–1746, 1731–1769, May 8, 1744, film 665425, image 218, Registros Parroquiales, Iglesia Sagrario de San Miguel, Culiacán, Sinaloa, Mexico (FamilySearch, https://familysearch.org).
250. Matrimonios 1731–1755 (incluye bautismos y defunciones), November 15, 1749, film 665426, image 54, Registros Parroquiales, Iglesia Sagrario de San Miguel, Culiacán, Sinaloa, Mexico (FamilySearch, https://familysearch.org).
251. Bautismos 1751–1794, matrimonios 1848, defunciones 1735–1752, film 666999, images 68–69, Registros Parroquiales, Iglesia de La Purísima Concepción, Álamos, Sonora, Mexico (FamilySearch, https://familysearch.org).
252. Matrimonios 1731–1755, August 15, 1755, film 665426, image 80, Registros Parroquiales, Iglesia Sagrario de San Miguel, Culiacán, Sinaloa, Mexico (FamilySearch, https://familysearch.org).
253. Bautismos 1755–1789, December 5, 1757, film 665427, image 21, Registros Parroquiales, Iglesia Sagrario de San Miguel, Culiacán, Sinaloa, Mexico (FamilySearch, https://familysearch.org).
254. Matrimonios 1731–1755 (incluye bautismos y defunciones), June 15, 1767, film 665426, image 279, Registros Parroquiales, Iglesia Sagrario de San Miguel, Culiacán, Sinaloa, Mexico (FamilySearch, https://familysearch.org).

vii.   **Miguel Joaquín Iturríos** was born before 1779. He died on August 23, 1779, in Culiacán. He was buried on August 24, 1779, at the church of the Sagrario de San Miguel in Culiacán.[255] His burial service was held with *cruz alta, capa, viligia, y misa de cuerpo presente*. Novenas and Masses for the repose of his soul were to be said. Miguel Joaquín received the last sacraments of the Catholic Church before death, but he did not receive the Holy Eucharist because the "violent" illness he suffered did not allow him to take the Host. He was interred in a burial site valued at ten pesos. The burial record stated that Miguel Joaquín was a single adult and named his parents as Thadeo Iturríos and Augustina Mallén (rather than Anguís).

97 viii.   **María Manuela Iturríos** was born about 1775 in Culiacán. She married Nicolás Inocencio Eseverri on January 10, 1795, in Cosalá, Sinaloa, New Spain and died on November 19, 1835 in Cosalá.

ix.   **José Quinto Iturríos** was born before April 5, 1791.[256] The cited burial record for his father, Thadeo Iturríos, named José Quinto as a surviving child.

x.   **Vicente Antonio Iturríos** was born before April 5, 1791.[257] The cited burial record for his father, Thadeo Iturríos, named Vicente Antonio Iturríos as a surviving child.

45. Thomas Antonio Anguís (María Mallén de Navarrete-5, Agustina Salvadora Esquer-4, Salvador-3, Salvador-2, Blas-1) was born about 1740.

Thomas Antonio Anguís and Juana de Dios María Gil Samaniego were married on November 22, 1763, at the church of the Purísima Concepción in Álamos.[258] The matrimonial record named Manuel Velarde and his wife Manuela Féliz as *padrinos*. Bachiller Juan Antonio de Anguís, Capitán Juan Augustín Yriarte and Joseph Gabriel Esquer were named as witnesses to the marriage. Parents were named, and the father of the bride was said be deceased.

He died on June 5, 1775, in Álamos. He was buried on June 6, 1775, at the church of the Purísima Concepción in Álamos.[259] His funeral service was held with *cruz alta, túmulo de tres cuerpos, caja y vigilia del cuerpo*. He was interred in a burial site valued at five pesos. The record stated that Thomas Antonio had been married to Juana Gil and that he had received the last sacraments of the Catholic Church and the indulgences provided by papal bull. Burial expenses were paid through charitable donations.

---

255. Defunciones 1746–1833, August 24,1779, film 674051, image 196, Registros Parroquiales, Iglesia Sagrario de San Miguel, Culiacán, Sinaloa, Mexico (FamilySearch, https://familysearch.org).
256. Defunciones 1746–1833, April 5, 1791, film 674051, image 102, Registros Parroquiales, Iglesia Sagrario de San Miguel, Culiacán, Sinaloa, Mexico (FamilySearch, https://familysearch.org).
257. Ibid.
258. Matrimonios 1758–1779, November 22,1763, film 666564, image 72, Registros Parroquiales, Iglesia de La Purísima Concepción, Álamos, Sonora, Mexico (FamilySearch, https://familysearch.org).
259. Defunciones 1717–1751,1764–1792, June 6, 1775, film 666995, image 240, Registros Parroquiales, Iglesia de La Purísima Concepción, Álamos, Sonora, Mexico (FamilySearch, https://familysearch.org).

Juana de Dios María Gil Samaniego, daughter of Juan Gil Samaniego and María Gertrudis de Rivera, was born about 1740.

Thomas Antonio Anguís and Juana de Dios María Gil Samaniego had the following known children:

98   i.   **Joseph Raphael Leandro Anguís** was born on 1766, in Álamos. He married María Francisca Gastélum on February 26, 1794, in Álamos and he later married María Manuela Gil Samaniego on October 30, 1797, in Álamos.

99   ii.   **María Loreto Anguís** was born on September 8, 1769, in Álamos and married José Joaquín Esquer on June 19, 1787, in Álamos. She died before October 20, 1793, in Álamos.

100 iii. **María Josepha Luisa Anguís** was born in 1772 in Álamos. She married Juan Antonio Avilés on December 21, 1788, in Álamos. She married Joseph Antonio Mucio Gil Samaniego, October 9, 1793, in Álamos.

46. Francisco Antonio Baptista Anguís (María Mallén de Navarrete-5, Agustina Salvadora Esquer-4, Salvador-3, Salvador-2, Blas-1) was born about 1734.

Francisco Antonio Baptista Anguís and Rosa Martínez Mendívil were married on August 16, 1754, at the church of the Purísima Concepción in Álamos.[260] The matrimonial record named Bachiller Joseph de Coronado and Bachiller Joaquín Esquer as witnesses to the marriage. Parents of the couple were not named in the marriage record, but they were named in the cited marriage information record dated July 1754.

Francisco Antonio Baptista Anguís died in 1775 in Álamos. He was buried on December 28, 1775, at the church of the Purísima Concepción in Álamos.[261] His funeral service was held with *cruz alta, capa, una mesa y caja*. His burial service was held with a *túmulo de cuartro cuerpo*s. The record stated that Francisco Antonio had been married to Rosa Mendívil.

Rosa Martínez Mendívil, daughter of Miguel Martínez Mendívil and María Teresa Rodríguez Correa, was born about 1736. She died on June 16, 1780, in Álamos. She was buried on June 17, 1780, at the church of the Purísima Concepción in Álamos.[262] The burial entry (barely legible) noted that she was the widow of Francisco Anguís, and it listed her surviving children.

---

260. Matrimonios 1716–1757, August 16, 1754, [no film number], images 186–187, Registros Parroquiales, Iglesia de La Purísima Concepción, Álamos, Sonora, Mexico (FamilySearch, https://familysearch.org); Información matrimonial 1731–1757, July 1754, film 667001, images 308–309, Registros Parroquiales, Iglesia de La Purísima Concepción, Álamos, Sonora, Mexico (FamilySearch, https://familysearch.org).
261. Defunciones 1717–1751, 1764–1792, December 28, 1775 film 666995, image 277, Registros Parroquiales, Iglesia de La Purísima Concepción, Álamos, Sonora, Mexico (FamilySearch, https://familysearch.org).
262. Defunciones 1717–1751, 1764–1792, June 17, 1780 film 666995, image 332, Registros Parroquiales, Iglesia de La Purísima Concepción, Álamos, Sonora, Mexico (FamilySearch, https://familysearch.org).

Francisco Antonio Baptista Anguís and Rosa Martínez Mendívil had the following known children:

i. **Augustina Antonia Gertrudis Anguís** was born in 1755 in Álamos. She was baptized on September 3, 1755, at the church of the Purísima Concepción in Álamos.[263] The baptismal record named Juan Augustín Yriarte and Michaela Mallén de Navarrete as her *padrinos*.

ii. **María Antonia Anguís** was born in 1759 in Álamos. She was baptized on January 30, 1759, at the church of the Purísima Concepción in Álamos.[264] The baptismal record named Fernando Barreda and Rafaela Esquer as her *padrinos*. She died on August 6, 1780, at the age of twenty-one in Álamos. María was buried on August 7, 1780, at the church of the Purísima Concepción in Álamos.[265] Her funeral service was held with a *cruz alta* and she was laid to rest in a burial site valued at ten pesos. María Antonia received the last sacraments of the Catholic Church. She also received plenary indulgences provided by papal bull. She was identified as a "maiden," and her parents were said to be deceased.

101 iii. **Juan Manuel Anguís** was born on April 7, 1762, in Álamos; he married Serafina González Barreda on December 30, 1794, in Álamos.

iv. **María Antonia Narcisa Anguís** was born in 1765 in Álamos. She was baptized on November 15, 1765, at the church of the Purísima Concepción in Álamos.[266] The baptismal record named Miguel de Rivera and Theresa Mallén de Navarrete as her *padrinos*. Others in attendance included Vicente Mallén de Navarrete, Teniente General Juan Augustín Yriarte, and Miguel Martínez. She died on August 13, 1766, at the age of ten in Álamos.[267] María was buried on August 14, 1766, at the church of the Purísima Concepción in Álamos.[268] The burial record appeared to identify "María Narcisa" as the deceased, but it was not clear. Her funeral service was held with a *cruz alta* and she was laid to rest in a burial site valued at ten pesos. There was no mention that the deceased was a child, as would normally have been the case.

---

263. Bautismos 1751–1794, matrimonios 1848, defunciones 1735–1752, September 3, 1755, film 666999, image 116, Registros Parroquiales, Iglesia de La Purísima Concepción, Álamos, Sonora, Mexico (FamilySearch, https://familysearch.org).

264. Bautismos 1751–1794, matrimonios 1848, defunciones 1735–1752, January 30, 1759, film 666999, image 172, Registros Parroquiales, Iglesia de La Purísima Concepción, Álamos, Sonora, Mexico (FamilySearch, https://familysearch.org).

265. Defunciones 1717–1751, 1764–1792, August 7, 1780, film 666995, images 335–336, Registros Parroquiales, Iglesia de La Purísima Concepción, Álamos, Sonora, Mexico (FamilySearch, https://familysearch.org).

266. Bautismos 1751–1794, matrimonios 1848, defunciones 1735–1752, November 15, 1765, film 666999, image 318, Registros Parroquiales, Iglesia de La Purísima Concepción, Álamos, Sonora, Mexico (FamilySearch, https://familysearch.org).

267. Defunciones 1717–1751, 1764–1792, August 14, 1776, film 666995, image 182, Registros Parroquiales, Iglesia de La Purísima Concepción, Álamos, Sonora, Mexico (FamilySearch, https://familysearch.org).

268. Ibid.

v. **Juan Francisco Anguís** was born in 1768 in Álamos. He was baptized on April 29, 1768, at the church of the Purísima Concepción in Álamos.[269] The baptismal record named Teniente General Juan Augustín Yriarte and his daughter María Balvanera de Yriarte as his *padrinos*. Thomas Anguís and Gabriel Carpena were named as witnesses to the sacrament of baptism. He died on April 3, 1781, at the age of twelve in Álamos. Juan was buried on April 4, 1781, at the church of the Purísima Concepción in Álamos.[270] Twenty-four hours after his death, a funeral service was held with *cruz alta, caja y una mesa*. He was laid to rest in a burial site valued at ten pesos. Juan Francisco was said to have been a single adult. He received the last sacraments of the Catholic Church before death. Juan Francisco did not receive Holy Communion because his throat illness did not permit him to swallow the Host. His parents were named and said to have been deceased. Juan Francisco was only thirteen years of age when he died, but the burial record describes an "adult" as the deceased. The burial of Juan Francisco as an adult conforms with contemporary burials of persons of his age.

47. **María Theresa Mallén de Navarrete** (Vicente-5, Agustina Salvadora Esquer-4, Salvador-3, Salvador-2, Blas-1) was born about 1730.

María Theresa Mallén de Navarrete and Miguel Alexandro Rivera were married after November 8, 1750, in Álamos.[271] The actual marriage record has not been located, but marriage is assumed to have taken place after the date of the cited marriage investigation.

The cited marriage investigation was a petition for permission to marry made by Miguel Alexandro Rivera and dated November 8, 1750. There was also another petition made during same time period (exact date not clear) by Father Juan Antonio de Anguís that said the marriage should be allowed to protect the honor of the bride.

María Theresa Mallén de Navarrete died on May 18, 1775, in Álamos. She was buried on May 19, 1775, at the church of the Purísima Concepción in Álamos.[272] Her funeral service was held with a *cruz alta* and she was laid to rest in burial site valued at five pesos. Her husband Miguel Alexandro Rivera was named in the record.

Miguel Alexandro Rivera, son of Lorenzo de Rivera and Andrea de Argüelles, was born about 1720.

269. Bautismos, matrimonios y defunciones 1696–1699 bautismos, 1768–1781, April 29, 1768, film 663487, image 106, Registros Parroquiales, Iglesia de La Purísima Concepción, Álamos, Sonora, Mexico (FamilySearch, https://familysearch.org).
270. Defunciones 1717–1751, 1764–1792, April 4, 178, film 666995, image 354, Registros Parroquiales, Iglesia de La Purísima Concepción, Álamos, Sonora, Mexico (FamilySearch, https://familysearch.org).
271. Información matrimonial 1731–1757, November 8, 1750, film 667001, images 165–166, Registros Parroquiales, Iglesia de La Purísima Concepción, Álamos, Sonora, Mexico (FamilySearch, https://familysearch.org).
272. Defunciones 1717–1751,1764–1792, May 19, 1775, film 666995, image 269, Registros Parroquiales, Iglesia de La Purísima Concepción, Álamos, Sonora, Mexico (FamilySearch, https://familysearch.org).

Miguel Alexandro Rivera and María Theresa Mallén de Navarrete had the following known children:

102 i.   **María Ysidora Rivera** was born in 1751 in Álamos; she married Joaquín Andrés Alcayde on April 22, 1772, in Álamos.

     ii.   **Manuel Antonio Rivera** was born in 1756 in Álamos. He was baptized on September 24, 1756, at the church of the Purísima Concepción in Álamos.[273] The baptismal record named Vicente Mallén de Navarrete and María Francisca de Amarillas as his *padrinos.*

     iii.   **María Guadalupe Lucía Rivera** was born in 1760 in Álamos. She was baptized on December 28, 1760, at the church of the Purísima Concepción in Álamos.[274] The baptismal record named Manuel Rivera and Augustina Valenzuela as her *padrinos.*

48. Gabriel Mallén de Navarrete (Vicente-5, Agustina Salvadora Esquer-4, Salvador-3, Salvador-2, Blas-1) was born about 1741.

Gabriel Mallén de Navarrete and Rita Antonia Gil Samaniego were married on December 28, 1761, at the church of the Purísima Concepción in Álamos.[275] The matrimonial record named Teniente General of the Province of Nueva Andalusia, Juan Augustín Yriarte, and his wife, Ana María Barreda, as *padrinos.* Sebastián López Bravo, Manuel Alexandro Rivera, and others present were identified as witnesses to the marriage. Parents were named, and the mother of the groom, María Francisca de Amarillas, was said to be deceased, as was the father of the bride, Juan Gil Samaniego. The bride's family was said to be from La Aduana. Gabriel Mallén de Navarrete at the time of his marriage held the title of *ensayador y balanzario* (assayer and balancer) for the province of Sinaloa.

Gabriel Mallén de Navarrete died on July 30, 1777, in Álamos. He was buried on July 31, 1777, at the church of the Purísima Concepción in Álamos.[276] Gabriel Mallén de Navarrete was buried in a plot valued at fifty pesos. His funeral service was elaborate, complete with *cruz alta, vigilia, túmulo de tres cuerpos, y caja.* He received the last sacraments of the Catholic Church. He gained plenary indulgences for sins committed during his lifetime through privileges granted by papal bull. The burial record stated that he left a will.

273. Bautismos 1751–1794, matrimonios 1848, defunciones 1735–1752, September 24, 1756, film 666999, image 133, Registros Parroquiales, Iglesia de La Purísima Concepción, Álamos, Sonora, Mexico (FamilySearch, https://familysearch.org).

274. Bautismos 1751–1794, matrimonios 1848, defunciones 1735–1752, December 28, 1760, film 666999, image 207, Registros Parroquiales, Iglesia de La Purísima Concepción, Álamos, Sonora, Mexico (FamilySearch, https://familysearch.org).

275. Matrimonios 1758–1779, December 28, 1761, film 666564, image 42, Registros Parroquiales, Iglesia de La Purísima Concepción, Álamos, Sonora, Mexico (FamilySearch, https://familysearch.org).

276. Defunciones 1717–1751, 1764–1792, July 31, 1777, film 666995, image 299, Registros Parroquiales, Iglesia de La Purísima Concepción, Álamos, Sonora, Mexico (FamilySearch, https://familysearch.org).

Rita Antonia Gil Samaniego, daughter of Juan Gil Samaniego and María Gertrudis de Rivera, was born about 1741 in Álamos.

Gabriel Mallén de Navarrete and Rita Antonia Gil Samaniego had the following known children:

i. **María Gertrudis del Carmen Mallén de Navarrete** was born in 1763 in Álamos. She was baptized on February 9, 1763, at the church of the Purísima Concepción in Álamos.[277] The baptismal record named Thomas Antonio Anguís and María Gertrudis Rivera as her *padrinos*. Bachiller Joaquín Antonio Esquer and Vicente Mallén de Navarrete, along with all those present at the ceremony, were identified as witnesses.

ii. **Manuel de Jesús de María Mallén de Navarrete** was born in 1764 in Álamos. He was baptized on December 26, 1764, at the church of the Purísima Concepción in Álamos.[278] The baptismal record named Bachiller Joseph de Avilés and Juana Gil Samaniego as his *padrinos*.

iii. **Joseph Gabriel Policarpo Mallén de Navarrete** was born in 1768 in Álamos. He was baptized on March 7, 1768, at the church of the Purísima Concepción in Álamos.[279] The baptismal record named Miguel de Rivera and Theresa Mallén de Navarrete as his *padrinos*. Bachiller Vicente Díaz de la Torre, Fernando González Barreda, and Thadeo Padilla were named as witnesses to the sacrament of baptism.

103 iv. **Joseph Antonio Mallén de Navarrete** was born in 1769 in Álamos. He married María Dolores Sabalza on February 13, 1798, in Álamos.

v. **María del Carmen Gertrudis Mallén de Navarrete** was born in 1771 in Álamos. She was baptized on March 2, 1771, at the church of the Purísima Concepción in Álamos.[280] The baptismal record named Bachiller Juan Mariano Gómez de Aguilar as her *padrino*. Bachiller Salvador de Castañeda, Juan Augustín de Yriarte, and Alfonso Ruiz Solorzano were named as witnesses to the sacrament of baptism.

vi. **María Dolores Mallén de Navarrete** was born about 1774. She died on April 11, 1781, in Álamos. She was buried on April 12, 1781, at the church of the Purísima Concepción in Álamos.[281] Her funeral service was held with *cruz alta y caja*. She was laid to rest in a burial site valued at five pesos. The record stated that María Dolores was a child of seven or eight years of age when she died.

---

277. Bautismos 1751–1794, matrimonios 1848, defunciones 1735–1752, February 7, film 666999, image 256, Registros Parroquiales, Iglesia de La Purísima Concepción, Álamos, Sonora, Mexico (FamilySearch, https:// familysearch.org).

278. Bautismos 1751–1794, matrimonios 1848, defunciones 1735–1752, December 26, 1764, film 666999, image 307, Registros Parroquiales, Iglesia de La Purísima Concepción, Álamos, Sonora, Mexico (FamilySearch, https://familysearch.org).

279. Bautismos, matrimonios y defunciones 1696–1699, bautismos 1768–1781, March 8, 1768, film 663487, image 101, Registros Parroquiales, Iglesia de La Purísima Concepción, Álamos, Sonora, Mexico (FamilySearch, https://familysearch.org).

280. Bautismos, matrimonios y defunciones 1696–1699, bautismos 1768–1781, March 2, 1771 film 663487, images 176–177, Registros Parroquiales, Iglesia de La Purísima Concepción, Álamos, Sonora, Mexico (FamilySearch, https:// familysearch.org).

281. Defunciones 1717–1751, 1764–1792, April 12, 1781, film 666995, images 357–358, Registros Parroquiales, Iglesia de La Purísima Concepción, Álamos, Sonora, Mexico (FamilySearch, https://familysearch. org).

vii. [*párvulo*] **Mallén de Navarrete** was born in 1775 in Álamos, he died on May 5, 1775, in Álamos. He was buried on May 6, 1775, at the church of the Purísima Concepción in Álamos.[282]

104 viii. **María Balvanera Mallén de Navarrete** was born in 1776, in Álamos. She married Santiago Peñúñuri on October 2, 1792, in Álamos.

105 ix. **Bernardo Mallén de Navarrete** was born about 1776; he married Gertrudis Sarmiento on November 21, 1799, in Rosario, Sinaloa, New Spain.

x. **Joseph Thomas Saturnino Mallén de Navarrete** was born in 1777 in Álamos. He was baptized on December 8, 1777, at the church of the Purísima Concepción in Álamos.[283] The baptismal record named his mother, Rita Gil Samaniego as his *madrina*. Vicente Mallén de Navarrete and Lucas Velarde were named as witnesses to the sacrament of baptism.

49. **Rita Antonia Mallén de Navarrete** (Vicente-5, Agustina Salvadora Esquer-4, Salvador-3, Salvador-2, Blas-1) was born about 1742.

Rita Antonia Mallén de Navarrete and Lorenzo Antonio Noriega were married on February 16, 1766, at the church of the Purísima Concepción in Álamos.[284] The matrimonial record named Vicente Mallén de Navarrete and Ana María González Barreda as *padrinos*. Juan Antonio de Anguís, Joseph de Avilés, and Vicente Díaz de la Torre were named as witnesses to the marriage. The groom was said to have originated in the Kingdom of Castile. Parents of the bride and groom were named, and the mother of the bride, María Francisca Amarillas, was said to have been deceased.

Lorenzo Antonio Noriega, son of Lorenzo Antonio Noriega and Isabel de Iglesias, was born about 1740 in Spain.

50. **Fernando Antonio González Barreda** (Micaela Salvadora Mallén de Navarrete-5, Agustina Salvadora Esquer-4, Salvador-3, Salvador-2, Blas-1) was born about 1733.

Fernando Antonio González Barreda and María Raphaela Esquer were married on April 1, 1750, at the parish of the Sagrario de San Miguel in Culiacán.[285] The matrimonial record named Francisco Ramos, and his wife Antonia Murillo as *padrinos*. Francisco Alcayde, Miguel Yturríos, and Ildefonso Verdugo were named as witnesses to the marriage. The marriage ceremony took

---

282. Burial record not located.

283. Bautismos, matrimonios y defunciones 1696–1699, bautismos 1768–1781, December 8, 1777, film 663487, image 360, Registros Parroquiales, Iglesia de La Purísima Concepción, Álamos, Sonora, Mexico (FamilySearch, https://familysearch.org).

284. Matrimonios 1758–1779, February 16, 1766, film 666564, image 84, Registros Parroquiales, Iglesia de La Purísima Concepción, Álamos, Sonora, Mexico (FamilySearch, https://familysearch.org).

285. Matrimonios 1731–1755, April 1, 1750, film 665426, images 104–105, Registros Parroquiales, Iglesia Sagrario de San Miguel, Culiacán, Sinaloa, Mexico (FamilySearch, https://familysearch.org); Matrimonios 1716–1757, August 30, 1750, [no film number], image 164, Registros Parroquiales, Iglesia de La Purísima Concepción, Álamos, Sonora, Mexico (FamilySearch, https://familysearch.org).

place in Culiacán at the home of Francisco Esquer. The couple received their nuptial blessing in Álamos on August 30, 1750, as noted in the matrimonial record. Manuel Sobarzo and Vicente Mallén de Navarrete were named as witnesses to the nuptial blessing.

Fernando Antonio González Barreda died before May 8, 1785. The cited burial record for his wife María Raphaela Esquer, dated May 8, 1785, stated that she was the widow of Fernando González Barreda. The cited baptismal records for his sons Joseph Fernando Antonio and Joseph Francisco stated that their father's name was "Fernando Antonio Barreda." Also, the cited record for his nuptial blessing noted his name as "Fernando Martín Antonio González Barreda."

María Raphaela Esquer, daughter of Francisco Joseph Esquer and María Nicolasa Murillo, was born in 1729 in Culiacán. She was baptized on November 8, 1729, at the church of the Sagrario de San Miguel in Culiacán.[286] Her baptismal record named Santiago Páez and María Rosa Páez as her *padrinos*. She died on May 7, 1785, at the age of fifty-six in Álamos. María Rafaela was buried on May 8, 1785, at the church of the Purísima Concepción in Álamos.[287] She was interred in a burial site valued at five pesos. Her funeral service was held with *capa y cruz alta*. The record stated that she had been the widow of Fernando Barreda. María Rafaela received the last sacraments of the Catholic Church before death.

Fernando Antonio González Barreda and María Raphaela Esquer had the following known children:

82 i.   **Joseph Fernando Antonio González Barreda** was born 1752 in Álamos; he married Maria Lucía Gastélum about 1778.

83 ii.   **Joseph Patricio Benito González Barreda** was born in 1754 in Álamos. He married María Guadalupe Amarillas on December 25, 1775, in Álamos and died on April 13, 1791, in Álamos.

    iii. **Joseph Francisco González Barreda** was born in 1756 in Álamos. He was baptized on June 7, 1756, at the church of the Purísima Concepción in Álamos.[288] The baptismal record named Juan Agustín de Yriarte and Anna Esquer as his *padrinos*.

84 iv.   **María de la Luz González Barreda** was born in 1758 in Álamos; she married José Pérez Contreras on July 21, 1772, in Álamos.

    v.   **María Phelipa Matilde González Barreda** was born in 1760 in Álamos. She was baptized on September 3, 1760, in Álamos.[289] The baptismal record named María Juana de Aragón as her *madrina*.

---

286. Bautismos 1690–1746, bautismos 1731–1769, film 665425, image 143, Registros Parroquiales, Iglesia Sagrario de San Miguel, Culiacán, Sinaloa, Mexico (FamilySearch, https://familysearch.org).

287. Defunciones 1717–1751, 1764–1792, May 8, 1785, film 666995, image 459, Registros Parroquiales, Iglesia de La Purísima Concepción, Álamos, Sonora, Mexico (FamilySearch, https://familysearch.org).

288. Bautismos 1751–1794, matrimonios 1848, defunciones 1735–1752, June 7, 1756, film 666999, image 130, Registros Parroquiales, Iglesia de La Purísima Concepción, Álamos, Sonora, Mexico (FamilySearch, https://familysearch.org).

289. Bautismos 1751–1794, matrimonios 1848, defunciones 1735–1752, September 3, 1760, film 666999, image 201, Registros Parroquiales, Iglesia de La Purísima Concepción, Álamos, Sonora, Mexico (FamilySearch, https://familysearch.org).

vi. **Joseph Luis Sepherino González Barreda** was born on August 25, 1762, in Álamos. The cited baptismal record stated that the child had been born eighteen days prior to his date of baptism. He was baptized on September 12, 1762, at the church of the Purísima Concepción in Álamos.[290] The baptismal record named Francisco Xavier Aragón and his sister Anna María Aragón as his *padrinos*. The *padrinos* were said to have been *vecinos* of La Aduana. Bachiller Juan Antonio de Anguís; Teniente General Juan Agustín de Yriarte; and Teniente de Cura, Bachiller Joaquín Antonio Esquer, were named as witnesses to the sacrament of baptism.

85 vii. **María Loreto González Barreda** was born about 1766; she married Juan José Timoteo Martínez Mendívil on June 11, 1787, in Álamos.

viii. **Josefa Antonia Demetria González Barreda** was born in 1768 in Álamos. It is assumed that she was born during the final days of 1768. The baptismal record did not indicate that the child was in danger of death, a situation that would have required baptism on the day of her birth. Josefa Antonia Demetria was baptized on January 1, 1769, at the church of the Purísima Concepción in Álamos.[291] The baptismal record named Vicente Mallén de Navarrete as her *padrino*. Lorenzo Noriega and Miguel Martínez were named as witnesses to the sacrament of baptism.

86 ix. **Serafina González Barreda** was born in 1768 in Álamos; she married Juan Manuel Anguís on December 30, 1794, in Álamos.

51. Ana María González Barreda (Micaela Salvadora Mallén de Navarrete-5, Agustina Salvadora Esquer-4, Salvador-3, Salvador-2, Blas-1) was born about 1732 in Álamos.

Ana María González Barreda and Juan Augustín de Yriarte were married on April 11, 1751, in Álamos.[292] The matrimonial record identified Teniente General y Capitán Salvador Esquer, Juan González de Zayas, and Manuel Velarde, among others present as witnesses to the marriage. The groom's place of birth was noted. Parents of the bride were named and her father was said to be deceased.

Juan Augustín de Yriarte was born about 1730 in the Valle de Roncal, Navarra, Spain.

Juan Augustín de Yriarte and Ana María González Barreda had the following known children:

i. **Juan Joseph Gabriel Yriarte** was born in 1759 in Álamos. He was baptized on March 28, 1759, at the church of the Purísima Concepción in Álamos.[293] The baptismal record named Gerónimo Tovar and Rafaela Esquer as his *padrinos*.

290. Bautismos 1751–1794, matrimonios 1848, defunciones 1735–1752, September 12, 1762, film 666999, image 248, Registros Parroquiales, Iglesia de La Purísima Concepción, Álamos, Sonora, Mexico (FamilySearch, https://familysearch.org).

291. Bautismos, matrimonios y defunciones 1696–1699, bautismos 1768–1781, January 1, 1769, film 663487, images 120–121, Registros Parroquiales, Iglesia de La Purísima Concepción, Álamos, Sonora, Mexico (FamilySearch, https://familysearch.org).

292. Matrimonios 1716–1757, April 11, 1751, film [no film number], images 168–169, Registros Parroquiales, Iglesia de La Purísima Concepción, Álamos, Sonora, Mexico (FamilySearch, https://familysearch.org).

293. Bautismos 1751–1794, matrimonios 1848, defunciones 1735–1752, March 28, 1759, film 666999, image 176, Registros Parroquiales, Iglesia de La Purísima Concepción, Álamos, Sonora, Mexico (FamilySearch, https://familysearch.org).

ii.   **María Michaela Yriarte** was born in 1756 in Álamos. She was baptized on September 23, 1756, at the church of the Purísima Concepción in Álamos.[294] The baptismal record named Fernando González Barreda and Josefa González Barreda as her *padrinos.*

106 iii.   **María Balvanera de Yriarte** was born about 1761 in Álamos; she married Miguel Alcayde Pérez de la Puente on December 6, 1775, in Álamos.

52. **Francisca Augustina Avilés** (Augustina Mallén de Navarrete-5, Agustina Salvadora Esquer-4, Salvador-3, Salvador-2, Blas-1) was born about 1740.

Francisca Augustina Avilés and Joseph Gabriel Esquer were married on January 1, 1762, at the church of the Purísima Concepción in Álamos.[295] The matrimonial record named Joseph Francisco de Avilés and Michaela Salvadora Mallén de Navarrete as *padrinos.* Michaela Salvadora Mallén de Navarrete was said to be a widow and aunt of both the bride and groom. Bachillers Juan Antonio de Anguís, Ygnacio Fernández Valdez, and Joaquín Antonio Esquer, among others present were identified as witnesses to the sacrament of marriage. The couple received a dispensation to marry because they were related in the third degree of consanguinity, meaning they were second cousins. Parents of the bride and groom were named in the record. Parents of the groom were said to be deceased, as was the mother of the bride.

Joseph Gabriel Esquer, son of Salvador Esquer (Amarillas) and María Rosa Nicolasa Anguís, was born in 1742.[296] Joseph Gabriel's year of birth is based on information he provided as a witness in the marriage investigation record of his second cousin, Gabriel Mallén de Navarrete, dated December 1761. In the record, he stated that he was nineteen years of age. Joseph Gabriel died on February 10, 1793, at the age of fifty-one in Álamos. He was buried on February 11, 1793, at the church of the Purísima Concepción in Álamos.[297] He was interred in a grave valued at four pesos, with *cruz alta y tres dobles.* The record stated that he had been married to Francisca Avilés and that there was a debt remaining for the funeral services.

Joseph Gabriel Esquer and Francisca Augustina Avilés had one known child:

i.   **María del Carmen Esquer** died on December 1, 1781, in Álamos. She was buried on December 2, 1781, at the church of the Purísima Concepción in Álamos.[298] Her funeral service was held with *cruz alta, capa y una mesa y caja.* She was interred in a grave site valued at ten pesos. The record appears to indicate that she was the adopted daughter of Joseph Gabriel Esquer and Francisca Augustina Avilés.

---

294. Bautismos 1751–1794, matrimonios 1848, defunciones 1735–1752, September 23, 1756 film 666999, image 133, Registros Parroquiales, Iglesia de La Purísima Concepción, Álamos, Sonora, Mexico (FamilySearch, https://familysearch.org).
295. Matrimonios 1758–1779, January 1, 1762, film 666564, image 43, Registros Parroquiales, Iglesia de La Purísima Concepción, Álamos, Sonora, Mexico (FamilySearch, https://familysearch.org).
296. Información matrimonial 1760–1799, December 1761, film 667002, image 67, Registros Parroquiales, Iglesia de La Purísima Concepción, Álamos, Sonora, Mexico (FamilySearch, https://familysearch.org).
297. Defunciones 1786–1819, February 11, 1793, film 666996, image 58, Registros Parroquiales, Iglesia de La Purísima Concepción, Álamos, Sonora, Mexico (FamilySearch, https://familysearch.org).
298. Defunciones 1717–1751, 1764–1792, December 2, 1781, film 666995, image 386, Registros Parroquiales, Iglesia de La Purísima Concepción, Álamos, Sonora, Mexico (FamilySearch, https://familysearch.org).

53. **José Claudio Esquer** (Joaquín-5, Blas Salvador-4, Salvador-3, Salvador-2, Blas-1) was born about 1761.

José Claudio Esquer and María Ignacia Mejia were married after July 6, 1794, at the church of the Sagrario de San Miguel in Culiacán.[299] Their actual matrimonial record has not been located. The cited marriage investigation record stated that the bride was a *mulata libre* and that the mother of the groom, Antonia Beltran, gave her consent to the marriage. Parents of the couple were named, and Joaquín Esquer, father of the groom was said to have been deceased. Ages of the groom and and bride were said to be twenty-five and thirty-eight, respectively. Neither had the ability to sign the document after giving testimony. No impediment to the marriage was found in the investigation.

María Ignacia Mejia, daughter of Juan María Mejia and María Canizalez, was born about 1769 in Culiacán.

José Claudio Esquer and María Ignacia Mejia had the following known children:

i. [*párvulo*] **Esquer** was born on February 3, 1798, in Culiacán. He was baptized on April 9, 1798, at the church of the Sagrario de San Miguel in Culiacán.[300] The baptismal record named Juan María Mejia and Juana María Canizales as his *padrinos*. The parents were said to be *vecinos* of the jurisdiction of San Benito.

ii. **María Francisca Esquer** was born on November 11, 1800, in Culiacán, according to the baptismal record. She was baptized on December 20, 1800, at the church of the Sagrario de San Miguel in Culiacán.[301] The baptismal record named Manuel Iturríos and Francisca Iturríos, siblings, as her *padrinos* who were said to be single and the children of Alexandro Iturríos.

54. **Joseph Mateo Miguel Ymaz Esquer y Luyando** (Juan Miguel Gordiano-5, Salvadora Manuela Silvestra Esquer-4, Salvador-3, Salvador-2, Blas-1) was born on September 21, 1728, in Mexico City, according to the cited baptismal record. He was baptized on October 2, 1728, at the parish church of the Asunción Sagrario Metropolitano in Mexico City.[302] The baptismal record named Bachiller Juan de Zúñiga [illegible], *vecino* of Mexico City, as his *padrino*.

Joseph Mateo Miguel Ymaz Esquer y Luyando and María Gertrudis de Olavarría Caballero de los Olivos were married on May 1, 1757, at the parish of the Asunción Sagrario Metropolitano in Mexico City.[303] The matrimonial record named Doctor Francisco Xavier Gómez, Doctor

---

299. Información matrimonial 1790–1794, 1820–1822, 1825–1827, July 6, 1794, film 673391, images 237–240, Registros Parroquiales, Iglesia Sagrario de San Miguel, Culiacán, Sinaloa, Mexico (FamilySearch, https://familysearch.org).

300. Bautismos 1789–1805, April 9, 1798, film 665428, image 200, Registros Parroquiales, Iglesia Sagrario de San Miguel, Culiacán, Sinaloa, Mexico (FamilySearch, https://familysearch.org).

301. Bautismos 1789–1805, December 20, 1800, film 665428, image 264, Registros Parroquiales, Iglesia Sagrario de San Miguel, Culiacán, Sinaloa, Mexico (FamilySearch, https://familysearch.org).

302. Bautismos de españoles 1724–1730, October 2, 1728, film 35180, image 775, Registros Parroquiales, Iglesia Asunción Sagrario Metropolitano, Mexico City, Mexico (FamilySearch, https://familysearch.org).

303. Matrimonios de españoles 1756–1757, 1760-1764, May 1, 1757, film 35274, image 107, Registros Parroquiales, Iglesia Asunción Sagrario Metropolitano, Mexico City, Mexico (FamilySearch, https://familysearch.org).

Mariano Gamboa, and Doctor Augustín Quintela as witnesses to the sacrament of marriage. The couple received a nuptial blessing, *velación*, on May 3, 1757, in the chapel of the royal university. Doctor Antonio de Santiago Ríos, Bachiller Manuel Joseph Monte, and Bachiller Nicolás Pérez de la Raya, all priests, were named witnesses to the marriage. The archbishop dispensed with two of the three required banns of marriage before the marriage. The marriage took place at the home of Gertrudis Caballero de los Olivos, in the Mayorazgo de Guerrero, located in the *plazuela* called El Volador. The time of the marriage ceremony was shortly after the evening prayers. Parents were not named in the record. María Gertrudis died before 1785.

Joseph Mateo Miguel Ymaz Esquer y Luyando and Ygnacia Josefa Bustamante were married on February 26, 1785, at the parish of the Asunción Sagrario Metropolitano in Mexico City.[304] The matrimonial record named Doctor Joaquín Ygnacio Rodríguez Gallardo, priest of the parish of Santa María and rector of the Real Pontificia Universidad, and Pedro María de Ymaz Esquer as witnesses to the marriage. The record stated that the groom was the widowed husband of María Gertrudis de Olavarría Caballero de los Olivos. The marriage ceremony took place at the house of Monroy located on the street of Los Cocheros. On April 4, 1785, the couple received a nuptial blessing at the parish church of Santa María. Parents of the bride were named in the record.

Joseph Mateo Miguel Ymaz Esquer y Luyando died on April 29, 1785, at the age of fifty-six in Mexico City.[305] Joseph was buried on April 30, 1785, at the parish of the Asunción Sagrario Metropolitano in Mexico City.[306] He was buried at the church of Jesús María. The record stated that he had been married to Ygnacia Josepha Bustamante, and that he had resided at the Real y Pontificia Universidad. Joseph Mateo Miguel held the position of Secretario de la Real y Pontificia Universidad.[307] The cited last testament written in 1784 for his brother, Bachiller Mariano Ymaz Esquer y Luyando, stated his title at the university. This was the same position once held by their father.

María Gertrudis de Olavarría Caballero de los Olivos was born about 1730. She died before 1785. This was the year her widowed husband married for a second time.

Joseph Mateo Miguel Ymaz Esquer y Luyando and María Gertrudis de Olavarría Caballero de los Olivos had the following known children:

107　i.　**Joseph María Ygnacio Pedro Mathias Severino Ymaz Esquer y Luyando** was born on February 21, 1758, in Mexico City; he married Margarita María Josefa Camacho Velasco y Negrín on December 2, 1786, in Mexico City.

---

304. Matrimonios de españoles 1769–1779, 1780–1781, 1785–1791, February 26, 1785, film 35276, image 534, Registros Parroquiales, Iglesia Asunción Sagrario Metropolitano, Mexico City, Mexico (FamilySearch, https://familysearch.org).
305. Bautismos de españoles 1785–1792, September 3, 1785, film 35192, image 86, Registros Parroquiales, Iglesia Asunción Sagrario Metropolitano, Mexico City, Mexico (FamilySearch, https://familysearch.org).
306. Defunciones de españoles 1779–1789, April 30, 1785, image 459, Registros Parroquiales, Iglesia Asunción Sagrario Metropolitano, Mexico City, Mexico (FamilySearch, https://familysearch.org).
307. Fernando Muñoz Altea, *Documentos Notariales, siglos XVII al XIX* (Mexico, D.F. n.d.: Francisco Muñoz Altea), Tomás Quintero (548) folio 67 vto., Testó 21–VIII–1784.

ii.   **Manuel María Joseph Ygnacio Gonzaga Julio Ymaz Esquer y Luyando** was born on December 19, 1759, in Mexico City, according to the cited baptismal record. He was baptized on December 21, 1759, at the parish church of San Miguel Arcángel in Mexico City.[308] The baptismal record named Gertrudis Prieto de Bonilla Caballero de los Olivos as his *madrina*.

iii.   **María Josepha Ygnacia de Jesús Joaquina Anna Apolinaria Ymaz Esquer y Luyando** was born on April 10, 1762, in Mexico City, according to the cited baptismal record. She was baptized on April 15, 1762, at the parish church of the Asunción Sagrario Metropolitano in Mexico City.[309] The baptismal record named Antonio Méndez Prieto as her *padrino*.

iv.   **Joseph María Ygnacio Domingo Jacobo Neri Ymaz Esquer y Luyando** was born on July 25, 1763, in Mexico City, according to the cited baptismal record. He was baptized on August 7, 1763, at the parish church of the Asunción Sagrario Metropolitano in Mexico City.[310] The baptismal record named Doctor Joseph Eusebio de Larragoiti, priest from Tacuba in Mexico City, as his *padrino*.

v.   **María Ygnacia Josepha Joaquina Juana Timotea Ymaz Esquer y Luyando** was born on August 22, 1764, in Mexico City, according to the cited baptismal record. She was baptized on August 26, 1764, at the parish church of the Asunción Sagrario Metropolitano in Mexico City.[311] The baptismal record named Doctor Juan Gregorio Campos as her *padrino*.

vi.   **Juana María Josepha Ygnacia Mathea Ymaz Esquer y Luyando** was born on February 21, 1765, in Mexico City, according to the cited baptismal record. She was baptized on February 23, 1765, at the parish church of the Asunción Sagrario Metropolitano in Mexico City.[312] The baptismal record named Francisco Gonzáles as her *padrino*.

vii.   **María Guadalupe Theresa Josepha Ygnacia Gonzaga Ymaz Esquer y Luyando** was born on December 5, 1767, in Mexico City, according to the cited baptismal record. She was baptized on December 7, 1767, at the parish church of the Asunción Sagrario Metropolitano in Mexico City.[313] The baptismal record named Doctor Thomas Gonzáles Calderón, second level graduate in Canon Law of the Catholic

308. Bautismos de españoles 1756–1759, December 21, 1759, film 35186, image 1180, Registros Parroquíales, Iglesia San Miguel Arcángel, Mexico City, Mexico (FamilySearch, https://familysearch.org).

309. Bautismos de españoles 1760–1763, April 15, 1762, film 35187, images 562–563, Registros Parroquiales, Iglesia Asunción Sagrario Metropolitano, Mexico City, Mexico (FamilySearch, https://familysearch.org).

310. Bautismos de españoles 1760–1763, August 7, 1763 film 35187, image 915, Registros Parroquiales, Iglesia Asunción Sagrario Metropolitano, Mexico City, Mexico (FamilySearch, https://familysearch.org).

311. Bautismos de españoles 1764–1769, August 26, 1764, film 35188, image 176, Registros Parroquiales, Iglesia Asunción Sagrario Metropolitano, Mexico City, Mexico (FamilySearch, https://familysearch.org).

312. Bautismos de españoles 1764–1769, February 23, 1765, film 35188, image 424, Registros Parroquiales, Iglesia Asunción Sagrario Metropolitano, Mexico City, Mexico (FamilySearch, https://familysearch.org).

313. Bautismos de españoles 1764–1769, December 7, 1767, film 35188, images 808–809, Registros Parroquiales, Iglesia Asunción Sagrario Metropolitano, Mexico City, Mexico (FamilySearch, https://familysearch.org).

Church at the Real Universidad de Mexico, as her *padrino*. The record stated that the child's father, Joseph Mateo Miguel Ymaz Esquer y Luyando held the title of Secretario de la Real Universidad.

Ygnacia Josefa Bustamante, daughter of Pedro Bustamante and Juana Bravo y Lagunas, was born in Chalco, New Spain, according to the cited matrimonial record.

Joseph Mateo Miguel Ymaz Esquer y Luyando and Ygnacia Josefa Bustamante had only one known child:

    i.   **María del Carmen Ymaz Esquer y Luyando** was born on September 3, 1785, in Mexico City, according to the baptismal record. She was baptized on September 3, 1785, at the parish church of the Asunción Sagrario Metropolitano in Mexico City.[314] The baptismal record named Josefa Moreno Monroy as her *madrina*. The record stated that the father of the child was deceased.

55. Pedro Martín Joseph Manuel Ymaz Esquer y Luyando (Juan Miguel Gordiano-5, Salvadora Manuela Silvestra Esquer-4, Salvador-3, Salvador-2, Blas-1) was born about 1743. According to the marriage solicitation document cited, he was twenty-three years of age at the time he and María Josepha Cabanillas were asking for permission to marry.[315]

Pedro Martín Joseph Manuel Ymaz Esquer y Luyando and María Josepha Regina Hidalgo Cabanillas were married on December 8, 1766, at the parish of the Asunción Sagrario Metropolitano in Mexico City.[316] The matrimonial record named Doctor Joseph Velasco de la Vara, Doctor Francisco Rangel, and Doctor Pedro Rangel, priests of the archdiocese, as witnesses to the marriage. The marriage ceremony took place at the home of the Secretario de la Real Universidad, located on the Calle del Correo Mayor. Although parents of the bride and groom were not named in the record, the location of the marriage ceremony strongly suggests that the ceremony took place at the home of the groom's brother, Joseph Matias. He held the title of Secretario de la Real Universidad at the time, having assumed the position after his father's death. The officiating priest at the ceremony was Father Mariano Ymaz y Luyando, brother of the groom.The cited marriage solicitation record confirmed that the intended bride was only thirteen years of age.

María Josepha Regina Hidalgo Cabanillas, daughter of Pedro Antonio Hidalgo Cabanillas and María Castillo de la Fuente, was born on September 7, 1753, in Mexico City, according to the cited baptismal record. She was baptized on September 10, 1753, at the parish church of the Asunción Sagrario Metropolitano in Mexico City.[317] The baptismal record named Mariana Carrión as her *madrina*.

---

314. Bautismos de españoles 1785–1792, September 3, 1785, film 35192, image 86, Registros Parroquiales, Iglesia Asunción Sagrario Metropolitano, Mexico City, Mexico (FamilySearch, https://familysearch.org).
315. Solicitud Matrimonial, Mexico, 1766, Instituciones Coloniales/Regio Patronato Indiano/ Matrimonios (069)/Expediente 64/ Volumen 125, Archivo General de la Nación, http://www.agn.gob.mx/guiageneral.
316. Matrimonios de españoles 1765–1766, December 8, 1766, film 35275, image 117, Registros Parroquiales, Iglesia Asunción Sagrario Metropolitano, Mexico City, Mexico (FamilySearch, https://familysearch.org); Solicitud Matrimonial, Mexico, 1766, Instituciones Coloniales/Regio Patronato Indiano/ Matrimonios (069)/ Expediente 64/ Volumen 125, Archivo General de la Nación, http://www.agn.gob.mx/guiageneral.
317. Bautismos de españoles 1751–1755, September 10, 1753, film 35185, image 565, Registros Parroquiales, Iglesia Asunción Sagrario Metropolitano, Mexico City, Mexico (FamilySearch, https://familysearch.org).

Pedro Martín Joseph Manuel Ymaz Esquer y Luyando and María Josepha Regina Hidalgo Cabanillas had one known child:

108 i.   **Manuel Joseph María Ygnacio Ymaz y Cabanillas** was born on May 27, 1769, in Mexico City; he married María Josefa Zeferina Arenas del Valle on October 14, 1798, in Mexico City.

56. Juan Antonio Joseph Chirlín (María Josepha Francisca Ymaz y Esquer-5, Salvadora Manuela Silvestra Esquer-4, Salvador-3, Salvador-2, Blas-1) was born on June 23, 1726, in Mexico City, according to the cited baptismal record. He was baptized on June 30, 1726, at the parish church of the Asunción Sagrario Metropolitano in Mexico City.[318] The baptismal record named Pedro Brendis and Mariana Rubio as his *padrinos*.

Juan Antonio Joseph Chirlín and Anna María de Tamariz y Gradillas were married on February 2, 1756, at the parish of the Asunción Sagrario Metropolitano in Mexico City.[319] The matrimonial record named Bachiller Manuel de Leca and Bachiller Mariano Patricio de Ymaz, priests in the Archdiocese of Mexico, as witnesses to the marriage. The marriage took place at the home of Licenciado Juan de Ymaz Esquer, which was located behind the Real Universidad. The following day the couple received a nuptial blessing at the chapel of the Real Universidad with the above-named witnesses present.

Anna María de Tamariz y Gradillas was born about 1738.

Juan Antonio Joseph Chirlín and Anna María de Tamariz y Gradillas had the following known children:

109 i.   **Manuel Joseph Narciso Thadeo Chirlín** was born on October 29, 1756, in Mexico City; he married Rosalía García y Salas on July 8, 1790, in Mexico City.

110 ii.   **Joseph María Martín Chirlín** was born on November 11, 1757, in Mexico City; he married Rosalía Ábrego y Cova on December 28, 1777, in Mexico City.

    iii.   **Manuel Joseph Antonio Xavier Chirlín** was born on December 23, 1758, in Mexico City, according to the baptismal record. He was baptized on December 26, 1758, at the parish church of the Asunción Sagrario Metropolitano in Mexico City.[320] The baptismal record named Licenciado Bernardo Joseph Carrasco, attorney for the Real Audiencia, as his *padrino*.

    iv.   **Juana María Josepha Ygnacia Chirlín** was born on June 24, 1760, in Mexico City, according to the baptismal record. She was baptized on June 29, 1760, at the parish

318. Bautismos de españoles 1724–1730, June 30, 1726, film 35180, image 393, Registros Parroquiales, Iglesia Asunción Sagrario Metropolitano, Mexico City, Mexico (FamilySearch, https://familysearch.org).

319. Matrimonios de españoles 1756–1757, 1760–1764, February 2, 1756, film 35274, image 6, Registros Parroquiales, Iglesia Asunción Sagrario Metropolitano, Mexico City, Mexico (FamilySearch, https://familysearch.org).

320. Bautismos de españoles 1756–1759, film 35186, image 895, Registros Parroquiales, Iglesia Asunción Sagrario Metropolitano, Mexico City, Mexico (FamilySearch, https://familysearch.org).

church of the Asunción Sagrario Metropolitano in Mexico City.[321] The baptismal record named Licenciado Antonio Leca [?] as her *padrino*.

v. **Ygnacio Joseph Simeón Chirlín** was born on February 18, 1762, in Mexico City, according to the baptismal record. He was baptized on February 23, 1762, at the parish church of the Asunción Sagrario Metropolitano in Mexico City.[322] The baptismal record named Raymundo Ymaz as his *padrino*.

111 vi. **María de Guadalupe Gertrudis Josepha Saturnina Chirlín** was born on February 11, 1764, in Mexico City; she married Diego Andrés Gradillas y Orejón on November 19, 1780, in Mexico City.

vii. **Augustín Joseph Policarpo Chirlín** was born on January 26, 1768, in Mexico City, according to the cited baptismal record. He was baptized on January 29, 1768, at the parish church of the Asunción Sagrario Metropolitano in Mexico City.[323] The baptismal record named María Antonia Tamariz as his *madrina*.

57. **Pablo Esquer** (Pedro Fernando-5, Miguel Fernando Simón-4, Salvador-3, Salvador-2, Blas-1) was born about 1755.

Pablo Esquer and María Dolores Valenzuela were married after November 13, 1779.[324] The actual matrimonial record has not been located. According to the cited marriage investigation, the couple were related in the third, with a fourth degree of consanguinity, meaning they were second cousins once removed. This investigation revealed that María Dolores Valenzuela's mother, María Antonia Mallén de Navarrete, was the illegitimate daughter of Vicente Mallén de Navarette. Vicente Mallén de Navarette was the uncle of Pablo Esquer. Pablo Esquer's parents were said to have been deceased. Testimony provided by Pablo Esquer and witnesses revealed that under a promise of marriage the couple, not knowing of their marriage impediment, had given birth to a daughter who was not named. It was Pablo's aunt, Manuela Esquer who stepped forward with the revelation. Both marriage candidates were said to have been *vecinos* of Río Chico, then located in the province of Ostimuri, Sonora. The marriage dispensation was granted by the bishop in Durango on November 13, 1779.

María Dolores Valenzuela, daughter of Felipe Valenzuela, was born in 1761. The cited marriage investigation stated that she was eighteen years of age in 1779.

---

321. Bautismos de españoles 1760–1763, June 29, 1760, film 35187, image 123, Registros Parroquiales, Iglesia Asunción Sagrario Metropolitano, Mexico City, Mexico (FamilySearch, https://familysearch.org).

322. Bautismos de españoles 1760–1763, February 23, 1762, film 35187, image 521, Registros Parroquiales, Iglesia Asunción Sagrario Metropolitano, Mexico City, Mexico (FamilySearch, https://familysearch.org).

323. Bautismos de españoles 1764–1769, January 29, 1768, film 35188, image 841, Registros Parroquiales, Iglesia Asunción Sagrario Metropolitano, Mexico City, Mexico (FamilySearch, https://familysearch.org).

324. Diligencias matrimoniales, Pablo de Esquerr y María Dolores de Valenzuela, Real de Río Chico, 1779, AHAD-30, frames 101–110, AHAD; Pablo Esquerr y María Dolores Valenzuela, Pueblo de Movas, 1779 AHAD–31, frames 429–443, AHAD.

Pablo Esquer and María Dolores Valenzuela had the following child:

i.   **[unnamed] Esquer**[325] was born before 1779. The only reference to the birth of this unnamed child was contained in the cited marriage investigation for her parents.

58. María Manuela Esquer (Pedro Fernando-5, Miguel Fernando Simón-4, Salvador-3, Salvador-2, Blas-1) was born about 1760.

María Manuela Esquer and Juan Francisco Campoy were married about 1776. Their marriage record has not been located.

Juan Francisco Campoy was born about 1757. He died on April 4, 1807, in Álamos. He was buried on April 5, 1807, at the church of the Purísima Concepción in Álamos.[326] He was laid to rest in a burial site valued at five pesos. Juan Francisco's funeral service was held with *cruz alta, capa y ataúd con caja al cadáver*. He received the last sacraments of the Catholic Church before death.

Juan Francisco Campoy and María Manuela Esquer had the following known children:

112 i.   **María Ygnacia Campoy** was born in 1777 in Álamos; she married José María Quirós y Mora on December 1, 1789, in Álamos.

ii.   **María Balvanera Viviana Campoy** was born on January 28, 1782, in Álamos, according to the baptismal record. She was baptized on February 8, 1782, at the church of the Purísima Concepción in Álamos. The baptismal record named Juan Manuel González de Zayas and Águeda González de Zayas as her *padrinos*.

iii.   **José Antonio de la Merced Campoy** was born on September 28, 1786, in Álamos. The cited baptismal record provided his date of birth. He was baptized on October 10, 1786, at the parish of the Purísima Concepción in Álamos.[327] The baptismal record named Ramón Soto, *vecino* of Río Chico, and Rafaela Esquer, *vecina* of La Aduana, as his *padrinos*. The baptism ceremony took place in the chapel of La Aduana.

iv.   **María Gertrudis Cecilia Campoy** was born on November 16, 1791, in Álamos, according to the cited baptismal record. She was baptized on November 22, 1791, at the parish of the Purísima Concepción in Álamos.[328] The baptismal record named the parish priest, Juan Nicolás Quirós y Mora and his sister, María Ysabel Quirós y Mora, as her *padrinos*. The baptism ceremony took place in the chapel of La Aduana, where the parents were said to have been *vecinos*. Grandparents were named in the record.

---

325. Diligencias matrimoniales, Pablo de Esquerr y María Dolores de Valenzuela, Real de Río Chico, 1779, AHAD-30, frames 101–110, AHAD; Pablo Esquerr y María Dolores Valenzuela, Pueblo de Movas, 1779 AHAD-31, frames 429–443, AHAD.
326. Defunciones 1786–1819, April 5, 1807 film, 666996, images 391–392, Registros Parroquiales, Iglesia de La Purísima Concepción, Álamos, Sonora, Mexico (FamilySearch, https://familysearch.org).
327. Bautismos 1781–1796, October 10, 1786, film 663488, image 208, Registros Parroquiales, Iglesia de La Purísima Concepción, Álamos, Sonora, Mexico (FamilySearch, https://familysearch.org).
328. Bautismos 1791–1796, 1805–1815, November 22, 1791, film 663996, image 13, Registros Parroquiales, Iglesia de La Purísima Concepción, Álamos, Sonora, Mexico (FamilySearch, https://familysearch.org).

v.   **María Manuela Campoy** was born about June 30, 1794, in Álamos. According to the cited baptismal record, she was born at the end of June. She was baptized on July 3, 1794, at the church of the Purísima Concepción in Álamos.[329] The baptismal record named Juan Manuel Ortiz and María Dolores Velarde as her *padrinos*.

vi.   **María Trinidad Dolores del Sacramento Campoy** was born in 1795 in Álamos. She was baptized on June 29, 1795, at the church of the Purísima Concepción in Álamos.[330]

---

329. Bautismos 1791–1796, 1805–1815, July 3, 1794, film 663996, image 134, Registros Parroquiales, Iglesia de La Purísima Concepción, Álamos, Sonora, Mexico (FamilySearch, https://familysearch.org).
330. Bautismos 1781–1796, June 29, 1795, film 663488, image [not located], Registros Parroquiales, Iglesia de La Purísima Concepción, Álamos, Sonora, Mexico (FamilySearch, https://familysearch.org).

Seventh Generation

59. **María Matilde de la Luz Alcayde Pérez de la Puente** (Francisco Xavier-6, Juana Esquer-5, Juan Salvador-4, Salvador-3, Salvador-2, Blas-1) was born in 1742 in Culiacán. She was baptized on June 16, 1742, at the parish church of the Sagrario de San Miguel in Culiacán.[331] Her baptismal record named Bachiller Diego Yturríos as her *padrino*.

María Matilde de la Luz Alcayde Pérez de la Puente and Bruno Joseph de Liceaga were married on February 26, 1758, at the church of the Sagrario de San Miguel in Culiacán.[332] The matrimonial record identified Manuel Ygnacio Fernández de Castañeda and Pedro Verdugo y Chávez, among many others present, as witnesses to the marriage. *Padrinos* were not named in the record. Parents of the bride and groom were named.

Bruno Joseph de Liceaga, son of Joseph de Liceaga and Catharina de Alonzo, was born about 1740 in Vizcaya, País Vasco, Spain. According to the cited matrimonial record, he was born *en los Reynos de Castilla, en Vizcaya*.

Bruno Joseph de Liceaga and María Matilde de la Luz Alcayde Pérez de la Puente had the following known children:

i. **María Theresa de Liceaga** was born in 1759 in Culiacán. She was baptized on April 21, 1759, at in the parish church of the Sagrario de San Miguel in Culiacán.[333] The baptismal record named María Teresa Montes as her *madrina*.

ii. **María Agripina de Liceaga** was born about 1764 in Culiacán. She died on August 14, 1814, in Culiacán. She was buried on August 15, 1814, at the church of the Sagrario de San Miguel in Culiacán.[334] Her funeral services were held with *cruz alta, caja y capa*. She was laid to rest in a burial site valued at five pesos. According to the record, she never married, and she died of natural causes.

iii. **Manuel María de Liceaga** was born in 1768 in Culiacán. He was baptized on June 4, 1768, at the church of the Sagrario de San Miguel in Culiacán.[335] The baptismal

331. Bautismos 1690–1746, 1731–1769, June 16,1742, film 665425, image 214, Registros Parroquiales, Iglesia Sagrario de San Miguel, Culiacán, Sinaloa, Mexico (FamilySearch, https://familysearch.org).

332. Matrimonios 1755–1784 [1794], February 26, 1758, film 673389, image 22, Registros Parroquiales, Iglesia Sagrario de San Miguel, Culiacán, Sinaloa, Mexico (FamilySearch, https://familysearch.org).

333. Bautismos 1755–1789, April 21, 1759, film 665427, image 35, Registros Parroquiales, Iglesia Sagrario de San Miguel, Culiacán, Sinaloa, Mexico (FamilySearch, https://familysearch.org).

334. Defunciones 1746–1833, August 15, 1814, film 674051, images 454–465, Registros parroquiales, Iglesia del Sagrario de San Miguel, Culiacán, Sinaloa, Mexico (FamilySearch, https://familysearch.org).

335. Defunciones 1731–1756, 1731–1755, June 4, 1768, film 665426, image 302, Registros Parroquiales, Iglesia Sagrario de San Miguel, Culiacán, Sinaloa, Mexico (FamilySearch, https://familysearch.org).

record named Joaquín Fernández Rojo as his *padrino*. The child was previously given the water of baptism on May 22 in the event he would not survive.

iv. **Xavier de Liceaga** was born about 1770. The cited burial record did not provide his age but did state that he was a child. He died on August 16, 1780, in Culiacán. He was buried on August 17, 1780, at the church of the Sagrario de San Miguel in Culiacán.[336] The burial record stated that Xavier had received the sacrament of extreme unction. He was buried on the same day as his brother Manuel Bruno.

v. **Manuel Bruno de Liceaga** was born about 1772 in Culiacán. He died on August 16, 1780, at the age of eight in Culiacán. He was buried on August 17, 1780, at the church of the Sagrario de San Miguel in Culiacán.[337] The burial record stated that Manuel Bruno was eight or nine years of age at the time of his death, and that he received the sacraments of penance and extreme unction. He was buried on the same day as his brother Xavier.

vi. **Joseph Joaquín María de Liceaga** was born in 1773 in Culiacán. He was baptized on October 17, 1773, at the church of the Sagrario de San Miguel in Culiacán.[338] The baptismal record named Francisco Amugra [?] as his *padrino*. The record named his father as Bruno Martínez.

60. Joaquín Andrés Alcayde (Francisco Xavier-6, Juana Esquer-5, Juan Salvador-4, Salvador-3, Salvador-2, Blas-1) was born about 1745 in Culiacán. He married María Ysidora Rivera on April 22, 1772, at the church of the Purísima Concepción in Álamos.[339] The matrimonial record named Teniente General Juan Augustín de Yriarte and Josephina González Barreda as his *padrinos*. Mariano Pantaleón Gómez and Felipe Goycochea were named as witnesses to the marriage. Parents of the bride and groom were named in the record.

Joaquín Andrés died on October 10, 1781, in Álamos. He was buried on October 11, 1781, at the church of the Purísima Concepción in Álamos.[340] Joaquín Andrés Alcayde died suddenly and was administered the sacrament of extreme unction after his death. His burial site was valued at five pesos, and his funeral was held with *cruz alta, vigilia, caja, y túmulo de dos cuerpos.* According to the burial record, he left four surviving children (only three have been identified).

---

336. Defunciones 1746–1833, August 27, 1780, film 674051, image 202, Registros Parroquiales, Iglesia Sagrario de San Miguel, Culiacán, Sinaloa, Mexico (FamilySearch, https://familysearch.org).
337. Ibid.
338. Bautismos 1755–1789, October 17, 1773, film 665427, image 321, Registros Parroquiales, Iglesia Sagrario de San Miguel, Culiacán, Sinaloa, Mexico (FamilySearch, https://familysearch.org).
339. Matrimonios 1758–1779, April 22, 1772, film 666564, image 147, Registros Parroquiales, Iglesia de La Purísima Concepción, Álamos, Sonora, Mexico (FamilySearch, https://familysearch.org).
340. Defunciones 1717–1751, 1764–1792, October 11, 1781, film 666995, image 384, Registros Parroquiales, Iglesia de La Purísima Concepción, Alamos, Sonora, Mexico (FamilySearch, https://familysearch.org).

María Ysidora Rivera, daughter of Miguel Alexandro Rivera and María Theresa Mallén de Navarrete, was born in 1751 in Álamos. She was baptized on April 27, 1751, at the church of the Purísima Concepción in Álamos.[341] The baptismal record is faded and for the most part illegible.

Joaquín Andrés Alcayde and María Ysidora Rivera had the following known children:

i.   **Bárbara Josefa Inés Alcayde** was born in 1777 in Álamos. She was baptized on January 30, 1777, at the church of the Purísima Concepción in Álamos.[342] The baptismal record named Miguel Alcayde and Michaela Yriarte as her *padrinos*. Lucas de la Serna, Juan de Fox, and Joseph Gabriel Esquer were named as witnesses to the baptism.

113 ii.   **Anna María Josefa Valentina Alcayde** was born in 1779 in Álamos; she married José Antonio Delgado in November 8, 1803, in Rosario, Sinaloa.

iii.   **José Julián Alcayde** was born on January 18, 1781, in Álamos, according to the baptismal record. He was baptized on February 6, 1781, at the church of the Purísima Concepción in Álamos.[343] The baptismal record named Miguel Alexandro de Rivera as his *padrino*. José Julián died on April 15, 1781, in Álamos, and was was buried on April 16, 1781, at the church of the Purísima Concepción in Álamos.[344] His funeral service was held with *cruz alta, capa, caja, y una mesa*. José Julián was buried in a grave valued at five pesos. The burial record stated that the deceased was a child and named the parents of the deceased child.

61. Miguel Alcayde Pérez de la Puente (Francisco Xavier-6, Juana Esquer-5, Juan Salvador-4, Salvador-3, Salvador-2, Blas-1) was born about 1744 in Culiacán. His place of birth was provided in the cited marriage dispensation record.

Miguel Alcayde Pérez de la Puente and María Balvanera de Yriarte were married on December 6, 1775, at the church of the Purísima Concepción in Álamos.[345] The matrimonial record named Juan Ortíz and María Dolores Velarde as *padrinos*. Parents of the bride and groom were named, and the record stated that the couple had received a nuptial blessing.

341. Bautismos 1751–1794, matrimonios 1848, defunciones 1735–1752, April 27, 1751, film 666999, image 40, Registros Parroquiales, Iglesia de La Purísima Concepción, Álamos, Sonora, Mexico (FamilySearch, https://familysearch.org).

342. Bautismos, matrimonios y defunciones 1696–1699, bautismos 1768–1781, film 663487, image 337, Registros Parroquiales, Iglesia de La Purísima Concepción, Álamos, Sonora, Mexico (FamilySearch, https://familysearch.org).

343. Bautismos, matrimonios y defunciones 1696–1699, bautismos 1768–1781, film 663487, image 505, Registros Parroquiales, Iglesia de La Purísima Concepción, Álamos, Sonora, Mexico (FamilySearch, https://familysearch.org).

344. Defunciones 1717–1751,1764–1792, April 16, 1781, film 666995, image 360, Registros Parroquiales, Iglesia de La Purísima Concepción, Álamos, Sonora, Mexico (FamilySearch, https://familysearch.org).

345. Matrimonios 1758–1779, December 6, 1775, film 666564, image 165, Registros Parroquiales, Iglesia de La Purísima Concepción, Álamos, Sonora, Mexico (FamilySearch, https://familysearch.org).

The bridal couple received a marriage dispensation on Oct 2, 1775, in Álamos.[346] The dispensation was required because the couple were related to the fourth degree of consanguinity: the father of the groom was the second cousin of the mother of the bride. María was said to have been a "poor demure child" and that the marriage would better serve God and the Holy Church. Parents of the bride and groom were named in the record. All were *vecinos* of Álamos. Vicente Mallén de Navarrete, Juan Manuel Morales, and Teniente Coronel Thadeo Padilla y Arnao served as witnessses in favor of the marriage dispensation. The marriage dispensation record used "Alcalde" as the family surname.

Miguel died on November 15, 1797, in Álamos. He was buried on November 16, 1797, at the church of the Purísima Concepción in Álamos.[347] His funeral service was held with *cruz alta, capa, incienso y caja*. He was laid to rest in a grave site valued at ten pesos. Miguel received the last sacraments of the Catholic Church before death. His wife was named in the record, and he was said not to have had any surviving children. He did not leave a will because there was no reason to do so, *"porque no hubo de qué."*

María Balvanera de Yriarte, daughter of Juan Augustín de Yriarte and Ana María González Barreda, was born about 1761 in Álamos.

Miguel Alcayde Pérez de la Puente and María Balvanera de Yriarte had the following known children:

i. **María Rosa Viterbo Cástula Alcayde Pérez de la Puente** was born in 1778 in Álamos. She was baptized on April 1, 1778, at the church of the Purísima Concepción in Álamos.[348] The baptismal record named Teniente del Gobernador Augustín Yriarte and Josefa González Barreda as her *padrinos.*

ii. **Juan Pablo de Jesús Alcayde Pérez de la Puente** was born on January 15, 1780, in Álamos. He was baptized on February 8, 1780, at the church of the Purísima Concepción in Álamos.[349] The baptismal record named Teniente del Gobernador Juan Augustín Yriarte and his daughter, Michaela Yriarte, as his *padrinos.* He died on October 4, 1782, at the age of two in Álamos. Juan was buried on October 5, 1782, at the church of the Purísima Concepción in Álamos.[350] His funeral service was held with *cruz alta, capa, una mesa y caja*. The little child was laid to rest at the Capilla de Jesús.

---

346. Diligencias matrimoniales, Miguel Alcalde y María Balbanera de Iriarte, Real de Álamos, 1775, AHAD-33, frames 601–605, AHAD.

347. Defunciones 1786–1819, November 16, 1797 film, 666996, image 280, Registros Parroquiales, Iglesia de La Purísima Concepción, Álamos, Sonora, Mexico (FamilySearch, https://familysearch.org).

348. Bautismos, matrimonios y defunciones 1696–1699 bautismos 1768–1781, film 663487, image 372, Registros Parroquiales, Iglesia de La Purísima Concepción, Álamos, Sonora, Mexico (FamilySearch, https:// familysearch.org).

349. Bautismos, matrimonios y defunciones 1696–1699, bautismos 1768–1781, February 8, 1780, film 663487, image 452, Registros Parroquiales, Iglesia de La Purísima Concepción, Álamos, Sonora, Mexico (FamilySearch, https:// familysearch.org).

350. Defunciones 1717–1751, 1764–1792, October 5, 1782, film 666995, images 406–407, Registros Parroquiales, Iglesia de La Purísima Concepción, Álamos, Sonora, Mexico (FamilySearch, https://familysearch. org).

62. **Anna María Esquer** (Juan Salvador-6, Salvador-5, Juan Salvador-4, Salvador-3, Salvador-2, Blas-1) was born before 1780.[351] The cited 1780 burial record for her mother lists Anna María Esquer as a surviving child.

Anna María Esquer and Juan Joseph Pantaleón Morales were married on July 4, 1808, at the church of the Purísima Concepción in Álamos.[352] The matrimonial record named Rafael Esquer and Rita Almagro as *padrinos*. Manuel Campoy and Juan Fox were named as witnesses to the marriage. According to the record, the groom was born in the mining town of Promontorios in the jurisdiction of Álamos and was widowed from his first wife, Michaela Valenzuela. Parents of the bride and groom were named in the record. The couple received a nuptial blessing on the day of their marriage.

Juan Joseph Pantaleón Morales, son of Juan Morales and Susana Esquerra y Rosas, was born on July 25, 1769, in Álamos, according to the baptismal record. He was baptized on September 6, 1769, at the church of the Purísima Concepción in Álamos.[353] The baptismal record named Joseph Esquerra y Rosas and Rosa Féliz as his *padrinos*. The waters of baptism had been previously administered out of necessity out of concern that the child would not survive.

Juan Joseph Pantaleón Morales and Anna María Esquer had only one known child:

    i.   **María Francisca Josefa Leandra Morales** was born on March 13, 1808, in Álamos, according to the cited baptismal record. She was baptized on March 15, 1808, at the church of the Purísima Concepción in Álamos.[354] The baptismal record named José Joaquín Elías González de Zayas and Águeda Josefa González de Zayas as her *padrinos*.

63. **José Rafael Esquer** (Juan Salvador-6, Salvador-5, Juan Salvador-4, Salvador-3, Salvador-2, Blas-1) was born in 1775 in Álamos.[355] The cited marriage information record stated he was twenty-two years of age in 1797 and had been born in Álamos.

José Rafael Esquer and María Rita Cano de los Ríos were married on July 27, 1797, at the church of the Purísima Concepción in Álamos.[356] The matrimonial record named Administrador de Azogues Bartolomé Salido and his wife María Bárbara González de Zayas as *padrinos*. Ygnacio Güereña, José Bustillos (*sacristán*) and José María Bustillos, among many others present, were identified as witnesses to the marriage. Parents of the bride and groom were named in the

---

351. Defunciones 1717–1751,1764–1792, September 8, 1780, film 666995, image 337, Registros Parroquiales, Iglesia de La Purísima Concepción, Álamos, Sonora, Mexico (FamilySearch, https://familysearch.org).
352. Matrimonios 1779–1817, July 4, 1808, film 666565, image 483, Registros Parroquiales, Iglesia de La Purísima Concepción, Álamos, Sonora, Mexico (FamilySearch, https://familysearch.org).
353. Bautismos, matrimonios y defunciones 1696–1699, bautismos 1768–1781, September 6, 1769, film 663487, image 137, Registros Parroquiales, Iglesia de La Purísima Concepción, Álamos, Sonora, Mexico (FamilySearch, https:// familysearch.org).
354. Bautismos 1791–1796, 1805–1815, March 15, 1808, film 663996, images 305–306, Registros Parroquiales, Iglesia de La Purísima Concepción, Álamos, Sonora, Mexico (FamilySearch, https://familysearch. org).
355. Defunciones 1717–1751,1764–1792, September 8, 1780, film 666995, image 337, Registros Parroquiales, Iglesia de La Purísima Concepción, Alamos, Sonora, Mexico (FamilySearch, https://familysearch.org).
356. Matrimonios 1779–1817, July 27, 1797, film 666565, images 334–335, Registros Parroquiales, Iglesia de La Purísima Concepción, Álamos, Sonora, Mexico (FamilySearch, https://familysearch.org).

record. Parents of the groom were said to have been deceased, as was the father of the bride. The couple received a nuptial blessing on the day of their marriage. The marriage information record, dated July 8, 1797, found no impediment to marriage.[357]

María Rita Cano de los Ríos, daughter of Toribio Cano de los Ríos and María Margarita Almagro, was born in 1770 in Álamos. The cited marriage information record stated that she was twenty-seven years of age in 1797 and had been born in Álamos.

José Rafael Esquer and María Rita Cano de los Ríos had the following known children:

     i. **María Trinidad Marcelina Dorotea Esquer** was born in 1798 in Álamos. She was baptized on June 2, 1798, at the church of the Purísima Concepción in Álamos.[358] The baptismal record named Juan José Fox and Margarita de Almagro as her *padrinos*.

    ii. **Juan Salvador Remigio Francisco Esquer** was born in 1799 in Álamos. He was baptized on July 12, 1799, at the church of the Purísima Concepción in Álamos.[359] The baptismal record named Juan José Fox and Anna María Esquer as his *padrinos*.

    iii. **María Andrea Diega Esquer** was born in 1800 in Álamos. She was baptized on November 14, 1800, at the church of the Purísima Concepción in Álamos.[360] The baptismal record named Antonio Almada and María de la Luz Alvarado as her *padrinos*.

    iv. **José Rafael Pedro de la Encarnación Esquer** was born in 1802 in Álamos. He was baptized on October 24, 1802, at the church of the Purísima Concepción in Álamos.[361] The baptismal record named Bartolomé Salido and María Bárbara González de Zayas as his *padrino*s.

114 v. **Bruno Dionicio Luis de Jesús Esquer** was born in 1804 in Álamos; he married María Josefa Figueroa about 1826.

115 vi. **José Francisco Evaristo de los Santos Esquer** was born on October 26, 1806, in Álamos; he married María Gertrudis Toledo sometime before 1830.

    vii. **José María Gumersindo Esquer** was born in 1808 in Álamos. He was baptized on January 13, 1808, at the church of the Purísima Concepción in Álamos.[362] The baptismal record named Antonia Zayas as his *madrina*.

    viii. **María de las Nieves Josefa Rita Anna Esquer** was born on August 5, 1811, in Álamos. According to the cited baptismal record, she was baptized the day she was

357. Información matrimonial 1795–1800, July 8, 1797, film 663809, images 298–303, Registros Parroquiales, Iglesia de La Purísima Concepción, Álamos, Sonora, Mexico (FamilySearch, https://familysearch.org).
358. Bautismos 1796–1805, June 2, 1798, film 663995, images 75–76, Registros Parroquiales, Iglesia de La Purísima Concepción, Álamos, Sonora, Mexico (FamilySearch, https://familysearch.org).
359. Bautismos 1796–1805, July 12, 1799, film 663995, image 105, Registros Parroquiales, Iglesia de La Purísima Concepción, Álamos, Sonora, Mexico (FamilySearch, https://familysearch.org).
360. Bautismos 1796–1805, November 14, 1800, film 663995, image 138, Registros Parroquiales, Iglesia de La Purísima Concepción, Álamos, Sonora, Mexico (FamilySearch, https://familysearch.org).
361. Bautismos 1796–1805, October 24, 1802, film 663995, image 180, Registros Parroquiales, Iglesia de La Purísima Concepción, Álamos, Sonora, Mexico (FamilySearch, https://familysearch.org).
362. Bautismos 1791–1796, 1805–1815, January 13, 1708, film 663996, images 299–300, Registros Parroquiales, Iglesia de La Purísima Concepción, Álamos, Sonora, Mexico (FamilySearch, https://familysearch.org).

born. She was baptized on August 5, 1811, at the church of the Purísima Concepción in Álamos.[363] The baptismal record named Ygnacio Almada and María Trinidad Salido as her *padrinos*.

64. María Gertrudis Esquer (Juan Salvador-6, Salvador-5, Juan Salvador-4, Salvador-3, Salvador-2, Blas-1) was born about 1777.[364] The cited 1780 burial record for her mother listed María Gertrudis Esquer as a surviving child.

María Gertrudis Esquer and Luis Juan Joseph Raphael Fox were married on March 28, 1797, at the church of the Purísima Concepción in Álamos.[365] The matrimonial record referred to the groom as "Juan José Fox." It named Juan Francisco Fox and María del Pilar, siblings of the groom, as *padrinos*. José Bustillos (*sacristán*) and Rafael Esquer, among many others present, were identified as witnesses to the marriage. The matrimonial record named the parents of the bride and groom. Parents of the bride were said to have been deceased. The couple received a nuptial blessing after the date of their marriage. According to the record the blessing was prohibited during the liturgical period when the marriage took place.

Luis Juan Joseph Raphael Fox, son of Juan Pablo Fox and María Loreto Esquer, was born in 1772 in Álamos. He was baptized on August 5, 1772, at the church of the Purísima Concepción in Álamos.[366] The baptismal record named Anna María Aragón as his *madrina*. Xavier de Aragón, Joaquín Ybáñez and Joaquín Gastélum were named as witnesses to the sacrament of baptism. He died before May 7, 1823.[367] The cited marriage record for his daughter María Petra Fox stated that Luis Juan Joseph Raphael Fox was deceased at the time of her marriage on May 7, 1823.

Luis Juan Joseph Raphael Fox and María Gertrudis Esquer had the following known children:

116 i.   **María Petra Fox** was born in 1797 in Álamos. She married José Manuel Tiburcio Quirós y Mora on May 7, 1823, in Álamos and died before December 3, 1868.

117 ii.   **María de Jesús del Mar Atilana Fox** was born in 1799 in Álamos; she married José Antonio Tena sometime before 1828.

iii.   **José Ygnacio de Jesús Francisco Sabino Fox** was born on December 30, 1801, in Álamos, according to the cited baptismal record. He was baptized on January 3, 1802, at the church of the Purísima Concepción in Álamos.[368] The baptismal record named his father Juan Fox and Anna María Esquer as his *padrinos*.

363. Bautismos 1791–1796, 1805–1815, August 5, 1811, film 663996, image 441, Registros Parroquiales, Iglesia de La Purísima Concepción, Álamos, Sonora, Mexico (FamilySearch, https://familysearch.org).

364. Defunciones 1717–1751, 1764–1792, September 8, 1780, film 666995, image 337, Registros Parroquiales, Iglesia de La Purísima Concepción, Alamos, Sonora, Mexico (FamilySearch, https://familysearch.org).

365. Matrimonios 1779–1817, March 28,1797, film 666565, images 322–323, Registros Parroquiales, Iglesia de La Purísima Concepción, Álamos, Sonora, Mexico (FamilySearch, https://familysearch.org).

366. Bautismos, matrimonios y defunciones 1696–1699, bautismos 1768–1781, film 663487, image 243, Registros Parroquiales, Iglesia de La Purísima Concepción, Álamos, Sonora, Mexico (FamilySearch, https://familysearch.org).

367. Matrimonios 1797–1833, 1846–1868, 1872–1877, May 7, 1823, film 666566, images 276–277, Registros Parroquiales, Iglesia de La Purísima Concepción, Álamos, Sonora, Mexico (FamilySearch, https://familysearch.org).

368. Bautismos 1796–1805, January 3, 1802, film 663995, image 164, Registros Parroquiales, Iglesia de La Purísima Concepción, Álamos, Sonora, Mexico (FamilySearch, https://familysearch.org).

118 iv.   **María Dolores Francisca de Jesús Candelaria Fox** was born on January 29, 1803, in Álamos.

    v.   **María de la Concepción Toribia Ignés Fox** was born on April 16, 1805, in Álamos, according to the cited baptismal record. She was baptized on April 20, 1805, at the church of the Purísima Concepción in Álamos.[369] The baptismal record named Manuel Anguís and Serafina Barreda as her *padrinos*.

    vi.   **José Ygnacio Genaro de Jesús Fox** was born on July 10, 1807, in Álamos, according to the cited baptismal record. He was baptized on July 15, 1807, at the church of the Purísima Concepción in Álamos.[370] The baptismal record named Mariano Pérez del Rey and María Gertrudis Goycochea as his *padrinos*.

    vii.   **María Balvanera Anastasia de Jesús Fox** was born in 1810 in Álamos. She was baptized on January 25, 1810, at the church of the Purísima Concepción in Álamos.[371] The baptismal record named Juan José Morales and María del Carmen Fox as her *padrinos*.

119 viii.   **María Antonia Francisca Feliciana Fox** was born in 1812 in Álamos; she married Guadalupe Sarracino on February 22, 1841, in Álamos.

    ix.   **María Guadalupe Leocadia Fox** was born in 1814 in Álamos. She was baptized on December 13, 1814, at the church of the Purísima Concepción in Álamos.[372] The baptismal record named Gertrudis Goycochea as her *madrina*.

65. María Ignacia de la Trinidad Esquer (Juan Salvador-6, Salvador-5, Juan Salvador-4, Salvador-3, Salvador-2, Blas-1) was born in 1779 in Álamos.[373] The cited burial record for María Manuela Campoy, her mother, listed Ignacia Esquer as a surviving child on September 8, 1780. She was baptized on July 12, 1779, at the church of the Purísima Concepción in Álamos.[374] The baptismal record named Francisco de Xruz [Cruz] and María Ignacia Campoy, his wife, as the child's *padrinos*.

María Ignacia de la Trinidad Esquer and Ignacio María Gonzáles de Zayas were married on February 24, 1800, at the church of the Purísima Concepción in Álamos.[375] The matrimonial

---

369. Bautismos 1796–1805, April 20, 1805, film 663995, image 270, Registros Parroquiales, Iglesia de La Purísima Concepción, Álamos, Sonora, Mexico (FamilySearch, https://familysearch.org).
370. Bautismos 1791–1796, 1805–1815, July 15,1807, film 663996, image 288, Registros Parroquiales, Iglesia de La Purísima Concepción, Álamos, Sonora, Mexico (FamilySearch, https://familysearch.org).
371. Bautismos 1791–1796, 1805–1815, January 25, 1810, film 663996, image 362, Registros Parroquiales, Iglesia de La Purísima Concepción, Álamos, Sonora, Mexico (FamilySearch, https://familysearch.org).
372. Bautismos 1791–1796, 1805–1815, December 13, 1814, film 663996, images 486-487, Registros Parroquiales, Iglesia de La Purísima Concepción, Álamos, Sonora, Mexico (FamilySearch, https://familysearch.org).
373. Defunciones 1717–1751, 1764–1792, September 8, 1780, film 666995, image 337, Registros Parroquiales, Iglesia de La Purísima Concepción, Álamos, Sonora, Mexico (FamilySearch, https://familysearch.org).
374. Bautismos, matrimonios y defunciones 1696–1699, bautismos 1768–1781, July 12, 1779, film 663487, image 272, Registros Parroquiales, Iglesia de La Purísima Concepción, Álamos, Sonora, Mexico (FamilySearch, https://familysearch.org).
375. Matrimonios 1779–1817, February 24, 1800, film, 666565, image 377, Registros Parroquiales, Iglesia de

record named Francisco Espinosa and María Gertrudis de Espinosa as *padrinos*. Manuel Zayas, among many others present, were identified as witnesses to the marriage. The couple received a nuptial blessing on the day of their marriage. Parents of the bride and groom were named in the record, and the parents of the bride were said to have been deceased.

Ignacio María Gonzáles de Zayas, son of Andrés Gonzáles de Zayas and María Yepes y Allora, was born in 1778 in Álamos. He was baptized on September 3, 1778, at the church of the Purísima Concepción in Álamos.[376] The cited baptisms for the children of Ignacio María Gonzáles de Zayas referred to him as simply "Zayas."

Ignacio María Gonzáles de Zayas and María Ignacia de la Trinidad Esquer had the following known children:

i.   **José de Jesús Andrés Abelino Gonzáles de Zayas** was born on November 10, 1803, in Álamos, according to the cited baptismal record. He was baptized on November 14, 1803, at the church of the Purísima Concepción in Álamos.[377] The baptismal record named José Fox and María Gertrudis Esquer as his *padrinos*.

ii. **María Dolores Gonzáles de Zayas** was born in 1806 in Álamos. She was baptized on May 13, 1806, at the parish of the Purísima Concepción in Álamos.[378] The baptism took place in the chapel of La Aduana, jurisdiction of Álamos. Francisco Espinosa and his sister María Francisca Espinosa were named as her *padrinos*.

iii. **María Trinidad Simona Gonzáles de Zayas** was born in 1809 in Álamos. She was baptized on February 21, 1809, at the church of the Purísima Concepción in Álamos.[379] The baptismal record named Ygnacio Yepes and Juana Pérez de Tagle as her *padrinos*.

iv. **Jesús Pedro Gonzáles de Zayas** was born in 1817 in Álamos. He was baptized on July 13, 1817, at the parish of the Purísima Concepción in Álamos.[380] The baptism took place in the chapel at La Aduana, jurisdiction of Álamos. Anna María Zayas was named as his *madrina*.

66. **Luis Juan Joseph Raphael Fox** (María Loreto Esquer-6, Salvador-5, Juan Salvador-4, Salvador-3, Salvador-2, Blas-1) was born in 1772 in Álamos. He was baptized on August 5,

---

La Purísima Concepción, Álamos, Sonora, Mexico (FamilySearch, https://familysearch.org).

376. Bautismos, matrimonios y defunciones 1696–1699, bautismos 1768–1781, September 3, 1778, film 663487, image [not located], Registros Parroquiales, Iglesia de La Purísima Concepción, Álamos, Sonora, Mexico (FamilySearch, https://familysearch.org).

377. Bautismos 1796–1805, November 14, 1803, film 663995, image 219, Registros Parroquiales, Iglesia de La Purísima Concepción, Álamos, Sonora, Mexico (FamilySearch, https://familysearch.org.

378. Bautismos 1791–1796, 1805–1815, May13, 1806, film 663996, image 246, Registros Parroquiales, Iglesia de La Purísima Concepción, Álamos, Sonora, Mexico (FamilySearch, https://familysearch.org.

379. Bautismos 1791–1796, 1805–1815, February 21, 1809, film 663996, image 327, Registros Parroquiales, Iglesia de La Purísima Concepción, Álamos, Sonora, Mexico (FamilySearch, https://familysearch.org.

380. Bautismos 1816–1825, 1827–1829, July 13,1817, film 663997, image 40, Registros Parroquiales, Iglesia de La Purísima Concepción, Álamos, Sonora, Mexico (FamilySearch, https://familysearch.org).

1772, at the church of the Purísima Concepción in Álamos.[381] The baptismal record named Anna María Aragón as his *madrina*. Xavier de Aragón, Joaquín Ybáñez and Joaquín Gastélum were named as witnesses to the sacrament of baptism.

Luis Juan Joseph Raphael Fox and María Gertrudis Esquer were married on March 28, 1797, at the church of the Purísima Concepción in Álamos.[382] The matrimonial record referred to the groom as "Juan José Fox." It named Juan Francisco Fox and María del Pilar, siblings of the groom, as *padrinos*. José Bustillos (*sacristán*) and Rafael Esquer, among many others present, were identified as witnesses to the marriage. The marriage record named the parents of the bride and groom. Parents of the bride were said to have been deceased. The couple received a nuptial blessing after the date of their marriage. According to the record the blessing was prohibited during the liturgical period when the marriage took place.

Luis Juan Joseph Raphael Fox died before May 7, 1823.[383] The cited marriage record for his daughter María Petra Fox stated that Luis Juan Joseph Raphael Fox was deceased at the time of her marriage on May 7, 1823.

María Gertrudis Esquer, daughter of Juan Salvador Esquer and María Manuela Campoy, was born about 1777.[384] The cited 1780 burial record for her mother listed María Gertrudis Esquer as a surviving child.

Luis Juan Joseph Raphael Fox and María Gertrudis Esquer had the following known children:

116 i.　**María Petra Fox** was born in 1797 in Álamos; she married José Manuel Tiburcio Quirós y Mora, on May 7, 1823, in Álamos; she died before December 3, 1868.

117 ii.　**María de Jesús del Mar Atilana Fox** was born in 1799 in Álamos; she married José Antonio Tena sometime before 1828.

　　iii.　**José Ygnacio de Jesús Francisco Sabino Fox** was born on December 30, 1801, in Álamos, according to the cited baptismal record. He was baptized on January 3, 1802, at the church of the Purísima Concepción in Álamos.[385] The baptismal record named his father Juan Fox and Anna María Esquer as his *padrinos*.

118 iv.　**María Dolores Francisca de Jesús Candelaria Fox** was born on January 29, 1803, in Álamos.

　　v.　**María de la Concepción Toribia Ignés Fox** was born on April 16, 1805, in Álamos, according to the cited baptismal record. She was baptized on April 20, 1805, at

381. Bautismos, matrimonios y defunciones 1696–1699, bautismos 1768–1781, film 663487, image 243, Registros Parroquiales, Iglesia de La Purísima Concepción, Álamos, Sonora, Mexico (FamilySearch, https://familysearch.org).

382. Matrimonios 1779–1817, March 28,1797, film 666565, images 322–323, Registros Parroquiales, Iglesia de La Purísima Concepción, Álamos, Sonora, Mexico (FamilySearch, https://familysearch.org).

383. Matrimonios 1797–1833, 1846–1868, 1872–1877, May 7, 1823, film 666566, images 276–277, Registros Parroquiales, Iglesia de La Purísima Concepción, Álamos, Sonora, Mexico (FamilySearch, https://familysearch.org).

384. Defunciones 1717–1751, 1764–1792, September 8, 1780, film 666995, image 337, Registros Parroquiales, Iglesia de La Purísima Concepción, Alamos, Sonora, Mexico (FamilySearch, https://familysearch.org).

385. Bautismos 1796–1805, January 3, 1802, film 663995, image 164, Registros Parroquiales, Iglesia de La Purísima Concepción, Álamos, Sonora, Mexico (FamilySearch, https://familysearch.org).

the church of the Purísima Concepción in Álamos.[386] The baptismal record named
Manuel Anguís and Serafina Barreda as her *padrinos*.

vi. **José Ygnacio Genaro de Jesús Fox** was born on July 10, 1807, in Álamos, according
to the cited baptismal record. He was baptized on July 15, 1807, at the church of the
Purísima Concepción in Álamos.[387] The baptismal record named Mariano Pérez del
Rey and María Gertrudis Goycochea as his *padrinos*.

vii. **María Balvanera Anastasia de Jesús Fox** was born in 1810 in Álamos. She was
baptized on January 25, 1810, at the church of the Purísima Concepción in Álamos.[388]
The baptismal record named Juan José Morales and María del Carmen Fox as her
padrinos.

119viii. **María Antonia Francisca Feliciana Fox** was born in 1812 in Álamos; she married
Guadalupe Sarracino on February 22, 1841, in Álamos.

ix. **María Guadalupe Leocadia Fox** was born in 1814 in Álamos. She was baptized on
December 13, 1814, at the church of the Purísima Concepción in Álamos.[389] The
baptismal record named Gertrudis Goycochea as her *madrina*.

67. Luis Juan Francisco Telmo Fox (María Loreto Esquer-6, Salvador-5, Juan Salvador-4,
Salvador-3, Salvador-2, Blas-1) was born in 1772 in Álamos. He was baptized on July 29, 1772,
at the parish church of the Purísima Concepción in Álamos.[390] The baptismal record named Juan
Augustín Yriarte and Josepha González Barreda as his *padrinos*. Ensayador Vicente Mallén de
Navarrete and Coronel Tadeo Padilla were named as witnesses, along with other persons whose
names are illegible.

Luis Juan Francisco Telmo Fox and María Petra Acuña were married on February 12, 1795,
at the parish church of the Purísima Concepción in Álamos.[391] The matrimonial record named
Eulogio Valenzuela and his wife María Micaela Esquer as *padrinos*. José Bustillos, Onofre Robles,
and Nepomuceno Anguís were named as witnesses to the marriage. Parents of the bride and
groom were named. The mother of the groom's name was written as "María Loreto Anguís,"
her maternal surname. The bride was said to have been the step-daughter of Faustino Torres.

386. Bautismos 1796–1805, April 20, 1805, film 663995, image 270, Registros Parroquiales, Iglesia de La
Purísima Concepción, Álamos, Sonora, Mexico (FamilySearch, https://familysearch.org).
387. Bautismos 1791–1796, 1805–1815, July 15,1807, film 663996, image 288, Registros Parroquiales, Iglesia
de La Purísima Concepción, Álamos, Sonora, Mexico (FamilySearch, https://familysearch.org).
388. Bautismos 1791–1796, 1805–1815, January 25, 1810, film 663996, image 362, Registros Parroquiales,
Iglesia de La Purísima Concepción, Álamos, Sonora, Mexico (FamilySearch, https://familysearch.org).
389. Bautismos 1791–1796, 1805–1815, December 13, 1814, film 663996, images 486-487, Registros
Parroquiales, Iglesia de La Purísima Concepción, Álamos, Sonora, Mexico (FamilySearch, https://familysearch.
org).
390. Bautismos 1751–1794, matrimonios 1848, defunciones 1735–1752, July 29, 1772, film 666999, image
351, Registros Parroquiales, Iglesia de La Purísima Concepción, Álamos, Sonora, Mexico (FamilySearch, https://
familysearch.org).
391. Matrimonios 1779–1817, February 12, 1795, film 666565, images 288–289, Registros Parroquiales, Iglesia
de La Purísima Concepción, Álamos, Sonora, Mexico (FamilySearch, https://familysearch.org).

María Petra Acuña, the natural daughter of Juana de Dios Acuña, was born about 1775. Her father has not been identified.

Luis Juan Francisco Telmo Fox and María Petra Acuña had the following known children:

120 i.   **María Dolores de Jesús Anselma Fox** was born in 1797in Álamos; she married José María de la Cruz Talamantes on May 4, 1824, in Álamos.

     ii.   **Francisca de Jesús Fox** was born on April 11, 1802, in Álamos, according to the cited baptismal record. She was baptized on April 18, 1802, at the parish church of the Purísima Concepción in Álamos.[392] The baptismal record named Juan José Fox and María Gertrudis Esquer as her *padrinos*.

   iii.   **Juan Francisco Gregorio Diego Fox** was born in 1804 in Álamos. He was baptized on November 17, 1804, at the church of the Purísima Concepción in Álamos.[393] The baptismal record named Juan de Fox and his daughter, María del Carmen Fox as the child's *padrinos*. His mother is identified as "María Petra Torres" in the record. Torres might be her paternal surname.

121 iv. **Manuel Fox** was born about 1807 in Álamos; he married María del Sacramento Ybarra in March 24, 1827, in Álamos.

     v.   **Juan Francisco de los Reyes Ynocente Fox** was born on December 28, 1809, in Álamos, according to the cited baptismal record. He was baptized on January 6, 1810, at the parish church of the Purísima Concepción in Álamos.[394] The baptismal record named Manuel Anguís and Balvanera Anguís as his *padrinos*.

68. María del Pilar Fox (María Loreto Esquer-6, Salvador-5, Juan Salvador-4, Salvador-3, Salvador-2, Blas-1) was born about 1779.[395] Evidence of parentage was provided in the cited marriage record for Luis Juan Joseph Raphael Fox and María Gertrudis Esquer. The record named María del Pilar as the sister of Juan Francisco Fox. Both were assumed to be siblings of the groom.

María del Pilar Fox had one known child:

     i.   **María de Jesús Paula de la luz Fox** was born on June 22, 1805, in Álamos. The cited baptismal record provided her date of birth. She was baptized on June 25, 1805, at the parish church of the Purísima Concepción in Álamos.[396] The baptismal record named Juan José Fox and María Gertrudis Esquer as her *padrinos*. The record

---

392. Bautismos 1796–1805, April18, 1802, film 663995, image 171, Registros Parroquiales, Iglesia de La Purísima Concepción, Álamos, Sonora, Mexico (FamilySearch, https://familysearch.org).

393. Bautismos 1796–1805, November17, 1804, film 663995, image 255, Registros Parroquiales, Iglesia de La Purísima Concepción, Álamos, Sonora, Mexico (FamilySearch, https://familysearch.org).

394. Bautismos 1791–1796,1805–1815, January 6,1810, film 663996, image 360, Registros Parroquiales, Iglesia de La Purísima Concepción, Álamos, Sonora, Mexico (FamilySearch, https://familysearch.org).

395. Matrimonios 1779–1817, March 28,1797, film 666565, images 322–323, Registros Parroquiales, Iglesia de La Purísima Concepción, Álamos, Sonora, Mexico (FamilySearch, https://familysearch.org).

396. Bautismos 1791–1796, 1805–1815, June 25, 1805, film 663996, image 222, Registros Parroquiales, Iglesia de La Purísima Concepción, Álamos, Sonora, Mexico (FamilySearch, https://familysearch.org).

stated that she was the natural daughter of María del Pilar Fox, and that her social status was the same as that of her unnamed father.

69. **María del Carmen Gertrudis Fox** (María Loreto Esquer-6, Salvador-5, Juan Salvador-4, Salvador-3, Salvador-2, Blas-1) was born on January 4, 1782, in Álamos, according to the cited baptismal record. She was baptized on January 13, 1782, at the church of the Purísima Concepción in Álamos.[397] The baptismal record named Juan Manuel Zavala and María Nicolasa Martínez as her *padrinos*.

María del Carmen Gertrudis Fox and Francisco Moreno y Ladosa were married on January 27, 1823, at the parish church of the Purísima Concepción in Álamos.[398] The matrimonial record named Juan José Morales and Gertrudis Esquer as *padrinos*. José María Gudiño and Ramón Navarrete were named as witnesses to the marriage. The groom was said to have been from Nochistlán, Guadalajara, and that he had been in Álamos for a period of two years. Parents of the bride and groom were named in the record. The father of the groom and both parents of the bride were said to have been deceased at the time of the marriage. The marriage record was placed under the heading "*Enero de 1823*," (January 1823), yet the text reads that the marriage took place in 1822. It appears this is a clerical error because the pattern persists in the records until March 1823.

Francisco Moreno y Ladosa, son of José María Moreno and Gregoria Márquez, was born about 1780 in Nochistlán, Guadalajara, New Spain. The cited marriage record provided his place of origin. Nochistlán is currently located in the Mexican state of Zacatecas.

70. **Petra María Gertrudis Féliz** (Manuela Antonia Esquer-6, Joseph Cayetano-5, Juan Salvador-4, Salvador-3, Salvador-2, Blas-1) was born about 1739 in Álamos. The cited marriage information record dated October 9, 1760, claimed that she was twenty-one or twenty-two years of age at the time.

Petra María Gertrudis Féliz and Francisco Antonio Martínez Mendívil were married on October 26, 1760, in Álamos.[399] The matrimonial record named Julián Samayoa and Hilaria de la Fuente y Valenzuela as *padrinos*. Juan Salvador Esquer and Joseph Cayetano Esquer were named as witnesses to the marriage. The family residence was in the Puesto de Las Haciendas (probably a military post), which was located one league distant from Álamos. The cited marriage information record stated that on October 9, 1760, the parish priest declared there was no impediment to marriage.

397. Bautismos 1781–1796, January 13, 1782, film 663488, image 14, Registros Parroquiales, Iglesia de La Purísima Concepción, Álamos, Sonora, Mexico (FamilySearch, https://familysearch.org).
398. Matrimonios 1797–1833, 1846–1868, 1872–1877, January 27, 1823, film 666566, image 271, Registros Parroquiales, Iglesia de La Purísima Concepción, Álamos, Sonora, Mexico (FamilySearch, https://familysearch.org).
399. Matrimonios 1758–1779, October 26, 1760, film 666564, image 30, Registros Parroquiales, Iglesia de La Purísima Concepción, Álamos, Sonora, Mexico (FamilySearch, https://familysearch.org); Información matrimonial 1760–1799, October 9, 1769, film 667002, images 29–33, Registros Parroquiales, Iglesia de La Purísima Concepción, Álamos, Sonora, Mexico (FamilySearch, https://familysearch.org).

Francisco Antonio Martínez Mendívil, son of Juan Ignacio Martínez Mendívil and Rosa Isabel Acuña, was born about 1741.

Francisco Antonio Martínez Mendívil and Petra María Gertrudis Féliz had the following known children:

i.   **Phelipe Miguel Martínez Mendívil** was born on May 15, 1762, in Álamos. The cited baptismal record claimed the child was eight days old at the time of his baptism. He was baptized on May 23, 1762, at the church of the Purísima Concepción in Álamos.[400] The baptismal record named Juan Crisóstomo González de Zayas and María Lucía González de Zayas as his *padrinos*. The record stated that his parents were *vecinos* of Álamos, living at the Puesto de las Haciendas.

122 ii.   **Simona María Gertrudis Martínez Mendívil** was born in 1763 in Álamos; she married Juan Francisco Padilla on September 25, 1784, in Álamos and died before 1800.

123 iii.   **Juan José Timoteo Martínez Mendívil** was born in 1766 in Álamos; he married María Loreto González Barreda on June 11, 1787, in Álamos.

124 iv.   **Luis María Antonio Martínez Mendívil** was born in 1768 in Álamos; he married María Gertrudis de Guadalupe Gerónima de Merced Muñoz on January 2, 1789, in Álamos.

v.   **María de los Santos Martínez Mendívil** was born in 1771 in Álamos. She was baptized on March 24, 1771, at the church of the Purísima Concepción in Álamos.[401] The baptismal record named Gabriel Mallén de Navarrete and María Francisca Mallén de Navarrete as her *padrinos*.

vi.   **Manuela Martínez Mendívil** was born about 1775 in Álamos. She died in 1792 in Álamos. She was buried on September 30, 1792, at the church of the Purísima Concepción in Álamos.[402] The burial record stated that she was an adult maiden, *doncella*. Her funeral service was held with *cruz alta, capa, e incensario*. She was laid to rest in a grave valued at five pesos.

125 vii.   **María Rosa Isabel Martínez Mendívil** was born in 1777 in Álamos; she married Juan Antonio López Bravo on May 2, 1793, in Álamos.

viii.   **Anna María Basilia Martínez Mendívil** was born on May 1, 1780, in Álamos, according to the baptismal record. She was baptized on May 3, 1780, at the church of the Purísima Concepción in Álamos.[403] The baptismal record named Anna María

---

400. Bautismos 1751–1794, matrimonios 1848, defunciones 1735–1752, May 23, 1762, film 666999, image 243, Registros Parroquiales, Iglesia de La Purísima Concepción, Álamos, Sonora, Mexico (FamilySearch, https://familysearch.org).

401. Bautismos, matrimonios y defunciones 1696–1699, bautismos 1768–1781, film 663487, image 178, Registros Parroquiales, Iglesia de La Purísima Concepción, Álamos, Sonora, Mexico (FamilySearch, https://familysearch.org).

402. Defunciones 1717–1751, 1764–1792, film 666995, image 561, Registros Parroquiales, Iglesia de La Purísima Concepción, Álamos, Sonora, Mexico (FamilySearch, https://familysearch.org).

403. Bautismos, matrimonios y defunciones 1696–1699, bautismos 1768–1781, May 3, 1780, film 663487, image 471, Registros Parroquiales, Iglesia de La Purísima Concepción, Álamos, Sonora, Mexico (FamilySearch,

Mendívil as her *madrina*. The family claimed their residency to be in El Chinal, in the jurisdiction of Álamos. She died on March 29, 1781, in Álamos. She was buried on March 30, 1781, at the church of the Purísima Concepción in Álamos.[404] Her funeral service was held with a *cruz alta y ataúd*, and she was laid to rest in a burial site valued at three pesos.

71. **Joseph Vicente Féliz** (Manuela Antonia Esquer-6, Joseph Cayetano-5, Juan Salvador-4, Salvador-3, Salvador-2, Blas-1) was born about 1741 in Álamos.

Joseph Vicente Féliz and Manuela Ygnacia López Peñuelas were married on July 13, 1760, at the church of the Purísima Concepción in Álamos.[405] The matrimonial record named Manuel Zazuela and Antonia de Aragón as *padrinos*. Joseph Féliz and Sebastián López Bravo were named as witnesses to to the marriage. The couple received a dispensation to marry because they were related in the second degree, with a third degree of consanguinity, meaning they were first cousins once removed. Parents of the bride and groom were named in the record. The family of the bride was said to have been from the Puesto de Casanate (probably a military post).

Joseph Vicente died on January 29, 1809, at the Santa Bárbara Presidio in Santa Bárbara, Alta California. He was buried on January 30, 1809, at Santa Bárbara Mission.[406] The burial record for Joseph Vicente Féliz stated that he was at the presidio of Santa Bárbara when he died and that he did not receive the last sacraments of the Catholic Church because his death was sudden. He was buried in the cemetery of Mission Santa Bárbara. Joseph Vicente Féliz was a soldier in the 1775–1776 Anza expedition that established a mission and presidio in San Francisco Bay.

Manuela Ygnacia López Peñuelas, daughter of Antonio López Peñuelas and Juana Agustina Murrieta, was born about 1744. She died on October 24, 1775.[407] Manuela López Peñuelas died at an encampment named La Canoa (later part of La Canoa Ranch, now in Arizona) at the start of the Anza expedition. She died after giving birth to her son, José Antonio de Capistrano. Her childbirth and death were described in the diaries of Juan Bautista de Anza and Father Pedro Font for the days of October 23 and October 24, 1775. She was buried on October 25, 1775, at Mission San Xavier del Bac.[408] The burial of Manuela López Peñuelas at Mission San Xavier del Bac, Sonora (now located in the American state of Arizona), was taken from the diary entries of Father Pedro Font. He recorded that she was was taken for burial to the mission of San Xavier del Bac and that she was buried on the morning of October 25 by Father Garcés who had accompanied the body from the campsite.

---

https://familysearch.org).
404. Defunciones 1717–1751, 1764–1792, March 30, 1781, film 666995, image 353, Registros Parroquiales, Iglesia de La Purísima Concepción, Álamos, Sonora, Mexico (FamilySearch, https://familysearch.org).
405. Matrimonios 1758–1779, July 13, 1760, film 666564, image 26, Registros Parroquiales, Iglesia de La Purísima Concepción, Álamos, Sonora, Mexico (FamilySearch, https://familysearch.org).
406. Santa Bárbara Presidio (BP), burial number 00127, January 30, 1809, The Huntington Library, Early California Population Project Database, 2006 (http://missions.huntington.org/SimpleQuery), hereafter ECPP, 2006.
407. Herbert Eugene Bolton, trans. *Anza's California Expeditions: The San Francisco Colony; Diaries of Anza, Font, and Eixarch, and Narratives by Palóu and Moraga.* (New York: Russell and Russell, 1966), vol. 3, pp 6–7.
408. Herbert Eugene Bolton, trans. *Anza's California Expeditions: Font's Complete Diary of the Second Anza Expedition.* (New York: Russell and Russell, 1966), vol. 4, p. 26.

Joseph Vicente Féliz and Manuela Ygnacia López Peñuelas had the following known children:

126 i.   **Joseph Francisco Féliz** was born on October 9, 1761, in Álamos; he married María Josefa Cota on January 29, 1788, and died in 1847.

127 ii.   **María Loreto Estéfana Féliz** was born on November 4, 1764, in Álamos; she married Joseph Ygnacio Olivera on December 8, 1778 and died on July 7, 1789.

128 iii. **Joseph Doroteo Féliz** was born about 1765 in Álamos; he married Juana Josefa Villalobo on March 3, 1787, in Santa Bárbara, Alta California. He died on September 29, 1832.

iv.   [*párvulo*] **Féliz** was born about 1767 in Álamos, New Spain. He died on April 17, 1767, in Álamos. He was buried on April 18, 1767, at the church of the Purísima Concepción in Álamos.[409] The funeral service for the unnamed infant was held with a *cruz baja*. He was interred in a burial site valued at five pesos.

v.   **María Antonia del Pilar Féliz** was born in 1768 in Álamos. She was baptized on June 26, 1768, at the church of the Purísima Concepción in Álamos.[410] The baptismal record named Juan Fox as her *padrino*. Blas Gutiérrez and Pedro Gutiérrez were named as witnesses. She died on July 5, 1780, at the age of twelve in San Diego, Alta California. María was buried on July 6, 1780, at the presidio in San Diego.[411] Her parents were named in the burial record.

129 vi.   **María Marcela Féliz** was born in 1770 in Álamos; she married Ygnacio Narciso Olivera on October 30, 1783.

130 vii. **Joseph Pablo de Jesús Féliz** was born in 1773 in Álamos; he married María Celia Cota on August 16, 1789, and died on December 25, 1837.

viii. **Joseph Antonio de Capistrano Féliz** was born on October 23, 1775, in La Canoa, Sonora (present-day Arizona).[412] Joseph Antonio de Capistrano Féliz was born during the first night of the Anza expedition.

> Juan Bautista de Anza wrote the following in his diary, dated Monday, October 23, 1775: "At the end of the afternoon today the wife of one of the soldiers of the expedition began to feel the first pains of childbirth. We aided her immediately with the shelter of a field tent and other things useful in the case and obtainable on the road, and she successfully gave birth to a very lusty boy at nine o'clock at night, the rest of which was passed without any other happening."

---

409. Defunciones 1717–1751,1764–1792, April 18, 1767, film 666995, image 187, Registros Parroquiales, Iglesia de La Purísima Concepción, Álamos, Sonora, Mexico (FamilySearch, https://familysearch.org).

410. Bautismos, matrimonios y defunciones 1696–1699, bautismos 1768–1781, July 26, 1768, film 663487, image 109, Registros Parroquiales, Iglesia de La Purísima Concepción, Álamos, Sonora, Mexico (FamilySearch, https://familysearch.org).

411. San Diego Mission (SD), death number 00124, July 6, 1780, ECPP, 2006.

412. Herbert Eugene Bolton, trans. *Anza's California Expeditions: The San Francisco Colony; Diaries of Anza, Font, and Eixarch, and Narratives by Palóu and Moraga* (New York: Russell and Russell, 1966), vol. 3, pp. 6–7.

Joseph Antonio de Capistrano was baptized on October 25, 1775, at Mission San Xavier del Bac.[413] The baptism is noted in Padre Pedro Font's diary for Wednesday, October 25, 1775: "In the afternoon Father Thomás baptized the boy who was born on the night of the 23rd." Joseph likely died on September 8, 1776. He was buried on September 9, 1776, at San Gabriel Arcángel Mission in Alta Calfornia.[414]

72. María Guadalupe Féliz (Manuela Antonia Esquer-6, Joseph Cayetano-5, Juan Salvador-4, Salvador-3, Salvador-2, Blas-1) was born about 1746 in Álamos.

María Guadalupe Féliz and Manuel Cornelio Maldonado were married on May 11, 1766, at the church of the Purísima Concepción in Álamos.[415] The matrimonial record named Miguel Mariscal and Ana María Morales as *padrinos.* Blas Gutiérrez and Melchor Amarillas were named as witnesses to the marriage. Parents of the bridal couple were named in the record.

She died on June 21, 1769, in Álamos. She was buried on June 22, 1769, at the church of the Purísima Concepción in Álamos.[416] The cited burial record for María Guadalupe Féliz does not actually name her as the deceased. Rather, it says that the wife of Manuel Maldonado and daughter of Joseph Féliz and Manuela Esquer was buried with a *cruz alta.* She likely died of complications of childbirth because her infant daughter, María Venancia, was baptized a few weeks later on July 15.

Manuel Cornelio Maldonado, son of Mateo Maldonado and María Magdalena de Apodaca, was born about 1740.

Manuel Cornelio Maldonado and María Guadalupe Féliz had one known child:

    i.   **María Venancia Marcelina Maldonado** was born in 1769 in Álamos. She was baptized on July 15, 1769, at the church of the Purísima Concepción in Álamos.[417] The baptismal record named Gertrudis Féliz as her *madrina.* Blas Gutiérrez and Francisco Gutiérrez were named as witnesses.

73. Joseph Salvador Féliz (Manuela Antonia Esquer-6, Joseph Cayetano-5, Juan Salvador-4, Salvador-3, Salvador-2, Blas-1) was born in 1752 in Álamos. He was baptized on April 9, 1752, at the church of the Purísima Concepción in Álamos.[418] The baptismal record named Thadeo Padilla de Arnao and María Isabel Ruiz de Guadiana as his *padrinos.*

413. Herbert Eugene Bolton, trans. *Anza's California Expeditions: Font's Complete Diary of the Second Anza Expedition*, vol. 4 (New York: Russell and Russell, 1966), p. 27.

414. San Gabriel Arcángel (SG), death number 00041, September 9, 1776, ECPP, 2006.

415. Matrimonios 1758–1779, film 666564, image 86, Registros Parroquiales, Iglesia de La PurísimaConcepción, Álamos, Sonora, Mexico (FamilySearch, https://familysearch.org).

416. Defunciones 1717–1751,1764–1792, June 22, 1769, film 666995, image 208, Registros Parroquiales, Iglesia de La Purísima Concepción, Álamos, Sonora, Mexico (FamilySearch, https://familysearch.org).

417. Bautismos, matrimonios y defunciones 1696–1699, bautismos 1768–1781, July 15, 1769, 663487, image 134, Registros Parroquiales, Iglesia de La Purísima Concepción, Álamos, Sonora, Mexico (FamilySearch, https://familysearch.org).

418. Bautismos 1751–1794, matrimonios 1848, defunciones 1735–1752, film 666999, image 59, Registros Parroquiales, Iglesia de La Purísima Concepción, Álamos, Sonora, Mexico (FamilySearch, https://familysearch.org).

Joseph Salvador Féliz and María Loreto Jacinta del Carmen Muñoz were married on July 5, 1791, at the church of the Purísima Concepción in Álamos.[419] The matrimonial record named Manuel Féliz and his sister María Gertrudis Féliz as *padrinos*. Pedro Bravo, Pedro Díaz Féliz, José Bustillos, the unnamed church sacristan, and many others in attendance at the marriage and nuptial blessing ceremonies were identified as witnesses. It was stated that the bride was originally from the Puesto de Bacamaya (likely a small military post or ranch), located in the jurisdiction of Álamos, and that she had resided in Álamos for a period of over one month.

María Loreto Jacinta del Carmen Muñoz, daughter of Joaquín Gabriel Muñoz and Anna Rosalía Gastélum, was born in 1771 in Álamos. She was baptized on September 8, 1771, at the church of the Purísima Concepción in Álamos.[420] The baptismal record named Joaquín Ybáñez and María del Carmen de Ybáñez as her *padrinos*. Francisco Cadenas and Joaquín Gastélum were named as witnesses to the baptism.

Joseph Salvador Féliz and María Loreto Jacinta del Carmen Muñoz had the following known children:

i.   **Joseph Antonio Matías Féliz** was born in 1794 in Álamos. He was baptized on March 17, 1794, in Álamos.[421] The baptismal record named Juan Francisco Mendívil and his wife Petra Gertrudis Féliz as his *padrinos*. They resided in El Chinal, jurisdiction of Álamos.

ii. **José Manuel Trinidad Féliz** was born in 1796 in Álamos. He was baptized on October 30, 1796, at the church of the Purísima Concepción in Álamos.[422] The baptismal record named José Manuel Féliz and Ignacia Pardo as his *padrinos*.

iii. **María Rosalia del Sacramento Féliz** was born in 1798. She was baptized on February 6, 1798, at the church of the Purísima Concepción in Álamos.[423] The baptismal record named José Mendívil and María Loreto Barreda as her *padrinos*.

iv. **José Salvador Basilio Antonio Féliz** was born in 1804 in Álamos. He was baptized on September 23, 1804, at the church of the Purísima Concepción in Álamos.[424] The baptismal record named Manuel Féliz and Anacleta Mendívil as his *padrinos*.

74. **Ana María Yrene Féliz** (Manuela Antonia Esquer-6, Joseph Cayetano-5, Juan Salvador-4, Salvador-3, Salvador-2, Blas-1) was born in 1757 in Álamos. She was baptized on November 7,

419. Matrimonios 1779–1817, July 5, 1791, film 666565, image 197, Registros Parroquiales, Iglesia de La Purísima Concepción, Álamos, Sonora, Mexico (FamilySearch, https://familysearch.org).
420. Bautismos, matrimonios y defunciones 1696–1699, bautismos 1768–1781, film 663487, image 238, Registros Parroquiales, Iglesia de La Purísima Concepción, Álamos, Sonora, Mexico (FamilySearch, https://familysearch.org).
421. Bautismos 1781–1796, March 17, 1794, film 663488, image 624, Registros Parroquiales, Iglesia de La Purísima Concepción, Álamos, Sonora, Mexico (FamilySearch, https://familysearch.org).
422. Bautismos 1796–1805, October 30, 1796, film 663995, image 17, Registros Parroquiales, Iglesia de La Purísima Concepción, Álamos, Sonora, Mexico (FamilySearch, https://familysearch.org).
423. Bautismos 1796–1805, February 6, 1798, film 663995, image 64, Registros Parroquiales, Iglesia de La Purísima Concepción, Álamos, Sonora, Mexico (FamilySearch, https://familysearch.org).
424. Bautismos 1796–1805, September 23, 1804, film 663995, image 251, Registros Parroquiales, Iglesia de La Purísima Concepción, Álamos, Sonora, Mexico (FamilySearch, https://familysearch.org).

1757, at the church of the Purísima Concepción in Álamos.[425] The baptismal record named Juan Agustín de Yriarte and Micaela Salvadora Mallén de Navarrete as her *padrinos.*

Ana María Yrene Féliz and José Ygnacio Ybarra were married on December 27, 1772, at the church of the Purísima Concepción in Álamos.[426] The matrimonial record named Raymundo Sabalza and Inés de Ybarra as *padrinos.* Nicolás Morales, Marcelo Morales, and Agustín Chavarría were named as witnesses to the marriarge. Parents of the bride and groom were also named in the record.

José Ygnacio Ybarra, son of José Ybarra and Rosa Valenzuela, was born about 1756.

75. **Manuel Féliz** (Manuela Antonia Esquer-6, Joseph Cayetano-5, Juan Salvador-4, Salvador-3, Salvador-2, Blas-1) was born about 1760.[427] The cited matrimonial record for Joseph Salvador Féliz named Manuel as the groom's brother and he is therefore included among the children of Joseph Saterino Féliz and Manuela Antonia Esquer. In addition, the marriage information for Manuel's son by his second marriage to María Francisca Padilla contained a genealogy that named Gertrudis Féliz, daughter of Joseph Saterino Féliz and Manuela Antonia Esquer, as his sister.

Manuel Féliz and María Ygnacia Pardo were married about 1784. The matrimonial record has not been located.

Manuel Féliz and María Ygnacia Pardo had the following known children:

131 i.   **Joseph Féliz**, was born about 1785 in Álamos; he married María Guadalupe Padilla on March 31, 1812, in Álamos.

132 ii.   **María Guadalupe Trinidad Cornelia Féliz** was born in 1796 in Álamos; she married José Francisco Padilla on June 5, 1820, in Álamos.

      iii.   **José Trinidad Féliz** was born on October 4, 1801, in Álamos, according to the baptismal record. He was baptized on November 10, 1801, at the church of the Purísima Concepción in Álamos.[428] The baptismal record named Francisco Mendívil and Gertrudis Féliz as his *padrinos.*

Manuel Féliz and María Francisca Padilla were married on May 15, 1822, at the church of the Purísima Concepción in Álamos.[429] The matrimonial record named José Francisco Padilla and

425. Bautismos 1751–1794, matrimonios 1848, defunciones 1735–1752, November 7, 1757, film 666999, images 154–155, Registros Parroquiales, Iglesia de La Purísima Concepción, Álamos, Sonora, Mexico (FamilySearch, https:// familysearch.org).
426. Matrimonios 1758–1779, December 27, 1772, film 666564, images 153–154, Registros Parroquiales, Iglesia de La Purísima Concepción, Álamos, Sonora, Mexico (FamilySearch, https://familysearch.org).
427. Matrimonios 1779–1817, July 5, 1791, film 666565, image 197, Registros Parroquiales, Iglesia de La Purísima Concepción, Álamos, Sonora, Mexico (FamilySearch, https://familysearch.org).
428. Bautismos 1796–1805, November 10, 1801, film 663995, image 161, Registros Parroquiales, Iglesia de La Purísima Concepción, Álamos, Sonora, Mexico (FamilySearch, https://familysearch.org).
429. Matrimonios 1797–1833, 1846–1868, 1872–1877, May 15, 1822, film 666566, images 261–262, Registros Parroquiales, Iglesia de La Purísima Concepción, Álamos, Sonora, Mexico (FamilySearch, https:// familysearch.org).

Guadalupe Féliz as *padrinos*. George Campoy and Ygnacio Anguís were named as witnesses to the marriage. The record stated that Manuel was the the widowed husband of Ygnacia Pardo. The couple received a dispensation for marriage because they were related in the third degree of consanguinity, meaning they were second cousins.

María Francisca Padilla, daughter of Juan Francisco Padilla and Simona María Gertrudis Martínez Mendívil, was born about 1796.

Manuel Féliz and María Francisca Padilla had one known child:

133   i.   **Juan José del Refugio Féliz** was born in 1823 in Álamos; he married María Teresa Martínez Mendívil on June 3, 1844, in Álamos.

76. **María Ynocencia Esquer** (Joseph Cayetano-6, Joseph Cayetano-5, Juan Salvador-4, Salvador-3, Salvador-2, Blas-1) was born in 1752 in Álamos. She was baptized on January 15, 1752, at the church of the Purísima Concepción in Álamos.[430] The baptismal record named Juan Salvador Esquer and María Jesús Esquer as her *padrinos*.

María Ynocencia Esquer and Juan Pedro Segundo Armenta were married on June 7, 1778, at the church of the Purísima Concepción in Álamos.[431] The matrimonial record named Joseph Arriola and his unnamed wife as *padrinos*. Joseph Bustillos and Joseph María Bustillos were named as witnesses to the marriage.

The marriage investigation cited, dated September 26, 1777, named María Ynocencia Esquer as the third wife of Pedro Armenta.[432] It further stated that María Ynocenica was related by blood in the third degree (second cousins) to Juan Pedro's first wife, Anna María Hurtado. The fathers of two wives (the first and the third) were first cousins, related by blood in the second degree. They were sons of two sisters who were not named. Juan Pedro's second wife, María Francisca Valenzuela, was related by blood to his third wife, María Ynocencia Esquer, in the fourth degree they were third cousins. Their fathers, Francisco Ygnacio Valenzuela and Joseph Cayetano Esquer, were second cousins, related by blood in the third degree as sons of two first cousins, related in the second degree. Those cousins were Nicolás Valenzuela and Nicolasa Valenzuela.

Juan Pedro Segundo Armenta, son of Juan Armenta and María de los Santos Carrasco, was born about 1740. He died on March 17, 1787, in Álamos. He was buried on March 18, 1787, at the church of the Purísima Concepción in Álamos.[433] The burial service for Juan Pedro was held with a *cruz baja*. He was buried in the cemetery. His burial occurred only five days after

---

430. Bautismos 1751–1794, matrimonios 1848, defunciones 1735–1752, January 15, 1752, film 666999, image 53, Registros Parroquiales, Iglesia de La Purísima Concepción, Álamos, Sonora, Mexico (FamilySearch, https://familysearch.org).
431. Matrimonios1758–1779, June 7, 1778, film 666564, image 181, Registros Parroquiales, Iglesia de La Purísima Concepción, Álamos, Sonora, Mexico (FamilySearch, https://familysearch.org).
432. Información matrimonial 1760–1799, September 26, 1777, film 667002, images 310–313, 330–331, Registros Parroquiales, Iglesia de La Purísima Concepción, Álamos, Sonora, Mexico (FamilySearch, https://familysearch.org).
433. Defunciones 1717–1751,1764–1792, March 18, 1787, film 666995, image 482, Registros Parroquiales, Iglesia de La Purísima Concepción, Álamos, Sonora, Mexico (FamilySearch, https://familysearch.org).

the burial of his father-in-law, Joseph Cayetano Esquer. Juan Pedro was named as "Juan Pedro Segundo" in the cited 1788 matrimonial record of his son born by his wife Ana María Hurtado, Antonio Guillermo Armenta.[434]

Juan Pedro Segundo Armenta and María Ynocencia Esquer had the following known children:

    i.   **José Ramón Gil Armenta** was born on September 1, 1780, in Álamos. He was baptized on October 22, 1780, at the church of the Purísima Concepción in Álamos.[435] The baptismal record named José Vicente Montiel and his sister María Balvanera Montiel as his *padrinos*. The parents were said to have lived in La Aduana in the parish of Álamos.

134 ii.   **Joseph Reyes Armenta** was born about 1782 in Álamos; he married María Ysidora Blancarte on July 30, 1806, in Álamos.

77. María Balvanera Antonia Esquer (Joseph Cayetano-6, Joseph Cayetano-5, Juan Salvador-4, Salvador-3, Salvador-2, Blas-1) was born in 1759 in Álamos. She was baptized on October 17, 1759, at the church of the Purísima Concepción in Álamos.[436] The baptismal record named Manuela Féliz and her son Policarpio Velarde as her *padrinos*. The child's mother was identified as "Juliana García" in the record.

María Balvanera Antonia Esquer and Salvador Manuel Víctor Corral were married on June 24, 1782, at the church of the Purísima Concepción in Álamos.[437] The matrimonial record named Miguel Alcayde and his wife María Balvanera Yriarte as *padrinos*. Ramón Montiel (over age fifty), Thadeo Hurtado (over age thirty), and Luis Ávila (over age twenty-five) were named witnesses as to the couple's liberty to marry. Miguel Guerra, José Bustillos, and José María Bustillos were named as witnesses to the marriage.

Salvador Manuel Víctor Corral, son of José Corral and Juana Díaz, was born in 1759 in Álamos. He was baptized on February 2, 1759, at the church of the Purísima Concepción in Álamos.[438] The baptismal record named Rosa Mendívil as his *madrina*. He died before June 1, 1808.[439] Salvador Corral was said to have been deceased in the cited marriage document for his daughter, María Antonia Petra Corral.

434. Información matrimonial 1760–1799, June 10, 1788, film 667002, image 573, Registros Parroquiales, Iglesia de La Purísima Concepción, Álamos, Sonora, Mexico (FamilySearch, https://familysearch.org).
435. Bautismos, matrimonios y defunciones 1696–1699, bautismos 1768–1781, October 22, 1780, film 663487, image 487, Registros Parroquiales, Iglesia de La Purísima Concepción, Álamos, Sonora, Mexico (FamilySearch, https://familysearch.org).
436. Bautismos 1751–1794, matrimonios 1848, defunciones 1735–1752, October 17, 1759, film 666999, image 180, Registros Parroquiales, Iglesia de La Purísima Concepción, Álamos, Sonora, Mexico (FamilySearch, https://familysearch.org).
437. Matrimonios 1779–1817, June 24, 1782, film 666565, image 48, Registros Parroquiales, Iglesia de La Purísima Concepción, Álamos, Sonora, Mexico (FamilySearch, https://familysearch.org).
438. Bautismos 1751–1794, matrimonios 1848, defunciones 1735–1752, February 2, 1759, film 666999, image 172, Registros Parroquiales, Iglesia de La Purísima Concepción, Álamos, Sonora, Mexico (FamilySearch, https://familysearch.org).
439. Matrimonios 1779–1817, June 1, 1808, film 666565, images 481-482, Registros Parroquiales, Iglesia de La Purísima Concepción, Álamos, Sonora, Mexico (FamilySearch, https://familysearch.org).

Salvador Manuel Víctor Corral and María Balvanera Antonia Esquer had the following known children:

i.   **José Antonio Corral** died on December 4, 1786, in Álamos. He was buried on December 5, 1786, at the church of the Purísima Concepción in Álamos.[440] The burial record stated that the deceased was a child whose burial service was held with a *cruz baja*. His parents were said to be the servants of José Jacinto Elías González de Zayas.

135 ii.   **María Antonia Petra Corral** was born in1787 in Álamos. She married José Salvador Figueroa on June 1, 1808, in Álamos and died on October 7, 1845, in Álamos.

136 iii.   **José Antonio Corral** was born about 1789; he married María Gertrudis Riveros on September 2, 1809, in Álamos.

iv.   **José Narciso Corral** was born about 1791 or 1792.[441] The cited record appears to be a census of the town of Conicari, province of Ostimuri, Sonora, taken in 1809 and 1810. It is a page fragment misplaced just under the cover of a marriage information book for Conicari. José Narciso's record stated that he was eighteen year of age. It was listed under his mother's name. By that time she must have been a widow. The text is difficult to decipher.

v.   **María Trinidad Corral** was born about 1793.[442] The cited record appears to be a census of the town of Conicari, province of Ostimuri, taken in 1809 and 1810. It is a page fragment misplaced just under the cover of a marriage information book for Conicari. María Trinidad, age sixteen, was listed under her mother's name. She by then must have been a widow. The text is difficult to decipher.

vi.   **María Manuela Josefa Corral** was born in 1795 in Álamos. She was baptized on February 2, 1795, at the church of the Purísima Concepción in Álamos.[443] The baptismal record named Juan Francisco Palomares and María Josefa Campoy as her *padrinos*.

vii.   **María de Jesús Corral** was born about 1796. The cited record appears to be a census of the town of Conicari, province of Ostimuri, taken in 1809 and 1810. It is a page fragment misplaced just under the cover of a marriage information book for Conicari. María de Jesús, age fourteen, is listed under his mother's name. She by then must have been a widow. The text is difficult to decipher.

---

440. Defunciones 1717–1751, 1764–1792, film 666995, image 472, Registros Parroquiales, Iglesia de La Purísima Concepción, Álamos, Sonora, Mexico (FamilySearch, https://familysearch.org).

441. Matrimonios 1797–1833, 1846–1868, 1872–1877, about 1809–1810, film 666566, image 6, Registros Parroquiales, Iglesia de La Purísima Concepción, Álamos, Sonora, Mexico (FamilySearch, https://familysearch.org).

442. Matrimonios 1797–1833, 1846–1868, 1872–1877, about 1809–1810, film 666566, image 6, Registros Parroquiales, Iglesia de La Purísima Concepción, Álamos, Sonora, Mexico (FamilySearch, https://familysearch.org).

443. Bautismos 1781–1796, February 2, 1795, film 663488, image 658, Registros Parroquiales, Iglesia de La Purísima Concepción, Álamos, Sonora, Mexico (FamilySearch, https://familysearch.org); Bautismos 1791–1796,1805–1815, February 2, 1795, film 663996, image 155, Registros Parroquiales, Iglesia de La Purísima Concepción, Álamos, Sonora, Mexico (FamilySearch, https://familysearch.org).

viii. **Juan José Gervacio Corral** was born in 1797 in Álamos. He was baptized on July 3, 1797, at the church of the Purísima Concepción in Álamos.[444] The baptimal record named Aniseto Figueroa and Guadalupe Acuña as his *padrinos*. He was socially classified as being a *mulato libre* in his baptismal record. He was also known as "Juan Corral."

ix. **José de Jesús Corral** was born about 1799 or 1800.[445] The cited record appears to be a census of the town of Conicari, province of Ostimuri, taken in 1809 and 1810. It is a page fragment misplaced just under the cover of a marriage information book for Conicari. José de Jesús, age ten, is listed under his mother's name. By then she must have been a widow. The text is difficult to decipher.

78. **María de la Merced Dolores Esquer** (Joseph Cayetano-6, Joseph Cayetano-5, Juan Salvador-4, Salvador-3, Salvador-2, Blas-1) was born in 1761 in Álamos. She was baptized on October 9, 1761, at the church of the Purísima Concepción in Álamos.[446] The baptismal record named Micaela Salvadora Esquer as her *madrina*.

María de la Merced Dolores Esquer and Guillermo Antonio Armenta were married on July 4, 1788, at the church of the Purísima Concepción in Álamos.[447] The matrimonial record named Alberto Moreno and María de Jesús Acuña as *padrinos*. José Bustillos, Luis Balderrain, and Pasqual de la Madrid were named as witnesses to the marriage. The couple received a nuptial blessing on the day of their marriage. Parents of the bride and groom were named. Parents of the groom and the father of the bride were said to have been deceased. The couple received a marriage dispensation on June 10, 1788. They were related by blood in the third with a fourth degree, meaning they were second cousins, once removed.[448]

Guillermo Antonio Armenta, son of Juan Pedro Segundo Armenta and Ana María Hurtado, was born in 1765 in Álamos. He was baptized on February 24, 1765, at the church of the Purísima Concepción in Álamos.[449] He died before May 5, 1790. The cited burial record for his unnamed son stated that Guillermo Antonio was already deceased.

---

444. Bautismos 1796–1805, July 3, 1797, film 663995, image 46, Registros Parroquiales, Iglesia de La Purísima Concepción, Álamos, Sonora, Mexico (FamilySearch, https://familysearch.org).
445. Matrimonios 1797–1833, 1846–1868, 1872–1877, about 1809–1810, film 666566, image 6, Registros Parroquiales, Iglesia de La Purísima Concepción, Álamos, Sonora, Mexico (FamilySearch, https://familysearch.org).
446. Bautismos 1751–1794, matrimonios 1848, defunciones 1735–1752, October 9, 1761, film 666999, image 219, Registros Parroquiales, Iglesia de La Purísima Concepción, Álamos, Sonora, Mexico (FamilySearch, https://familysearch.org).
447. Matrimonios 1779–1817, July 4, 1788, film 666565, image 129, Registros Parroquiales, Iglesia de La Purísima Concepción, Álamos, Sonora, Mexico (FamilySearch, https://familysearch.org).
448. Información matrimonial 1760–1799, June 10, 1788, film 667002, image 573, Registros Parroquiales, Iglesia de La Purísima Concepción, Álamos, Sonora, Mexico (FamilySearch, https://familysearch.org).
449. Bautismos, matrimonios y defunciones 1696–1699, bautismos 1768–1781, February 24, 1765, film 663487, [image not located], Registros Parroquiales, Iglesia de La Purísima Concepción, Álamos, Sonora, Mexico (FamilySearch, https://familysearch.org).

Guillermo Antonio Armenta and María de la Merced Dolores Esquer had the following child:

    i.   **[*párvulo*] Armenta** was born about 1790 in Álamos. He died in 1790 in Álamos. He was buried on May 5, 1790, at the church of the Purísima Concepción in Álamos.[450] The unnamed child was buried beneath the choir loft and his service was held with a *cruz baja*. The cost of burial was placed on the account of Antonio Palacio. The father of the child was said to have been deceased.

79. **María Gertrudis Esquer** (Joseph Cayetano-6, Joseph Cayetano-5, Juan Salvador-4, Salvador-3, Salvador-2, Blas-1) was born in 1768 in Álamos. She was baptized on October 12, 1768, at the church of the Purísima Concepción in Álamos.[451] The baptismal record named Agustina de Arballo, wife of Antonio Corral, as her *madrina*. Pedro Corral and Blas Gutiérrez were named as witnesses to the sacrament of baptism.

María Gertrudis Esquer and Agustín Castro were married on June 18, 1798, at the church of the Purísima Concepción in Álamos.[452] The matrimonial record named Pedro José García and Serafina Gongora as *padrinos*. José Bustillos, *sacristán*, and Pedro Mallén, among others present, were identified as witnesses to the marriage. Agustín Castro, socially identified as *como español*, had been married first to María Antonia Montiel who was deceased. The couple received a nuptial blessing on the day of their marriage. Parents of the bride and groom were named. The father of the bride and the parents of the groom were said to have been deceased.

María Gertrudis Esquer died on June 2, 1811, at the age of forty-three in Álamos. She was buried on June 3, 1811, at the parish of the Purísima Concepción in Álamos.[453] She received the last rites of the Catholic Church and was buried at the cemetery. Her burial service was held with a *cruz baja*.

Agustín Castro, son of Nicolás Castro and Loreto Martín Bernal, was born about 1758 in Sivirijoa, Sinaloa. The cited matrimonial record provided his place of birth.

Agustín Castro and María Gertrudis Esquer had the following known children:

    i.   **José Eduviges Castro** was born in 1799 in Álamos. He was baptized on June 11, 1799, at the church of the Purísima Concepción in Álamos.[454] The baptismal record socially identified the child as *como español* and named José Ygnacio Ortiz and Dolores Velarde as his *padrinos*.

    ii.   **María Rosalía Castro** was born in 1801 in Álamos. She was baptized on January 8, 1801, at the church of the Purísima Concepción in Álamos.[455] The baptismal record

---

450. Defunciones 1786–1819, May 5, 1790, film 666996, image 39, Registros Parroquiales, Iglesia de La Purísima Concepción, Álamos, Sonora, Mexico (FamilySearch, https://familysearch.org).
451. Bautismos, matrimonios y defunciones 1696–1699, bautismos 1768–1781, October 12, 1768, film 663487, image 114, Registros Parroquiales, Iglesia de La Purísima Concepción, Álamos, Sonora, Mexico (FamilySearch, https://familysearch.org).
452. Matrimonios 1779–1817, June 18, 1798, film 666565, image 352, Registros Parroquiales, Iglesia de La Purísima Concepción, Álamos, Sonora, Mexico (FamilySearch, https://familysearch.org).
453. Defunciones 1786–1819, June 3, 1811, film 666996, image 445, Registros Parroquiales, Iglesia de La Purísima Concepción, Álamos, Sonora, Mexico (FamilySearch, https://familysearch.org).
454. Bautismos 1796–1805, June 11, 1799, film 663995, image 103, Registros Parroquiales, Iglesia de La Purísima Concepción, Álamos, Sonora, Mexico (FamilySearch, https://familysearch.org).
455. Bautismos 1796–1805, January 8, 1801, film 663995, images 141–142, Registros Parroquiales, Iglesia de La Purísima Concepción, Álamos, Sonora, Mexico (FamilySearch, https://familysearch.org).

named María Úrsula Ruiz de Eguino as her *madrina*. The child was socially classified as a *mulata libre*. That classification was later crossed out.

iii. **José María de Jesús Castro** was born in 1803 in Álamos. He was baptized on October 9, 1803, at the church of the Purísima Concepción in Álamos.[456] The baptismal record named Juan de Dios Hurtado and María Basilia Valenzuela as his *padrinos*.

iv. **José Marcelino Castro** was born in 1811 in Álamos. He was baptized on June 14, 1811, at the church of the Purísima Concepción in Álamos.[457] The baptismal record named José Esquer and María Juliana García as his *padrinos*.

80. **José Joaquín Esquer** (Joseph Cayetano-6, Joseph Cayetano-5, Juan Salvador-4, Salvador-3, Salvador-2, Blas-1) was born about 1768.

José Joaquín Esquer and María Manuela del Carmen Hurtado were married on June 18, 1787, in Álamos.[458] The matrimonial record named Manuel Esquer and his unnamed wife as *padrinos*. Antonio Zapopa, twenty-five years of age, and Francisco García, twenty-eight years of age were named as witnesses to the couple's eligibility to marry. Francisco Padilla and Melchor Amarillas were named as witnesses to the marriage.

The cited June 8, 1787, marriage information record for José Joaquín Antonio Esquer gave his age as nineteen, and María Manuela Hurtado's, as twenty-three.[459] The record also provided testimony that the couple had no impediment to marriage, and that both were single and free enter into matrimony.

José Joaquín Esquer died on December 15, 1796, in Álamos. He was buried on December 16, 1796, at the church of the Purísima Concepción in Álamos. His burial service was held with *cruz alta, capa y andas*, and he was laid to rest in a in a burial site valued at five pesos. The baptismal records for the children of the marriage of José Joaquín Esquer and María Manuela Hurtado identify him as "Joaquín Antonio Esquer," "José Joaquín Esquer," and "Joaquín Esquer."

María Manuela del Carmen Hurtado, daughter of Felipe Hurtado and Gertrudis Ávila, was born in 1761 in Álamos. She was baptized on January 22, 1761, at the church of the Purísima Concepción in Álamos.[460] The baptismal record named Francisco Diaz de la Torre and Josepha Diaz de la Torre as her *padrinos*.

---

456. Bautismos 1796–1805, October 9, 1803, film 663995, image 217, Registros Parroquiales, Iglesia de La Purísima Concepción, Álamos, Sonora, Mexico (FamilySearch, https://familysearch.org).
457. Bautismos 1791–1796,1805–1815, June 14, 1811, film 663996, image 439, Registros Parroquiales, Iglesia de La Purísima Concepción, Álamos, Sonora, Mexico (FamilySearch, https://familysearch.org).
458. Matrimonios 1779–1817, June 18, 1787, film 666565, images 112–113, Registros Parroquiales, Iglesia de La Purísima Concepción, Álamos, Sonora, Mexico (FamilySearch, https://familysearch.org).
459. Información matrimonial 1760–1799, June 8, 1787, film 667002, images 494–496, Registros Parroquiales, Iglesia de La Purísima Concepción, Álamos, Sonora, Mexico (FamilySearch, https://familysearch.org).
460. Bautismos 1751–1794, matrimonios 1848, defunciones 1735–1752, January 22, 1761, film 666999, image 208, Registros Parroquiales, Iglesia de La Purísima Concepción, Álamos, Sonora, Mexico (FamilySearch, https://familysearch.org).

José Joaquín Esquer and María Manuela del Carmen Hurtado had the following known children:

i.   **María Gertrudis Esquer** was born on February 2, 1785, in Álamos, according to the baptismal record. She was baptized on June 7, 1785, at the parish of the Purísima Concepción in Álamos.[461] The baptismal record named José Joaquín Esquer and María de las Mercedes Esquer as her *padrinos*. The child was classified as *hija ligitima*, even though her parents did not marry until two years after her birth.

ii.   **María Rosalía Esquer** died on October 14, 1787, in Álamos. She was born before October 15, 1787. She was buried on October 15, 1787, at the church of the Purísima Concepción in Álamos.[462] She was identified as a child (*párvula*) in the record. María Rosalía's burial service was held with a *cruz alta*.

137 iii.   **José Salvador Esquer**, was born on March 13, 1789, in Álamos; he married Juana María Josefa Méndez on November 4, 1809, in Álamos.

iv.   **José María Crisanto Esquer** was born on October 26, 1791, in Álamos, according to the cited baptismal record. He was baptized on October 30, 1791, at the church of the Purísima Concepción in Álamos.[463] The baptismal record named Ana Pérez de la Fuente as his *madrina*.

v.   **María Josefa Guadalupe Esquer** was born in 1794 in Álamos. She was baptized on April 11, 1794, at the church of the Purísima Concepción in Álamos.[464] The baptismal record named bachiller Juan Villa Sánchez and María Ynocencia Esquer as her *padrinos*.

vi.   **José Ygnacio del Sacramento Esquer** was born in 1796 in Álamos. He was baptized on July 31, 1796, at the church of the Purísima Concepción in Álamos.[465] The baptismal record named María Dolores Salido as his *madrina*.

81. Joseph Julián Esquer (Joseph Cayetano-6, Joseph Cayetano-5, Juan Salvador-4, Salvador-3, Salvador-2, Blas-1) was born on February 15, 1770, in Álamos. The cited baptismal record stated that Joseph Julián Esquer was born nine days prior to his baptism. He was baptized on February 24, 1770, at the church of the Purísima Concepción in Álamos.[466] The baptismal record named Phelipe Hurtado and Gertrudis de Ávila as his *padrinos*. The children of Joseph Julián Esquer

---

461. Bautismos 1781–1796, June 7, 1785, film 663488, image 189, Registros Parroquiales, Iglesia de La Purísima Concepción, Álamos, Sonora, Mexico (FamilySearch, https://familysearch.org).
462. Defunciones 1717–1751,1764–1792, October 15, 1787, film 666995, Registros Parroquiales, Iglesia de La Purísima Concepción, Álamos, Sonora, Mexico (FamilySearch, https://familysearch.org).
463. Bautismos 1791–1796,1805–1815, October 30, 1791, film 663996, image 8, Registros Parroquiales, Iglesia de La Purísima Concepción, Álamos, Sonora, Mexico (FamilySearch, https://familysearch.org).
464. Bautismos 1791–1796,1805–1815, April 11, 1794, film 663996, image 125, Registros Parroquiales, Iglesia de La Purísima Concepción, Álamos, Sonora, Mexico (FamilySearch, https://familysearch.org).
465. Bautismos 1791–1796, 1805–1815, July 31, 1796, film 663996, image 210, Registros Parroquiales, Iglesia de La Purísima Concepción, Álamos, Sonora, Mexico (FamilySearch, https://familysearch.org).
466. Bautismos, matrimonios y defunciones 1696–1699 bautismos 1768–1781, film 663487, image 144, Registros Parroquiales, Iglesia de La Purísima Concepción, Álamos, Sonora, Mexico (FamilySearch, https://familysearch.org).

and María Juliana García were identified by the priest at baptism as *como españoles*, or *dicen ser españoles*. These social identifications suggested that the children, even if of mixed racial heritage, had European facial features and were light skinned. Joseph Julián Esquer and María Juliana García were married on November 13, 1795, at the church of the Purísima Concepción in Álamos.[467] The matrimonial record named José Joaquín Esquer and Manuela Hurtado as *padrinos*. José Bustillos, Antonio Gil, and many others present were identified as witnesses.

The petition to the bishop of Sonora for a marriage dispensation for Joseph Julian Esquer and María Juliana García was made by Father Juan Nicolás Quirós y Mora. The petition stated that the candidate bride (about sixteen years of age) and groom (about twenty-five years of age) were related by blood in a second with third a degree, meaning they were first cousins once removed. Father Quirós y Mora recommended that the dispensation be granted in the name of charity and mercy. The reason was that the father of María Juliana García was elderly, poor, and unable to support his family. The petition provided a genealogy chart showing the family relationship between the bride and groom. The marriage dispensation was granted on September 22, 1795, by the bishop of Sonora from the Real del Rosario, Sinaloa.[468]

Joseph Julián Esquer and María Juliana García had the following known children:

i. **María Loreta Gorgonia Eustaquia Esquer** was born in 1796 in Álamos. She was baptized on September 19, 1796, at the church of the Purísima Concepción in Álamos.[469] The baptismal record named Vicente Ávila and Josefa Ávila as her *padrinos*.

ii. **José Julián Esquer** was born in 1799 in Álamos. He was baptized on January 2, 1799, at the church of the Purísima Concepción in Álamos.[470] The baptismal record named Juan Agustín [Ruiz de] Eguino and his sister, María Dolores [Ruiz de] Eguino, as his *padrinos*.

iii. **José Jesús Quirino Esquer** was born in 1801 in Álamos. He was baptized on June 14, 1801, at the church of the Purísima Concepción in Álamos.[471] The baptismal record named Prudencio Ruiz and María Dolores Eguino as his *padrinos*.

iv. **Pedro Esquer** was born about 1804 in Álamos.[472] He was listed in what appears to be a page of a census placed in front of marriage records. Pedro Esquer was said to have been six years of age in 1810.

---

467. Matrimonios 1779–1817, November 13, 1795, film 666565, images 300–301, Registros Parroquiales, Iglesia de La Purísima Concepción, Álamos, Sonora, Mexico (FamilySearch, https://familysearch.org).

468. Información matrimonial 1760–1799, September 22, 1795, film 667002, images 630–636, Registros Parroquiales, Iglesia de La Purísima Concepción, Álamos, Sonora, Mexico (FamilySearch, https://familysearch. org).

469. Bautismos 1796–1805, September 19, 1796, film 663995, image 11, Registros Parroquiales, Iglesia de La Purísima Concepción, Álamos, Sonora, Mexico (FamilySearch, https://familysearch.org).

470. Bautismos 1796–1805, January 2, 1799, film 663995, image 93, Registros Parroquiales, Iglesia de La Purísima Concepción, Álamos, Sonora, Mexico (FamilySearch, https://familysearch.org).

471. Bautismos 1796–1805, June 14, 1801, film 663995, image 154, Registros Parroquiales, Iglesia de La Purísima Concepción, Álamos, Sonora, Mexico (FamilySearch, https://familysearch.org).

472. Matrimonios 1797–1833, 1846–1868, 1872–1877, about 1810, film 666566, image 6, Registros Parroquiales, Iglesia de La Purísima Concepción, Álamos, Sonora, Mexico (FamilySearch, https://familysearch. org). .

v.   **Vicente Ávila Esquer** was born on April 29, 1804, in Álamos, according to the baptismal record. He was baptized on May 6, 1804, at the church of the Purísima Concepción in Álamos.[473] The baptismal record stated that he was baptized conditionally by Father Nicolás Quirós y Mora out of necessity for fear of the infant's death. On April 29, 1804, the waters of baptism were poured over the infant. The priest performed the baptismal ceremony at the church on May 6. José Aniceto Figueroa and María Guadalupe Corral were named as his *padrinos*.

vi.   **José de Jesús del Pilar Esquer** was born in 1806 in Álamos. He was baptized on October 20, 1806, at the parish church of the Purísima Concepción. in Álamos.[474] The baptismal record named José Salvador Esquer and Manuela Hurtado as his *padrinos*. The child was socially classified as *como español*.

vii.   **María Dolores Sebastiana Esquer** was born in 1809 in Álamos. She was baptized on January 22, 1809, at the church of the Purísima Concepción in Álamos.[475] The baptismal record named Manuel Anguís and Serafina Barreda as her *padrinos*.

viii.   **José Felipe Esquer** was born on July 26, 1812, in Álamos. The baptismal record stated that he was born seven days before his baptism. He was baptized on August 1, 1812, at the church of the Purísima Concepción in Álamos.[476] The baptismal record named José Antonio Corral and Gertrudis Marroquín as his *padrinos*.

82. Joseph Fernando Antonio González Barreda (María Raphaela Esquer-6, Francisco Joseph-5, Juan Salvador-4, Salvador-3, Salvador-2, Blas-1) was born in 1752 in Álamos. He was baptized on June 24, 1752, at the church of the Purísima Concepción in Álamos.[477] His baptismal record named Juan Agustín de Yriarte and Micaela Mallén de Navarrete as his *padrinos*. His father's name was recorded as Fernando Antonio Barreda.

Joseph Fernando Antonio González Barreda and Maria Lucía Gastélum were married about 1778. The matrimonial record has not been located.

Maria Lucía Gastélum was born about 1760.

Joseph Fernando Antonio González Barreda and Maria Lucía Gastélum had the following known children:

i.   **José Francisco González Barreda** was born on January 31, 1780, in Álamos, according to the baptismal record. He was baptized on March 12, 1780, at the

---

473. Bautismos 1796–1805, May 6, 1804, film 663995, image 239, Registros Parroquiales, Iglesia de La Purísima Concepción, Álamos, Sonora, Mexico (FamilySearch, https://familysearch.org).
474. Bautismos 1791–1796, 1805–1815, October 20, 1806, film 663996, image 260, Registros Parroquiales, Iglesia de La Purísima Concepción, Álamos, Sonora, Mexico (FamilySearch, https://familysearch.org).
475. Bautismos 1791–1796,1805–1815, January 22, 1809, film 663996, image 324, Registros Parroquiales, Iglesia de La Purísima Concepción, Álamos, Sonora, Mexico (FamilySearch, https://familysearch.org).
476. Bautismos 1791–1796, 1805–1815, August 1, 1812, film 663996, image 435, Registros Parroquiales, Iglesia de La Purísima Concepción, Álamos, Sonora, Mexico (FamilySearch, https://familysearch.org).
477. Bautismos 1751–1794, matrimonios 1848, defunciones 1735–1752, June 24, 1752, film 666999, image 63, Registros Parroquiales, Iglesia de La Purísima Concepción, Álamos, Sonora, Mexico (FamilySearch, https:// familysearch.org).

church of the Purísima Concepción in Álamos.[478] The baptismal record named Pedro Sebastián Esquer and Ana María Murrieta as his *padrinos*. The record identified his mother as "Lucía Castéla." It stated that his parents were legally married and born in Álamos.

138 ii.   **Juana Leocadia González Barreda** was born about 1781; she married Agustín Esquerra y Rosas on April 21, 1800, in Álamos.

iii.   **José Antonio Antonino González Barreda** was born on May 11, 1784, in Álamos, according to the baptismal record. He was baptized on August 22, 1784, at the church of the Purísima Concepción in Álamos.[479] The baptismal record named Miguel Alcalde and Anna María González Barreda as his *padrinos*.

iv.   **José Luis González Barreda** was born on August 19, 1785, in Álamos, according to the baptismal record. He was baptized on November 27, 1785, at the church of the Purísima Concepción in Álamos.[480] The baptismal record named Manuel Sol de Villa Ruiz and Matilde Barreda as his *padrinos*.

v.   **José Gerónimo González Barreda** was born on October 6, 1787, in Álamos, according to the baptismal record. He was baptized on October 30, 1787, at the church of the Purísima Concepción in Álamos.[481] The baptismal record named José Luis Barreda and Josefa Anguís as his *padrinos*.

139 vi.   **José Ygnacio de Jesús González Barreda** was born in 1789 in Álamos; he married María Gertrudis Gastélum, May 3, 1821, Álamos.

vii.   **María Josefa Francisca Xaviera González Barreda** was born in 1796 in Álamos. She was baptized on January 29, 1796, at the parish of the Purísima Concepción in Álamos.[482] The baptismal record named Manuel Anguís and María Serafina Barreda as his *padrinos*. The baptism took place at the chapel of La Aduana.

140 viii.   **Fernando González Barreda** was born about 1798; he married Josefa Martina Acosta on May 9, 1820, in Álamos.

ix.   **María Manuela Rita Quiteria González Barreda** was born in 1799 in Álamos. She was baptized on June 2, 1799, at the church of the Purísima Concepción in Álamos.[483]

478. Bautismos, matrimonios y defunciones 1696–1699, bautismos 1768–1781, March 12, 1780, film 663487, image 457, Registros Parroquiales, Iglesia de La Purísima Concepción, Álamos, Sonora, Mexico (FamilySearch, https:// familysearch.org).

479. Bautismos 1781–1796, August 22,1784, film 663488, image 157, Registros Parroquiales, Iglesia de La Purísima Concepción, Álamos, Sonora, Mexico (FamilySearch, https://familysearch.org).

480. Bautismos 1781–1796, November 27, 1785, film 663488, image 199, Registros Parroquiales, Iglesia de La Purísima Concepción, Álamos, Sonora, Mexico (FamilySearch, https://familysearch.org).

481. Bautismos 1781–1796, October 30, 1787, film 663488, image 236, Registros Parroquiales, Iglesia de La Purísima Concepción, Álamos, Sonora, Mexico (FamilySearch, https://familysearch.org).

482. Bautismos 1781–1796, January 29,1796, film 663488, image 690, Registros Parroquiales, Iglesia de La Purísima Concepción, Álamos, Sonora, Mexico (FamilySearch, https://familysearch.org); Bautismos 1791–1796, 1805–1815, January 29, 1796, film 663996, image 189, Registros Parroquiales, Iglesia de La Purísima Concepción, Álamos, Sonora, Mexico (FamilySearch, https://familysearch.org).

483. Bautismos 1796–1805, June 2, 1799, film 663995, image 103, Registros Parroquiales, Iglesia de La Purísima Concepción, Álamos, Sonora, Mexico (FamilySearch, https://familysearch.org).

The baptismal record named Agustín [Esquerra y] Rosas and María Loreto Barreda as her *padrinos*.

    x.   **José Manuel de Jesús Thomas González Barreda** was born in 1801 in Álamos. He was baptized on April 30, 1801, at the church of the Purísima Concepción in Álamos.[484] The baptismal record named Balvanera Yriarte as his *madrina*.

    xi.   **José María Guadalupe González Barreda** was born in 1805 in Álamos. He was baptized on May 8, 1805, at the church of the Purísima Concepción in Álamos.[485] The baptismal record named Juan Agustín Ruiz de Eguino and his mother Ana María Tovar as his *padrinos*.

83. Joseph Patricio Benito González Barreda (María Raphaela Esquer-6, Francisco Joseph-5, Juan Salvador-4, Salvador-3, Salvador-2, Blas-1) was born in 1754 in Álamos. He was baptized on March 23, 1754, at the church of the Purísima Concepción in Álamos.[486] The baptismal record named the Jesuit priest, Antonio Merino, and Micaela Mallén de Navarrete as his *padrinos*.

Joseph Patricio Benito González Barreda and María Guadalupe Amarillas were married on December 25, 1775, at the church of the Purísima Concepción in Álamos.[487] The matrimonial record named Antonio Salcido and María de la Luz Barreda as *padrinos*. Parents of the bride and groom were named in the record. The couple did not receive a nuptial blessing on the day of their marriage because it was prohibited during that time period in the liturgical calendar of the Catholic Church. The bride and groom had a fourth with a third degree relationship of consanguinity, meaning they were third cousins once removed.

Joseph Patricio Benito died on April 13, 1791, at the age of thirty-seven in Álamos. He was buried beneath the choir of the church on April 14, 1791, at the church of the Purísima Concepción in Álamos.[488] His funeral service was held with *cruz alta, capa, una mesa, y caja*. He received all the last sacraments of the Catholic Church. The burial record stated that Joseph Patricio Benito had been married to Guadalupe Amarillas, and that he predeceased three sons and two unnamed daughters. The record claimed that his widow was pregnant at the time of his death, and that he left a will. He was also known as "Patricio Barreda."

María Guadalupe Amarillas, daughter of Domingo Francisco Amarillas and Micaela Carrasco, was born about 1750.

---

484. Bautismos 1796–1805, April 30, 1801, film 663995, image 153, Registros Parroquiales, Iglesia de La Purísima Concepción, Álamos, Sonora, Mexico (FamilySearch, https://familysearch.org).
485. Bautismos 1796–1805, May 8, 1805, film 663995, image 272, Registros Parroquiales, Iglesia de La Purísima Concepción, Álamos, Sonora, Mexicon (FamilySearch, https://familysearch.org).
486. Bautismos 1751–1794, matrimonios 1848, defunciones 1735–1752, March 23, 1754, film 666999, image 92, Registros Parroquiales, Iglesia de La Purísima Concepción, Álamos, Sonora, Mexico (FamilySearch, https://familysearch.org).
487. Matrimonios 1758–1779, December 25, 1775, film 666564, image 165, Registros Parroquiales, Iglesia de La Purísima Concepción, Álamos, Sonora, Mexico (FamilySearch, https://familysearch.org).
488. Defunciones 1717–1751, 1764–1792, April 14, 1791, film 666995, images 540–541, Registros Parroquiales, Iglesia de La Purísima Concepción, Álamos, Sonora, Mexico (FamilySearch, https://familysearch.org).

Joseph Patricio Benito González Barreda and María Guadalupe Amarillas had the following known children:

    i.   **María Vicenta Rafaela González Barreda** was born in 1776 in Álamos. She was baptized on November 3, 1776, at the church of the Purísima Concepción in Álamos.[489] The baptismal record named María Rafaela Esquer as her *madrina*.

    ii.   **Joseph Patricio González Barreda** was born in 1778 in Álamos. He was baptized on December 7, 1778, at the church of the Purísima Concepción in Álamos.[490] The baptismal record named Rafaela Esquer as his *madrina*. Juan Antonio Esquer and Joseph Bustillos were named as witnesses to the sacrament of baptism.

    iii.   **José Francisco de Jesús González Barreda** was born on February 5, 1781, in Álamos, according to the baptismal record. He was baptized on February 12, 1781, at the church of the Purísima Concepción in Álamos.[491] The baptismal record named Francisco Amarillas and Matilde Barreda as his *padrinos*.

141 iv.   **Patricio Alfonso González Barreda** was born on January 11, 1783, in Álamos. He married Anastasia Mendívil, July 20, 1814, Álamos and later married María del Rosario Rodríguez after October 28, 1848, in Álamos.

142 v.   **María Francisca González Barreda** was born on October 10, 1786, in Álamos; she married José Manuel Gil de Lamadrid on April 23, 1807, in Álamos.

143 vi.   **María Ignacia González Barreda** was born about 1788; she married Tomás Rodríguez on May 8, 1814, in Álamos.

84. María de la Luz González Barreda (María Raphaela Esquer-6, Francisco Joseph-5, Juan Salvador-4, Salvador-3, Salvador-2, Blas-1) was born in 1758 in Álamos. She was baptized on July 16, 1758, at the church of the Purísima Concepción in Álamos.[492] The baptismal record named Bachiller Joaquín Antonio Esquer and María Theresa Esquer as her *padrinos*.

María de la Luz González Barreda and José Pérez Contreras were married on July 21, 1772, at the church of the Purísima Concepción in Álamos.[493] The matrimonial record named Teniente General Antonio Casimiro Esparza and Rafaela Esquer as *padrinos*. *Notarios* Juan Fox and

489. Bautismos, matrimonios y defunciones 1696–1699, bautismos 1768–1781, November 3, 1776, film 663487, image 330, Registros Parroquiales, Iglesia de La Purísima Concepción, Álamos, Sonora, Mexico (FamilySearch, https:// familysearch.org).
490. Bautismos, matrimonios y defunciones 1696–1699, bautismos 1768–1781, December 7, 1778, film 663487, image 394, Registros Parroquiales, Iglesia de La Purísima Concepción, Álamos, Sonora, Mexico (FamilySearch, https:// familysearch.org).
491. Bautismos, matrimonios y defunciones 1696–1699, bautismos 1768–1781, February 12, 1781, film 663487, image 505, Registros Parroquiales, Iglesia de La Purísima Concepción, Álamos, Sonora, Mexico (FamilySearch, https:// familysearch.org).
492. Bautismos 1751–1794, matrimonios 1848, defunciones 1735–1752, July 16, 1758, film 666999, image 166, Registros Parroquiales, Iglesia de La Purísima Concepción, Álamos, Sonora, Mexico (FamilySearch, https:// familysearch.org).
493. Matrimonios 1758–1779, July 21, 1772, film 666564, image 149, Registros Parroquiales, Iglesia de La Purísima Concepción, Álamos, Sonora, Mexico (FamilySearch, https://familysearch.org).

Antonio Cosío were named as witnesses to the marriage. Parents of the bride and groom were named in the record.

José Pérez Contreras, son of Alonso Pérez de Contreras and María Anna de Olachea, was born about 1752 in Guadalajara, New Spain (currently in the Mexican state of Jalisco).

José Pérez Contreras and María de la Luz González Barreda had the following known children:

i. **Andrés Avelino Pérez Contreras** was born in 1792 in Culiacán. He was baptized on November 24, 1792, at the church of the Sagrario de San Miguel in Culiacán.[494] The baptismal record named Luis Antonio Esquer and María Benigna Esquer as his *padrinos*.

ii. **Juan José Pérez Contreras** was born on December 26, 1794, in Culiacán. The cited burial record stated that the child was three days old when he died. He was baptized on December 26, 1794, at the church of the Sagrario de San Miguel in Culiacán.[495] The cited burial record stated that Juan José was baptized on the day he was born because he was not expected to survive. He died on December 28, 1794, in Culiacán. He was buried on December 29, 1794, at the church of the Sagrario de San Miguel in Culiacán.[496] His funeral service was held with *cruz alta y capa*.

85. **María Loreto González Barreda** (María Raphaela Esquer-6, Francisco Joseph-5, Juan Salvador-4, Salvador-3, Salvador-2, Blas-1) was born about 1766.

María Loreto González Barreda and Juan José Timoteo Martínez Mendívil were married on June 11, 1787, at the church of the Purísima Concepción in Álamos.[497] The matrimonial record named Luis Martínez de Mendívil and María Lucía Martínez de Mendívil as *padrinos*. Juan Thomas Padilla, sixty-one years of age; Miguel de Lara, over fifty years of age; and Antonio Ybarra, over forty years of age, were named as witnesses to the couple's eligibility to marry. Juan Francisco Padilla and Melchor Amarillas were named as witnesses to the marriage. Parents of the bride and groom were named in the record. Parents of the bride were said to be deceased. The couple received a nuptial blessing on the same day as their marriage.

The marriage investigation, dated May 21, 1787, stated that Juan José Timoteo Martínez Mendívil and María Loreto González Barreda were related in the third, with fourth degree of consanguinity, meaning they were second cousins one generation removed.[498] Because of this blood relationship they were required to receive a dispensation to marry. The marriage investigation revealed no other impediments to their marriage.

494. Bautismos 1789–1805, November 24,1792, film 665428, image 52, Registros Parroquiales, Iglesia Sagrario de San Miguel, Culiacán, Sinaloa, Mexico (FamilySearch, https://familysearch.org).
495. Defunciones 1746–1833, December 29,1794, film 674051, image 111, Registros Parroquiales, Iglesia Sagrario de San Miguel, Culiacán, Sinaloa, Mexico (FamilySearch, https://familysearch.org).
496. Defunciones 1746–1833, December 29, 1794, film 674051, image 111, Registros Parroquiales, Iglesia Sagrario de San Miguel, Culiacán, Sinaloa, Mexico (FamilySearch, https://familysearch.org).
497. Matrimonios 1779–1817, June 11, 1787, film 666565, image 112, Registros Parroquiales, Iglesia de La Purísima Concepción, Álamos, Sonora, Mexico (FamilySearch, https://familysearch.org).
498. Información matrimonial 1760–1799, May 21, 1787, film 667002, images 523–524, Registros Parroquiales, Iglesia de La Purísima Concepción, Álamos, Sonora, Mexico (FamilySearch, https://familysearch.org).

Juan José Timoteo Martínez Mendívil, son of Francisco Antonio Martínez Mendívil and Petra María Gertrudis Féliz, was born in 1766 in Álamos. He was baptized on February 5, 1766, at the church of the Purísima Concepción in Álamos.[499] The baptismal record named Joseph Prudencio Mendívil and Juana María Mendívil as his *padrinos*. Bachiller Juan Joseph de Avilés and Blas Gutiérrez were named as witnesses to the sacrament of baptism. His surname in some records appeared simply as "Mendívil."

Juan José Timoteo Martínez Mendívil and María Loreto González Barreda had the following known children:

144 i. **José Fernando Trinidad Martínez Mendívil** was born on May 31, 1791, in Álamos; he died on September 16, 1792, in Álamos.

ii. **María Rafaela Gerónima Martínez Mendívil** was born in 1793 in Álamos. She was baptized on October 6, 1793, at the parish of the Purísima Concepción in Álamos.[500] The baptismal record named José Carrillo and María Matilde Barreda as her *padrinos*.

iii. **María del Carmen Cayetana Martínez Mendívil** was born in 1795 in Álamos. She was baptized on August 15, 1795, at the parish of the Purísima Concepción in Álamos.[501] The baptismal record named Manuel Anguís and Serafina Barreda as her *padrinos*. The baptism ceremony took place at the chapel of La Aduana.

145 iv. **José Fernando Casimiro Martínez Mendívil** was born in 1797 in Álamos; he married María Isidora Tomasa Gaxiola on July 21, 1828, in Álamos.

146 v. **Manuel de Jesús Esteban Martínez Mendívil** was born in 1798 in Álamos; he married María Encarnación Carrasco about 1821.

147 vi. **María Gertrudis Catarina Martínez Mendívil** was born in 1801 in Álamos; she married José Francisco Yepes on February 6, 1821, in Álamos.

vii. **José Andrés de Jesús Martínez Mendívil** was born in 1804 in Álamos. He was baptized on February 11, 1804, at the church of the Purísima Concepción in Álamos.[502] The baptismal record named Agustín Esquerra y Rosas and María de la Luz González Barreda as his *padrinos*.

viii. **José de Jesús Máximo Martínez Mendívil** was born in 1806 in Álamos. He was baptized on July 1, 1806, at the church of the Purísima Concepción in Álamos.[503] The baptismal record named Luis Mendívil and Simona Muñoz as his *padrinos*.

499. Bautismos 1751–1794, matrimonios 1848, defunciones 1735–1752, February 5, 1766, film 666999, image 323, Registros Parroquiales, Iglesia de La Purísima Concepción, Álamos, Sonora, Mexico (FamilySearch, https://familysearch.org).
500. Bautismos 1781–1796, October 6, 1793, film 663488, image 604, Registros Parroquiales, Iglesia de La Purísima Concepción, Álamos, Sonora, Mexico (FamilySearch, https://familysearch.org).
501. Bautismos 1781–1796, August 15, 1795, film 663488, image 675, Registros Parroquiales, Iglesia de La Purísima Concepción, Álamos, Sonora, Mexico (FamilySearch, https://familysearch.org).
502. Bautismos 1796–1805, February 11, 1804, film 663995, image 227, Registros Parroquiales, Iglesia de La Purísima Concepción, Álamos, Sonora, Mexico (FamilySearch, https://familysearch.org).
503. Bautismos 1791–1796,1805–1815, July 1, 1806, film 663996, image 250, Registros Parroquiales, Iglesia de La Purísima Concepción, Álamos, Sonora, Mexico (FamilySearch, https://familysearch.org).

86. Serafina González Barreda (María Raphaela Esquer-6, Francisco Joseph-5, Juan Salvador-4, Salvador-3, Salvador-2, Blas-1) was born in 1768 in Álamos. The cited marriage investigation for Serafina González Barreda stated that she was twenty-six years of age in 1794 and that she had been born in Álamos.

Serafina González Barreda and Juan Manuel Anguís were married on December 30, 1794, at the church of the Purísima Concepción in Álamos.[504] The matrimonial record named Prudencio Ruiz de Eguino and Anna María Tovar as *padrinos*. Bachiller José Joaquín Elías de Zayas and Subdelegado Rafael Valenzuela were identified as witnesses to the marriage. Parents of the bride and groom were named in the record and all were said to be deceased at the time of the marriage. A marriage dispensation was required because the couple were related in the third and fourth degrees of consanguinity, meaning they were both second and third cousins.

The cited marriage investigation record, dated December 24, 1794, noted that Juan Manuel Anguís was engaged in commerce in La Aduana.[505] The cited letter dated November 25, 1794, from Licenciado Manuel María Moreno, lawyer for the Audiencia of Mexico City spoke on behalf of providing the bridal couple with a dispensation to marry.[506]

Juan Manuel Anguís, son of Francisco Antonio Baptista Anguís and Rosa Martínez Mendívil, was born on April 7, 1762, in Álamos. The cited baptismal record stated that he was born twenty-eight days prior to his date of baptism. He was baptized on May 5, 1762, at the church of the Purísima Concepción in Álamos.[507] The baptismal record named Bachiller Juan Antonio de Anguís and Gertrudis de Anguís, his sister, as the child's *padrinos*. The waters of baptism had already been poured on the child at birth, fearing he might not survive.

Juan Manuel Anguís and Serafina González Barreda had the following known children:

148 i.   **María Dolores de Jesús Josefa Gregoria Anguís** was born in 1797 in Álamos; she married José Pasqual Prudencio Ygnacio de la Cruz Gómez Lamadrid on October 10, 1813, in Álamos.

ii.   **María Balvanera del Carmen Juana de la Cruz Anguís** was born on December 24, 1799, in Álamos, according to the baptismal record. She was baptized on December 31, 1799, at the church of the Purísima Concepción in Álamos.[508] The baptismal record named Bachiller Pedro Pablo González Barreda and Juana Gil Samaniego as her *padrinos*.

---

504. Matrimonios 1779–1817, December 30, 1794, film 666565, images 285–286, Registros Parroquiales, Iglesia de La Purísima Concepción, Álamos, Sonora, Mexico (FamilySearch, https://familysearch.org).
505. Información matrimonial 1793–1798, December 24, 1794, film 663808, images 147–152, Registros Parroquiales, Iglesia de La Purísima Concepción, Álamos, Sonora, Mexico (FamilySearch, https://familysearch.org).
506. Información matrimonial 1760–1799, November 25, 1794, film 667002, images 615–616, Registros Parroquiales, Iglesia de La Purísima Concepción, Álamos, Sonora, Mexico (FamilySearch, https://familysearch.org).
507. Bautismos 1751–1794, matrimonios 1848, defunciones 1735–1752, May 5, 1762, film 666999, images 227–228 and 242–243, Registros Parroquiales, Iglesia de La Purísima Concepción, Álamos, Sonora, Mexico (FamilySearch, https:// familysearch.org).
508. Bautismos 1796–1805, December 31, 1799, film 663995, image 113, Registros Parroquiales, Iglesia de La Purísima Concepción, Álamos, Sonora, Mexico (FamilySearch, https://familysearch.org).

iii.   **María Concepción Juana Paula Anguís** was born on June 18, 1801, in Álamos, according to the baptismal record. She was baptized on June 24, 1801, at the church of the Purísima Concepción in Álamos.[509] The baptismal record named Prudencio Ruiz de Eguino and Anna María Fabar, his wife, as her *padrinos*.

iv.   **María del Carmen Juana Ladislao Anguís** was born in 1803 in Álamos. She was baptized on July 3, 1803, at the church of the Purísima Concepción in Álamos.[510] The baptismal record named the parish priest, Nicolás Quirós y Mora, and Isabel Quirós y Mora as her *padrinos*. Those present included Juan Fox Fernández and Juan Miguel Santini, among others.

v.   **Juana Bautista María Juliana Anguís** was born in February 1810 in Álamos. The cited baptismal record stated that she was born the same month in which she was baptized. The day of the month was not clearly indicated. She was baptized on February 25, 1810, at the church of the Purísima Concepción in Álamos.[511] The baptismal record named Bachiller José Rosas and Rita Gil Samaniego as her *padrinos*.

87. **María Guadalupe de la Merced de Quirós y Mora** (Micaela Matilde Esquer-6, Francisco Joseph-5, Juan Salvador-4, Salvador-3, Salvador-2, Blas-1) was born in 1753 in Culiacán. She was baptized on October 12, 1753, at the church of the Sagrario de San Miguel in Culiacán.[512] The baptismal record named Joaquín Esquer and Juana Esquer as her *padrinos*.

María Guadalupe de la Merced de Quirós y Mora and Francisco Ochoa were married on June 24, 1782, at the parish of the Sagrario de San Miguel in Culiacán.[513] The matrimonial record named Francisco Samaniego and María Francisca de Quirós as *padrinos*. Agustín Beltrán and Juan Ochoa were named as witnesses to the marriage. Parents of the bride and groom were named in the record. The couple received a nuptial blessing on the day of their wedding. The marriage took place at the church of the pueblo of Imala, jurisdiction of Culiacán. The record claimed that the groom was originally from Cosalá, Sinaloa, and that he had resided in Palo Alto, jurisdiction of Culiacán for a period of seven months.

Francisco Ochoa, son of Felipe Ochoa and Inés López de Siqueiros, was born about 1750 in Cosalá, Sinaloa. The cited marriage record stated that he originated in Cosalá, jurisdiction of Culiacán.

---

509. Bautismos 1796–1805, June 24, 1801, film 663995, image 155, Registros Parroquiales, Iglesia de La Purísima Concepción, Álamos, Sonora, Mexico (FamilySearch, https://familysearch.org).

510. Bautismos 1796–1805, July 3, 1803, film 663995, images 202–203, Registros Parroquiales, Iglesia de La Purísima Concepción, Álamos, Sonora, Mexico (FamilySearch, https://familysearch.org).

511. Bautismos 1791–1796, 1805–1815, February 25, 1810, film 663996, image 365, Registros Parroquiales, Iglesia de La Purísima Concepción, Álamos, Sonora, Mexico (FamilySearch, https://familysearch.org).

512. Matrimonios 1731–1755 (incluye bautismos y defunciones), October 12, 1753, film 665426, images 192–193, Registros Parroquiales, Iglesia Sagrario de San Miguel, Culiacán, Sinaloa, Mexico (FamilySearch, https://familysearch.org).

513. Matrimonios 1755–1829, June 24, 1782, film 673378, image 123, Registros Parroquiales, Iglesia Sagrario de San Miguel, Culiacán, Sinaloa, Mexico (FamilySearch, https://familysearch.org).

88. **José Miguel Quirós y Mora** (Micaela Matilde Esquer-6, Francisco Joseph-5, Juan Salvador-4, Salvador-3, Salvador-2, Blas-1) was born about 1773 in Culiacán. José Miguel Quirós y Mora and Juana Rosa Millán were married on September 28, 1793, at the church of Santa Úrsula in Cosalá, Sinaloa.[514] The matrimonial record named Juan Alexo Moreno and María del Carmen Moreno as *padrinos*. Diego Muñoz and Celestino Eseverri were named as witnesses to the marriage. Parents of the couple were named and the father of the bride was said to have been deceased. The couple received a nuptial blessimg on the day of their wedding. The record stated that José Miguel was born in the Real de Palo Alto, jurisdiction of Culiacán, and had been a *vecino* of Cosalá for ten years. Juana Rosa Millán was said to have been born in Soquititán, jurisdiction of Culiacán, and it continued to be her place of residence.

Juana Rosa Millán, daughter of Manuel Millán and Juana de Salazar, was born about 1775.

José Miguel Quirós y Mora and Juana Rosa Millán had the following known children:

149 i. **María Sixta de la Trinidad Quirós y Mora** was born on March 28, 1802, in Cosalá; she married Quirino Solís on June 30, 1823, in Cosalá.

150 ii. **Pablo Quirós y Mora** was born about 1794 in Culiacán; he married Manuela Ponce, May 30, 1822, Culiacán.

89. **María Irene Esquer** (Francisco Gabriel-6, Francisco Joseph-5, Juan Salvador-4, Salvador-3, Salvador-2, Blas-1) was born about 1768.

María Irene Esquer and Francisco Xavier Sambade were married on April 24, 1786, in Culiacán.[515] The matrimonial record named José Verdugo and Nicolasa Verdugo as *padrinos* and Miguel Mojardín and Martín León as witnesses to the marriage. Parents of the bride and groom were named in the record and the couple received a nuptial blessing the day of their marriage. There are no known children from the marriage of Francisco Xavier Sambade and María Irene Esquer.

María Irene Esquer died on September 9, 1787, in Culiacán and was was buried on September 10, 1787, at the church of the Sagrario de San Miguel in Culiacán.[516] She was buried at a site along the side door of the church and her funeral service was held with a *cruz alta*. Her burial record stated that she had been the wife of Francisco Sambade, and that she had received the last sacraments of the Catholic Church before death.

Francisco Xavier Sambade, son of Phelipe Sambade and María López de Siqueiros, was born on September 24, 1763, in Culiacán. The cited baptismal record stated that he was born thirteen days prior to his day of baptism. Francisco Xavier was baptized on October 7, 1763, at the

---

514. Información matrimonial 1793–1801, 1831–1832, September 28, 1793, film 665883, images 21–22, Registros Parroquiales, Iglesia de Santa Úrsula, Cosalá, Sinaloa, Mexico (FamilySearch, https://familysearch.org).
515. Matrimonios 1755–1784 [1794], April 24, 1786, film 673389, image 278, Registros Parroquiales, Iglesia Sagrario de San Miguel, Culiacán, Sinaloa, Mexico (FamilySearch, https://familysearch.org).
516. Defunciones 1746–1833, September 10, 1787, film 674051, image 237, Registros Parroquiales, Iglesia Sagrario de San Miguel, Culiacán, Sinaloa, Mexico (FamilySearch, https://familysearch.org).

church of the Sagrario de San Miguel in Culiacán.[517] The baptismal record named María Rosa de Urrea as his *madrina*.

90. **María Manuela Esquer** (Francisco Gabriel-6, Francisco Joseph-5, Juan Salvador-4, Salvador-3, Salvador-2, Blas-1) was born about 1771 in Culiacán. The cited matrimonial record provided her place of birth. María Manuela Esquer and Felipe Timoteo Verdugo were married on December 29, 1786, in Culiacán.[518] The matrimonial record named José Urrea and Quirina Verdugo as *padrinos*. Ignacio Avilés and José Urtuzuástegui were identified as witnesses to the marriage, along with others present at the marriage ceremony. Parents of the bride and groom were named in the record.

María Manuela Esquer and Pedro Zazueta were married on November 8, 1793, at the church of the Sagrario de San Miguel in Culiacán.[519] The cited marriage investigation record dated November 8, 1793, stated that Pedro Zazueta and María Manuela Esquer were both widowed at the time of their marriage. Felipe Verdugo, María Manuela's first husband, and Pedro's first wife, Isabel Policarpa Verdugo, were siblings. They received a dispensation to marry having to do with a second degree of affinity because of licit relations within their previous marriages. Parents of the bride and groom were named in the record. Parents of the groom were said to have been deceased. The actual matrimonial record has not been located.

María Manuela Esquer died on June 20, 1831, in Culiacán. She was buried on June 21, 1831, at the church of the Sagrario de San Miguel in Culiacán.[520] María Manuela Esquer's funeral service was held with *cruz alta, cajón, misa, y vigilia*. She was interred in a burial site valued at five pesos. The burial record claimed that María Manuela had been the widow of her second husband, Pedro Zazueta, and that she received the last rites of the Catholic Church.

Felipe Timoteo Verdugo, son of Alonso Verdugo and Isabel Beltrán, was born about 1766 in Culiacán. The cited matrimonial record stated that he had originated in Culiacán.

Felipe Timoteo Verdugo and María Manuela Esquer had the following known children:

151 i.   **Manuel Eusebio Verdugo** was born on November 14, 1787, in Culiacán; he married Narcisa Ibarra about 1805.

    ii.   **María Patricia Verdugo** was born in 1792 in Culiacán. She was baptized on March 27, 1792, at the church of the Sagrario de San Miguel in Culiacán.[521] The baptismal record named Nicolasa Esquer as her *madrina*.

---

517. Bautismos 1755–1789, October 7, 1763, film 665427, image 111, Registros Parroquiales, Iglesia Sagrario de San Miguel, Culiacán, Sinaloa, Mexico (FamilySearch, https://familysearch.org).
518. Matrimonios 1755–1784 [1794], December 29, 1786, film 673389, images 286–287, Registros Parroquiales, Iglesia Sagrario de San Miguel, Culiacán, Sinaloa, Mexico (FamilySearch, https://familysearch.org).
519. Información matrimonial 1769–1796, November 8, 1793, film 673448, images 599–600, Registros Parroquiales, Iglesia Sagrario de San Miguel, Culiacán, Sinaloa, Mexico (FamilySearch, https://familysearch.org).
520. Defunciones 1746–1833, June 21, 1831 film 674051, image 691, Registros Parroquiales, Iglesia Sagrario de San Miguel, Culiacán, Sinaloa, Mexico (FamilySearch, https://familysearch.org).
521. Bautismos 1789–1805, March 27, 1792, film 665428, image 37, Registros Parroquiales, Iglesia Sagrario de San Miguel, Culiacán, Sinaloa, Mexico (FamilySearch, https://familysearch.org).

152 iii. **Manuela Verdugo** was born about 1794; she married Nicolás Verdugo about 1819.

153 iv. **María Serafina Verdugo** was born in 1789 in Culiacán; she married Antonio Zazueta, after October 3, 1806, in Culiacán; she died on May 12, 1836, in Culiacán.

Pedro Zazueta, son of Juan Zazueta and Juana Josefa Beltrán, was born about 1750.

Pedro Zazueta and María Manuela Esquer had the following known children:

    i. **José María Germán Zazueta** was born in 1794 in Culiacán. He was baptized on December 21, 1794, at the church of the Sagrario de San Miguel in Culiacán.[522] The baptismal record named María Josepha Páez as his *madrina*.

154 ii. **María Petra Zazueta** was born on May 14, 1797 in Culiacán; she married Manuel Páez on December 3, 1827, in Culiacán.

155 iii. **José Esteban Zazueta** was born on August 8, 1799, in Culiacán; he married Gertrudis Hernández on November 3, 1843, in Culiacán.

    iv. **Miguel Zazueta** was born on November 27, 1802, in Culiacán. The cited baptismal record provided his date of birth. He was baptized on December 4, 1802, at the church of the Sagrario de San Miguel in Culiacán.[523] The baptismal record named Miguel Antonio González Posada and María Josefa González Posada as his *padrinos*.

156 v. **Pedro Zazueta** was born about 1803; he married María de Jesús Palazuelos in April 4, 1837, in Culiacán.

157 vi. **María Rafaela Zazueta** was born on June 12, 1808, in Culiacán; she married Pedro Juan Tomás Verdugo about 1831 Culiacán and died on December 9, 1881, in Culiacán.

    vii. **María Basilia Zazueta** was born about 1810.[524] The cited baptismal record for Miguel María Verdugo Zazueta named Pedro and María Basilia Zazueta y Esquer as his *padrinos*. This helps make the case that María Basilia was the daughter of Pedro Zazueta and María Manuela Esquer.

91. María Josefa Esquer (Francisco Gabriel-6, Francisco Joseph-5, Juan Salvador-4, Salvador-3, Salvador-2, Blas-1) was born in 1772 in Culiacán. She was baptized on February 24, 1772, in Culiacán.[525] The baptismal record named José Esquer and Juana Cárdenas as her *padrinos*.

María Josefa Esquer and Francisco Rodríguez de la Rodriguera were married on September 13, 1790, at the church of the Sagrario de San Miguel in Culiacán.[526] The matrimonial record

522. Bautismos 1789–1805, December 21, 1794, film 665428, image 89, Registros Parroquiales, Iglesia Sagrario de San Miguel, Culiacán, Sinaloa, Mexico (FamilySearch, https://familysearch.org).
523. Bautismos 1789–1805, December 4, 1802, film 665428, image 298, Registros Parroquiales, Iglesia Sagrario de San Miguel, Culiacán, Sinaloa, Mexico (FamilySearch, https://familysearch.org).
524. Bautismos 1831–1838, October 10,1834, film 665431, image 273, Registros Parroquiales, Iglesia Sagrario de San Miguel, Culiacán, Sinaloa, Mexico (FamilySearch, https://familysearch.org).
525. Bautismos 1755–1789, February 24, 1772, film 665427, image 272, Registros Parroquiales, Iglesia Sagrario de San Miguel, Culiacán, Sinaloa, Mexico (FamilySearch, https://familysearch.org).
526. Matrimonios 1755–1784 [1794], September 13, 1790, film 673389, images 314–315, Registros

named Manuel Avellanar and Ygnacia Avilés [husband and wife] as *padrinos*. He was said to be twenty-five years of age at the time of his marriage.

Francisco Rodríguez de la Rodriguera, son of Francisco Rodríguez de la Rodriguera and Rita Astorga, was born about 1765 in Culiacán. The cited marriage record stated that he was born in Culiacán. He died on April 21, 1840, in Culiacán. He was buried on April 22, 1840, at the church of the Sagrario de San Miguel in Culiacán.[527] His funeral service was held with a *cruz alta*, and he was laid to rest in a burial site valued at three pesos.

Francisco Rodríguez de la Rodriguera and María Josefa Esquer had the following known children:

158 i.   **Yrene Rodríguez de la Rodriguera** was born about 1792; she married Francisco Palma y Mesa on July 28, 1812, in Culiacán.

    ii.   **Luis Seferino Rodríguez de la Rodriguera** was born in 1793 in Culiacán. He was baptized on September 27, 1793, at the church of the Sagrario de San Miguel in Culiacán.[528] The baptismal record named Luis Zasueta and Seferina Zasueta as his *padrinos*.

    iii.   **José María Rodríguez de la Rodriguera** was born between 1798 and 1805 in Culiacán. He died on December 1, 1805, in Culiacán. He was buried on December 2, 1805, at the church of the Sagrario de San Miguel in Culiacán.[529] His funeral service was held with a *cruz alta*, and the small child, *párvulo*, was laid to rest in a burial site valued at three pesos. His parents were named in the record.

    iv.   **María Manuela Severiana Rodríguez de la Rodriguera** was born on August 10, 1798, in Culiacán. The cited baptism record stated that she was born twenty-four days prior to her date of baptism. She was baptized on September 3, 1798, at the church of the Sagrario de San Miguel in Culiacán.[530] The baptismal record named Pedro Zasueta and his wife, Manuela Zasueta, as her *padrinos*.

159 v.   **María Teresa Cecilia Rodríguez de la Rodriguera** was born on February 1, 1801, in Culiacán; she married Pedro Suárez after August 20, 1837, in Culiacán.

    vi.   **Juan Francisco Rodríguez de la Rodriguera** was born on August 14, 1803, in Culiacán, according to the baptismal record. He was baptized on August 24, 1803, at the church of the Sagrario de San Miguel in Culiacán.[531] The baptismal record named Manuel Rojo and his wife, Nicolasa Esquer, as his *padrinos*.

Parroquiales, Iglesia Sagrario de San Miguel, Culiacán, Sinaloa, Mexico (FamilySearch, https://familysearch.org).

527. Defunciones 1933–1956, April 22, 1840, film 674052, image 130, Registros Parroquiales, Iglesia Sagrario de San Miguel, Culiacán, Sinaloa, Mexico (FamilySearch, https://familysearch.org).

528. Bautismos 1789–1805, September 27, 1793, film 665428, image 67, Registros Parroquiales, Iglesia Sagrario de San Miguel, Culiacán, Sinaloa, Mexico (FamilySearch, https://familysearch.org).

529. Defunciones 1746–1833, December 2, 1805, film 674051, image 331, Registros Parroquiales, Iglesia Sagrario de San Miguel, Culiacán, Sinaloa, Mexico (FamilySearch, https://familysearch.org).

530. Bautismos 1796–1818, September 3, 1798, film 665429, image 50, Registros Parroquiales, Iglesia Sagrario de San Miguel, Culiacán, Sinaloa, Mexico (FamilySearch, https://familysearch.org).

531. Bautismos 1789–1805, August 24, 1803, film 665428, image 315, Registros Parroquiales, Iglesia Sagrario de San Miguel, Culiacán, Sinaloa, Mexico (FamilySearch, https://familysearch.org).

160vii.   **María Rafaela Rodríguez de la Rodriguera** was born on March 4, 1807, in Culiacán; she married Claudio Zepeda on March 2, 1835, in Culiacán.

viii.   **María Josefa Úrsula Rodríguez de la Rodriguera** was born on October 22, 1809, in Culiacán, according to the baptismal record. She was baptized on November 1, 1809, at the church of the Sagrario de San Miguel in Culiacán.[532] The baptismal record named Rita Astorga, widow of Francisco Rodríguez de la Rodriguera as her *madrina*.

ix.   **Maria de Jesús Salomé Rodríguez de la Rodriguera** was born on October 22, 1814, in Culiacán, according to the baptismal record. She was baptized on October 25, 1814, at the church of the Sagrario de San Miguel in Culiacán.[533] The baptismal record named José María Trapero and Rosa Cadenas as her *padrinos*.

92. José Vicente Esquer (Luis Antonio-6, Francisco Joseph-5, Juan Salvador-4, Salvador-3, Salvador-2, Blas-1) was born in 1775 in Culiacán. He was baptized on December 1, 1775, in Culiacán.[534] The baptismal record named Marcos José de Guzmán as his *padrino*. Guzmán was said to have been from the city of Guadalajara, and was currently living in Culiacán.

José Vicente Esquer and Juana María Cayetana Fernández Rojo were married on November 4, 1795, at the church of the Sagrario de San Miguel in Culiacán.[535] The marriage record identified Nicolás Yturríos, Estanislao Vega, and Francisco Esteban de la Vega, among many others present, as witnesses to the marriage. Parents of the bride and groom were named, stating that the mother of the groom was deceased, as were the parents of the bride.

José Vicente died about 1798.[536] The cited baptismal record for his daughter Juana Paula Esquer, dated January 24, 1798, stated that he had died before she was born.

Juana María Cayetana Fernández Rojo, daughter of Francisco Fernández Rojo and Juana Alcayde, was born in 1772 in Culiacán. She was baptized on August 17, 1772, at the church of the Sagrario de San Miguel in Culiacán.[537] The baptismal record named Rosa María de Avilés as her *madrina*.

José Vicente Esquer and Juana María Cayetana Fernández Rojo had the following known children:

---

532. Bautismos 1796–1818, film 665429, November 1, 1809, image 295, Registros Parroquiales, Iglesia Sagrario de San Miguel, Culiacán, Sinaloa, Mexico (FamilySearch, https://familysearch.org).

533. Bautismos 1796–1818, October 25, 1814, film 665429, image 468, Registros Parroquiales, Iglesia Sagrario de San Miguel, Culiacán, Sinaloa, Mexico (FamilySearch, https://familysearch.org).

534. Bautismos 1755–1789, December 1, 1775, film 665427, image 355, Registros Parroquiales, Iglesia Sagrario de San Miguel, Culiacán, Sinaloa, Mexico (FamilySearch, https://familysearch.org).

535. Matrimonios 1755–1829, November 4, 1795, film 673378, images 214–215, Registros Parroquiales, Iglesia Sagrario de San Miguel, Culiacán, Sinaloa, Mexico (FamilySearch, https://familysearch.org).

536. Bautismos 1796–1818, January 28, 1798, film 665429, images 37–38, Registros Parroquiales, Iglesia Sagrario de San Miguel, Culiacán, Sinaloa, Mexico (FamilySearch, https://familysearch.org).

537. Bautismos 1755–1789, August 17, 1772, film 665427, image 293, Registros Parroquiales, Iglesia Sagrario de San Miguel, Culiacán, Sinaloa, Mexico (FamilySearch, https://familysearch.org).

i.   **María Asención Esquer** was born about 1796 in Culiacán.[538]

ii.   **Máximo Esquer** was born about 1797 in Culiacán.[539]

iii.   **Juana Paula Esquer** was born on January 24, 1798, in Culiacán. The baptismal record stated that she was born four days prior to her day of baptism. She was baptized on January 28, 1798, at the church of the Sagrario de San Miguel in Culiacán.[540] The baptismal record named Luis Esquer and Antonia Alcayde as her *padrinos*. The record appears to say that her father José Vicente Esquer died before Juana Paula was born.

93. José Joaquín Esquer (Pedro Sebastián-6, Francisco Joseph-5, Juan Salvador-4, Salvador-3, Salvador-2, Blas-1) was born about 1768. José Joaquín Esquer and María Loreto Anguís were married on June 19, 1787, at the church of the Purísima Concepción in Álamos.[541] The matrimonial record named Manuel Anguís and Augustina Anguís as *padrinos*. Juan Tomás Padilla, age sixty-one; José Padilla, age sixty-two; and Pedro Bravo, more than forty years of age, were named as witnesses to the couple's liberty to marry. Juan Francisco Padilla and Melchor Amarillas were named as witnesses to the marriage. The bride and groom were related in the fourth degree of consanguinity, meaning they were third cousins. For that reason, a marriage dispensation was required.

As per the cited marriage investigation, the dispensation was issued on June 12, 1787.[542] Parents of the couple were named in the record. The bride's father was said to have been deceased.

María Loreto Anguís, daughter of Thomas Antonio Anguís and Juana de Dios María Gil Samaniego, was born on September 8, 1769, in Álamos, according to the baptismal record. She was baptized on September 17, 1769, at the church of the Purísima Concepción in Álamos.[543] The baptismal record named Policarpo Velarde and Francisca Mallén de Navarrete as her *padrinos*. María Loreto died before October 20, 1793, in Álamos. The cited baptismal record for her infant daughter María Tomasa Loreto del Carmen stated that her mother was deceased.

José Joaquín Esquer and María Loreto Anguís had the following known children:

161   i.   **Miguel Ygnacio Dolores Antonio de la Luz Esquer** was born September 29, 1788, in Álamos; he married María del Carmen Martínez Mendívil on May 11, 1831, in Álamos.

---

538. Padrones del estado de Sinaloa, Mexico 1778–1804, Archivo Franciscano de la Biblioteca Nacional de México. Padrón de la Villa de Culiacán, 1804, item 2, caja 37, exp. 821, pp 1–24v, film 1149545 Item 2 (FamilySearch, https://familysearch.org).

539. Ibid.

540. Bautismos 1796–1818, January 28, 1798, film 665429, images 37–38, Registros Parroquiales, Iglesia Sagrario de San Miguel, Culiacán, Sinaloa, Mexico (FamilySearch, https://familysearch.org).

541. Matrimonios 1779–1817, June 19, 1787, film 666565, image 113, Registros Parroquiales, Iglesia de La Purísima Concepción, Álamos, Sonora, Mexico (FamilySearch, https://familysearch.org).

542. Información matrimonial 1760–1799, June 12, 1787, film 667002, images 482–483, Registros Parroquiales, Iglesia de La Purísima Concepción, Álamos, Sonora, Mexico (FamilySearch, https://familysearch.org).

543. Bautismos, matrimonios y defunciones 1696–1699 bautismos 1768–1781, September 17, 1769, film 663487, image 138, Registros Parroquiales, Iglesia de La Purísima Concepción, Álamos, Sonora, Mexico (FamilySearch, https://familysearch.org).

162 ii. **María Josefa Dolores Esquer** was born on July 8, 1790, in El Fuerte; she married Juan José Trinidad Francisco Vicente Gervasio Ortíz, on June 11, 1808, in Álamos and died on November 24, 1868, in Álamos.

iii. **Ygnacio Esquer** was born before September 22, 1792. He died on September 22, 1792, in Álamos. Ygnacio was buried on September 23, 1792, at the church of the Purísima Concepción in Álamos.[544] His funeral service was held with *cruz alta, capa e incensario y caja*. He was interred in a burial site valued at five pesos.

iv. **María Tomasa Loreto del Carmen Esquer** was born on September 18, 1793, in Álamos, according to the baptismal record. She was baptized on October 20, 1793, at the church of the Purísima Concepción in Álamos.[545] The baptismal record named her father José Joaquín Esquer and her grandmother Juana Gil Samaniego as her *padrinos*. The record stated that the child's mother was deceased. The child must have received the waters of baptism before this date because the record stated that she was baptized conditionally on October 20, 1793. In all likelihood her mother died in childbirth, and the baby was thought to have been in danger of death.

94. José Miguel Rojo (María Nicolasa Esquer-6, Francisco Joseph-5, Juan Salvador-4, Salvador-3, Salvador-2, Blas-1) was born on February 19, 1765, in Culiacán. The baptismal record stated that he was born eight days prior to his date of baptism. He was baptized on February 27, 1765, at the church of the Sagrario de San Miguel in Culiacán.[546] The baptismal record named Ygnacio López and Cleta de Esquer as his *padrinos*.

José Miguel Rojo and Josefa Amarillas were married on July 9, 1788, at the church of the Sagrario de San Miguel in Culiacán.[547] The matrimonial record named Miguel Pérez and Martín de León as witnesses to the marriage. The couple received a dispensation to marry because they were related both in the second, with a third degree of consanguinity, and also in the fourth degree of consanguinity. This means they were first cousins, once removed, and also third cousins. The couple received a nuptial blessing on the day of their marriage. Parents of the bride and groom were named in the record.

José Miguel Rojo died before July 8, 1830.[548] The cited marriage record for his daughter, María Guadalupe, stated that he was deceased at the time the marriage took place.

---

544. Defunciones 1717–1751, 1764–1792, September 23, 1792, film 666995, image 561, Registros Parroquiales, Iglesia de La Purísima Concepción, Álamos, Sonora, Mexico (FamilySearch, https://familysearch.org).
545. Bautismos 1781–1796, October 20, 1793, film 663488, image 606, Registros Parroquiales, Iglesia de La Purísima Concepción, Álamos, Sonora, Mexico (FamilySearch, https://familysearch.org).
546. Matrimonios 1731–1755, February 27, film 665426, image 228, Registros Parroquiales, Iglesia Sagrario de San Miguel, Culiacán, Sinaloa, Mexico (FamilySearch, https://familysearch.org).
547. Matrimonios 1755–1784, July 9, 1788, film 673389, image 301, Registros Parroquiales, Iglesia Sagrario de San Miguel, Culiacán, Sinaloa, Mexico (FamilySearch, https://familysearch.org).
548. Matrimonios 1830–1856, July 8, 1830, film 673379, image 13, Registros Parroquiales, Iglesia Sagrario de San Miguel, Culiacán, Sinaloa, Mexico (FamilySearch, https://familysearch.org).

Josefa Amarillas, daughter of José María Amarillas and Micaela López, was born about 1767. She died before April 17, 1824.[549] The cited marriage information record dated April 17, 1824, provided testimony for her widowed husband to remarry. The record stated that Josefa Amarillas was deceased at the time.

José Miguel Rojo and Josefa Amarillas had the following known children:

i.   **María Nicolasa Simona Rojo** was born in 1790 in Culiacán. She was baptized on November 18, 1790, at the church of the Sagrario de San Miguel in Culiacán.[550] The baptismal record named María Francisca Fernández Rojo y Alcayde as her *madrina*. She appeared in the census in 1804 in Culiacán.[551]

ii.   **José María Fernández Rojo** was born between 1796 and 1803. He died on July 21, 1803, in Culiacán. He was buried on July 22, 1803, at the church of the Sagrario de San Miguel in Culiacán.[552] José María Fernández Rojo died as a child, *párvulo*, and was buried under the choir of the church. His parents were named in the burial record.

163 iii.   **Seferina Rojo** was born in 1800 in Culiacán; she married Rafael Féliz on January 9, 1827, in Culiacán.

iv.   **Juana Josefa Paula Rojo** was born on January 25, 1802, in Culiacán according to the baptismal record. She was baptized on February 7, 1802, at the church of the Sagrario de San Miguel in Culiacán.[553] The baptismal record named María Gertrudis Páez, wife of José Antonio López, as her *madrina*. She appeared in the census in 1804 in Culiacán.[554] Juana Josefa Paula died on January 13, 1885, at the age of eighty-two in Culiacán. Juana was buried on January 14, 1885, at the church of the Sagrario de San Miguel in Culiacán.[555] Her funeral service was held with a *cruz baja*. Juana Josefa Paula received the last sacraments of the Catholic Church before her death. Her parents were named in the burial record.

v.   **Gregorio Rojo** was born before 1804 in Culiacán. He appeared in the census in 1804 in Culiacán.[556] He died on December 28, 1835, at the age of 31 in Culiacán.

549. Información matrimonial 1819–1830, April 17, 1824, film 673451, images 173–174, Registros Parroquiales, Iglesia Sagrario de San Miguel, Culiacán, Sinaloa, Mexico (FamilySearch, https://familysearch.org).

550. Bautismos 1789–1805, November 18, 1790, film 665428, image 18, Registros Parroquiales, Iglesia Sagrario de San Miguel, Culiacán, Sinaloa, Mexico (FamilySearch, https://familysearch.org).

551. Padrones del estado de Sinaloa, Mexico 1778–1804, Archivo Franciscano de la Biblioteca Nacional de México. Padrón de la Villa de Culiacán, 1804, item 2, caja 37, exp. 821, pp 1–24v, film 1149545 Item 2 (FamilySearch, https:// familysearch.org).

552. Defunciones 1746–1833, July 22, 1803, film 674051, image 414, Registros Parroquiales, Iglesia Sagrario de San Miguel, Culiacán, Sinaloa, Mexico (FamilySearch, https://familysearch.org).

553. Bautismos 1789–1805, February 7, 1802, film 665428, images 286–287, Registros Parroquiales, Iglesia Sagrario de San Miguel, Culiacán, Sinaloa, Mexico (FamilySearch, https://familysearch.org).

554. Padrones del estado de Sinaloa, Mexico 1778–1804, Archivo Franciscano de la Biblioteca Nacional de México. Padrón de la Villa de Culiacán, 1804, item 2, caja 37, exp. 821, pp 1–24v, film 1149545 Item 2 (FamilySearch, https://familysearch.org).

555. Defunciones 1856–1919, image 325, Registros Parroquiales, Iglesia Sagrario de San Miguel, Culiacán, Sinaloa, Mexico (FamilySearch, https://familysearch.org).

556. Padrones del estado de Sinaloa, Mexico 1778–1804, Archivo Franciscano de la Biblioteca Nacional de México. Padrón de la Villa de Culiacán, 1804, item 2, caja 37, exp. 821, pp 1–24v, film 1149545 Item 2

Gregorio was buried on December 29, 1835, at the church of the Sagrario de San Miguel in Culiacán.[557] Gregorio was identified as a single adult. His funeral service was held with a *cruz baja*. He was interred in a burial site valued at three pesos. The burial record stated that he died of a fever related to a wound on his arm, and that he received the last sacraments of the Catholic Church. His parents were named.

164 vi.   **José Antonio Rojo** was born before 1804 in Culiacán; he married María Guadalupe Rojo on October 1, 1828, in Culiacán.

vii.   **Francisco Rojo** was born before 1804 in Culiacán. He appeared in the census in 1804 in Culiacán.[558]

165 viii.   **José de Jesús Rojo**, was born about 1809; he married Ana María López on October 25, 1837, in Culiacán.

166 ix.   **María Guadalupe Rojo** was born about 1816; she married Pedro Amarillas on July 8, 1830, in Culiacán.

José Miguel Rojo and Gertrudis Medina were married on April 26, 1824, at the church of the Sagrario de San Miguel in Culiacán.[559] The matrimonial record named Manuel Romero and Manuel Avilés as witnesses to the act of matrimony. The record stated that the groom was a widower, having previously been married to María Josefa Amarillas. The couple received a nuptial blessing on the day of their marriage. Parents of the bride were named.

The cited marriage information record, dated April 17, 1824, found no impediment to marriage.[560] The bride and groom were said to be forty and fifty-five years of age, respectively. However, the cited baptism record for José Miguel figured that he was actually fifty-nine years of age in 1824. Only the parents of the bride were named in the record. There are no known children from this marriage.

Gertrudis Medina, daughter of José Medina and Manuela López, was born in 1784. The cited marriage information record for Gertrudis Medina stated that she was forty years of age at the time of her marriage.

95. María Juana Rafaela Rojo (María Nicolasa Esquer-6, Francisco Joseph-5, Juan Salvador-4, Salvador-3, Salvador-2, Blas-1) was born about 1767 in Culiacán. The cited marriage record stated that she originated in Culiacán. She was also known as "Rafaela Rojo."

(FamilySearch, https:// familysearch.org).

557. Defunciones 1933–1956, December 29, 1835, film 674052, image 54, Registros Parroquiales, Iglesia Sagrario de San Miguel, Culiacán, Sinaloa, Mexico (FamilySearch, https://familysearch.org).

558. Padrones del estado de Sinaloa, Mexico 1778–1804, Archivo Franciscano de la Biblioteca Nacional de México. Padrón de la Villa de Culiacán, 1804, item 2, caja 37, exp. 821, pp 1–24v, film 1149545 Item 2 (FamilySearch, https:// familysearch.org).

559. Matrimonios 1755–1829, April 26, 1824, film 673378, image 437, Registros Parroquiales, Iglesia Sagrario de San Miguel, Culiacán, Sinaloa, Mexico (FamilySearch, https://familysearch.org).

560. Información matrimonial 1819–1830, April 17, 1824, film 673451, images 173–174, Registros Parroquiales, Iglesia Sagrario de San Miguel, Culiacán, Sinaloa, Mexico (FamilySearch, https://familysearch.org).

María Juana Rafaela Rojo and José Manuel Palazuelos were married on May 16, 1788, at the church of the Sagrario de San Miguel in Culiacán.[561] The matrimonial record named Manuel Romero, Dionisio de León, and Martín de León as witnesses to the marriage. The couple received a nuptial blessing on the day of their marriage. Parents of the bride and groom were not named.

José Manuel Palazuelos was born about 1758 in Culiacán. The marriage record stated that he was born in Culiacán. He died on June 10, 1813, in Culiacán. He was buried on June 11, 1813, at the church of the Sagrario de San Miguel in Culiacán.[562] His funeral service was held with a *cruz alta* and he was laid to rest in a burial site valued at three pesos. The record stated that José Manuel died of natural causes at the age of fifty-five, and that he had been married to Juana Rafaela Rojo.

José Manuel Palazuelos and María Juana Rafaela Rojo had the following known children:

167 i.   **José María Palazuelos** was born about 1791; he married María Isabel Castro on April 23, 1813, in Culiacán.

    ii.   **Ana Palazuelos** was born in 1792. She died on September 25, 1814, of natural causes at the age of twenty-two in Culiacán. Ana was buried on September 26, 1814, at the church of the Sagrario de San Miguel in Culiacán.[563] Her funeral service was held with a *cruz baja* and she was buried in a site valued at three pesos. The record stated that Ana was single, and the daughter of José Manuel Palazuelos and Rafaela Rojo. She received the sacrament of penance and the Holy Eucharist before her death.

168 iii.   **José Manuel Palazuelos** was born in 1795. He married three times, first to María Loreto Baldenegro on September 28, 1824; next to María Josefa Isideria Páez on November 17, 1831, and last to María Gertrudis Rodríguez de la Rodriguera on March 7, 1840. All three marriages were in Culiacán.

    iv.   **María Benigna Estéfana Palazuelos** was born on December 27, 1798, in Culiacán, according to the baptismal record. She was baptized on January 2, 1799, at the church of the Sagrario de San Miguel in Culiacán.[564] The baptismal record named Nicolás Iturríos and María Nicolasa Esquer as her *padrinos*.

169 v.   **José Laureano Palazuelos** was born on June 4, 1800, in Culiacán; he married Concepción Murrieta on April 28, 1829, in Culiacán.

170 vi.   **María Rosa Palazuelos** was born about 1801; she married Timoteo Hernández on July 2, 1826, in Culiacán.

171 vii.   **María Antonia Palazuelos** was born on May 6, 1803, in Culiacán; she married Pedro José Páez on November 3, 1824, in Culiacán.

561. Matrimonios 1755–1784, May 16, 1788, film 673389, images 300–301, Registros Parroquiales, Iglesia Sagrario de San Miguel, Culiacán, Sinaloa, Mexico (FamilySearch, https://familysearch.org).
562. Defunciones 1746–1833, June 11, 1813, film 674051, image 453, Registros Parroquiales, Iglesia Sagrario de San Miguel, Culiacán, Sinaloa, Mexico (FamilySearch, https://familysearch.org).
563. Defunciones 1746–1833, September 26, 1814, film 674051, images 465–466, Registros Parroquiales, Iglesia Sagrario de San Miguel, Culiacán, Sinaloa, Mexico (FamilySearch, https://familysearch.org).
564. Bautismos 1796–1818, January 2, 1799, film 665429, image 59, Registros Parroquiales, Iglesia Sagrario de San Miguel, Culiacán, Sinaloa, Mexico (FamilySearch, https://familysearch.org).

172viii.   **Justo Palazuelos** was born about 1810; he married María de Jesús Castro on
November 15, 1832, in Culiacán.

173 ix.   **Casimiro Palazuelos** was born about 1812; he married María Josefa Niebla on
August 31, 1842, Culiacán.

96. **José Manuel Rojo** (María Nicolasa Esquer-6, Francisco Joseph-5, Juan Salvador-4,
Salvador-3, Salvador-2, Blas-1) was born in 1771 in Culiacán. He was baptized on August 9,
1771, at the church of the Sagrario de San Miguel in Culiacán.[565] The baptismal record named
Francisco de la Vega and Loreto Verdugo y Chávez as his *padrinos*.

José Manuel Rojo and Rafaela Palazuelos Cárdenas were married about 1791. The matrimonial
record has not been located, but the cited burial record for Rafaela Palazuelos stated that she had
been married to Manuel Rojo.

Rafaela Palazuelos Cárdenas died on January 28, 1823, in Culiacán. She was buried on January
29, 1823, at the church of the Sagrario de San Miguel in Culiacán.[566] Her funeral service was
held with a *cruz alta* and she was buried in a plot valued at three pesos. The burial record named
Manuel Rojo as her husband.

97. **María Manuela Iturríos** (Augustina Anguís-6, María Mallén de Navarrete-5, Agustina Salvadora Esquer-4, Salvador-3, Salvador-2, Blas-1) was born about 1775 in Culiacán. The cited
matrimonial record stated that she had originated in Culiacán.

María Manuela Iturríos and Nicolás Inocencio Eseverri were married on January 10, 1795,
at the church of Santa Úrsula in Cosalá.[567] The matrimonial record named Francisco Cruz de
Echeverría and Ana Maria Morales as *padrinos*. Ramón Imperial and Diego Muñoz were named
as witnesses to the marriage. Parents of the bride and groom were named in the record, and the
father of the bride was said to have been deceased. The couple received a nuptial blessing on
their wedding day.

María Manuela Iturríos died on November 19, 1835, in Cosalá. She was buried on November
20, 1835, at the church of Santa Úrsula in Cosalá.[568] The burial record is difficult to read but
stated that she was the widow of Inocencio Eseverri and that she was survived by three children,
two sons and one daughter. The children were not named. She died of a urinary condition, *mal
de orina*.

Nicolás Inocencio Eseverri, son of Juan Miguel Eseverri and María Antonia Rita Elizalde, was
born about 1775. The cited burial record stated that he was forty years of age at the time of his

565. Bautismos 1755–1789, August 9, 1771, film 665427, image 260, Registros Parroquiales, Iglesia Sagrario de
San Miguel, Culiacán, Sinaloa, Mexico (FamilySearch, https://familysearch.org).
566. Defunciones 1746–1833, January 29, 1823, film 674051, image 570, Registros Parroquiales, Iglesia
Sagrario de San Miguel, Culiacán, Sinaloa, Mexico (FamilySearch, https://familysearch.org).
567. Información matrimonial 1793–1801, 1831–1832, January 10, 1795, film 665883, image 42, Registros
Parroquiales, Iglesia de Santa Úrsula, Cosalá, Sinaloa, Mexico (FamilySearch, https://familysearch.org).
568. Defunciones 1818–1837, November 20, 1835, film 665901, image 499, Registros Parroquiales, Iglesia de
Santa Úrsula, Cosalá, Sinaloa, Mexico (FamilySearch, https://familysearch.org).

death. That presents a problem because it would have made him twelve years of age at the time of his marriage. His birth year has been adjusted to reflect that he was about twenty years of age at the time of his marriage. He died on August 24, 1823, in Cosalá. He was buried on August 25, 1823, at the church of Santa Úrsula in Cosalá.[569] His funeral service was held with *cruz alta, ataúd, y dos mesas*. He was said to have died of a [presumed] sudden respiratory attack (*insulto de aire*) and that he had been married to María Manuela Iturríos. He was administered the last sacraments of the Catholic Church before his death. He was interred in a in a burial site valued at twenty-five pesos.

Nicolás Inocencio Eseverri and María Manuela Iturríos had the following known children:

    i.   **Mariana Eseverri** was born between 1795 and 1800 in Culiacán. She died on March 29, 1800, in Culiacán. She was buried on March 30, 1800, at the church of the Sagrario de San Miguel in Culiacán.[570] She was said to have been a small child, *párvula*, and that her funeral service was held with *cruz alta, capa y caja*. The record named her parents, stating that they were *vecinos* of Cosalá.

    ii.   **Pedro Ignacio Eseverri** was born about 1797. The cited burial record stated that he was fifty-four years of age at death. He died on August 3, 1851, in Cosalá. He was buried on August 4, 1851, in Cosalá.[571] His burial service was held with *cruz baja y ataúd*. He was buried in the cemetery (details for locating the burial site were provided in the record). He died of cholera and received the last sacraments of the Catholic Church before death. His parents were named in the record.

    iii.   **José María Eseverri** was born about 1796 in Cosalá. The cited burial record claimed that he was over sixty years of age when he died. He died on December 15, 1856, in Cosalá. He was buried on December 16, 1856, in Cosalá.[572] His funeral service was held with *cruz alta y dos mesas*. He was interred in the cemetery in a site valued at five pesos (details for locating the burial site were provided in the record). The record stated that he was single, that he died of an inflammation, and that he had received the last sacraments of the Catholic Church before death.

98. Joseph Raphael Leandro Anguís (Thomas Antonio-6, María Mallén de Navarrete-5, Agustina Salvadora Esquer-4, Salvador-3, Salvador-2, Blas-1) was born in 1766 in Álamos. He was baptized on March 6, 1766, at the church of the Purísima Concepción in Álamos.[573] The baptismal record named Pedro Gil Samaniego and María Balvanera Velarde as his *padrinos*.

---

569. Defunciones 1818–1837, August 25, 1823, film 665901, image 121, Registros Parroquiales, Iglesia de Santa Úrsula, Cosalá, Sinaloa, Mexico (FamilySearch, https://familysearch.org).

570. Defunciones 1746–1833, March 30, 1800 film 674051, image 394, Registros Parroquiales, Iglesia Sagrario de San Miguel, Culiacán, Sinaloa, Mexico (FamilySearch, https://familysearch.org).

571. Defunciones 1845–1855, August 4, 1851, film 665904, image 317, Registros Parroquiales, Iglesia de Santa Úrsula, Cosalá, Sinaloa, Mexico (FamilySearch, https://familysearch.org).

572. Defunciones 1845–1855, December 16, 1856, film 665904, image 554, Registros Parroquiales, Iglesia de Santa Úrsula, Cosalá, Sinaloa, Mexico (FamilySearch, https://familysearch.org).

573. Bautismos 1751–1794, matrimonios 1848, defunciones 1735–1752, March 6, 1766, film 666999, image 325, Registros Parroquiales, Iglesia de La Purísima Concepción, Álamos, Sonora, Mexico (FamilySearch, https://familysearch.org).

Those present included Juan Antonio de Anguís, Julián de Alvarado, and others from within the vicinity.

Joseph Raphael Leandro Anguís and María Francisca Gastélum were married on February 26, 1794, at the church of the Purísima Concepción in Álamos.[574] The marriage record named Sebastián Esquer and Rita Gil Samaniego as *padrinos*. José Bustillos and José María Bustillos, among many others, were said to have been present at the marriage. Parents of the bride and groom were named in the record. Thomas Anguís, father of the groom, and Joaquín Gastélum, father of the bride, were said to have been deceased.

María Francisca Gastélum, daughter of Joaquín Gastélum and María Gertrudis Perpetua de Murrieta, was born about 1777 in Álamos. The cited matrimonial record stated that María Francisca Gastélum originated in the Puesto de Casanate. She died on September 1, 1795, in Álamos. She was buried on September 2, 1795, at the church of the Purísima Concepción in Álamos.[575] María Francisca's funeral service was held with *cruz alta, capa, incensario, y ataúd.* Her husband was said to have owed for the burial expenses. The variant spelling "Castelo," rather than "Gastélum" was used in the burial record.

Joseph Raphael Leandro Anguís and María Francisca Gastélum had one known child:

i.   **José Ygnacio de Jesús Anguís** was born in 1795 in Álamos. He was baptized on March 26, 1795, at the church of the Purísima Concepción in Álamos.[576] The baptismal record named Juana Gil Samaniego as his *madrina*. He was buried on September 2, 1795, at the church of the Purísima Concepción in Álamos.[577] The burial record simply identifies the child as a *párvulo*. His funeral service and burial were held *bajo del coro, con cruz alta.* It was noted that there was an outstanding balance due for the funeral.

Joseph Raphael Leandro Anguís and María Manuela Gil Samaniego were married on October 30, 1797, at the church of the Purísima Concepción in Álamos.[578] The matrimonial record stated that the bride and groom were related in the third degree of consanguinity, meaning they are second cousins. They were also related to the fourth degree in affinity. For these reasons they received a dispensation from the bishop of Sonora for their marriage. José Mendívil and Rita Gil Samaniego were named as *padrinos*. José Bustillos, Ignacio Güereña, Gabriel Lara, and Ramón Gil were named as witnesses to the marriage. Parents of the bride and groom were named. The father of the groom was said to have been deceased, as were both parents of the bride.

574. Matrimonios 1779–1817, February 26, 1794, film 666565, image 271, Registros Parroquiales, Iglesia de La Purísima Concepción, Álamos, Sonora, Mexico (FamilySearch, https://familysearch.org).
575. Defunciones 1786–1819, September 2, 1795, film 666996, image 71, Registros Parroquiales, Iglesia de La Purísima Concepción, Álamos, Sonora, Mexico (FamilySearch, https://familysearch.org).
576. Bautismos 1791–1796,1805–1815, March 26, 1795, film 663996, images 161–162, Registros Parroquiales, Iglesia de La Purísima Concepción, Álamos, Sonora, Mexico (FamilySearch, https://familysearch.org).
577. Defunciones 1786–1819, September 2, 1795, film 666996, image 71, Registros Parroquiales, Iglesia de La Purísima Concepción, Álamos, Sonora, Mexico (FamilySearch, https://familysearch.org).
578. Matrimonios 1779–1817, October 30, 1797, film 666565, image 338, Registros Parroquiales, Iglesia de La Purísima Concepción, Álamos, Sonora, Mexico (FamilySearch, https://familysearch.org).

The cited marriage information, dated February 2, 1797, disclosed that the relationship of fourth degree in affinity was due to the familial relationship between the two wives.[579] Note was also made that Joseph Raphael Leonardo Anguís had been previously married to María Francisca Gastélum.

María Manuela Gil Samaniego, daughter of Pedro Joseph Gil Samaniego and Juana María Urvina, was born about 1775 in Álamos. The cited matrimonial record provided her place of birth.

Joseph Raphael Leandro Anguís and María Manuela Gil Samaniego had the following known children:

i. **José Atanasio Agustín Antonio de Jesús Anguís** was born in 1807 in Álamos. He was baptized on May 4, 1807, at the church of the Purísima Concepción in Álamos.[580] The baptismal record named Francisco Gil Samaniego and Loreto Esquer as his *padrinos*.

ii. **José Rafael Nicolás de la Concepción Anguís** was born in 1808 in Álamos. He was baptized on December 7, 1808, at the church of the Purísima Concepción in Álamos.[581] The baptismal record named Manuel Ygnacio Gil Samaniego and María Dolores Avilés as his *padrinos*.

iii. **María Ignacia Anguís** died on May 17, 1826, in Álamos. She was buried on May 18, 1826, in Álamos.[582] Her funeral service was held with *cruz alta, incensario, cajón con tapa y mesa*. She was interred in a burial site valued at five pesos.

99. **María Loreto Anguís** (Thomas Antonio-6, María Mallén de Navarrete-5, Agustina Salvadora Esquer-4, Salvador-3, Salvador-2, Blas-1) was born on September 8, 1769, in Álamos, according to the baptismal record. She was baptized on September 17, 1769, at the church of the Purísima Concepción in Álamos.[583] The baptismal record named Policarpo Velarde and Francisca Mallén de Navarrete as her *padrinos*.

María Loreto Anguís and José Joaquín Esquer were married on June 19, 1787, at the church of the Purísima Concepción in Álamos.[584] The matrimonial record named Manuel Anguís and

579. Información matrimonial 1760–1799, February 2, 1797, film 667002, images 656–657, Registros Parroquiales, Iglesia de La Purísima Concepción, Álamos, Sonora, Mexico (FamilySearch, https://familysearch.org).

580. Bautismos 1791–1796, 1805–1815, May 4, 1807, film 663996, image 281, Registros Parroquiales, Iglesia de La Purísima Concepción, Álamos, Sonora, Mexico (FamilySearch, https://familysearch.org).

581. Bautismos 1791–1796, 1805–1815, December 7, 1808, film 663996, image 318, Registros Parroquiales, Iglesia de La Purísima Concepción, Álamos, Sonora, Mexico (FamilySearch, https://familysearch.org).

582. Defunciones 1809–1842, May 18, 1826, film 666997, image 116, RegistrosParroquiales, Iglesia de La Purísima Concepción, Álamos, Sonora, Mexico (FamilySearch, https://familysearch.org).

583. Bautismos, matrimonios y defunciones 1696–1699 bautismos 1768–1781, September 17, 1769, film 663487, image 138, Registros Parroquiales, Iglesia de La Purísima Concepción, Álamos, Sonora, Mexico (FamilySearch, https:// familysearch.org).

584. Matrimonios 1779–1817, June 19, 1787, film 666565, image 113, Registros Parroquiales, Iglesia de La Purísima Concepción, Álamos, Sonora, Mexico (FamilySearch, https://familysearch.org).

Augustina Anguís as *padrinos*. Juan Tomás Padilla, age sixty-one; José Padilla, age sixty-two; and Pedro Bravo, more than forty years of age, were named as witnesses to the couple's liberty to marry. Juan Francisco Padilla and Melchor Amarillas were named as witnesses to the marriage. The bride and groom were related in the fourth degree of consanguinity, meaning they were third cousins. For that reason, a marriage dispensation was required. As per the cited marriage investigation, the dispensation was issued on June 12, 1787.[585] Parents of the couple were named in the record. The bride's father was said to have been deceased.

María Loreto died before October 20, 1793, in Álamos. The cited baptismal record for her infant daughter María Tomasa Loreto del Carmen stated that her mother was deceased.

José Joaquín Esquer, son of Pedro Sebastián Esquer and Anna María Murrieta, was born about 1768.

José Joaquín Esquer and María Loreto Anguís had the following known children:

161 i.   **Miguel Ygnacio Dolores Antonio de la Luz Esquer** was born on September 29, 1788 in Álamos; he married María del Carmen Martínez Mendívil on May 11, 1831, in Álamos.

162 ii.   **María Josefa Dolores Esquer** wa born on July 8, 1790, in El Fuerte; she married Juan José Trinidad Francisco Vicente Gervasio Ortíz on June 11, 1808, in Álamos, and she died on November 24, 1868, in Álamos.

iii.   **Ygnacio Esquer** was born before September 22, 1792. He died on September 22, 1792, in Álamos. Ygnacio was buried on September 23, 1792, at the church of the Purísima Concepción in Álamos.[586] His funeral service was held with *cruz alta, capa e incensario y caja*. He was interred in a burial site valued at five pesos.

iv.   **María Tomasa Loreto del Carmen Esquer** was born on September 18, 1793, in Álamos, according to the baptismal record. She was baptized on October 20, 1793, at the church of the Purísima Concepción in Álamos.[587] The baptismal record named her father José Joaquín Esquer and her grandmother Juana Gil Samaniego as her *padrinos*. The record stated that the child's mother was deceased. The child must have received the waters of baptism before this date because the record stated that she was baptized conditionally on October 20, 1793. In all likelihood her mother died in childbirth and the baby was thought to have been in danger of death.

100. **María Josepha Luisa Anguís** (Thomas Antonio6, María Mallén de Navarrete-5, Agustina Salvadora Esquer-4, Salvador-3, Salvador-2, Blas-1) was born in 1772 in Álamos. She was baptized

585. Información matrimonial 1760–1799, June 12, 1787, film 667002, images 482–483, Registros Parroquiales, Iglesia de La Purísima Concepción, Álamos, Sonora, Mexico (FamilySearch, https://familysearch. org).
586. Defunciones 1717–1751, 1764–1792, September 23, 1792, film 666995, image 561, Registros Parroquiales, Iglesia de La Purísima Concepción, Álamos, Sonora, Mexico (FamilySearch, https://familysearch. org).
587. Bautismos 1781–1796, October 20, 1793, film 663488, image 606, Registros Parroquiales, Iglesia de La Purísima Concepción, Álamos, Sonora, Mexico (FamilySearch, https://familysearch.org).

on March 8, 1772, at the church of the Purísima Concepción in Álamos.[588] The baptismal record did not name *padrinos*.

María Josepha Luisa Anguís and Juan Antonio Avilés were married on December 21, 1788, at the parish of the Purísima Concepción in Álamos.[589] The matrimonial record named Manuel Anguís and Andrea Gil Samaniego as *padrinos*. José Francisco Rosas, Ignacio Beldarraín, Luis María Beldarraín, and José Bustillos, among others were identified as witnesses to the marriage. Parents of the bride and groom were named. The marriage took place at the home of Lucas de la Serna. A dispensation, dated December 17, 1788, was necessary because the couple were related in the third degree of consanguinity, meaning they were second cousins. The record stated that Juan Antonio Avilés had first been married to María de la Luz Martín Bernal.

Juan Antonio Avilés, son of Juan Miguel Avilés and María Antonia Zamorano, was born about 1768.

Juan Antonio Avilés and María Josepha Luisa Anguís had one known child:

i. **María Dolores Avilés** was born on May 16, 1790, in El Fuerte, according to the baptismal record. She was baptized on June 12, 1790, at the church of the Sagrado Corazón in El Fuerte.[590] The baptismal record named Raphael Anguís and Juana Gil as her *padrinos*.

María Josepha Luisa Anguís and Joseph Antonio Mucio Gil Samaniego were married on October 9, 1793, at the church of the Purísima Concepción in Álamos.[591] The matrimonial record named Antonio Gil Samaniego, the groom's brother, and Andrea Gil as *padrinos*. José Bustillos and Blas Miranda, among others were identified as witnesses to the marriage. Parents of the bride and groom were also named. The record stated that María Josefa Luisa Anguís was the widow of Juan Antonio Avilés, and that the couple had received a dispensation to marry from the bishop. Thomas Anguís, father of the bride was said to have been deceased at the time. The couple received a nuptial blessing on the day they were married.

The dispensation for marriage was granted on September 14, 1793.[592] The cited marriage investigation claimed that the couple were related in the third degree of consanguinity, meaning they were second cousins. They were also related by affinity in the third degree for *cópula lícita* (permitted sexual relations) in which they were legally bound to contract marriage. Both bride and groom were said to have originated in the town of La Aduana, in the jurisdiction of Álamos. María Josefa Luisa Anguís was noted as the widow of Juan Antonio Avilés.

---

588. Bautismos 1751–1794, matrimonios 1848, defunciones 1735–1752, March 8, 1772, film 666999, image 344, Registros Parroquiales, Iglesia de La Purísima Concepción, Álamos, Sonora, Mexico (FamilySearch, https://familysearch.org).
589. Matrimonios 1779–1817, December 21, 1788, film 666565, image 143, Registros Parroquiales, Iglesia de La Purísima Concepción, Álamos, Sonora, Mexico (FamilySearch, https://familysearch.org).
590. Bautismos 1783–1799, 1806–1829, June 12, 1790, image 94, Registros Parroquiales, Iglesia Sagrado Corazón, El Fuerte, Sinaloa, Mexico (FamilySearch, https://familysearch.org).
591. Matrimonios 1779–1817, October 9, 1793, film 666565, image 254, Registros Parroquiales, Iglesia de La Purísima Concepción, Álamos, Sonora, Mexico (FamilySearch, https://familysearch.org).
592. Información matrimonial 1760–1799, September 14, 1793, film 667002, images 653–654, Registros Parroquiales, Iglesia de La Purísima Concepción, Álamos, Sonora, Mexico (FamilySearch, https://familysearch.org).

Joseph Antonio Mucio Gil Samaniego, son of Juan Gil Samaniego and Juana Paula Gaxiola, was born in 1771 in Álamos. The cited matrimonial record for Joseph Antonio Gil Samaniego and María Josefa Luisa Anguís stated that the groom originated in the town of La Aduana, jurisdiction of Álamos. He was baptized on May 26, 1771, at the church of the Purísima Concepción in Álamos.[593] The baptismal record named Juan Manuel de Ortiz and María Dolores Velarde as his *padrinos*. All were *vecinos* of La Aduana.

Joseph Antonio Mucio Gil Samaniego and María Josepha Luisa Anguís had the following known children:

i. **María del Carmen Josepha Damiana Gil Samaniego** was born in 1794 in Álamos. She was baptized on October 18, 1794, at the church of the Purísima Concepción in Álamos.[594] The baptismal record named Joaquín Esquer and Andrea Gil Samaniego as her *padrinos*.

ii. **María Valvanera Juana de los Dolores Gil Samaniego** was born in 1801 in Álamos. She was baptized on July 28, 1801, at the church of the Purísima Concepción in Álamos.[595] The baptismal record named Manuel Espinosa and María Gertrudis Espinosa as her *padrinos*.

iii. **María Francisca Romualda Gil Samaniego** was born in 1805 in Álamos. She was baptized on February 17, 1805, at the church of the Purísima Concepción in Álamos.[596] The baptismal record named Antonio Gil de Lamadrid and Gertrudis Tagle as her *padrinos*.

101. **Juan Manuel Anguís** (Francisco Antonio Baptista-6, María Mallén de Navarrete-5, Agustina Salvadora Esquer-4, Salvador-3, Salvador-2, Blas-1) was born on April 7, 1762, in Álamos. The cited baptismal record stated that he was born twenty-eight days prior to his date of baptism. He was baptized on May 5, 1762, at the church of the Purísima Concepción in Álamos.[597] The baptismal record named Bachiller Juan Antonio de Anguís and Gertrudis de Anguís, his sister, as the child's *padrinos*. The waters of baptism had already been poured on the child at birth, fearing he might not survive.

Juan Manuel Anguís and Serafina González Barreda were married on December 30, 1794, at the church of the Purísima Concepción in Álamos.[598] The matrimonial record named Prudencio

---

593. Bautismos, matrimonios y defunciones 1696–1699, bautismos 1768–1781, May 26, 1771, film 663487, image 184, Registros Parroquiales, Iglesia de La Purísima Concepción, Álamos, Sonora, Mexico (FamilySearch, https://familysearch.org).

594. Bautismos 1781–1796, October 18, 1794, film 663488, image 648, Registros Parroquiales, Iglesia de La Purísima Concepción, Álamos, Sonora, Mexico (FamilySearch, https://familysearch.org).

595. Bautismos 1796–1805, July 28, 1801, film 663995, images 155–156, Registros Parroquiales, Iglesia de La Purísima Concepción, Álamos, Sonora, Mexico (FamilySearch, https://familysearch.org).

596. Bautismos 1796–1805, February 17, 1805, film 663995, image 264, Registros Parroquiales, Iglesia de La Purísima Concepción, Álamos, Sonora, Mexico (FamilySearch, https://familysearch.org).

597. Bautismos 1751–1794, matrimonios 1848, defunciones 1735–1752, May 5, 1762, film 666999, images 227–228 and 242–243, Registros Parroquiales, Iglesia de La Purísima Concepción, Álamos, Sonora, Mexico (FamilySearch, https:// familysearch.org).

598. Matrimonios 1779–1817, December 30, 1794, film 666565, images 285–286, Registros Parroquiales,

Ruiz de Eguino and Anna María Tovar as *padrinos*. Bachiller José Joaquín Elías de Zayas and Subdelegado Rafael Valenzuela were identified as witnesses to the marriage. Parents of the bride and groom were named in the record and all were said to have been deceased at the time of the marriage. A marriage dispensation was required because the couple were related in the third and fourth degrees of consanguinity, meaning they were both second and third cousins.

The cited marriage investigation record, dated December 24, 1794, noted that Juan Manuel Anguís was engaged in commerce in La Aduana. [599] The cited letter dated November 25, 1794, from Licenciado Manuel María Moreno, lawyer for the Audiencia of Mexico City spoke on behalf of providing the bridal couple with a dispensation to marry.[600]

Serafina González Barreda, daughter of Fernando Antonio González Barreda and María Raphaela Esquer, was born in 1768 in Álamos. The cited marriage investigation for Serafina González Barreda stated that she was twenty-six years of age in 1794 and that she originated in Álamos.

Juan Manuel Anguís and Serafina González Barreda had the following known children:

148 i. **María Dolores de Jesús Josefa Gregoria Anguís** was born in 1797 in Álamos; she married José Pasqual Prudencio Ygnacio de la Cruz Gómez Lamadrid on October 10, 1813, in Álamos.

ii. **María Balvanera del Carmen Juana de la Cruz Anguís** was born on December 24, 1799, in Álamos, according to the baptismal record. She was baptized on December 31, 1799, at the church of the Purísima Concepción in Álamos.[601] The baptismal record named Bachiller Pedro Pablo González Barreda and Juana Gil Samaniego as her *padrinos*.

iii. **María Concepción Juana Paula Anguís** was born on June 18, 1801, in Álamos, according to the baptismal record. She was baptized on June 24, 1801, at the church of the Purísima Concepción in Álamos.[602] The baptismal record named Prudencio Ruiz de Eguino and Anna María Fabar, his wife, as her *padrinos*.

iv. **María del Carmen Juana Ladislao Anguís** was born in 1803 in Álamos. She was baptized on July 3, 1803, at the church of the Purísima Concepción in Álamos.[603]

Iglesia de La Purísima Concepción, Álamos, Sonora, Mexico (FamilySearch, https://familysearch.org).

599. Información matrimonial 1793–1798, December 24, 1794, film 663808, images 147–152, Registros Parroquiales, Iglesia de La Purísima Concepción, Álamos, Sonora, Mexico (FamilySearch, https://familysearch.org).

600. Información matrimonial 1760–1799, November 25, 1794, film 667002, images 615–616, Registros Parroquiales, Iglesia de La Purísima Concepción, Álamos, Sonora, Mexico (FamilySearch, https://familysearch.org).

601. Bautismos 1796–1805, December 31, 1799, film 663995, image 113, Registros Parroquiales, Iglesia de La Purísima Concepción, Álamos, Sonora, Mexico (FamilySearch, https://familysearch.org).

602. Bautismos 1796–1805, June 24, 1801, film 663995, image 155, Registros Parroquiales, Iglesia de La Purísima Concepción, Álamos, Sonora, Mexico (FamilySearch, https://familysearch.org).

603. Bautismos 1796–1805, July 3, 1803, film 663995, images 202–203, Registros Parroquiales, Iglesia de La Purísima Concepción, Álamos, Sonora, Mexico (FamilySearch, https://familysearch.org).

The baptismal record named the parish priest, Nicolás Quirós y Mora, and Isabel Quirós y Mora as her *padrinos*. Those present included Juan Fox Fernández and Juan Miguel Santini, among others.

    v.   **Juana Bautista María Juliana Anguís** was born in February 1810 in Álamos. The cited baptismal record stated that she was born the same month in which she was baptized. The day of the month was not clearly indicated. She was baptized on February 25, 1810, at the church of the Purísima Concepción in Álamos.[604] The baptismal record named Bachiller José Rosas and Rita Gil Samaniego as her *padrinos*.

102. **María Ysidora Rivera** (María Theresa Mallén de Navarrete-6, Vicente-5, Agustina Salvadora Esquer-4, Salvador-3, Salvador-2, Blas-1) was born in 1751 in Álamos. She was baptized on April 27, 1751, at the church of the Purísima Concepción in Álamos.[605] The baptismal record is faded and for the most part illegible.

María Ysidora Rivera and Joaquín Andrés Alcayde were married on April 22, 1772, at the church of the Purísima Concepción in Álamos.[606] The matrimonial record named Teniente General Juan Augustín de Yriarte and Josephina González Barreda as his *padrinos*. Mariano Pantaleón Gómez and Felipe Goycochea were named as witnesses to the marriage. Parents of the bride and groom were named in the record.

Joaquín Andrés Alcayde, son of Francisco Xavier Alcayde Pérez de la Puente and Ana Antonia del Castillo y Cabanillas, was born about 1745 in Culiacán. He died on October 10, 1781, in Álamos. He was buried on October 11, 1781, at the church of the Purísima Concepción in Álamos.[607] Joaquín Andrés Alcayde died suddenly and was administered the sacrament of extreme unction after his death. His burial site was valued at five pesos, and his funeral was held with *cruz alta, vigilia, caja, y túmulo de dos cuerpos*. According to the burial record, Joaquín Andrés originated in Culiacán and had been married to María Ysidora Rivera. He left four surviving children (only three children have been identified).

Joaquín Andrés Alcayde and María Ysidora Rivera had the following known children:

    i.   **Bárbara Josefa Inés Alcayde** was born in 1777 in Álamos. She was baptized on January 30, 1777, at the church of the Purísima Concepción in Álamos.[608] The baptismal record named Miguel Alcayde and Michaela Yriarte as her *padrinos*. Lucas de la Serna, Juan de Fox, and Joseph Gabriel Esquer were named as witnesses to the baptism.

604. Bautismos 1791–1796, 1805–1815, February 25, 1810, film 663996, image 365, Registros Parroquiales, Iglesia de La Purísima Concepción, Álamos, Sonora, Mexico (FamilySearch, https://familysearch.org).

605. Bautismos 1751–1794, matrimonios 1848, defunciones 1735–1752, April 27, 1751, film 666999, image 40, Registros Parroquiales, Iglesia de La Purísima Concepción, Álamos, Sonora, Mexico (FamilySearch, https://familysearch.org).

606. Matrimonios 1758–1779, April 22, 1772, film 666564, image 147, Registros Parroquiales, Iglesia de La Purísima Concepción, Álamos, Sonora, Mexico (FamilySearch, https://familysearch.org).

607. Defunciones 1717–1751, 1764–1792, October 11, 1781, film 666995, image 384, Registros Parroquiales, Iglesia de La Purísima Concepción, Alamos, Sonora, Mexico (FamilySearch, https://familysearch.org).

608. Bautismos, matrimonios y defunciones 1696–1699, bautismos 1768–1781, film 663487, image 337, Registros Parroquiales, Iglesia de La Purísima Concepción, Álamos, Sonora, Mexico (FamilySearch, https://familysearch.org).

113 ii. **Anna María Josefa Valentina Alcayde** was born in 1779 in Álamos; she married José Antonio Delgado on November 8, 1803, in Rosario.

iii. **José Julián Alcayde** was born on January 18, 1781, in Álamos, according to the baptismal record. He was baptized on February 6, 1781, at the church of the Purísima Concepción in Álamos.[609] The baptismal record named Miguel Alexandro de Rivera as his *padrino*. José Julián died on April 15, 1781, in Álamos. He was was buried on April 16, 1781, at the church of the Purísima Concepción in Álamos.[610] His funeral service was held with *cruz alta, capa, caja, y una mesa*. José Julián was buried in a grave valued at five pesos. The burial record named the parents of the deceased child.

103. Joseph Antonio Mallén de Navarrete (Gabriel-6, Vicente-5, Agustina Salvadora Esquer-4, Salvador-3, Salvador-2, Blas-1) was born in 1769 in Álamos. He was baptized on July 14, 1769, at the church of the Purísima Concepción in Álamos.[611] The baptismal record named Juan Thomas Padilla and Rosa González as his *padrinos*. Juan de Fox and Miguel Martínez were named as witnesses to the baptism.

Joseph Antonio Mallén de Navarrete and María Dolores Sabalza were married on February 13, 1798, at the church of the Purísima Concepción in Álamos.[612] The matrimonial record named Rafael Ayon and Francisca Sabalza as *padrinos*. Juan Francisco Fox, Andrés Díaz, and those present at the ceremony were identified, as witnesses to the marriage. Parents of the bride and groom were named. Both parents of the bride were said to have been deceased.

María Dolores Sabalza, daughter of Raymundo Sabalza and Ignés Ybarra, was born about 1780.

Joseph Antonio Mallén de Navarrete and María Dolores Sabalza had the following known children:

i. **María Josefa Agapita Mallén de Navarrete** was born in 1797 in Álamos. She was baptized on October 17, 1797, at the church of the Purísima Concepción in Álamos.[613] The baptismal record named Toribio Diego de la Puente and Petra Ibarra as her *padrinos*. The child was identified as the *hija natural* of her parents.

ii. **María Petra Francisca Mallén de Navarrete** was born in 1800 in Álamos. She was baptized on February 6, 1800, at the church of the Purísima Concepción in Álamos.[614] The baptismal record named Francisco Algorre as her *padrino*.

---

609. Bautismos, matrimonios y defunciones 1696–1699, bautismos 1768–1781, film 663487, image 505, Registros Parroquiales, Iglesia de La Purísima Concepción, Álamos, Sonora, Mexico (FamilySearch, https://familysearch.org).

610. Defunciones 1717–1751,1764–1792, April 16, 1781, film 666995, image 360, Registros Parroquiales, Iglesia de La Purísima Concepción, Álamos, Sonora, Mexico (FamilySearch, https://familysearch.org).

611. Bautismos, matrimonios y defunciones 1696–1699 bautismos 1768–1781, July 14, 1769, film 663487, image 134, Registros Parroquiales, Iglesia de La Purísima Concepción, Álamos, Sonora, Mexico (FamilySearch, https://familysearch.org).

612. Matrimonios 1779–1817, February 13,1798, film 666565, images 343–344, Registros Parroquiales, Iglesia de La Purísima Concepción, Álamos, Sonora, Mexico (FamilySearch, https://familysearch.org).

613. Bautismos 1796–1805, October 17, 1797, film 663995, image 54, Registros Parroquiales, Iglesia de La Purísima Concepción, Álamos, Sonora, Mexico (FamilySearch, https://familysearch.org).

614. Bautismos 1796–1805, February 6, 1800, film 663995, image 117, Registros Parroquiales, Iglesia de La

iii. **José Ciriaco de los Dolores Mallén de Navarrete** was born in 1801 in Álamos. He was baptized on August 13, 1801, at the church of the Purísima Concepción in Álamos.[615] The baptismal record named Bernardo Andrade and his sister Ana María Andrade as his *padrinos.*

104. María Balvanera Mallén de Navarrete (Gabriel-6, Vicente-5, Agustina Salvadora Esquer-4, Salvador-3, Salvador-2, Blas-1) was born in 1776 in Álamos. She was baptized on June 7, 1776, at the church of the Purísima Concepción in Álamos.[616] The baptismal record named Bachiller Vicente Díaz de la Torre and Gertrudis Rivera as her *padrinos.* Joseph Bustillos, Manuel *"el músico,"* and Melchor Amarillas were named as witnesses to the baptism.

María Balvanera Mallén de Navarrete and Santiago Peñúñuri were married on October 2, 1792, at the church of the Purísima Concepción in Álamos.[617] The matrimonial record named Manuel Anguís and Josefa Anguís as *padrinos.* Joseph Bustillos, Pedro Francisco Quirós y Mora, and Pedro Mallén were named as witnesses to the marriage. Parents of the couple were named. The mother of the groom, María Reyes Padilla, and the father of the bride, Gabriel Mallén de Navarrete were said to have been deceased.

Santiago Peñúñuri, son of Manuel Peñúñuri and María Reyes Padilla, was born about 1776. He died before March 11, 1817. The cited baptismal record for his son José Antonio Romero stated that Santiago Peñúñuri was deceased at the time of the baptism.

Santiago Peñúñuri and María Balvanera Mallén de Navarrete had the following known children:

i. **María Dolores Peñúñuri** was born on August 18, 1793, in Álamos, according to the baptismal record. She was baptized on August 24, 1793, at the parish of the Purísima Concepción in Álamos.[618] The baptismal record named Manuel Anguís and Rita Gil Samaniego as her *padrinos.* The service took place at the chapel of La Aduana.

ii. **José de Jesús de Sacramento Peñúñuri** was born in 1796 in Álamos. He was baptized on January 4, 1796, at the parish of the Purísima Concepción in Álamos.[619] The baptismal record named Antonio Gil Samaniego and María Gertrudis Yepes de Tagle as his *padrinos.* The baptism took place at the chapel of the La Virgen de la Balvanera in La Aduana.

iii. **María Josefa Antonia del Sacramento Peñúñuri** was born in 1798 in Álamos. She was baptized on March 26, 1798, at the parish of the Purísima Concepción in

Purísima Concepción, Álamos, Sonora, Mexico (FamilySearch, https://familysearch.org).

615. Bautismos 1796–1805, August 13, 1801, film 663995, image 156, Registros Parroquiales, Iglesia de La Purísima Concepción, Álamos, Sonora, Mexico (FamilySearch, https://familysearch.org).

616. Bautismos, matrimonios y defunciones 1696–1699 bautismos 1768–1781, June 7, 1776, film 663487, images 320–321, Registros Parroquiales, Iglesia de La Purísima Concepción, Álamos, Sonora, Mexico (FamilySearch, https:// familysearch.org).

617. Matrimonios 1779–1817, October 2,1792 film 666565, images 230–231, Registros Parroquiales, Iglesia de La Purísima Concepción, Álamos, Sonora, Mexico (FamilySearch, https://familysearch.org).

618. Bautismos 1791–1796, 1805–1815, August 24, 1793, film 663996, image 95, Registros Parroquiales, Iglesia de La Purísima Concepción, Álamos, Sonora, Mexico (FamilySearch, https://familysearch.org).

619. Bautismos 1791–1796,1805–1815, January 4, 1796, film 663996, image 204, Registros Parroquiales, Iglesia de La Purísima Concepción, Álamos, Sonora, Mexico (FamilySearch, https://familysearch.org).

Álamos.[620] The baptismal record named Manuel Anguís and Serafina Barreda as her *padrinos*. The service was held at the chapel of La Aduana.

174 iv. **José Ignacio Dionisio Peñúñuri** was born in 1803 in Álamos.

v. **María Bárbara Dolores de la Santísima Trinidad Peñúñuri** was born in 1804 in Álamos. She was baptized on December 16, 1804, at the parish of the Purísima Concepción in Álamos.[621] The baptismal record named Father José Rosas, the officiating priest, and Rita Gil Samaniego as her *padrinos*. The service was held at the chapel of La Aduana.

vi. **María Dolores Josefa Andrea Peñúñuri** was born on November 26, 1806, in Álamos, according to the baptismal record. She was baptized on November 30, 1806, at the church of the Purísima Concepción in Álamos.[622] The baptismal record named María Gertrudis Mallén as her *madrina*.

vii. **José Thomas Antonio Macedonio Peñúñuri** was born in 1808 in Álamos. He was baptized on September 16, 1808, at the parish of the Purísima Concepción in Álamos.[623] The baptismal record named Manuel Ygnacio Gil and María Gertrudis Mallén as his *padrinos*. The baptism took place at the chapel of the La Virgen de la Balvanera in La Aduana.

viii. **Francisca María Loreto del Sacramento Peñúñuri** was born in 1810 in Álamos. She was baptized on December 10, 1810, at the church of the Purísima Concepción in Álamos.[624] The baptismal record named Pedro Francisco Quirós and María Isabel Quirós as her *padrinos*.

ix. **María Dolores Peñúñuri** was born in 1812 in Álamos. She was baptized on October 19, 1812, at the parish of the Purísima Concepción in Álamos.[625] The baptismal record named María Magdalena Tagle as her *madrina*. The service took place at the chapel of La Aduana.

x. **José del Carmen Antonio Peñúñuri** was born in 1815 in Álamos. He was baptized on April 2, 1815, at the church of the Purísima Concepción in Álamos.[626] The baptismal

---

620. Bautismos 1796–1805, March 26, 1798, film 663995, image 70, Registros Parroquiales, Iglesia de La Purísima Concepción, Álamos, Sonora, Mexico (FamilySearch, https://familysearch.org).

621. Bautismos 1796–1805, December 16, 1804, film 663995, image 257, Registros Parroquiales, Iglesia de La Purísima Concepción, Álamos, Sonora, Mexico (FamilySearch, https://familysearch.org).

622. Bautismos 1791–1796, 1805–1815, November 30, 1806, film 663996, images 264–265, Registros Parroquiales, Iglesia de La Purísima Concepción, Álamos, Sonora, Mexico (FamilySearch, https://famiysearch.org).

623. Bautismos 1791–1796, 1805–1815, September 16, 1808, film 663996, image 314, Registros Parroquiales, Iglesia de La Purísima Concepción, Álamos, Sonora, Mexico (FamilySearch, https://familysearch.org).

624. Bautismos 1791–1796, 1805–1815, December 10, 1810, film 663996, images 403–404, Registros Parroquiales, Iglesia de La Purísima Concepción, Álamos, Sonora, Mexico (FamilySearch, https://familysearch.org).

625. Bautismos 1791–1796, 1805–1815, October 19, 1812, film 663996, image 445, Registros Parroquiales, Iglesia de La Purísima Concepción, Álamos, Sonora, Mexico (FamilySearch, https://familysearch.org).

626. Bautismos 1791–1796, 1805–1815, April 2, 1815, film 663996, image 494, Registros Parroquiales, Iglesia de La Purísima Concepción, Álamos, Sonora, Mexico (FamilySearch, https://familysearch.org).

record named Ygnacio María Campoy and María Lucía Tagle as his *padrinos*.

xi. **José Antonio Romano Eulogio Peñúñuri** was born in 1817 in Álamos. He was baptized on March 11, 1817, at the parish of the Purísima Concepción in Álamos.[627] The baptismal record named José Jesús Peñúñuri and María Peñuñuri as his *padrinos*. The child's father, Santiago Peñúñuri was said to have been deceased. The baptism took place at chapel of La Aduana.

105. Bernardo Mallén de Navarrete (Gabriel-6, Vicente-5, Agustina Salvadora Esquer-4, Salvador-3, Salvador-2, Blas-1) was born about 1776. Bernardo Mallén de Navarrete and Gertrudis Sarmiento were married on November 21, 1799, at the church of Nuestra Señora del Rosario in Rosario, Sinaloa.[628] The matrimonial record named Antonio Navarro and Augustín Portillo, Ministro de la Real Hacienda in Rosario, as witnesses to the marriage. Parents of the bride and groom were named in the record, stating that Gabriel Mallén de Navarrete, father of the groom, was deceased. The marriage ceremony took place at the home of the bride's father. On the following day, the couple received a nuptial blessing at the church.

Gertrudis Sarmiento, daughter of Phelipe Sarmiento and Petra de Uzeta, was born on December 7, 1781, in Rosario, Sinaloa, according to the baptismal record. She was baptized on December 17, 1781, at the church of Nuestra Señora del Rosario in Rosario. The baptismal record named Manuel Balmasada and María Uzuta as her *padrinos*. The child's father was identified as a *mestizo* and her mother as an *española*.

Bernardo Mallén de Navarrete and Gertrudis Sarmiento had the following child:

i. **José Bernardo Catharino Mallén de Navarrete** was born on November 25, 1800, in Rosario, according to the baptismal record. He was baptized on December 10, 1800, at the church of Nuestra Señora del Rosario in Rosario.[629] The baptismal record did not name *padrinos*. The child was baptized provisionally at his birth, in the event he would not survive.

106. María Balvanera de Yriarte (Ana María González Barreda-6, Micaela Salvadora Mallén de Navarrete-5, Agustina Salvadora Esquer-4, Salvador-3, Salvador-2, Blas-1) was born about 1761 in Álamos.

María Balvanera de Yriarte and Miguel Alcayde Pérez de la Puente were married on December 6, 1775, at the church of the Purísima Concepción in Álamos.[630] The matrimonial record named Juan Ortíz and María Dolores Velarde as *padrinos*. Parents of the bride and groom were named, and the record stated that the couple had received a nuptial blessing.

---

627. Bautismos 1816–1825,1827–1829, March 11, 1817, film 663997, image 30, Registros Parroquiales, Iglesia de La Purísima Concepción, Álamos, Sonora, Mexico (FamilySearch, https://familysearch.org).
628. Matrimonios 1776–1806, 1823–1830, 1849–1858, 1863–1869, film 676111, image 248, Registros Parroquiales, Iglesia de Nuestra Señora del Rosario, Sinaloa, Mexico (FamilySearch, https://familysearch.org).
629. Bautismos 1789–1801, December 10, 1800, film 676094, image 533, Registros Parroquiales, Iglesia de Nuestra Señora del Rosario, Sinaloa, Mexico (FamilySearch, https://familysearch.org).
630. Matrimonios 1758–1779, December 6, 1775, film 666564, image 165, Registros Parroquiales, Iglesia de La Purísima Concepción, Álamos, Sonora, Mexico (FamilySearch, https://familysearch.org).

The bridal couple received a marriage dispensation on Oct 2, 1775, in Álamos.[631] The dispensation was required because the couple were related to the fourth degree of consanguinity since the father of the groom was the second cousin of the mother of the bride. María was said to have been a "poor, demure child" and that the marriage would better serve God and the Holy Church. Parents of the bride and groom were named in the record. All were *vecinos* of Álamos. Vicente Mallén de Navarrete, Juan Manuel Morales, and Teniente Coronel Thadeo Padilla y Arnao served as witnessses in favor of the marriage dispensation. The marriage dispensation record used "Alcalde" as the family surname.

Miguel Alcayde Pérez de la Puente, son of Francisco Xavier Alcayde Pérez de la Puente and Ana Antonia del Castillo y Cabanillas, was born about 1744 in Culiacán. His place of birth was provided in the cited marriage dispensation record. He died on November 15, 1797, in Álamos. He was buried on November 16, 1797, at the church of the Purísima Concepción in Álamos.[632] His funeral service was held with *cruz alta, capa, incienso y caja.* He was laid to rest in a grave site valued at ten pesos. Miguel received the last sacraments of the Catholic Church before death. His wife was named in the record, and he was said not to have had any surviving children. He did not leave a will because there was no reason to do so, *"porque no hubo de qué."*

Miguel Alcayde Pérez de la Puente and María Balvanera de Yriarte had the following known children:

i. **María Rosa Viterbo Cástula Alcayde Pérez de la Puente** was born in 1778 in Álamos. She was baptized on April 1, 1778, at the church of the Purísima Concepción in Álamos.[633] The baptismal record named Teniente de Gobernador Augustín Yriarte and Josefa González Barreda as her *padrinos.*

ii. **Juan Pablo de Jesús Alcayde Pérez de la Puente** was born on January 15, 1780, in Álamos. He was baptized on February 8, 1780, at the church of the Purísima Concepción in Álamos.[634] The baptismal record named Teniente de Gobernador Juan Augustín Yriarte, and his daughter Michaela Yriarte as his *padrinos.* He died on October 4, 1782, at the age of two in Álamos. Juan was buried on October 5, 1782, at the church of the Purísima Concepción in Álamos.[635] His funeral service was held with *cruz alta, capa, una mesa y caja.* The little child was laid to rest at the Capilla de Jesús.

---

631. Diligencias matrimoniales, Miguel Alcalde y María Balbanera de Iriarte, Real de Álamos, 1775, AHAD-33, frames 601–605, AHAD.
632. Defunciones 1786–1819, November 16, 1797 film, 666996, image 280, Registros Parroquiales, Iglesia de La Purísima Concepción, Álamos, Sonora, Mexico (FamilySearch, https://familysearch.org).
633. Bautismos, matrimonios y defunciones 1696–1699 bautismos 1768–1781, film 663487, image 372, Registros Parroquiales, Iglesia de La Purísima Concepción, Álamos, Sonora, Mexico (FamilySearch, https:// familysearch.org).
634. Bautismos, matrimonios y defunciones 1696–1699, bautismos 1768–1781, February 8, 1780, film 663487, image 452, Registros Parroquiales, Iglesia de La Purísima Concepción, Álamos, Sonora, Mexico (FamilySearch, https:// familysearch.org).
635. Defunciones 1717–1751, 1764–1792, October 5, 1782, film 666995, images 406–407, Registros Parroquiales, Iglesia de La Purísima Concepción, Álamos, Sonora, Mexico (FamilySearch, https://familysearch. org).

107. **Joseph María Ygnacio Pedro Mathias Severino Ymaz Esquer y Luyando** (Joseph Mateo Miguel-6, Juan Miguel Gordiano-5, Salvadora Manuela Silvestra Esquer-4, Salvador-3, Salvador-2, Blas-1) was born on February 21, 1758, in Mexico City. The cited baptismal record provided his date of birth. He was baptized on February 24, 1758, at the parish church of the Asunción Sagrario Metropolitano in Mexico City.[636] The baptismal record named Licenciado Juan de Ymaz Esquer, Abogado de la Real Audiencia y Secretario de la Real Universidad, as his *padrino*.

Joseph María Ygnacio Pedro Mathias Severino Ymaz Esquer y Luyando and Margarita María Josefa Camacho Velasco y Negrín were married on December 2, 1786, at the parish of San Miguel Arcángel in Mexico City.[637] The matrimonial record named Cirilo Camacho, José Domingo Ramírez, and Joseph Antonio Aguero as witnesses to the marriage. The marriage took place at the chapel of San Joseph at seven in the morning. The couple received a nuptial blessing on the day of their wedding. Parents of the bride and groom were named in the record.

Margarita María Josefa Camacho Velasco y Negrín, daughter of Cirilo Joseph Camacho de Almonarriz and María Manuela de Velasco y Negrín, was born about 1768. The cited baptismal record for her daughter, Maria Josefa Ygnacia Cornellia, added "Margarita" to her mother's name, "Margarita María Josefa."

Joseph María Ygnacio Pedro Mathias Severino Ymaz Esquer y Luyando and Margarita María Josefa Camacho Velasco y Negrín had the following known children:

175 i.   **Catharina María Loreto Josepha Ygnacia Gertrudis Ymaz Camacho** was born on November 25, 1788, in Mexico City; she married José Francisco Pérez de León Aguiar y Seixas on February 19, 1807, in Mexico City.

   ii.   **María Josefa Ygnacia Cornelia Ymaz Esquer y Luyando** was born on September 16, 1790, in Mexico City, according to the baptismal record. She was baptized on September 16, 1790, at the parish church of the Asunción Sagrario Metropolitano in Mexico City.[638] The baptismal record named Escribano Francisco Celapiola y Nabos and María Antonia de Cordova as her *padrinos*. Paternal and maternal grandparents were named in the record.

108. **Manuel Joseph María Ygnacio Ymaz y Cabanillas** (Pedro Martín Joseph Manuel-6, Juan Miguel Gordiano-5, Salvadora Manuela Silvestra Esquer-4, Salvador-3, Salvador-2, Blas-1) was born on May 27, 1769, in Mexico City. The cited baptismal record provided his date of birth. He was baptized on May 30, 1769, at the parish church of the Asunción Sagrario Metropolitano in Mexico City.[639] The baptismal record named Teniente Coronel del Regimiento Provincial de Milicias Luis María de Luyando as his *padrino*.

---

636. Bautismos de españoles 1756–1759, February 24, 1758, film 35186, image 674, Registros Parroquiales, Iglesia Asunción Sagrario Metropolitano, Mexico City, Mexico (FamilySearch, https://familysearch.org).
637. Matrimonios de españoles 1761–1790, December 2, 1786, film 206002, image 427, Registros Parroquíales, Iglesia San Miguel Arcángel, Mexico City, Mexico (FamilySearch, https://familysearch.org).
638. Bautismos de españoles 1785–1792, September 16, 1790, film 35192, image 716, Registros Parroquiales, Iglesia Asunción Sagrario Metropolitano, Mexico City, Mexico (FamilySearch, https://familysearch.org).
639. Bautismos de españoles 1769–1774, May 30, 1769, film 35189, image 41, Registros Parroquiales, Iglesia Asunción Sagrario Metropolitano, Mexico City, Mexico (FamilySearch, https://familysearch.org).

Manuel Joseph María Ygnacio Ymaz y Cabanillas and María Josefa Zeferina Arenas del Valle were married on October 14, 1798, at the parish church of the Asunción Sagrario Metropolitano in Mexico City.[640] The matrimonial record named Gabriel de Lugo and Bachiller Francisco Gasca as witnesses to the marriage. Parents were named in the record.

María Josefa Zeferina Arenas del Valle, daughter of Lucas Arenas del Valle and María del Loreto de la Peña, was born about 1780. She was also known as "María Zeferina," according the the cited matrimonial record for her son, José María Nicolás Francisco.[641]

Manuel Joseph María Ygnacio Ymaz y Cabanillas and María Josefa Zeferina Arenas del Valle had the following known children:

176 i. **José María Antonio Francisco de Paula Juan Nepomuceno Luis Gonzaga Ymaz** was born on February 15, 1799, in Mexico City; he married María del Carmen Pérez Anca on September 20, 1820, in Mexico City and he died on April 8, 1864, in Mexico City.

ii. **Ygnacio María Francisco Cosme Damián Ymaz** was born on September 27, 1800, in Mexico City. The cited baptismal record provided his date of birth. He was baptized on September 27, 1800, at the parish church of the Asunción Sagrario Metropolitano in Mexico City.[642] The baptismal record named José Manuel Varo y Ibáñez as his *padrino*. Paternal and maternal grandparents were named in the record.

iii. **María Francisca Ignacia Josefa Catharina Plácida Loreto de Jesús Ymaz** was born on October 12, 1801, in Mexico City, according to the baptismal record. She was baptized on October 12, 1801, at the church of Santa Veracruz in Mexico City.[643] The baptismal record named Teniente de Comercio José Rodríguez Alemán and María Ygnacia de la Peña as her as her *padrinos*. Paternal and maternal grandparents were named in the record.

iv. **Anna María Joaquina Narcisa Petra de Alcántara Luisa Gonzaga Ymaz** was born on October 29, 1802, in Mexico City, according to the cited baptismal record. She was baptized on November 2, 1802, at the parish church of Santa Veracruz in Mexico City.[644] The baptismal record named Miguel Cruzado as a proxy *padrino* for José María Cacho. Paternal and maternal grandparents were named in the record.

---

640. Matrimonios de españoles 1792–1796, 1799–1803, October 14, 1798, film 35277, image 503, Registros Parroquiales, Iglesia Asunción Sagrario Metropolitano, Mexico City, Mexico (FamilySearch, https://familysearch.org).
641. Matrimonios 1824–1878, June 28, 1854, film 35852, image 756, Registros Parroquíales, Iglesia de Santa Veracruz, Mexico City, Mexico (FamilySearch, https://familysearch.org).
642. Bautismos de españoles 1799–1803, September 27, 1800, film 35194, image 307, Registros Parroquiales, Iglesia Asunción Sagrario Metropolitano, Mexico City, Mexico (FamilySearch, https://familysearch.org).
643. Bautismos de españoles 1772–1804, October 12, 1801, film 35825, image 895, Registros Parroquíales, Iglesia de Santa Veracruz, Mexico City, Mexico (FamilySearch, https://familysearch.org).
644. Bautismos de españoles 1772–1804, November 2, 1802, film 35825, image 927, Registros Parroquíales, Iglesia de Santa Veracruz, Mexico City, Mexico (FamilySearch, https://familysearch.org).

v.   **María Isabel Josefa Nicolasa Ymaz** was born on July 3, 1805, in Mexico City, according to the baptismal record. She was baptized on July 3, 1805, at the parish church of Santa Veracruz in Mexico City.[645] The baptismal record named María de la Peña as her *madrina*. Paternal and maternal grandparents were named in the record.

vi.   **María Dolores Eduviges Josefa Francisca Nicolasa Luisa Gonzaga Ymaz** was born on October 17, 1806, in Mexico City, according to the cited baptismal record. She was baptized on October 18, 1806, at the parish church of Santa Veracruz in Mexico City.[646] The baptismal record named Lucas Arenas del Valle, maternal grandfather, as a proxy *padrino* for Bachiller Juan José Villasusán, Cura y Juez Eclesiástico de Acapulco. Paternal and maternal grandparents were named in the record.

vii.   **Joseph María Francisco Luis Cecilio Nicolás Ymaz** was born on November 22, 1807, in Mexico City. The cited baptismal record provided his date of birth. He was baptized on November 23, 1807, at the parish church of Santa Veracruz in Mexico City.[647] The baptismal record named Vicente de Eguía and Josefa Anselmo Carrasco as his *padrinos*. Paternal and maternal grandparents were named in the record.

177 viii. **José María Nicolás Francisco Ymaz** was born on December 22, 1808, in Mexico City; he married Nicolasa Urquiaga on June 28, 1854, in Mexico City.

ix.   **María Dolores Francisca Ygnacia Josefa Nicolasa Luisa Felipa Dominga Ymaz** was born on August 11, 1812, in Mexico City. The cited baptismal record provided her date of birth. She was baptized on August 11, 1812, at the parish church of Santa Veracruz in Mexico City.[648] The baptismal record named José María Fernández Pallardo and María Joaquina de Castro as her *padrinos*. Paternal and maternal grandparents were named in the record.

x.   **María de la Soledad Francisca Josefa Nicolasa Ana Joaquina Ymaz** was born on April 2, 1815, in Mexico City. The cited baptismal record provided her date of birth. She was baptized on April 3, 1815, at the parish church of Santa Veracruz in Mexico City.[649] The baptismal record named Agustina Álvarez as her *madrina*. Paternal and maternal grandparents were named in the record.

109. Manuel Joseph Narciso Thadeo Chirlín (Juan Antonio Joseph-6, María Josepha Francisca Ymaz y Esquer-5, Salvadora Manuela Silvestra Esquer-4, Salvador-3, Salvador-2, Blas-1) was

645. Bautismos de españoles 1804–1826, July 3, 1805, film 35826, image 45, Registros Parroquíales, Iglesia de Santa Veracruz, Mexico City, Mexico (FamilySearch, https://familysearch.org).
646. Bautismos de españoles 1804–1826, October 18, 1806 film 35826, image 91, Registros Parroquíales, Iglesia de Santa Veracruz, Mexico City, Mexico (FamilySearch, https://familysearch.org).
647. Bautismos de españoles 1804–1826, November 23, 1807, film 35826, image 143, Registros Parroquíales, Iglesia de Santa Veracruz, Mexico City, Mexico (FamilySearch, https://familysearch.org).
648. Bautismos de españoles 1804–1826, August 11, 1812, film 35826, image 378, Registros Parroquíales, Iglesia de Santa Veracruz, Mexico City, Mexico (FamilySearch, https://familysearch.org).
649. Bautismos de españoles 1804–1826, April 3, 1815, film 35826, image 468, Registros Parroquíales, Iglesia de Santa Veracruz, Mexico City, Mexico (FamilySearch, https://familysearch.org).

born on October 29, 1756, in Mexico City. The cited baptismal record provided his date of birth. He was baptized on November 5, 1756, at the parish church of the Asunción Sagrario Metropolitano in Mexico City.[650] The baptismal record named Félix Sandoval, Oficial Mayor de Gobierno, and María Dolores de Zelada as his *padrino*s.

Manuel Joseph Narciso Thadeo Chirlín and Rosalía García y Salas were married on July 8, 1790, at the parish church of the Asunción Sagrario Metropolitano in Mexico City.[651] The matrimonial record named José Norzagaray and Bachiller Tomás Martínez as witnesses to the marriage. The bride was said to have been the widow of Julián Pacheco, alias "*Falcón*." Only the parents of the groom were named. There are no known children of this marriage.

Rosalía García y Salas was born about 1772.

110. **Joseph María Martín Chirlín** (Juan Antonio Joseph-6, María Josepha Francisca Ymaz y Esquer-5, Salvadora Manuela Silvestra Esquer-4, Salvador-3, Salvador-2, Blas-1) was born on November 11, 1757, in Mexico City, according to the baptismal record. He was baptized on November 13, 1757, at the parish church of the Asunción Sagrario Metropolitano in Mexico City.[652] The baptismal record named Licenciado Juan de Ymaz Esquer, Abogado de la Real Audiencia de Mexico, as his *padrino*.

Joseph María Martín Chirlín and Rosalía Ábrego y Cova were married on December 28, 1777, at the parish church of the Asunción Sagrario Metropolitano in Mexico City.[653] The matrimonial record named Tomás Miguel del Pozo and Pedro Flores as witnesses to the marriage. Parents of the bride and groom were named in the record. The record identified the bride with her paternal and maternal compounded surname, Ábrego y Cova.

Rosalía Ábrego y Cova, daughter of Miguel Ábrego and Anna de la Cova y Vera, was born about 1759.

Joseph María Martín Chirlín and Rosalía Ábrego y Cova had one known child:

i.	**María Dolores Josepha Dionisia Chirlín** was born on April 8, 1778, in Mexico City. Her baptismal record provided her date of birth. She was baptized on April 9, 1778, at the parish church of the Asunción Sagrario Metropolitano in Mexico City.[654] The baptismal record named the child's maternal grandfather, Miguel Ábrego, as her *padrino*. Paternal and maternal grandparents were named in the record.

---

650. Bautismos de españoles 1756–1759, November 5, 1756, film 35186, image 278, Registros Parroquiales, Iglesia Asunción Sagrario Metropolitano, Mexico City, Mexico (FamilySearch, https://familysearch.org).
651. Matrimonios de españoles 1769–1779, 1780–1781,1785–1791, July 8, 1790, film 35276, image 868, Registros Parroquiales, Iglesia Asunción Sagrario Metropolitano, Mexico City, Mexico (FamilySearch, https://familysearch.org).
652. Bautismos de españoles 1756–1759, November13, 1757, film 35186, image 607, Registros Parroquiales, Iglesia Asunción Sagrario Metropolitano, Mexico City, Mexico (FamilySearch, https://familysearch.org).
653. Matrimonios de españoles 1765–1766, December 28, 1777, film 35275, image 767, Registros Parroquiales, Iglesia Asunción Sagrario Metropolitano, Mexico City, Mexico (FamilySearch, https://familysearch.org).
654. Bautismos de españoles 1774–1778, April 9, 1778, film 35190, image 720, Registros Parroquiales, Iglesia Asunción Sagrario Metropolitano, Mexico City, Mexico (FamilySearch, https://familysearch.org).

111. **María de Guadalupe Gertrudis Josepha Saturnina Chirlín** (Juan Antonio Joseph-6, María Josepha Francisca Ymaz y Esquer-5, Salvadora Manuela Silvestra Esquer-4, Salvador-3, Sal-vador-2, Blas-1) was born on February 11, 1764, in Mexico City, according to the baptismal record. She was baptized on February 23, 1764, at the parish church of the Asunción Sagrario Metropolitano in Mexico City.[655] The baptismal record named Augustín Aresti as her *padrino*.

María de Guadalupe Gertrudis Josepha Saturnina Chirlín and Diego Andrés Gradillas y Orejón were married on November 19, 1780, at the parish of the Asunción Sagrario Metropolitano in Mexico City.[656] The matrimonial record named Licenciado Juan Monroy and Mariano Pérez de Tagle as witnesses to the marriage. The wedding ceremony took place at a house numbered fifty-six on the Calle de la Merced, at about six in the evening. The following day the couple received a nuptial blessing at the chapel of the Real Universidad. Parents of the bride and groom were named in the record.

Diego Andrés Gradillas y Orejón, son of Diego Gradillas and Anna Rosa Arvizu, was born about 1760 in Durango, New Spain. The cited marriage record stated that Diego Andrés Gradillas y Orejón was born in (*natural de*) the Archdiocese of Durango.

Diego Andrés Gradillas y Orejón and María de Guadalupe Gertrudis Josepha Saturnina Chirlín had one known child:

    i.   **María Josefa Hipólita Rita Gradillas** was born on August 13, 1782, in Mexico City, the baptismal record provided her date of birth. She was baptized on August 15, 1782, at the parish church of the Asunción Sagrario Metropolitano in Mexico City.[657] The baptismal record named Juan Minges del Real as her *padrino*. Her father was said to have been born in the city of Guatemala and that he was an *escribano publico*, public scribe, in Cuautla, Mexico. Her father's birthplace in his marriage record states that he was born in Durango. It seems possible that the child is identified with the wrong set of parents.

112. **María Ygnacia Campoy** (María Manuela Esquer-6, Pedro Fernando-5, Miguel Fernando Simón-4, Salvador-3, Salvador-2, Blas-1) was born in 1777 in Álamos. She was baptized on January 26, 1777, at the church of the Purísima Concepción in Álamos.[658] The baptismal record named María Elvira Esquer [?] as her *madrina*. The child previously had received the waters of baptism, out of necessity should she not survive.

---

655. Bautismos de españoles 1764–1769, February 23, 1764, film 35188, image 45, Registros Parroquiales, Iglesia Asunción Sagrario Metropolitano, Mexico City, Mexico (FamilySearch, https://familysearch.org).
656. Matrimonios de españoles 1769–1779, 1780–1781, 1785–1791, film 35276, image 68, Registros Parroquiales, Iglesia Asunción Sagrario Metropolitano, Mexico City, Mexico (FamilySearch, https://familysearch.org).
657. Bautismos de españoles 1779–1784, August 15, 1782, film 35191, image 680, Registros Parroquiales, Iglesia Asunción Sagrario Metropolitano, Mexico City, Mexico (FamilySearch, https://familysearch.org).
658. Bautismos, matrimonios y defunciones 1696–1699, bautismos 1768–1781, January 26, 1777, film 663487, image 257, Registros Parroquiales, Iglesia de La Purísima Concepción, Álamos, Sonora, Mexico (FamilySearch, https:// familysearch.org).

María Ygnacia Campoy and José María Quirós y Mora were married on December 1, 1789, at the parish of the Purísima Concepción in Álamos.[659] The matrimonial record named Francisco Campoy and Manuela Esquer, parents of the bride, as *padrinos*. The record stated that on November 2, 1789, documents were sent to the bishop of Sonora to petition a dispensation because the couple were said to be related through marriage in the third with a second degree of affinity. The dispensation was granted. However, there seems to be a scriber's error. The couple actually had a confirmed relationship in the third with second degree of consanguinity, meaning they were second cousins, once removed.

The parish priest, Father Juan Nicolás y Mora wrote that he had made the journey to the town of La Aduana to officiate at the marriage at the home of María Quirós y Mora. the couple received a nuptial blessing on January 19, 1790. Parents of the bride and groom were named, and the parents of the groom were said to have been deceased. Manuel Ruiz, Manuel Espinosa, and Manuel Anguís, among various others, were identified as being present at the marriage. The bride and her family were identified as "Campoy y Quirós" in the record.

In contrast to what was recorded in the marriage record, the marriage information record, dated November 18, 1789, found that the couple were related in the fourth degree with a third degree of consanguinity.[660] It stated that the groom was born in Culiacán and was twenty-three years of age and that he had resided in Álamos for two years. María Ygnacia was said to have been born in La Aduana and was thirteen years of age at the time she gave testimony. José María testified, wanting to clear his conscience, that he had previously given his word to marry two other women with whom he was blood related. The marriages were suspended because of mutual parental agreement, also because of close familial blood ties between himself and his intended brides.

José María Quirós y Mora, son of Pedro Quirós y Mora and Ana María Verdugo, was born about 1766 in Culiacán. The cited marriage information record provided his place of birth and his age. José María Quirós y Mora and María Ygnacia Campoy had the following known children:

i. **Juana María Guadalupe Quirós y Mora** was born on December 31, 1790 in La Aduana. She was baptized on January 30, 1791, at the parish of the Purísima Concepción in Álamos.[661] The baptismal record named Juan Francisco Campoy y Quirós and María Manuela Esquer as her *padrinos*. The baptismal ceremony took place in the chapel of La Aduana, jurisdiction of Álamos. She had previously been poured the waters of baptism by Juan Antonio Formoso on the day of her birth, should she not survive.

---

659. Matrimonios 1779–1817, December 1, 1789, film 666565, image 172–173, Registros Parroquiales, Iglesia de La Purísima Concepción, Álamos, Sonora, Mexico (FamilySearch, https://familysearch.org).
660. Información matrimonial 1788–1790, Novmeber 18, 1789, [no film number], images 232–238, Registros Parroquiales, Iglesia de La Purísima Concepción, Álamos, Sonora, Mexico (FamilySearch, https://familysearch.org).
661. Bautismos 1781–1796, January 30, 1791, film 663488, image 364, Registros Parroquiales, Iglesia de La Purísima Concepción, Álamos, Sonora, Mexico (FamilySearch, https://familysearch.org).

178 ii.   **José Trinidad Feliciano Quirós y Mora** was born in 1794 in San Pedro de Quila, Sinaloa; he married María Francisca Gil Samaniego on November 19, 1822, in Álamos.

179 iii.   **María Isabel Quirós y Mora** was born about 1795; she married José María Almada on April 18, 1813, in Álamos.

180 iv.   **José Manuel Tiburcio Quirós y Mora** was born about 1800 in Culiacán; he married María Petra Fox on May 7, 1823, in Álamos and died before December 26, 1868.

181 v.   **Pedro Francisco Quirós y Mora** was born on August 4, 1804, in Álamos; he married María Balvanera de Lamadrid, about 1824.

    vi.   **José Eugenio de Jesús Quirós y Mora** was born on November 15, 1807, in Álamos, according to the baptismal record. He was baptized on November 17, 1807, at the church of the Purísima Concepción in Álamos.[662] The baptismal record named Pedro Francisco Quirós as his *padrino*. José Tiburcio Quirós y Mora and Francisco Xavier Navarro were named as witnesses.

182 vii.   **Juan Hipólito de Jesús Quirós y Mora**, was born on August 13, 1817; he married María Josefa Torres Gil, after June 19, 1847, in Álamos.

---

662. Bautismos 1791–1796, 1805–1815, November 17, 1807, film 663996, image 296, Registros Parroquiales, Iglesia de La Purísima Concepción, Álamos, Sonora, Mexico (FamilySearch, https://familysearch.org).

Eighth Generation

113. **Anna María Josefa Valentina Alcayde** (Joaquín Andrés-7, Francisco Xavier-6, Juana Esquer-5, Juan Salvador-4, Salvador-3, Salvador-2, Blas-1) was born in 1779 in Álamos. She was baptized on February 20, 1779, at the church of the Purísima Concepción in Álamos.[663] The baptismal record named Juan Manuel González de Zayas and Guadalupe Rivera as her *padrinos*. Miguel Alcayde and Joseph Bustillos were named as witnesses to the sacrament of baptism.

Anna María Josefa Valentina Alcayde and José Antonio Delgado were married on November 8, 1803, at the church of Nuestra Señora del Rosario in Rosario.[664] The matrimonial record named Francisco de Ontiveros and his son Juan Nepomueno Ontiveros as witnesses to the marriage. Parents of the bridal couple were named. The bride and groom received a nuptial blessing on the day of their marriage. the groom was said to be the widowed husband of María de Osuna.

José Antonio Delgado and Anna María Josefa Valentina Alcayde had one known child:

    i.   **José María Escolástico Delgado** was born on February 10, 1806, in Rosario, according to the baptismal record. He was baptized on February 16, 1806, at the church of Nuestra Señora del Rosario in Rosario.[665] The baptismal record named Bárbara López Portillo as his *madrina*.

114. **Bruno Dionicio Luis de Jesús Esquer** (José Rafael-7, Juan Salvador-6, Salvador-5, Juan Salvador-4, Salvador-3, Salvador-2, Blas-1) was born in 1804 in Álamos. He was baptized on October 8, 1804, at the church of the Purísima Concepción in Álamos.[666] The baptismal record named Juan de Fox and María Gertrudis Esquer as his *padrinos*.

Bruno Dionicio Luis de Jesús Esquer and María Josefa Figueroa were married about 1826. The marriage record has not been located. Evidence of marriage was provided in the baptismal records of their children where they were identified as *hijos legítimos*.

---

663. Bautismos, matrimonios y defunciones 1696–1699, bautismos 1768–1781, film 663487, images 400–401, Registros Parroquiales, Iglesia de La Purísima Concepción, Álamos, Sonora, Mexico, (FamilySearch, https://familysearch.org).
664. Matrimonios 1776–1806, 1823–1830, 1849–1858, 1863–1869, November 8, 1803, film 676111, image 285, Registros Parroquiales, Iglesia de Nuestra Señora del Rosario, Rosario, Sinaloa, Mexico (FamilySearch, https://familysearch.org).
665. Bautismos 1804–1814, February 16, 1806, film 676095, image 54, Registros Parroquiales, Iglesia de Nuestra Señora del Rosario, Rosario, Sinaloa, Mexico (FamilySearch, https://familysearch.org).
666. Bautismos 1796–1805, October 8, 1804, film 663995, image 252, Registros Parroquiales, Iglesia de La Purísima Concepción, Álamos, Sonora, Mexico (FamilySearch, https://familysearch.org).

María Josefa Figueroa, daughter of Joseph Joaquín Figueroa and María Gertrudis Montiel, was born in 1804 in Álamos, according to the cited civil death record. She died on February 24, 1872, at the age of sixty-eight in Álamos.[667] The civil death record named her husband and parents.

Bruno Dionicio Luis de Jesús Esquer and María Josefa Figueroa had the following children:

i. **José María de la Asunción Esquer** was born in 1827 in Álamos. He was baptized on August 16, 1827, at the church of the Purísima Concepción in Álamos.[668] The baptismal record named José María Verdugo and Gertrudis Figueroa as his *padrinos*.

ii. **Bruno Eutimio Esquer** was born in 1829 in Álamos. He was baptized on March 15, 1829, at the church of the Purísima Concepción in Álamos.[669] The baptismal record named Joaquín Figueroa and María Gertrudis Montiel as his *padrinos*.

iii. **María de las Nieves Esquer** was born in 1830 in Álamos. She was baptized on August 12, 1830, at the church of the Purísima Concepción in Álamos.[670] The baptismal record named Salvador Esquer and Rita Cano de los Ríos as her *padrinos*.

iv. **María Guadalupe Margarita Esquer** was born in 1833 in Álamos. She was baptized on June 9, 1833, at the church of the Purísima Concepción in Álamos.[671] The baptismal record named José Montiel and María Guadalupe de la Fuente as her *padrinos*.

v. **Rómulo Eulalio Esquer** was born in 1835 in Álamos. He was baptized on February 12, 1835, at the church of the Purísima Concepción in Álamos.[672] The baptismal record named José María Esquer and Trinidad Esquer as his *padrinos*.

vi. **Wenceslao Zenón Esquer** was born in 1836 in Álamos. He was baptized on June 23, 1836, at the church of the Purísima Concepción in Álamos.[673] The baptismal record named José María Esquer and Nieves Esquer as his *padrinos*.

---

667. Defunciones 1868–1887, February 24, 1872, film [none] image 205, Civil Registrations, Álamos, Sonora, Mexico (FamilySearch, https://familysearch.org).
668. Bautismos 1816–1825, 1827–1829, August 16, 1827, film 663997, image 457, Registros Parroquiales, Iglesia de La Purísima Concepción, Álamos, Sonora, Mexico (FamilySearch, https://familysearch.org).
669. Bautismos 1816–1825, 1827–1829, March 15, 1829, film 663997, images 541–542, Registros Parroquiales, Iglesia de La Purísima Concepción, Álamos, Sonora, Mexico (FamilySearch, https://familysearch.org).
670. Bautismos 1829–1838, August 12, 1830, film 666560, image 35, Registros Parroquiales, Iglesia de La Purísima Concepción, Álamos, Sonora, Mexico (FamilySearch, https://familysearch.org).
671. Bautismos 1829–1838, June 9, 1833, film 666560, image 157, Registros Parroquiales, Iglesia de La Purísima Concepción, Álamos, Sonora, Mexico (FamilySearch, https://familysearch.org).
672. Bautismos 1829–1838, February 12, 1835, film 666560, image 279, Registros Parroquiales, Iglesia de La Purísima Concepción, Álamos, Sonora, Mexico (FamilySearch, https://familysearch.org).
673. Bautismos 1829–1838, June 23, 1836, film 666560, image 361, Registros Parroquiales, Iglesia de La Purísima Concepción, Álamos, Sonora, Mexico (FamilySearch, https://familysearch.org).

115. **José Francisco Evaristo de los Santos Esquer** (José Rafael-7, Juan Salvador-6, Salvador-5, Juan Salvador-4, Salvador-3, Salvador-2, Blas-1) was born on October 26, 1806, in Álamos. The cited baptismal record provided his date of birth. He was baptized on November 1, 1806, at the church of the Purísima Concepción in Álamos.[674] The baptismal record named Juan José Fox and Liberata Almagro as his *padrinos*.

José Francisco Evaristo de los Santos Esquer and María Gertrudis Toledo were married before 1830.[675] The actual marriage record has not been located. Proof of marriage was taken from the cited baptismal record for their son José Salvador Román Francisco Esquer.

María Gertrudis Toledo, daughter of Tiburcio Toledo, was born about 1808.

José Francisco Evaristo de los Santos Esquer and María Gertrudis Toledo had the following known children:

i. **José Salvador Román Francisco Esquer** was born in 1830 in Álamos. He was baptized on March 2, 1830, in Álamos.[676] He married Trinidad Amarillas sometime before 1857. The marriage record has not been located.

ii. **José de Jesús Esquer** was born on April 15, 1839, in Álamos. The baptismal record stated that he was one day old the day of his baptism. He was baptized on April 16, 1839, at the church of Nuestra Señora de Loreto in Baroyeca, Sonora.[677] The baptismal record named Verónica Ángel de Toledo as his *madrina*. The child's mother's name was written in the record as "Plutarca Gertrudis Ángel de Toledo." The baptism took place in the mining town of Baroyeca.

iii. **Delfín Eutimio de Jesús Esquer** was born on December 23, 1842 in Baroyeca. The baptismal record stated that he was three days old when baptized. He was baptized on December 26, 1842, at the church of Nuestra Señora de Loreto in Baroyeca, Sonora.[678] The baptismal record named Juan Nepomuceno Ángel de Toledo and María Loreto Ángel de Toledo as his *padrinos*. The child's mother was identified as "Plutarca Gertrudis Ángel de Toledo." The baptism took place in the town of Tesopaco, Sonora.

---

674. Bautismos 1791–1796, 1805–1815, November 1, 1806, film 663996, image 262, Registros Parroquiales, Iglesia de La Purísima Concepción, Álamos, Sonora, Mexico (FamilySearch, https://familysearch.org).
675. Bautismos 1829–1838, March 2, 1830, film 666560, image 19, Registros Parroquiales, Iglesia de La Purísima Concepción, Álamos, Sonora, Mexico (FamilySearch, https://familysearch.org).
676. Bautismos 1829–1838, March 2, 1830, film 666560, image 19, Registros Parroquiales, Iglesia de La Purísima Concepción, Álamos, Sonora, Mexico (FamilySearch, https://familysearch.org).
677. Bautismos 1838–1856, April 16, 1839, film 663998, image 15, Registros Parroquiales, Iglesia de La Purísima Concepción, Álamos, Sonora, Mexico (FamilySearch, https://familysearch.org).
678. Bautismos 1838–1856, December 26, 1842, film 663998, image 57, Registros Parroquiales, Iglesia de La Purísima Concepción, Álamos, Sonora, Mexico (FamilySearch, https://familysearch.org).

116. **María Petra Fox** (María Gertrudis Esquer-7, Juan Salvador-6, Salvador-5, Juan Salvador-4, Salvador-3, Salvador-2, Blas-1) was born in 1797 in Álamos. She was baptized on July 8, 1797, at the church of the Purísima Concepción in Álamos.[679] The baptismal record named Juan Fox and María Loreto Anguís as her *padrinos*.

María Petra Fox and José Manuel Tiburcio Quirós y Mora were married on May 7, 1823, at the church of the Purísima Concepción in Álamos.[680] The matrimonial record named José María Almada and Ysabel Quirós y Mora as *padrinos* to the marriage. Ygnacio Fox and Pedro Quirós y Mora, among others, were said to have been present at the ceremony. The couple received a nuptial blessing on the day of their marriage. Parents of the bride and groom were named in the record, and the father of the bride was said to have been deceased at the time. The couple received a marriage dispensation for having been related in the fourth degree of consanguinity, meaning they were third cousins.

María Petra Fox died before December 3, 1868.[681] The cited matrimonial record for her son Domingo stated that his mother was deceased on the date of his marriage, December 3, 1868.

José Manuel Tiburcio Quirós y Mora, son of José María Quirós y Mora and María Ygnacia Campoy, was born about 1800 in Culiacán. The cited marriage record provided his place of birth. He died before December 26, 1868. The cited matrimonial record for his son Domingo stated that his father was deceased on the date of his marriage. His name appeared as "José Manuel Quirós" in most of his children's baptismal records. "José Manuel Tiburcio Quirós" was used in the baptismal record of his daughter Bernarda.

José Manuel Tiburcio Quirós y Mora and María Petra Fox had the following known children:

i. **José Pascual Bernardino de Jesús Quirós y Mora** was born in 1824 in Álamos. He was baptized on May 20, 1824, at the church of the Purísima Concepción in Álamos.[682] The baptismal record named José María Quirós and María Ignacia Campoy as his *padrinos*.

ii. **Juan José Secundino Quirós y Mora** was born in 1827 in Álamos. He was baptized on July 5, 1827, at the church of the Purísima Concepción in Álamos.[683] The baptismal record named José María Almada and María Isabel Quirós as his *padrinos*.

iii. **María Josefa Quirós y Mora** was born in 1829 in Álamos. She was baptized on March 29, 1829, at the parish of the Purísima Concepción in Álamos.[684] The baptismal

679. Bautismos 1796–1805, July 8, 1797, film 663995, image 47, Registros Parroquiales, Iglesia de La Purísima Concepción, Álamos, Sonora, Mexico (FamilySearch, https://familysearch.org).

680. Matrimonios 1797–1833, 1846–1868, 1872–1877, May 7, 1823, film 666566, images 276–277, Registros Parroquiales, Iglesia de La Purísima Concepción, Álamos, Sonora, Mexico (FamilySearch, https://familysearch.org).

681. Matrimonios 1851–1909, 1911–1917, December 3, 1868, film 687240, image 153, Registros Parroquiales, Iglesia de Nuestra Señora de Guadalupe, Altar, Sonora, Mexico (FamilySearch, https://familysearch.org).

682. Bautismos 1816–1825, 1827–1829, May 20, 1824, film 663997, image 272, Registros Parroquiales, Iglesia de La Purísima Concepción, Álamos, Sonora, Mexico (FamilySearch, https://familysearch.org).

683. Bautismos 1816–1825, 1827–1829, July 5, 1827, film 663997, image 454, Registros Parroquiales, Iglesia de La Purísima Concepción, Álamos, Sonora, Mexico (FamilySearch, https://familysearch.org).

684. Bautismos 1816–1825, 1827–1829, March 29, 1829, film 663997, image 542, Registros Parroquiales, Iglesia de La Purísima Concepción, Álamos, Sonora, Mexico (FamilySearch, https://familysearch.org).

record named Ygnacio Fox and María Gertrudis Esquer as her *padrinos*. The baptism took place at the chapel of La Aduana.

iv. **Bernarda María del Carmen Quirós y Mora** was born in 1832 in Álamos. She was baptized on August 20, 1832, at the church of the Purísima Concepción in Álamos.[685] The baptismal record named the officiating priest, Father Nicolás Quirós, and Isabel Quirós as her *padrinos*.

v. **Francisco María de Candelaria Quirós y Mora** was born on January 29, 1835 in Álamos, according to the baptismal record. He was baptized on February 2, 1835, at the church of the Purísima Concepción in Álamos.[686] The baptismal record named José María Almada and María Isabel Quirós as his *padrinos*.

vi. **Domingo Quirós y Mora** was born about 1840 in Álamos. He married María de Jesús Carmelo on December 3, 1868 in Altar, Sonora, Mexico.[687]

117. **María de Jesús del Mar Atilana Fox** (María Gertrudis Esquer-7, Juan Salvador-6, Salvador-5, Juan Salvador-4, Salvador-3, Salvador-2, Blas-1) was born in 1799 in Álamos. She was baptized on October 11, 1799, at the church of the Purísima Concepción in Álamos.[688] The baptismal record named Bachiller Pedro Joaquín Campoy as her *padrino*.

María de Jesús del Mar Atilana Fox and José Antonio Tena were married sometime before 1828. The matrimonial record has not been located. The marriage date was estimated to be around the time of their first child's birth.

José Antonio Tena was born about 1797.

José Antonio Tena and María de Jesús del Mar Atilana Fox had the following known children:

i. **Jose Ygnacio Teofilo de Jesús Tena** was born in 1828 in Álamos. He was baptized on December 13, 1828, at the church of the Purísima Concepción in Álamos.[689]

ii. **Jose Antonio Bonifacio de Jesús Tena** was born in 1830 in Álamos. He was baptized on May 14, 1830, at the church of the Purísima Concepción in Álamos.[690] The baptismal record named José Ygnacio Fox and María Gertrudis Esquer [mother and son] as his *padrinos*.

685. Bautismos 1829–1838, August 20, 1832, film 666560, image 123, Registros Parroquiales, Iglesia de La Purísima Concepción, Álamos, Sonora, Mexico (FamilySearch, https://familysearch.org).
686. Bautismos 1829–1838, February 2, 1835, film 666560, image 261, Registros Parroquiales, Iglesia de La Purísima Concepción, Álamos, Sonora, Mexico (FamilySearch, https://familysearch.org).
687. Matrimonios 1851–1909, 1911–1917, December 3, 1868, film 687240, image 153, Registros Parroquiales, Iglesia de Nuestra Señora de Guadalupe, Altar, Sonora, Mexico (FamilySearch, https://familysearch.org).
688. Bautismos 1796–1805, October 11, 1799, film 663995, image 109, Registros Parroquiales, Iglesia de La Purísima Concepción, Álamos, Sonora, Mexico (FamilySearch, https://familysearch.org).
689. Bautismos 1816–1825, 1827–1829, December 13, 1828, film 663997, image [not located], Registros Parroquiales, Iglesia de La Purísima Concepción, Álamos, Sonora, Mexico (FamilySearch, https://familysearch.org).
690. Bautismos 1829–1838, May 14, 1830, film 666560, images 27–28, Registros Parroquiales, Iglesia de La Purísima Concepción, Álamos, Sonora, Mexico (FamilySearch, https://familysearch.org).

iii. **Jesús María Narciso Tena** was born in 1832 in Álamos. He was baptized on October 31, 1832, in Álamos.[691] The baptismal record named Belén Tena and Francisca Tena as his *padrinos.*

iv. **José Antonio Rufo Tena** was born in 1835 in Álamos. He was baptized on August 27, 1835 in Álamos.[692] He married Loreto Esquer on February 6, 1864, in Álamos.[693]

v. **Buenaventura Carmen de Jesús Tena** was born in 1841 in Álamos. He was baptized on July 16, 1841, at the church of the Purísima Concepción in Álamos.[694] The baptismal record named Jesús and Trinidad Esquerra as his *padrinos.*

118. María Dolores Francisca de Jesús Candelaria Fox (María Gertrudis Esquer-7, Juan Salvador-6, Salvador-5, Juan Salvador-4, Salvador-3, Salvador-2, Blas-1) was born on January 29, 1803, in Álamos, according to the baptismal record. She was baptized on February 4, 1803, at the church of the Purísima Concepción in Álamos.[695] The baptismal record named María Petra de Goycochea as her *madrina.*

119. María Antonia Francisca Feliciana Fox (María Gertrudis Esquer-7, Juan Salvador-6, Salvador-5, Juan Salvador-4, Salvador-3, Salvador-2, Blas-1) was born in 1812 in Álamos. She was baptized on June 14, 1812, at the church of the Purísima Concepción in Álamos.[696] The baptismal record named Petra Mariana de Goycochea as her *madrina.*

María Antonia Francisca Feliciana Fox and Guadalupe Sarracino were married on February 22, 1841, at the church of the Purísima Concepción in Álamos.[697] The matrimonial record named Pasqual Quirós and María Petra Fox as *padrinos.* Arnelo Inocencio García, and Julián Ybarra were named as witnesses to the marriage. Parents of the bridal couple were named, and the father of the bride was said to be deceased. The matrimonial record is attached to the cited marriage information record dated January 18, 1841.

691. Bautismos 1829–1838, October 31,1832, film 666560, image 133, Registros Parroquiales, Iglesia de La Purísima Concepción, Álamos, Sonora, Mexico (FamilySearch, https://familysearch.org).

692. Bautismos 1829–1838, August 27, 1835, film 666560, images 315–316, Registros Parroquiales, Iglesia de La Purísima Concepción, Álamos, Sonora, Mexico (FamilySearch, https://familysearch.org).

693. Matrimonios 1797–1833, 1846–1868, 1872–1877, February 6, 1864, film 666566, image 470, Registros Parroquiales, Iglesia de La Purísima Concepción, Álamos, Sonora, Mexico (FamilySearch, https://familysearch.org); Información matrimonial 1862–1868, January 16, 1865, film 666573, images 136–138, Registros Parroquiales, Iglesia de La Purísima Concepción, Álamos, Sonora, Mexico (FamilySearch, https://familysearch.org).

694. Bautismos 1838–1871, July 16, 1841, film 667000, image 203, Registros Parroquiales, Iglesia de La Purísima Concepción, Álamos, Sonora, Mexico (FamilySearch, https://familysearch.org).

695. Bautismos 1796–1805, February 4, 1803, film 663995, image 189, Registros Parroquiales, Iglesia de La Purísima Concepción, Álamos, Sonora, Mexico (FamilySearch, https://familysearch.org).

696. Bautismos 1791–1796, 1805–1815, June 14, 1812, film 663996, image 433, Registros Parroquiales, Iglesia de La Purísima Concepción, Álamos, Sonora, Mexico (FamilySearch, https://familysearch.org).

697. Información matrimonial 1840–1849, February 22, 1841, film 663814, images 77–82, Registros Parroquiales, Iglesia de La Purísima Concepción, Álamos, Sonora, Mexico (FamilySearch, https://familysearch.org).

The marriage investigation revealed that the groom was engaged in business and originally from New Mexico. He had resided in La Aduana, jurisdiction of Álamos for one year. The record further stated that the bride's family was poor and that the household consisted of only women. Witnesses attested that there were no impediments to marriage. A dispensation by the bishop of Sonora was granted on January 29, 1841, after it was determined that both candidates were free to marry. There are no known children of this marriage.

Guadalupe Sarracino, son of Francisco Sarracino and Gertrudis Telles, was born in 1816 in New Mexico, New Spain. According to the cited marrige information record he was twenty-five years of age when he married.

120. **María Dolores de Jesús Anselma Fox** (Luis Juan Francisco Telmo-7, María Loreto Esquer-6, Salvador-5, Juan Salvador-4, Salvador-3, Salvador-2, Blas-1) was born in 1797 in Álamos. She was baptized on April 27, 1797, at the parish church of the Purísima Concepción in Álamos.[698] The baptismal record named Juan Fox and Ysabel Esquer as her *padrinos*.

María Dolores de Jesús Anselma Fox and José María de la Cruz Talamantes were married on May 4, 1824, at the parish of the Purísima Concepción in Álamos.[699] The matrimonial record named José María Quirós y Mora and María Dolores Fox as *padrinos*. Manuel Fox and Ignacio Fox were said to have been present at the ceremony. Parents of the bride and groom were named. The mother of the bride was identified as what appears to be "Petra Torres."

José María de la Cruz Talamantes, son of José María Talamantes and Balvanera Montiel, was born in 1799 in Álamos. He was baptized on May 12, 1799, at the church of the Purísima Concepción in Álamos.[700] The baptismal record named Miguel Aguilar and Agustina Aguilar as his *padrinos*. The record identified the child as a mestizo. The baptism took place at the chapel of La Aduana.

José María de la Cruz Talamantes and María Dolores de Jesús Anselma Fox had the following known children:

i. **Juana Paula Talamantes** was born in 1825 in Álamos. She was baptized on July 4, 1825, at the church of the Purísima Concepción in Álamos.[701]

ii. **María Carlota Felipa Dorotea Talamantes** was born in 1831 in Álamos. She was baptized on June 5, 1831, at the parish of the Purísima Concepción in Álamos.[702] The baptismal record named Juan Francisco Fox and María Anastasia Talamantes

698. Bautismos 1796–1805, April 27, 1797, film 663995, image 40, Registros Parroquiales, Iglesia de La Purísima Concepción, Álamos, Sonora, Mexico (FamilySearch, https://familysearch.org).
699. Matrimonios 1797–1833, 1846–1868, 1872-1877, May 2, 1824, film 666566, images 290–291, Registros Parroquiales, Iglesia de La Purísima Concepción, Álamos, Sonora, Mexico (FamilySearch, https://familysearch. org).
700. Bautismos 1796–1805, May 12, 1799, film 663995, images 101–102, Registros Parroquiales, Iglesia de La Purísima Concepción, Álamos, Sonora, Mexico (FamilySearch, https://familysearch.org).
701. Bautismos 1816–1825, 1827–1829, July 4, 1825, film 663997, image [not located], Registros Parroquiales, Iglesia de La Purísima Concepción, Álamos, Sonora, Mexico (FamilySearch, https://familysearch.org).
702. Bautismos 1829–1838, June 5, 1831, film 666560, image 78, Registros Parroquiales, Iglesia de La Purísima Concepción, Álamos, Sonora, Mexico (FamilySearch, https://familysearch.org).

as her *padrinos*. The baptism took place at the chapel of La Aduana in the parish of Álamos.

    iii.   **Francisco Damián Talamantes** was born in 1833 in Álamos. He was baptized on October 4, 1833, at the church of the Purísima Concepción in Álamos.[703] The baptismal record named Vicente Ortiz and Dolores Esquer as his *padrinos*.

121. **Manuel Fox** (Luis Juan Francisco Telmo-7, María Loreto Esquer-6, Salvador-5, Juan Salvador-4, Salvador-3, Salvador-2, Blas-1) was born about 1807 in Álamos.

Manuel Fox and María del Sacramento Ybarra were married on March 24, 1827, at the parish church of the Purísima Concepción in Álamos.[704] The matrimonial record named Ramón Navarro and Ygnacio Malo as witnesses to the marriage. The couple received a nuptial blessing on the day of their marriage. Both the bride and groom were said to have originated in Álamos. Parents of the bridal couple were named in the record. The mother of the groom was identified in the record as María Petra Torres.

María del Sacramento Ybarra, daughter of Francisco Ybarra and María Francisca Pacheco, was born about 1809 in Álamos.

Manuel Fox and María del Sacramento Ybarra had the following known children:

    i.   **Juan José Policarpo Fox** was born in 1828 in Álamos. He was baptized on February 3, 1828, at the parish church of the Purísima Concepción in Álamos.[705] The baptismal record named José María Talamantes and María Dolores Fox as his *padrinos*.

    ii.   **María Guadalupe Sebastiana Fox** was born on January 19, 1838, in Álamos. She was baptized on January 28, 1838, at the parish church of the Purísima Concepción in Álamos.[706] The baptismal record named José Ygnacio Moreno and María Ybarra as her *padrinos*. She was said have been nine days old on the day of her baptism.

    iii.   **María Guadalupe Crecencia Fox** was born on December 25, 1845 in Álamos. The baptismal record stated she was born twelve days before her date of baptism. She was baptized on January 6, 1846, at the parish church of the Purísima Concepción in Álamos.[707]

---

703. Bautismos 1829–1838, October 4, 1833, film 666560, image 172, Registros Parroquiales, Iglesia de La Purísima Concepción, Álamos, Sonora, Mexico (FamilySearch, https://familysearch.org).
704. Matrimonios 1797–1833, 1846–1868, 1872–1877, March 24, 1827, film 666566, image 315, Registros Parroquiales, Iglesia de La Purísima Concepción, Álamos, Sonora, Mexico (FamilySearch, https://familysearch.org).
705. Bautismos 1816–1825,1827–1829, February 3, 1828, film 663997, image 481, Registros Parroquiales, Iglesia de La Purísima Concepción, Álamos, Sonora, Mexico (FamilySearch, https://familysearch.org).
706. Bautismos 1829–1838, January 28,1838, film 666560, image 433, Registros Parroquiales, Iglesia de La Purísima Concepción, Álamos, Sonora, Mexico (FamilySearch, https://familysearch.org).
707. Bautismos 1838–1856, January 6, 1846, film 663998, image 205, Registros Parroquiales, Iglesia de La Purísima Concepción, Álamos, Sonora, Mexico (FamilySearch, https://familysearch.org).

122. **Simona María Gertrudis Martínez Mendívil** (Petra María Gertrudis Féliz-7, Manuela Antonia Esquer-6, Joseph Cayetano-5, Juan Salvador-4, Salvador-3, Salvador-2, Blas-1) was born in 1763 in Álamos. She was baptized on November 13, 1763, at the church of the Purísima Concepción in Álamos.[708] The baptismal record named Víctor Morales and Juana María de Urvina as her *padrinos*.

Simona María Gertrudis Martínez Mendívil and Juan Francisco Padilla were married on September 25, 1784, at the church of the Purísima Concepción in Álamos.[709] The matrimonial record named Juan Ignacio Mendívil and Ana María Mendívil as *padrinos*. Marcelo Morales, over sixty years of age; Josef Antonio Gutiérrez, over forty years of age; and Josef Rosas, over forty years of age, were named as witnesses to the couple's eligibility to marry. Parents of the bride and groom were named. The record also stated that the groom had been the widowed husband of Mariana de Ochoa.

Simona María Gertrudis Martínez Mendívil died before 1800. The cited matrimonial record for her daughter, María de Carmen, stated that her mother was deceased on the day of the marriage, October 8, 1800.

Juan Francisco Padilla, son of Joseph Padilla and Juana Calvo, was born about 1750 in Álamos. The cited matrimonial record provided his place of birth.

Juan Francisco Padilla and Simona María Gertrudis Martínez Mendívil had the following known children:

i. **José Francisco Padilla** was born about 1784 in Álamos; he married María Guadalupe Trinidad Cornelia Féliz on June 5, 1820, in Álamos.[710]

ii. **María del Carmen Padilla Arnao** was born about 1785 in Álamos; she married Joseph Ygnacio Gastélum on October 8, 1800, in Álamos.[711]

iii. **María Dolores Padilla Arnao** was born about 1788 in Álamos; she married Joseph Casiano Gil de Lamadrid on February 26, 1805, in Álamos.[712]

iv. **María Guadalupe Padilla** was born about 1795; she married Joseph Féliz on March 31, 1812, in Álamos.[713]

---

708. Bautismos 1751–1794, matrimonios 1848, defunciones 1735–1752, November 13, 1763, film 666999, image 269, Registros Parroquiales, Iglesia de La Purísima Concepción, Álamos, Sonora, Mexico (FamilySearch, https://familysearch.org).
709. Matrimonios 1779–1817, September 25, 1784, film 666565, image 96, Registros Parroquiales, Iglesia de La Purísima Concepción, Álamos, Sonora, Mexico (FamilySearch, https://familysearch.org).
710. Matrimonios 1797–1833, 1846–1868, 1872–1877, June 5, 1820, film 666566, image 237, Registros Parroquiales, Iglesia de La Purísima Concepción, Álamos, Sonora, Mexico (FamilySearch, https://familysearch.org).
711. Matrimonios 1779–1817, October 8, 1800, flm 666565, image 384, Registros Parroquiales, Iglesia de La Purísima Concepción, Álamos, Sonora, Mexico (FamilySearch, https://familysearch.org).
712. Matrimonios 1779–1817, February 26, 1805, flm 666565, image 453, Registros Parroquiales, Iglesia de La Purísima Concepción, Álamos, Sonora, Mexico (FamilySearch, https://familysearch.org).
713. Matrimonios 1779–1817, March 31, 1812, film 666565, image 512, Registros Parroquiales, Iglesia de La Purísima Concepción, Álamos, Sonora, Mexico (FamilySearch, https://familysearch.org).

v.   **María Francisca Padilla** was born about 1796; she married Manuel Féliz on May 15, 1822, in Álamos.[714]

123. Juan José Timoteo Martínez Mendívil (Petra María Gertrudis Féliz-7, Manuela Antonia Esquer-6, Joseph Cayetano-5, Juan Salvador-4, Salvador-3, Salvador-2, Blas-1) was born in 1766 in Álamos. He was baptized on February 5, 1766, at the church of the Purísima Concepción in Álamos.[715] The baptismal record named Joseph Prudencio Mendívil and Juana María Mendívil as his *padrinos*. Bachiller Juan Joseph de Avilés and Blas Gutiérrez were named as witnesses to the sacrament of baptism. His surname in some records appeared simply as "Mendívil."

Juan José Timoteo Martínez Mendívil and María Loreto González Barreda were married on June 11, 1787, at the church of the Purísima Concepción in Álamos.[716] The matrimonial record named Luis Martínez de Mendívil and María Lucía Martínez de Mendívil as *padrinos*. Juan Thomas Padilla, sixty-one years of age; Miguel de Lara, over fifty years of age; and Antonio Ybarra, over forty years of age, were named as witnesses to the couple's eligibility to marry. Juan Francisco Padilla and Melchor Amarillas were named as witnesses to the marriage. Parents of the bride and groom were named in the record. Parents of the bride were said to be deceased. The couple received a nuptial blessing on the same day as their marriage.

The marriage investigation, dated May 21, 1787, stated that Juan José Timoteo Martínez Mendívil and María Loreto González Barreda were related in the third, with fourth degree of consanguinity, meaning they were second cousins, one generation removed.[717] Because of this blood relationship they were required to receive a dispensation to marry. The marriage investigation revealed no other impediments to their marriage.

María Loreto González Barreda, daughter of Fernando Antonio González Barreda and María Raphaela Esquer, was born about 1766.

Juan José Timoteo Martínez Mendívil and María Loreto González Barreda had the following known children:

i.   **José Fernando Trinidad Martínez Mendívil** was born on May 31, 1791, in Álamos. He was baptized on June 5, 1791, in Álamos.[718] He died on September 16, 1792 in Álamos and was buried on September 17, 1792, in Álamos.[719]

---

714. Matrimonios 1797–1833, 1846–1868, 1872–1877, May 15, 1822, film 666566, images 261–262, Registros Parroquiales, Iglesia de La Purísima Concepción, Álamos, Sonora, Mexico (FamilySearch, https://familysearch.org).

715. Bautismos 1751–1794, matrimonios 1848, defunciones 1735–1752, February 5, 1766, film 666999, image 323, Registros Parroquiales, Iglesia de La Purísima Concepción, Álamos, Sonora, Mexico (FamilySearch, https://familysearch.org).

716. Matrimonios 1779–1817, June 11, 1787, film 666565, image 112, Registros Parroquiales, Iglesia de La Purísima Concepción, Álamos, Sonora, Mexico (FamilySearch, https://familysearch.org).

717. Información matrimonial 1760–1799, May 21, 1787, film 667002, images 523–524, Registros Parroquiales, Iglesia de La Purísima Concepción, Álamos, Sonora, Mexico (FamilySearch, https://familysearch.org).

718. Bautismos 1781–1796, June 5, 1791, film 663488, images 377–378, Registros Parroquiales, Iglesia de La Purísima Concepción, Álamos, Sonora, Mexico (FamilySearch, https://familysearch.org).

719. Defunciones 1786–1819, September 17, 1792, film 666996, image 55, Registros Parroquiales, Iglesia de La Purísima Concepción, Álamos, Sonora, Mexico (FamilySearch, https://familysearch.org).

ii.   **María Rafaela Gerónima Martínez Mendívil** was born in 1793 in Álamos. She was baptized on October 6, 1793, at the parish of the Purísima Concepción in Álamos.[720] The baptismal record named José Carrillo and María Matilde Barreda as her *padrinos*.

iii.   **María del Carmen Cayetana Martínez Mendívil** was born in 1795 in Álamos. She was baptized on August 15, 1795, at the parish of the Purísima Concepción in Álamos.[721] The baptismal record named Manuel Anguís and Serafina Barreda as her *padrinos*. The baptism ceremony took place at the chapel of La Aduana.

iv.   **José Fernando Casimiro Martínez Mendívil** was born in 1797 in Álamos. He was baptized on May 12, 1797, in Álamos.[722] He married María Isidora Tomasa Gaxiola on July 21, 1828, in Álamos.[723]

v.   **Manuel de Jesús Esteban Martínez Mendívil** was born in 1798, in Álamos, and he was baptized on December 31, 1798, in Álamos. [724] He married María Encarnación Carrasco in about 1821 in Álamos.[725]

vi.   **María Gertrudis Catarina Martínez Mendívil** was born in 1801 in Álamos, and she was baptized on April 30, 1801, in Álamos.[726] She married José Francisco Yepes on February 6, 1821, in Álamos.[727]

vii.   **José Andrés de Jesús Martínez Mendívil** was born in 1804 in Álamos. He was baptized on February 11, 1804, at the church of the Purísima Concepción in Álamos.[728] The baptismal record named Agustín Esquerra y Rosas and María de la Luz González Barreda as his *padrinos*.

---

720. Bautismos 1781–1796, October 6, 1793, film 663488, image 604, Registros Parroquiales, Iglesia de La Purísima Concepción, Álamos, Sonora, Mexico (FamilySearch, https://familysearch.org).

721. Bautismos 1781–1796, August 15, 1795, film 663488, image 675, Registros Parroquiales, Iglesia de La Purísima Concepción, Álamos, Sonora, Mexico (FamilySearch, https://familysearch.org).

722. Bautismos 1796–1805, March 12, 1797, film 663995, image 34, Registros Parroquiales, Iglesia de La Purísima Concepción, Álamos, Sonora, Mexico (FamilySearch, https://familysearch.org).

723. Matrimonios 1797–1833, 1846–1868, 1872–1877, July 21, 1828, film 666566, images 326–327, Registros Parroquiales, Iglesia de La Purísima Concepción, Álamos, Sonora, Mexico (FamilySearch, https://familysearch.org); Información matrimonial 1800–1855, June 10, 1828, film 663811, images 400–401, Registros Parroquiales, Iglesia de La Purísima Concepción, Álamos, Sonora, Mexico (FamilySearch, https://familysearch.org).

724. Bautismos 1796–1805, December 31, 1798, film 663995, image 89, Registros Parroquiales, Iglesia de La Purísima Concepción, Álamos, Sonora, Mexico (FamilySearch, https://familysearch.org).

725. Información matrimonial 1800–1855, about 1820, film 663811, image 89, Registros Parroquiales, Iglesia de La Purísima Concepción, Álamos, Sonora, Mexico (FamilySearch, https://familysearch.org).

726. Bautismos 1796–1805, April 30, 1801, film 663995, image 153, Registros Parroquiales, Iglesia de La Purísima Concepción, Álamos, Sonora, Mexico (FamilySearch, https://familysearch.org).

727. Matrimonios 1797–1833, 1846–1868, 1872–1877, February 6, 1821, film 666566, image 246, Registros Parroquiales, Iglesia de La Purísima Concepción, Álamos, Sonora, Mexico (FamilySearch, https://familysearch.org).

728. Bautismos 1796–1805, February 11, 1804, film 663995, image 227, Registros Parroquiales, Iglesia de La Purísima Concepción, Álamos, Sonora, Mexico (FamilySearch, https://familysearch.org).

viii.   **José de Jesús Máximo Martínez Mendívil** was born in 1806 in Álamos. He was baptized on July 1, 1806, at the church of the Purísima Concepción in Álamos.[729] The baptismal record named Luis Mendívil and Simona Muñoz as his *padrinos*.

124. Luis María Antonio Martínez Mendívil (Petra María Gertrudis Féliz-7, Manuela Antonia Esquer-6, Joseph Cayetano-5, Juan Salvador-4, Salvador-3, Salvador-2, Blas-1) was born in 1768 in Álamos. He was baptized on September 8, 1768, at the church of the Purísima Concepción in Álamos.[730] The baptismal record named Joseph Martínez Mendívil and Lucía Mendívil as his *padrinos*.

Luis María Antonio Martínez Mendívil and María Gertrudis de Guadalupe Gerónima de Merced Muñoz were married on January 2, 1789, at the church of the Purísima Concepción in Álamos.[731] The matrimonial record named José Mendívil, and his wife, María Loreto Barreda as *padrinos*. Parents of the bride and groom, along with Francisco Mendívil; Joaquín Muñoz; Juan José Fox; Jose Bustillos, *sacristán*; and many others were witnesses to the sacrament of marriage. The couple received a nuptial blessing on the day of their marriage. The bride was said to have originated in Álamos, and that she was a resident of Bacamaya, currently in the jurisdiction of Álamos. Bacamaya was, at the time of the marriage, in the jurisdiction of El Fuerte, Sinaloa.

The cited marriage investigation, dated December 13, 1788, provided testimony from the marriage candidates, as well as three witnesses.[732] Luis María Antonio testified to be twenty-one years of age, a *vecino* of Álamos, single with no impediment to marriage. His intended bride testified to be more than fifteen years of age, a maiden, and that she was from Bacamaya. José Francisco Esquerra de Rosas, married, forty years of age, and *vecino* of Álamos; Manuel de Orrantia, married, more than forty years of age, *vecino* of Álamos, originally from the Kingdom of Castile, Spain; and Juan Gil Samaniego, married, over fifty years of age, and *vecino* of Álamos, were named as witnesses to the couple's eligibility to marry. The investigation was concluded on December 23, 1788.

María Gertrudis de Guadalupe Gerónima de Merced Muñoz, daughter of Joaquín Gabriel Muñoz and Anna Rosalía Gastélum, was born in 1770 in Álamos. She was baptized on September 30, 1770, at the church of the Purísima Concepción in Álamos.[733] The baptismal record named Raymundo Antonio Campoy and María Lucía Gastélum as her *padrinos*. Francisco Manuel

---

729. Bautismos 1791–1796,1805–1815, July 1, 1806, film 663996, image 250, Registros Parroquiales, Iglesia de La Purísima Concepción, Álamos, Sonora, Mexico (FamilySearch, https://familysearch.org).

730. Bautismos, matrimonios y defunciones 1696–1699, bautismos 1768–1781, September 8, 1768, film 663487, image 113, Registros Parroquiales, Iglesia de La Purísima Concepción, Álamos, Sonora, Mexico (FamilySearch, https:// familysearch.org).

731. Matrimonios 1779–1817, January 2, 1790, film 666565, image 145, Registros Parroquiales, Iglesia de La Purísima Concepción, Álamos, Sonora, Mexico (FamilySearch, https://familysearch.org).

732. Información matrimonial 1788–1790, December 13, 1789, [no film number], images 63–68, Registros Parroquiales, Iglesia de La Purísima Concepción, Álamos, Sonora, Mexico (FamilySearch, https://familysearch. org).

733. Bautismos, matrimonios y defunciones 1696–1699, bautismos 1768–1781, September 30, 1770, film 663487, image 234, Registros Parroquiales, Iglesia de La Purísima Concepción, Álamos, Sonora, Mexico (FamilySearch, https://familysearch.org).

Campoy and Joaquín Gastélum were named as witnesses. The baptism took place at the chapel of La Aduana.

Luis María Antonio Martínez Mendívil and María Gertrudis de Guadalupe Gerónima de Merced Muñoz had the following known children:

 i. **Luis Martínez Mendívil** married María Domínguez. The marriage record has not been located.

 ii. **José Merced Martínez Mendívil** married Inés Domíngues. The marriage record has not been located.

 iii. **Francisco Antonio Martínez Mendívil** was born on December 11, 1790, at the church of the Purísima Concepción in Álamos, according to the baptismal record. He was baptized on February 8, 1791, at the church of the Purísima Concepción in Álamos.[734] The baptismal record named Francisco Mendívil and María Petra Féliz as his *padrinos.*

 iv. **Manuela Martínez Mendívil** was born about 1796; she married José Joaquín Domínguez on June 1, 1814, in Álamos.[735]

 v. **José Antonio Sotero Martínez Mendívil** was born in 1799 in Álamos, and he was baptized on May 15, 1799, in Álamos.[736] He married María Josefa Murrieta. The marriage record has not been located.

 vi. **María Josepha Marcos Martínez Mendívil** was born in 1803 in Álamos. She was baptized on June 7, 1803, at the church of the Purísima Concepción in Álamos.[737] The baptismal record named Salvador Féliz and María Loreto Muñoz as her *padrinos.*

 vii. **José de Jesús Guadalupe Martínez Mendívil** was born in 1805 in Álamos, and he was baptized on January 24, 1805, in Álamos.[738]

 viii. **María del Carmen Martínez Mendívil** was born about 1811; she married Miguel Ygnacio Dolores Antonio de la Luz Esquer on May 11, 1831, Álamos.[739]

125. María Rosa Isabel Martínez Mendívil (Petra María Gertrudis Féliz-7, Manuela Antonia Esquer-6, Joseph Cayetano-5, Juan Salvador-4, Salvador-3, Salvador-2, Blas-1) was born in 1777 in Álamos. She was baptized on April 2, 1777, at the church of the Purísima Concepción

---

734. Bautismos 1781–1796, February 8, 1791, film 663489, images 365–366, Registros Parroquiales, Iglesia de La Purísima Concepción, Álamos, Sonora, Mexico (FamilySearch, https://familysearch.org).
735. Matrimonios 1779–1817, June 1, 1814, film 666565, image 525, Registros Parroquiales, Iglesia de La Purísima Concepción, Álamos, Sonora, Mexico (FamilySearch, https://familysearch.org).
736. Bautismos 1796–1805, May 15, 1799, film 663995, image 102, Registros Parroquiales, Iglesia de La Purísima Concepción, Álamos, Sonora, Mexico (FamilySearch, https://familysearch.org).
737. Bautismos 1796–1805, June 7, 1803, film 663995, image 200, Registros Parroquiales, Iglesia de La Purísima Concepción, Álamos, Sonora, Mexico (FamilySearch, https://familysearch.org).
738. Bautismos 1796–1805, January 24, 1805, film 663995, image 260, Registros Parroquiales, Iglesia de La Purísima Concepción, Álamos, Sonora, Mexico (FamilySearch, https://familysearch.org).
739. Bautismos 1796–1805, January 24, 1805, film 663995, image 260, Registros Parroquiales, Iglesia de La Purísima Concepción, Álamos, Sonora, Mexico (FamilySearch, https://familysearch.org).

in Álamos.[740] The baptismal record named Joseph Carrillo and Anna María Francisca Mendívil as her *padrinos*.

María Rosa Isabel Martínez Mendívil and Juan Antonio López Bravo were married on May 2, 1793, at the church of the Purísima Concepción in Álamos.[741] The matrimonial record claimed they were related in the third, with a fourth degree of consanguinity. They were second cousins once removed. The record named Agustín Rosas and Anna María Mendívil as *padrinos*. José Bustillos, Francisco Mariño, Xavier Acuña, among others, were named as witnesses to to marriage. The couple received a nuptial blessing on the day of their marriage. Parents of the bride and groom were also named in the record. The bride's family was said to have been from the Puesto de Chinal, jurisdiction of Álamos.

The cited marriage investigation, dated April 13, 1793, provided a letter from the bishop of Sonora giving the couple a dispensation to marry and to receive a nuptial blessing.[742] Parents were named, and the mother of the groom, María Francisca Ruiz, was said to have been deceased.

Juan Antonio López Bravo, son of Pedro López Bravo and María Micaela Francisca Ruiz de Ayllón, was born about 1770 in Álamos. The cited baptismal record for his daughter María Guadalupe claimed he used the alias "*El Cuervo*" (The Crow).

Juan Antonio López Bravo and María Rosa Isabel Martínez Mendívil had the following known children:

i. **María Guadalupe George López Bravo** was born in 1795 in Álamos. She was baptized on April 17, 1795, at the church of the Purísima Concepción in Álamos.[743] The baptismal record named Francisco Mendívil and Petra Gertrudis Féliz as her *padrinos*.

ii. **José Víctor López Bravo** was born about March 12, 1806, in Álamos. He died about March 12, 1806, in Álamos. He was buried on March 12, 1806, in Álamos.[744] The burial record stated that he was buried beneath the choir *con cruz baja*. The officiating priest recorded that the little child just barely lived long enough to receive the waters of baptism, "*apenas alcanzó el agua*." Parents of the deceased child were named in the record.

iii. **María Gertrudis López Bravo** died in 1809 in Álamos. She was born about 1809 in Álamos. She was buried on February 18, 1809, at the church of the Purísima

---

740. Bautismos, matrimonios y defunciones 1696–1699, bautismos 1768–1781, film 663487, image 343, Registros Parroquiales, Iglesia de La Purísima Concepción, Álamos, Sonora, Mexico (FamilySearch, https://familysearch.org).
741. Matrimonios 1779–1817, May 2, 1793, film 666565, image 242, Registros Parroquiales, Iglesia de La Purísima Concepción, Álamos, Sonora, Mexico (FamilySearch, https://familysearch.org).
742. Información matrimonial 1760–1799, film 667002, images 612–613, Registros Parroquiales, Iglesia de La Purísima Concepción, Álamos, Sonora, Mexico (FamilySearch, https://familysearch.org).
743. Bautismos 1781–1796, April 17, 1795, film 663488, image 669, Registros Parroquiales, Iglesia de La Purísima Concepción, Álamos, Sonora, Mexico (FamilySearch, https://familysearch.org).
744. Defunciones 1786–1819, March 12, 1806, film 666996, image 378, Registros Parroquiales, Iglesia de La Purísima Concepción, Álamos, Sonora, Mexico (FamilySearch, https://familysearch.org).

Concepción in Álamos.[745] María Gertrudis López Bravo died as a child (*párvula*), and she was buried beneath the choir of the church. Her funeral service was held with a *cruz baja*.

126. Joseph Francisco Féliz (Joseph Vicente-7, Manuela Antonia Esquer-6, Joseph Cayetano-5, Juan Salvador-4, Salvador-3, Salvador-2, Blas-1) was born on October 9, 1761 in Álamos. The cited baptismal record claimed that he was born eleven days prior to his date of baptism. He was baptized on October 20, 1761, in Álamos.[746] The baptismal record named Gabriel Mallén de Navarette and Rita Antonia Mallén de Navarrete, his sister, as the child's *padrinos*. The family was said to have been living at the *puesto*, likely a military post, named Las Haciendas, one league distance from Álamos, traveling east. He died in 1847, at the age of eighty-six. Joseph was buried on March 21, 1847, at San Gabriel Arcángel Mission, Alta California, New Spain.[747]

Joseph Francisco Féliz and María Josefa Cota were married on January 29, 1788, at San Gabriel Arcángel Mission.[748] The marriage record named Crispín Pérez and Joseph Manuel Pérez as witnesses to the couple's eligibility to marry without impediment. María Alvarado and Juan de Osuna were named witnesses to the marriage. Parents of the bride and groom were named in the record. At the time of his marriage, Joseph Francisco Féliz was a soldier stationed at the presidio in San Diego, Alta California, New Spain.

María Josefa Cota, daughter of Roque Jacinto Cota and Juana María Verdugo, was born about 1773 in Loreto, Baja California, New Spain. She died on April 14, 1836. The cited burial record noted that she had died two days before her burial. She was buried on April 16, 1836, at San Fernando Rey de España Mission.[749] María Josefa Cota was buried in the mission cemetery. She received the last sacraments of the Catholic Church before death. Her husband Francisco Féliz was named, and she was identified as having been a *vecina* of the Pueblo de Nuestra Señora la Reina de los Ángeles de Porciúncula (also known as Pueblo de los Ángeles), Alta California, New Spain.

Joseph Francisco Féliz and María Josefa Cota had the following known children:

i. **Adriano Francisco Féliz** was born on March 1, 1792, at the San Diego Presidio, according to the baptismal record. He was baptized on March 2, 1792, at the San Diego Mission in San Diego, Alta California.[750] The baptismal record named Juan Francisco Padilla and María Gertrudis Rodríguez as his *padrinos*. His father was said to have been a soldier at the presidio. Adriano Francisco died on January 3, 1813, at the age of twenty. He was buried on January 4, 1813, at San Gabriel Arcángel

745. Bautismos 1791–1796, 1805–1815, February 18, 1809, film 663996, image 414, Registros Parroquiales, Iglesia de La Purísima Concepción, Álamos, Sonora, Mexico (FamilySearch, https://familysearch.org).
746. Bautismos 1751–1794, matrimonios 1848, defunciones 1735–1752, October 20, 1761, film 666999, image 220, Registros Parroquiales, Iglesia de La Purísima Concepción, Álamos, Sonora, Mexico (FamilySearch, https://familysearch.org).
747. Burials 1774–1855, March 21, 1847, film 2646, [no image number], Catholic Church Records, San Gabriel Arcángel Mission, San Gabriel, California, USA, (FamilySearch, https://familysearch.org).
748. San Gabriel Arcángel Mission (SG), marriage number 00302, January 29, 1788, ECPP, 2006.
749. San Fernando Rey Mission (SFR), death record 02082, April 16, 1836, ECPP, 2006.
750. San Diego Mission (SD), baptism number 01524, March 2, 1792, ECPP, 2006.

Mission in the mission cemetery[751] He had resided at the Rancho de los Féliz before his death.

ii. **José Thomas Féliz** was born about 1793; he married María de Jesus López Salgado on January 5, 1815 at San Fernando Rey Mission.[752] He died on November 11, 1830, and he was buried on November 12, 1830, at the Los Angeles Plaza Church.[753]

iii. **María Marcelina Luciana Féliz** was born in 1796. She was baptized on June 3, 1796, at San Gabriel Arcángel Mission.[754] The baptismal record named María Josefa de la Luz Heredia and Juan Padilla as her *padrinos*. She died on March 27, 1840. María was buried on March 28, 1840, at the Los Angeles Plaza Church.[755]

iv. **Josef Vicente Valentín Féliz** was born in 1797. He was baptized on December 17, 1797, at San Gabriel Arcángel Mission.[756] The baptismal record named María Gertrudis Valenzuela and Anastasio Féliz as his *padrinos*.

v. **María Francisca Féliz** was born on October 10, 1799, and she was baptized on October 11, 1799 at the San Gabriel Arcángel Mission.[757] She married José Domingo Romero Salgado on April 11, 1815, at the San Fernando Rey Mission.[758]

vi. **María de Gracia Féliz** was born on March 7, 1801. She was baptized on March 8, 1801, at San Gabriel Arcángel Mission.[759] The baptismal record named Anna Gerónima Féliz and Francisco Bruno García as her *padrinos*. She died on November 26, 1823, at the age of twenty-two. María was buried on November 27, 1823, at San Gabriel Arcángel Mission in the mission cemetery.[760] She received the last sacraments of the Catholic Church. The record stated that she died on November 28, 1823, which is in error, given her burial was recorded as November 27, 1823.

vii. **María Rosalía Féliz** was born on December 13, 1802, according to the baptismal record. She was baptized on December 14, 1802, at the San Gabriel Arcángel Mission.[761] The baptismal record named María Luisa Cota and Claudio López as her *padrinos*. She died on April 29, 1813, at the age of ten. María was buried on April 30, 1813, at San Gabriel Arcángel Mission, in the mission cemetery.[762]

viii. **José Antonio Féliz** was born on April 2, 1804. He was baptized on April 4, 1804, at San Gabriel Arcángel Mission.[763] The baptismal record named Luisa Cota and Josef Antonio López as his *padrinos*.

---

751. San Gabriel Arcángel Mission (SG), death number 03291, January 4, 1813, ECPP, 2006.
752. San Fernando Rey Mission (SFR), Marriage number 00597, January 5, 1815, ECPP, 2006.
753. Los Angeles Plaza Church (LA), death number 00112, November 12, 1830, ECPP, 2006.
754. San Gabriel Arcángel Mission, baptism number 02721, June 3, 1796, ECPP, 2006.
755. Los Angeles Plaza Church (LA), death number 00482, March 28, 1840, ECPP, 2006.
756. San Gabriel Arcángel Mission (SG), baptism number 02883, December 17, 1797, ECPP, 2006.
757. San Gabriel Arcángel Mission (SG), baptism number 03071, October 11, 1799, ECPP, 2006.
758. San Fernando Rey Mission (SFR), marriage number 00598, April 11, 1815, ECPP, 2006.
759. San Gabriel Arcángel Mission (SG), baptism number 03247, March 8, 1801, ECPP, 2006.
760. San Gabriel Arcángel Mission (SG), death number 04754, November 27, 1823, ECPP, 2006.
761. San Gabriel Arcángel Mission (SG), baptism number 03394, December 14, 1802, ECPP, 2006.
762. San Gabriel Arcángel Mission (SG), death number 03325, April 30, 1813, ECPP, 2006.
763. San Gabriel Arcángel Mission (SG), baptism number 03735, April 4, 1804, ECPP, 2006.

ix. **José Domingo Féliz** was born in 1805, and he was baptized on November 18, 1805 at the San Gabriel Arcángel Mission.[764] He married María del Rosario Villa on June 2, 1829, at the San Gabriel Arcángel Mission.[765] He died on March 27, 1836, and he was buried on March 28, 1836 at Los Angeles Plaza Church.[766]

x. **José Cristóbal Féliz** was born in 1807. He was baptized on August 1, 1807, at San Gabriel Arcángel Mission.[767] The baptismal record did not name his *padrinos*. He died on August 31, 1819, at the age of twelve at the Rancho de los Feliz.[768] José was buried on September 1, 1819, at San Gabriel Arcángel Mission, in the mission cemetery.[769] He died from a fall in a horseback riding accident. He did not receive the last sacraments of the Catholic Church before death. His family were residents of the Rancho de los Féliz.

xi. **María del Pilar Féliz** was born on March 8, 1809, in the Pueblo de los Ángeles, according to the baptismal record. She was baptized on March 8, 1809, at San Gabriel Arcángel Mission.[770] The baptismal record named Luisa Cota and Claudio López as her *padrinos*.

xii. **María Dolores Féliz** was born in 1813. She was baptized on April 10, 1813, at San Gabriel Arcángel Mission.[771] The baptismal record named María Briones and Leandro Duarte as her *padrinos*.

xiii. **María de la Trinidad Féliz** was born in 1811. She was baptized on June 11, 1811, at San Gabriel Arcángel Mission.[772] The baptismal record named María Luisa Cota as her *madrina*.

xiv. **María de la Ascención Féliz** was born on May 4, 1815, according to the baptismal record. She was baptized on May 8, 1815, at San Gabriel Arcángel Mission.[773] The baptismal record named María Ygnacia Amador and José Ygnacio Lugo as her *padrinos*. The parents were said to be *vecinos* of the Rancho de San José.

xv. **Saturnina Féliz** was born about 1818 in San Gabriel, Alta California.[774]

127. **María Loreto Estéfana Féliz** (Joseph Vicente-7, Manuela Antonia Esquer-6, Joseph Cayetano-5, Juan Salvador-4, Salvador-3, Salvador-2, Blas-1) was born on November 4, 1764, in Álamos. The cited baptismal record stated that she was baptized provisionally because of fear

764. San Gabriel Acrangel Mission (SG), baptism number 04025, November 18, 1805, ECPP, 2006.
765. San Gabriel Arcángel Mission (SG), marriage number 01841, June 2, 1829, ECPP, 2006.
766. Los Angeles Plaza Church (LA), death number 00268, March 28, 1836, ECPP, 2006.
767. San Gabriel Arcángel Mission (SG), baptism number 04160, August 1, 1807, ECPP, 2006.
768. San Gabriel Arcángel Mission (SG), death number 04182, September 1, 1819, ECPP, 2006.
769. Ibid.
770. San Gabriel Arcángel Mission (SG), baptism number 04260, March 8, 1809, ECPP, 2006.
771. San Gabriel Arcángel Mission (SG), baptism number 05259, April 10, 1813, ECPP, 2006.
772. San Gabriel Arcángel Mission (SG), baptism number 05022, June 11, 1811, ECPP, 2006.
773. San Gabriel Arcángel Mission (SG), baptism number 05721, May 8, 1815, ECPP, 2006.
774. Marie E. Northrop, *Spanish-Mexican families of Early California: Los Pobladores de la Reina de Los Angeles*, volume III (Burbank, Calif: Southern California Genealogical Society, Inc., 2004), p. 107.

of death. This is evidence that she was born and baptized on the same day. She was baptized on November 4, 1764, in Álamos.[775] The baptismal record named Joseph Francisco Esquerra de Rosas and María Susana Esquerra de Rosas as her *padrinos*. Francisco Betilla and Blas Gutiérrez were named as witnesses.

María Loreto Estéfana Féliz and Joseph Ygnacio Olivera were married on December 8, 1778, at San Gabriel Arcángel Mission.[776] The matrimonial record named Juan Joseph Domínguez, Pedro Lisalde, Francisco Raphael Márquez, and Santiago Pico as witnesses to the couple's eligibility to marry without impediment. Leonardo Verdugo and Ignacia Carrillo, among various others, were identified as witnesses to the marriage. Parents of the bride and groom were named in the record.

María Loreto Estéfana Féliz died on July 7, 1789, at the age of twenty-four. She was buried on July 8, 1789, at San Gabriel Arcángel Mission.[777] The burial record stated that she had originated in Álamos, and that she had been married to Joseph Ygnacio Olivera, a sergeant at the Santa Bárbara presidio at the time of her death.

Joseph Ygnacio Olivera, son of Martín Olivera and María Micaela Carrillo, was born about 1752. The cited marriage record claimed that he had originated in Loreto, Baja California, and that his father was soldier stationed at the presidio in Loreto. He died in 1794, and he was buried on April 26, 1794, at Santa Bárbara Mission.[778]

Joseph Ygnacio Olivera and María Loreto Estéfana Féliz had one known child:

    i.   **María Estéfana Olivera** was born on August 3, 1788, and she was baptized on August 4, 1788 at San Buenaventura Mission.[779] She married Joseph Vicente Ortega López on January 11, 1807, at Santa Ynez Mission.[780] María Estéfana died on June 10, 1830, and he was buried on June 11, 1830, at Santa Bárbara Mission.[781]

128. **Joseph Doroteo Féliz** (Joseph Vicente-7, Manuela Antonia Esquer-6, Joseph Cayetano-5, Juan Salvador-4, Salvador-3, Salvador-2, Blas-1) was born about 1765 in Álamos.

Joseph Doroteo Féliz and Juana Josefa Villalobo were married on March 3, 1787, at the chapel of the presidio in Santa Bárbara, Alta California.[782] The marriage record named Pedro Amador and Mariano Cota as witnesses to the marriage. Parents of the bride and groom were named in the record. The groom was said to be a soldier at the presidio of Santa Bárbara.

775. Bautismos 1751–1794, matrimonios 1848, defunciones 1735–1752, November 4, 1764, film 666999, image 314, Registros Parroquiales, Iglesia de La Purísima Concepción, Álamos, Sonora, Mexico (FamilySearch, https://familysearch.org).
776. San Gabriel Arcángel Mission (SG), Marriage number 00100, December 8, 1778, ECPP, 2006.
777. San Gabriel Arcángel Mission (SG), death number 00644, July 8, 1789, ECPP, 2006.
778. Santa Bárbara Presidio (BP), death number 00034, April 26, 1794, ECPP, 2006.
779. San Buenaventura Mission (SBV), baptism number 00387, August 4, 1788, ECPP, 2006.
780. Santa Ynes Mission (SI), marriage number 00101, January 11, 1807, ECPP, 2006.
781. Santa Bárbara Presidio (BP), death number 00274, June 11, 1830, ECPP, 2006.
782. Santa Bárbara Presidio (BP), marriage number 00002, March 3, 1787, ECPP, 2006.

Joseph Doroteo Féliz died on September 29, 1832. The cited burial record noted that he had died the day before his burial at the age of seventy-two. He was buried on September 30, 1832, at San Carlos Borromeo Mission in Monterey, Alta California.[783] The following details of his death were paraphrased from information contained in the burial record:

Father Patricio Yrlandes crossed the Monterey River to a ranch where don Juan Mararin kept his livestock, for the purpose of hearing the confession of Joseph Doroteo Féliz. On that same day, Féliz was placed on a *carreta*, cart, to be taken to the presidio. He died while in route without the priest administering to him. He was buried in the cemetery of San Carlos Borromeo Mission. He had been married to Juana Villalobo.

Juana Josefa Villalobo, daughter of Juan José Miguel Villalobo and María Nicolasa Beltrán, was born about 1769 in Sinaloa. The cited burial record for her husband Doroteo Féliz stated that she was from the Villa de Sinaloa. She died on March 6, 1834. She was buried on March 7, 1834, at San Carlos Borromeo Mission in Monterey, Alta California.[784] The burial record noted that she had died the day before her burial and that she had received the last sacraments of the Catholic Church.

Joseph Doroteo Féliz and Juana Josefa Villalobo had the following known children:

i.   **Juan Féliz** was born on February 25, 1788, according the the baptismal record. He was baptized on February 25, 1788, at San Antonio de Padua Mission.[785] The baptismal record named Vicente Briones as his *padrino*. He died on March 18, 1788. Juan was buried on March 19, 1788, at San Antonio de Padua Mission.[786] The burial record stated the deceased was a small child.

ii.   **María Martina Petra Féliz** was born on January 30, 1789, at the Pueblo de los Ángeles, Alta California, and she was baptized on January 31, 1789, at San Gabriel Arcángel Mission.[787] She married twice: Miguel Blanco on April 22, 1805, at San Gabriel Arcángel Mission, and Pablo Rodríguez on August 22, 1829, at the San Diego presidio.[788]

iii.   **María Concepción Antonia Vicenta Féliz** was born on January 22, 1792, and was baptized on January 23, 1792 at San Diego de Alcalá Mission.[789] She married José Antonio Botiller on August 10, 1810, at San Gabriel Arcángel Mission.[790] María Concepción died on May 16, 1811, and was buried on May 17, 1811, at San Antonio de Padua Mission.[791]

---

783. San Carlos Borromeo Mission (SC), death number 02828, September 30, 1832, ECPP, 2006.

784. San Carlos Borromeo Mission (SC), Death number 02859, March 7, 1834, ECPP, 2006.

785. San Antonio Mission (SAP), baptism number 01533, February 25, 1788, ECPP, 2006.

786. San Antonio Mission (SAP), death number 00519, March 19, 1788, ECPP, 2006.

787. San Gabriel Arcángel Mission (SG), baptism number 01661, January 31, 1789, ECPP, 2006.

788. San Gabrie Arcángel Mission (SG), marriage number 00927, April 22, 1805, ECPP, 2006; San Diego (SD), marriage number 01714, August 22, 1829, ECPP, 2006.

789. San Diego de Alcalá Mission (SD), baptism number 01521, January 23, 1792, ECPP, 2006.

790. San Gabriel Arcángel Mission (SG), marriage number 01096, August 10, 1810, ECPP, 2006.

791. San Antonio Mission (SAP), death number 02307, May 17, 1811, ECPP, 2006.

iv.   **María Antonia Féliz** was born on June 17, 1794 and was baptized on June 19, 1794, at San Diego de Alcalá Mission.[792] She married Joseph Antonio María Valenzuela on September 22, 1807, at San Gabriel Arcángel Mission.[793]

v.   **José Féliz** was born on March 31, 1796, according to the baptismal record. He was baptized on April 1, 1796, at San Juan Capistrano Mission.[794] The baptismal record named José María Monroy and María Teresa Graciana as his *padrinos*.

vi.   **José Luciano María Féliz** was born on January 7, 1798, and was baptized on January 14, 1798, at San Diego de Alcalá Mission.[795] He married María Marcela Higuera on November 8, 1817, at San Gabriel Arcángel Mission.[796]

vii.   **María Antonia Féliz** was born on February 23, 1800, according to the baptismal record. She was baptized on February 24, 1800, at San Gabriel Arcángel Mission.[797] The baptismal record named María Gertrudis Valenzuela and Anastasio María Féliz as her *padrinos*.

viii.   **Juana Francisca Féliz** was born in 1804. She was baptized on May 6, 1804, at San Gabriel Arcángel Mission.[798] The baptismal record named Miguel Ortega as her *padrino*. She died on February 17, 1806, at the age of two. Juana was buried on February 18, 1806, at San Gabriel Arcángel Mission.[799]

ix.   **Vicente Antonio Féliz** was born in 1805 and was baptized on November 13, 1805, at San Gabriel Arcángel Mission.[800] He married Juana María Antonia Villavicencio on March 1, 1829, at San Carlos Borromeo Mission. He died on July 14, 1844, and he was buried on July 15, 1844, at the Camposanto de Monterey.[801]

x.   **Juan Diego Féliz** was born in 1807. He was baptized on November 13, 1807.[802] He married María Rosario Alviso. The marriage record has not been located. Juan Diego died on April 8, 1840, and was buried on April 9, 1840, at San Carlos Borromeo Mission.[803]

xi.   **José María Féliz** was born in 1809. He was baptized on February 3, 1809, at San Gabriel Arcángel Mission.[804] The baptismal record named María Luz Castro and Adriano Féliz as his *padrinos*. He died on September 28, 1823, at the age of fourteen. José was buried on September 29, 1823, at San Carlos Borromeo Mission.[805]

---

792. San Diego de Alcalá Mission (SD), baptism number 01629, January 19, 1794, ECPP, 2006.

793. San Gabriel Arcángel Mission, marriage number 00989, September 22, 1807, ECPP, 2006.

794. San Juan Capistrano Mission (SJC), baptism number 01590, April 1, 1796, ECPP, 2006.

795. San Diego Mission (SD), baptism number 02428, January 14, 1798, ECPP, 2006.

796. San Gabriel Arcángel Mission (SG), marriage number 01458, November 8, 1817, ECPP, 2006.

797. San Gabriel Arcángel Mission (SG), baptism number 03107, February 24, 1800, ECPP, 2006.

798. San Gabriel Mission Arcángel (SG), baptism number 03745, May 6, 1804, ECPP, 2006.

799. San Gabriel Arcángel Mission (SG), death number 02542, February 18, 1806, ECPP, 2006.

800. San Gabriel Arcángel Mission (SG), baptism number 04023, November 13, 1805, ECPP, 2006.

801. San Carlos Borromeo Mission (SC), death number 03246Y, July 15, 1844, ECPP, 2006.

802. San Carlos Borromeo Mission (SC), baptism number 04181, November 13, 1807, ECPP, 2006.

803. San Carlos Borromeo Mission (SC), death number 03029Y, April 9, 1840, ECPP, 2006.

804. San Gabriel Arcángel Mission (SG), baptism number 04251, February 3, 1809, ECPP, 2006.

805. San Carlos Borromeo Mission (SC), death number 02469, September 29, 1823, ECPP, 2006.

xii.   **Juana Féliz** was born on June 24, 1813, and was baptized on June 27, 1813, at San Gabriel Arcángel Mission.[806] She married twice: Emeterio Espinosa on October 30, 1830, at San Carlos Borromeo Mission then Gabriel de la Torre on August 10, 1838, at San Carlos Borromeo Mission.[807] Juana died died on August 1, 1894, and was buried on August 2, 1894, at San Carlos Borromeo Mission.[808]

129. María Marcela Féliz (Joseph Vicente-7, Manuela Antonia Esquer-6, Joseph Cayetano-5, Juan Salvador-4, Salvador-3, Salvador-2, Blas-1) was born in 1770 in Álamos. She was baptized on November 11, 1770, at the church of the Purísima Concepción in Álamos.[809] The baptismal record for María Marcela Féliz named Francisco Mendívil and Petra Gertrudis Féliz as her *padrinos.*

María Marcela Féliz and Ygnacio Narciso Olivera were married on October 30, 1783, at San Gabriel Arcángel Mission.[810] The matrimonial record named [unstated] Silva, Joseph María Verdugo, among other as witnesses to the sacrament of marriage. The groom was said to have been a soldier at the presidio of Santa Bárbara. Parents of the bride and groom were named.

Ygnacio Narciso Olivera, son of Martín Olivera and María Micaela Carrillo, was born about 1758 in San Antonio, Baja California, New Spain. He died on May 15, 1814. He was buried on May 16, 1814, at Santa Bárbara Mission, in the mission cemetery.[811] He held the title of *sargento retirado*, retired sergeant, at the time of his death.

Ygnacio Narciso Olivera and María Marcela Féliz had the following known children:

i.   **Antonio María Olivera** was born in 1785 and was baptized on May 26, 1785, at San Buenaventura Mission.[812] He married María Tomasa de Gracia Cota on April 10, 1809, at the chapel of the Santa Bárbara Presidio.[813]

ii.   **José Tomás Antonio Olivera** was born on December 19, 1787, and was baptized on December 21, 1787, at the Santa Bárbara Presidio.[814] He married María Antonia Marta Cota on February 1, 1816, at the Santa Barbara Presidio.[815] He died on July 27, 1848, and was buried at San Luis Obispo Mission.[816]

---

806. San Gabriel Arcángel Mission (SG), baptism number 05399, June 27, 1813, ECPP, 2006.

807. San Carlos Borromeo Mission (SC), marriage number 00999, October 30, 1830, ECPP, 2006; San Carlos Borromeo Mission (SC), marriage number 01081, August 10, 1838, ECPP, 2006.

808. Marie E. Northrop, *Spanish-Mexican families of Early California: Los Pobladores de la Reina de Los Angeles*, volume III (Burbank, Calif: Southern California Genealogical Society, Inc., 2004), p. 103.

809. Bautismos, matrimonios y defunciones 1696–1699, bautismos 1768–1781, November 30, 1783, film 663487, image 166, Registros Parroquiales, Iglesia de La Purísima Concepción, Álamos, Sonora, Mexico (FamilySearch, https:// familysearch.org).

810. San Gabriel Arcángel Mission (SG), marriage number 00186, October 30, 1783, ECPP, 2006.

811. Santa Bárbara Presidio (BP), death number 00169, May 16, 1814, ECPP, 2006.

812. San Buenaventura Mission (SPV), baptism number 00113, May 26, 1785, ECPP, 2006.

813. Santa Bárbara Presidio (BP), marriage number 00066, April 10, 1809, ECPP, 2006.

814. Santa Bárbara Presidio (BP), baptism number 00043, December 21, 1787, ECPP, 2006.

815. Santa Bárbara Presidio (BP), marriage number 00094, February 1, 1816, ECPP, 2006.

816. Marie E. Northrop, *Spanish-Mexican families of Early California: Los Pobladores de la Reina de Los Angeles*, volume III (Burbank, Calif: Southern California Genealogical Society, Inc., 2004), pp. 112–113.

130. **Joseph Pablo de Jesús Féliz** (Joseph Vicente-7, Manuela Antonia Esquer-6, Joseph Cayetano-5, Juan Salvador-4, Salvador-3, Salvador-2, Blas-1) was born in 1773 in Álamos. He was baptized on January 3, 1773, at the church of the Purísima Concepción in Álamos.[817] The baptismal record named Pedro Goycochea and Juana Lorenza Goycochea as his *padrinos*. Joaquín Gastélum was named as a witness.

Joseph Pablo de Jesús Féliz and María Celia Cota were married on August 16, 1789, at San Gabriel Arcángel Mission.[818] The matrimonial record named Ramón Buelna, Joseph María Duarte, and Manuel Pérez Nieto as witnesses to the couple's eligibility to marry without impediments. Luisa Cota and Claudio López were named witnesses to the sacrament of marriage.

The cited marriage investigation record, dated July 26, 1789, claimed that the couple had no impediment to marriage. Manuel Pérez Nieto, soldier at the presidio of San Diego; Ramón Buelna, native of Sinaloa, and soldier at that presidio; and José María Duarte, native of Sonora, gave testimony. The record stated that the groom was eighteen years of age and that the bride was the widow of Juan Antonio Botiller, native of *la antigua California*, Baja California.

Joseph Pablo died on December 25, 1837, at the age of sixty-four. Joseph was buried on December 26, 1837, in the cemetery at the Los Angeles Plaza Church.[819]

María Celia Cota, daughter of Roque Jacinto Cota and Juana María Verdugo, was born about 1758 in Loreto, Baja California. She died on May 1, 1847, according to the burial record. She was buried on May 2, 1847, at the cemetery of the Santa Bárbara Presidio in Santa Bárbara, Alta California.[820] She received the last sacraments of the Catholic Church before she died.

Joseph Pablo de Jesús Féliz and María Celia Cota had the following children:

    i.   **Juana Gertrudis Féliz** was born on July 11, 1790, and was baptized on July 12, 1790, at San Gabriel Arcángel Mission.[821] She married José Antonio Gil López on May 25, 1804, at San Gabriel Arcángel Mission.[822]

    ii.   **Leonardo María Féliz** was born on November 6, 1792, according to the baptismal record. He was baptized on November 7, 1792, at San Diego de Alcalá Mission.[823] The baptismal record named Juan Francisco Padilla and Thomasa Lugo as his *padrinos*.

    iii.   **Fernando de la Trinidad Féliz** was born on May 30, 1795. He was baptized on May 31, 1795, at San Gabriel Arcángel Mission.[824] The baptismal record named María

---

817. Bautismos, matrimonios y defunciones 1696–1699, bautismos 1768–1781, January 3, 1773, film 663487, image 245, Registros Parroquiales, Iglesia de La Purísima Concepción, Álamos, Sonora, Mexico (FamilySearch, https://familysearch.org).

818. San Gabriel Arcángel (SG), marriage number 00351, August 16, 1789, ECPP, 2006; Matrimonial investigation records of the San Gabriel Mission, José Féliz and María Celia (Cota) Botiller marriage record, July 26, 1789, Honnold Mudd Library, Claremont College, Claremont, CA. Special Collections (http://ccdl.libraries.claremont.edu/cdm/landingpage/ collection/mir).

819. Los Angeles Plaza Church (LA), death number 00330, December 26, 1837, ECPP, 2006.

820. Santa Bárbara Presidio (BP), death number 00749, May 2, 1847, ECPP, 2006.

821. San Gabriel Arcángel Mission (SG), baptism number 01848, July 12, 1790, ECPP, 2006.

822. San Gabriel Arcángel Mission (SG), marriage number 00864, May 25, 1804, ECPP, 2006.

823. San Diego de Alcalá Mission (SD), baptism number 01559, November 7, 1792, ECPP, 2006.

824. San Gabriel Arcángel Mission (SG), baptism number 02573, May 31, 1795, ECPP, 2006..

Duarte and Joseph María Duarte as his *padrinos*. He died on November 12, 1859, at the age of sixty-four at Rancho Sanel in Hopeland, Mendocino County, California, United States. Fernando was buried, at Hopeland Cemetery.[825] The inscription on his gravestone provided his date of death, saying we was sixty-three years of age at the time of death.

   iv.   **Antonio Rafael Féliz** was born on June 11, 1798, according to the baptismal record. He was baptized on June 12, 1798, at San Gabriel Arcángel Mission.[826] The baptismal record named María Silvas and Francisco Serrano as his *padrinos*. He died about July 26, 1850, at the age of fifty-two. Antonio was buried on July 27, 1850, at Santa Clara Mission, Alta California.[827]

   v.   **María Antonia Féliz** was born on November 16, 1800 and baptized on November 17, 1800, at San Gabriel Arcángel Mission.[828] She married José Francisco de Gracia López Salgado on September 10, 1822, at the Santa Bárbara Presidio.[829]

131. **Joseph Féliz** (Manuel-7, Manuela Antonia Esquer-6, Joseph Cayetano-5, Juan Salvador-4, Salvador-3, Salvador-2, Blas-1) was born about 1785 in Álamos. The matrimonial record for Joseph Féliz stated that he originated in El Chinal, jurisdiction of Álamos.

Joseph Féliz and María Guadalupe Padilla were married on March 31, 1812, at the church of the Purísima Concepción in Álamos.[830] The matrimonial record named Laureano Ybarra and Juana Féliz as *padrinos*. A marriage dispensation was granted because they were related in the second with third degree of consanguinity, meaning they were first cousins, once removed. Parents of the bride and groom were named in the record. There are no know children of this marriage.

María Guadalupe Padilla, daughter of Juan Francisco Padilla and Simona María Gertrudis Martínez Mendívil, was born about 1795.

132. **María Guadalupe Trinidad Cornelia Féliz** (Manuel-7, Manuela Antonia Esquer-6, Joseph Cayetano-5, Juan Salvador-4, Salvador-3, Salvador-2, Blas-1) was born in 1796 in Álamos. She was baptized on October 30, 1796, at the church of the Purísima Concepción in Álamos.[831] The baptism record named Manuel de Jesús Esquerra de Rosas and Anna María Martínez de Mendívil as her *padrinos*.

825. Fernando Feliz Memorial number 70734867, November 12, 1859, Hopeland Cemetery, Hopeland, Mendocino County, USA, Find a Grave (https://www.findagrave.com/memorial/70734867).
826. San Gabriel Arcángel Mission (SG), baptism number 02940, June 12, 1798, ECPP, 2006.
827. Marie E. Northrop, *Spanish-Mexican families of Early California: Los Pobladores de la Reina de Los Angeles*, volume III (Burbank, Calif: Southern California Genealogical Society, Inc., 2004), p. 110.
828. San Gabriel Arcángel Mission (SG), baptism number 03175, November 17, 1800, ECPP, 2006.
829. Santa Bárbara Presidio (BP) marriage number 00117, September 10, 1822, ECPP, 2006.
830. Matrimonios 1779–1817, March 31, 1812, film 666565, image 512, Registros Parroquiales, Iglesia de La Purísima Concepción, Álamos, Sonora, Mexico (FamilySearch, https://familysearch.org).
831. Bautismos 1796–1805, October 30, 1796, film 663995, image 17, Registros Parroquiales, Iglesia de La Purísima Concepción, Álamos, Sonora, Mexico (FamilySearch, https://familysearch.org).

María Guadalupe Trinidad Cornelia Féliz and José Francisco Padilla were married on June 5, 1820, at the church of the Purísima Concepción in Álamos.[832] The matrimonial record named Juan José Alvarez and María Candelaria Padilla as *padrinos*. The couple received a marriage dispensation because they were related in the second with third degree of consanguinity, meaning they were second cousins once removed. Parents were named in the record. The groom's family was said to have been from El Chinal, jurisdiction of Álamos.

José Francisco Padilla, son of Juan Francisco Padilla and Simona María Gertrudis Martínez Mendívil, was born about 1784 in Álamos. The cited matrimonial record for José Francico Padilla stated that he originated in Álamos.

José Francisco Padilla and María Guadalupe Trinidad Cornelia Féliz had one known child:

i.   **María del Carmen Victoria Padilla** was born on March 1, 1820, in Álamos, according the the baptismal record. She was baptized on April 8, 1820, at the church of the Purísima Concepción in Álamos.[833] The baptismal record named José Féliz and Candelaria Padilla as her *padrino*s.

133. Juan José del Refugio Féliz (Manuel-7, Manuela Antonia Esquer-6, Joseph Cayetano-5, Juan Salvador-4, Salvador-3, Salvador-2, Blas-1) was born in 1823 in Álamos. He was baptized on March 18, 1823, at the church of the Purísima Concepción in Álamos.[834] The baptismal record named Francisco Féliz and either María or Francisca Padilla as his *padrinos* (copy is very light).

Juan José del Refugio Féliz and María Teresa Martínez Mendívil were married on June 3, 1844, at the church of the Purísima Concepción in Álamos.[835] The matrimonial record, is included within the cited marriage information record dated April 29, 1844. The record named José María Álvarez and María Álvarez as *padrinos*. José [?] López, among others as witnesses to the marriage. The couple received a marriage dispensation from the bishop of Sonora on May 17, 1844, because, according to the genealogical tree provided, they were related in the third degree of consanguinity (second cousins) on one side and in the fourth with a second degree of consanguinity on the other. Parents of the bridal couple were named.

The groom, who was twenty years of age, was said to be the widowed husband of Josefa Barreda and that he was from the town of Tapizuelas, jurisdiction of Álamos. The bride was said to also be twenty years of age and that she was born in El Chinal, jurisdiction of Álamos. The marriage information record contained a family tree that demonstrated the familial relationship of the couple.

---

832. Matrimonios 1797–1833, 1846–1868, 1872–1877, June 5, 1820, film 666566, image 237, Registros Parroquiales, Iglesia de La Purísima Concepción, Álamos, Sonora, Mexico (FamilySearch, https://familysearch.org).
833. Bautismos 1816–1825, 1827–1829, April 8, 1820, film 663997, image 109, Registros Parroquiales, Iglesia de La Purísima Concepción, Álamos, Sonora, Mexico (FamilySearch, https://familysearch.org).
834. Bautismos 1816–1825, 1827–1829, March 18, 1823, film 663997, image 222, Registros Parroquiales, Iglesia de La Purísima Concepción, Álamos, Sonora, Mexico (FamilySearch, https://familysearch.org).
835. Información matrimonial 1840–1849, June 3, 1844, film 663814, images 230–234, Registros Parroquiales, Iglesia de La Purísima Concepción, Álamos, Sonora, Mexico (FamilySearch, https://familysearch.org).

María Teresa Martínez Mendívil, daughter of Luis Martínez Mendívil and María Dominguez, was born about 1824 in El Chinal.

Juan José del Refugio Féliz and María Teresa Martínez Mendívil had the following known children:

    i.   **Esteban Cristino Féliz** was born in 1848 in Álamos. He was baptized on October 1, 1848, at the church of the Purísima Concepción in Álamos.[836] The baptismal record named Esteban Mendívil and María Victoria Padilla as his *padrinos*.

    ii.   **María del Carmen Tirso Féliz** was born in 1850 in Álamos. She was baptized on March 20, 1850, at the church of the Purísima Concepción in Álamos.[837] The baptismal record named Pedro Mendívil and Dolores Mendívil as her *padrinos*.

134. Joseph Reyes Armenta (María Ynocencia Esquer-7, Joseph Cayetano-6, Joseph Cayetano-5, Juan Salvador-4, Salvador-3, Salvador-2, Blas-1) was born about 1782 in Álamos.

Joseph Reyes Armenta and María Ysidora Blancarte were married on July 30, 1806, at the church of the Purísima Concepción in Álamos.[838] The matrimonial record named Juan Agustín Eguino and Ana Esquer as *padrinos*. Ramón Eguino and Miguel Santini were named as witnesses to the marriage. Parents of the bride and groom were named. Joseph Reyes was said to have been from Álamos but had lived in the pueblo of Movas in the jurisdiction of Rosario, Sonora, for several years with his widowed mother.

María Ysidora Blancarte, daughter of Francisco Blancarte and Ysidora Rivera, was born about 1784.

Joseph Reyes Armenta and María Ysidora Blancarte had one known child:

    i.   **María Josefa Armenta** was born about 1808 in Álamos; she married Pedro Ignacio de Jesús Rochín on February 6, 1848, in Culiacán.[839]

135. María Antonia Petra Corral (María Balvanera Antonia Esquer-7, Joseph Cayetano-6, Joseph Cayetano-5, Juan Salvador-4, Salvador-3, Salvador-2, Blas-1) was born in 1787 in Álamos. She was baptized on September 12, 1787, at the church of the Purísima Concepción in Álamos.[840] The baptismal record named Francisco Ybarra and Petra Corral as her *padrinos*.

---

836. Bautismos 1838–1856, October 1, 1848, film 663998, image 357, Registros Parroquiales, Iglesia de La Purísima Concepción, Álamos, Sonora, Mexico (FamilySearch, https://familysearch.org).
837. Bautismos 1838–1856, March 20, 1850, film 663998, image 401, Registros Parroquiales, Iglesia de La Purísima Concepción, Álamos, Sonora, Mexico (FamilySearch, https://familysearch.org).
838. Matrimonios 1779–1817, July 30, 1806, film 666565, image 465, Registros Parroquiales, Iglesia de La Purísima Concepción, Álamos, Sonora, Mexico (FamilySearch, https://familysearch.org).
839. Matrimonios 1830–1856, February 6, 1848, film 673379, images 401–402, Registros Parroquiales, Iglesia Sagrario de San Miguel, Culiacán, Sinaloa, Mexico (FamilySearch, https://familysearch.org).
840. Bautismos 1781–1796, September 12, 1787, film 663488, image 230, Registros Parroquiales, Iglesia de La Purísima Concepción, Álamos, Sonora, Mexico (FamilySearch, https://familysearch.org).

María Antonia Petra Corral and José Salvador Figueroa were married on June 1, 1808, at the church of the Purísima Concepción in Álamos.[841] The matrimonial record named Joaquín Esquer and María Gertrudis Montiel as *padrinos*. Parents of the bridal couple were named, and the bride's father was said to have been deceased. After the death of Blas Antonio Figueroa in 1780, it is assumed that his widow remarried to Blas Manuel Esquer. It appears that the surname "Esquer" was recorded in error. It should have been entered as "Figueroa."

María Antonia died on October 7, 1845, at the age of fifty-eight in Álamos. She was buried on October 8, 1845, at the parish of the Purísima Concepción in Álamos.[842] The burial record noted that she had received the last sacraments of the Catholic Church. Her husband was named in the record. The death and burial took place in La Aduana in the jurisdiction of Álamos. She was also known as "María Petra Corral."

José Salvador Figueroa, son of Blas Antonio Figueroa and María Manuela Serafina Góngora, was born before 1780 in Álamos. The time of his birth was determined by the year of his father's death in 1780.

José Salvador Figueroa and María Antonia Petra Corral had the following known children:

i. **Francisco Ramón Figueroa** was born in 1809 in Álamos. He was baptized on March 12, 1809, at the church of the Purísima Concepción in Álamos.[843] The baptismal record named José Aniceto Figueroa and Josefa Figueroa as his *padrinos*. The margin of the entry noted that the person baptized was female, but within the actual entry the child was classified as male.

ii. **José Francisco Figueroa** was born about 1810 in Álamos; he married María Josefa Apodaca after May 4, 1833, in Álamos.[844]

iii. **María Josefa Lorenza del Sacramento Figueroa** was born in 1811 in Álamos and baptized on August 12, 1811, in Álamos.[845] She married Severiano de Jesús Gamez on February 23, 1831, in Álamos.[846]

iv. **José Antonio Balvanera Figueroa** was born in 1813 in Álamos. He was baptized on December 2, 1823, at the church of the Purísima Concepción in Álamos.[847] The

---

841. Matrimonios 1779–1817, June 1, 1808, film 666565, images 481-482, Registros Parroquiales, Iglesia de La Purísima Concepción, Álamos, Sonora, Mexico (FamilySearch, https://familysearch.org).
842. Defunciones 1843–1862, 1920–1960, October 8, 1845, film 666998, image 24, Registros Parroquiales, Iglesia de La Purísima Concepción, Álamos, Sonora, Mexico (FamilySearch, https://familysearch.org). .
843. Bautismos 1791–1796, 1805–1815, March 12, 1809, film 663996, images 328–329, Registros Parroquiales, Iglesia de La Purísima Concepción, Álamos, Sonora, Mexico (FamilySearch, https://familysearch.org).
844. Información matrimonial 1832–1834, after May 4, 1833, film 680063, images 368–369, Cathedral La Asunción, Hermosillo, Sonora Mexico (FamilySearch, https://familysearch.org).
845. Bautismos 1791–1796, 1805–1815, August 12, 1811, film 663996, image 441, Registros Parroquiales, Iglesia de La Purísima Concepción, Álamos, Sonora, Mexico (FamilySearch, https://familysearch.org).
846. Matrimonios 1797–1833, 1846–1868, 1872–1877, February 23, 1831, film 666566, image 335, Registros Parroquiales, Iglesia de La Purísima Concepción, Álamos, Sonora, Mexico (FamilySearch, https://familysearch.org).
847. Bautismos 1791–1796, 1805–1815, December 2, 1823, film 663996, image 465, Registros Parroquiales, Iglesia de La Purísima Concepción, Álamos, Sonora, Mexico (FamilySearch, https://familysearch.org).

baptismal record named José Esquer and Juliana García as his *padrinos*. The child was ethnically identified as *como español,* meaning he was likely light skinned in a racially mixed family.

v.   **José Francisco Figueroa** died on August 23, 1814, in Álamos. He was born before August 24, 1814 in Álamos. He was buried on August 24, 1814, at the church of the Purísima Concepción in Álamos.[848] His funeral service was held with a *cruz baja* and he was buried beneath the choir. The record identified him as a small child.

vi.   **María Gertrudis Damasa Figueroa** was born on December 11, 1817, in Álamos, according to the baptismal record. She was baptized on December 16, 1817, at the church of the Purísima Concepción in Álamos.[849] The baptismal record named Joaquín Figueroa and Gertrudis Montiel as her *padrinos.*

vii.   **José María Benedicto Figueroa** was born on April 27, 1819, in Álamos, according to the baptismal record. He was baptized on May 5, 1819, at the church of the Purísima Concepción in Álamos.[850] The baptismal record named Pasqual Gómez and María Dolores Anguís as his *padrinos.*

viii.   **[*párvulo*] Figueroa** was born about 1821 in Álamos. He was buried on October 23, 1821, at the parish of the Purísima Concepción in Álamos.[851] His funeral service was held with *cruz baja* and the small child was buried beneath the choir of the chapel of La Aduana.

ix.   **José Antonio María Balvanera Figueroa** was born in 1822 in Álamos. He was baptized on January 22, 1822, at the church of the Purísima Concepción in Álamos.[852] The baptismal record named María Balvanera Anguís as his *madrina.*

x.   **María Balvarena Trinidad Agatona Figueroa** was born in 1824 in Álamos. She was baptized on January 18, 1824, at the church of the Purísima Concepción in Álamos.[853] The baptismal record named María Balvanera Gómez as her *madrina.*

xi.   **Manuel María Marcos Lino Figueroa** was born on April 25, 1825, in Álamos, according to the baptismal record. He was baptized on April 29, 1825, at the church of the Purísima Concepción in Álamos.[854] The baptismal record named María Concepción Anguís as his *madrina.*

---

848. Defunciones 1786–1819, August 24, 1814, film 666996, image 474, Registros Parroquiales, Iglesia de La Purísima Concepción, Álamos, Sonora, Mexico (FamilySearch, https://familysearch.org).
849. Bautismos 1816–1825, 1827–1829, December 16, 1817, film 663997, image 51, Registros Parroquiales, Iglesia de La Purísima Concepción, Álamos, Sonora, Mexico (FamilySearch, https://familysearch.org).
850. Bautismos 1816–1825, 1827–1829, May 5, 1819, film 663997, image 82, Registros Parroquiales, Iglesia de La Purísima Concepción, Álamos, Sonora, Mexico (FamilySearch, https://familysearch.org).
851. Defunciones 1809–1842, October 23, 1821, film 666997, image 42, Registros Parroquiales, Iglesia de La Purísima Concepción, Álamos, Sonora, Mexico (FamilySearch, https://familysearch.org).
852. Bautismos 1816–1825, 1827–1829, January 22, 1822, film 663997, image 172, Registros Parroquiales, Iglesia de La Purísima Concepción, Álamos, Sonora, Mexico (FamilySearch, https://familysearch.org).
853. Bautismos 1816–1825, 1827–1829, January 18, 1824, film 663997, image 255, Registros Parroquiales, Iglesia de La Purísima Concepción, Álamos, Sonora, Mexico (FamilySearch, https://familysearch.org).
854. Bautismos 1816–1825, 1827–1829, April 29, 1825, film 663997, image 320, Registros Parroquiales, Iglesia de La Purísima Concepción, Álamos, Sonora, Mexico (FamilySearch, https://familysearch.org).

xii. **José Ignacio Figueroa** was born about 1826 in Álamos; he married María Trinidad Moreno on March 25, 1846, in Álamos.[855]

xiii. **María Francisca Alvina Figueroa** was born in 1827 in Álamos. She was baptized on December 18, 1827, at the church of the Purísima Concepción in Álamos.[856] The baptismal record named Trinidad Quirós y Campoy and Francisca Gil Samaniego as her *padrinos*.

xiv. **José de Jesús Pio Figueroa** was born in 1831 in Álamos. He was baptized on May 15, 1831, at the church of the Purísima Concepción in Álamos.[857] The baptismal record is in poor condition and difficult to read the named *padrinos*.

136. José Antonio Corral (María Balvanera Antonia Esquer-7, Joseph Cayetano-6, Joseph Cayetano-5, Juan Salvador-4, Salvador-3, Salvador-2, Blas-1) was born about 1789.

José Antonio Corral and María Gertrudis Riveros were married on September 2, 1809, at the church of the Purísima Concepción in Álamos.[858] The matrimonial record named Xavier Navarro and Camilo Comun [?] as witnesses to the marriage. The couple received a marriage dispensation on August 1, 1809, because they were third cousins, related in the fourth degree of consanguinity. Parents of the groom were named. The bride was classified as an *hija natural* of her mother, María Josefa Marroquín Riveros. Her father was not identified.

María Gertrudis Riveros, daughter of Josefa Marroquin Riveros, was born about 1791. She was also known as "Gertrudis Astorga."

José Antonio Corral and María Gertrudis Riveros had the following known children:

i. **María Antonia Corral** was born in 1811 in Álamos. She was baptized on June 15, 1811, at the church of the Purísima Concepción in Álamos.[859] The baptismal record named Balvanera Esquer as her *madrina*.

ii. **Juan José Corral**, married María Trinidad Manuela Esquer, April 30, 1846, in Álamos.

---

855. Información matrimonial 1800–1855, March 25, 1846, film 663811, image 791, Registros Parroquiales, Iglesia de La Purísima Concepción, Álamos, Sonora, Mexico (FamilySearch, https://familysearch.org); Información matrimonial 1840–1849, February 16, 1846, film 663814, images 303–310, Registros Parroquiales, Iglesia de La Purísima Concepción, Álamos, Sonora, Mexico (FamilySearch, https://familysearch.org).

856. Bautismos 1816–1825, 1827–1829, December 18, 1827, film 663997, image 472, Registros Parroquiales, Iglesia de La Purísima Concepción, Álamos, Sonora, Mexico (FamilySearch, https://familysearch.org).

857. Bautismos 1829–1838, May 15, 1831, film 666560, image 74, Registros Parroquiales, Iglesia de La Purísima Concepción, Álamos, Sonora, Mexico (FamilySearch, https://familysearch.org).

858. Matrimonios 1779–1817, September 2, 1809, film 666565, image 492, Registros Parroquiales, Iglesia de La Purísima Concepción, Álamos, Sonora, Mexico (FamilySearch, https://familysearch.org).

859. Bautismos 1791–1796, 1805–1815, June 15, 1811, film 663996, image 439, Registros Parroquiales, Iglesia de La Purísima Concepción, Álamos, Sonora, Mexico (FamilySearch, https://familysearch.org).

137. **José Salvador Esquer** (José Joaquín-7, Joseph Cayetano-6, Joseph Cayetano-5, Juan Salvador-4, Salvador-3, Salvador-2, Blas-1) was born on March 13, 1789, in Álamos. The cited baptismal record stated he was seventeen days old when he was baptized. He was baptized on March 30, 1789, at the church of the Purísima Concepción in Álamos.[860] The baptismal record named Salvador Corral and María Balvanera Esquer as his *padrinos*.

José Salvador Esquer and Juana María Josefa Méndez were married on November 4, 1809, at the church of the Purísima Concepción in Álamos.[861] The matrimonial record named José María Espinosa and Josefa Esquer as *padrinos*. Parents of the bridal couple were named. The couple had a marriage impediment in the fourth degree of consanguinity, meaning they were third cousins. For that reason they required a marriage dispensation from the bishop.

The cited marriage information record noted that the marriage dispensation was granted on October 10, 1809, and that the couple received their nuptial blessing on November 5, 1809.[862]

Juana María Josefa Méndez was born about 1791.

José Salvador Esquer and Juana María Josefa Méndez had one known child:

    i.   **María Ramona Justa Esquer** was born in 1810 in Álamos. She was baptized on September 23, 1810, at the parish of the Purísima Concepción in Álamos.[863] The baptismal record named Ramón Eguino and María Balvanera Yriarte as her *padrinos*. The ceremony took place in the pueblo de Camoa in jurisdiction of Navojoa.

138. **Juana Leocadia González Barreda** (Joseph Fernando Antonio-7, María Raphaela Esquer-6, Francisco Joseph-5, Juan Salvador-4, Salvador-3, Salvador-2, Blas-1) was born about 1781. She was also known as "Juana Leocadia Barreda."

Juana Leocadia González Barreda and Agustín Esquerra y Rosas were married on April 21, 1800, in Álamos.[864] The matrimonial record stated that the marriage required a dispensation from the bishop because the couple were related in the third degree, with a fourth degree "*transversal*" consanguinity (collateral) family line. Parents of the bride and groom were named, and the parents of the groom were said to have been deceased. All were said to have originated in Álamos. José Mendívil and Loreto González Barreda, husband and wife, were named as *padrinos*.

---

860. Bautismos 1781–1796, March 30, 1789, film 663488, image 288, Registros Parroquiales, Iglesia de La Purísima Concepción, Álamos, Sonora, Mexico (FamilySearch, https://familysearch.org).

861. Matrimonios 1779–1817, November 4, 1809, film 666565, image 494, Registros Parroquiales, Iglesia de La Purísima Concepción, Álamos, Sonora, Mexico (FamilySearch, https://familysearch.org).

862. Información matrimonial 1800–1855 (incluye matrimonios, 1835 y bautismos, 1835), October 10, 1809, film 667003, images 41–42, Registros Parroquiales, Iglesia de La Purísima Concepción, Álamos, Sonora, Mexico (FamilySearch, https:// familysearch.org).

863. Bautismos 1791–1796, 1805–1815, September 23, 1810, film 663996, image 398, Registros Parroquiales, Iglesia de La Purísima Concepción, Álamos, Sonora, Mexico (FamilySearch, https://familysearch.org).

864. Matrimonios 1779–1817, April 21,1800, film 666565, images 377–378, Registros Parroquiales, Iglesia de La Purísima Concepción, Álamos, Sonora, Mexico (FamilySearch, https://familysearch.org).

Over time the couple chose to drop their compound surnames for simply Rosas and Barreda. Some of their children's sacramental records reflect that change. In order to maintain consistency, compounded surnames were maintained for children's baptisms. The only exception is their son José Felipe de Jesús, who later chose to use Rosas as his surname at marriage.

Agustín Esquerra y Rosas, son of Agustín Esquerra y Rosas and Juana Mendívil, was born about 1760. He was also known as "Agustín Rosas."

Agustín Esquerra y Rosas and Juana Leocadia González Barreda had the following known children:

i. **María Josefa Petra Esquerra y Rosas** was born in 1801 in Álamos. She was baptized on June 28, 1801, at the church of the Purísima Concepción in Álamos.[865] The baptismal record named José Rosas and María Balvanera Iriarte as her *padrinos*.

ii. **José María Olayo Esquerra y Rosas** was born on February 12, 1803, in Álamos. He was baptized on February 19, 1803, at the church of the Purísima Concepción in Álamos.[866] The baptismal record named Fernando Barreda and María Luisa Gastelo [Gastélum] as his *padrinos*.

iii. **José Felipe Esquerra y Rosas** was born in 1805 in Álamos and was baptized on May 9, 1805, in Álamos.[867] He married María Rosa Mendívil on June 22, 1831, in Álamos.[868]

iv. **José María Macedonio Esquerra y Rosas** was born in 1809 in Álamos. He was baptized on September 19, 1809, at the parish of the Purísima Concepción in Álamos.[869] The baptismal record named Antonio Almada as his *padrino*. The baptismal ceremony took place at the chapel of La Aduana.

v. **María Josefa Juana Nepomucena Esquerra y Rosas** was born in 1811 in Álamos. She was baptized on July 22, 1811, at the church of the Purísima Concepción in Álamos.[870] The baptismal record named José Antonio Barreda and María Josefa Barreda as her *padrinos*.

vi. **María Bernardina Esquerra y Rosas** was born in 1813 in Álamos. She was baptized on May 31, 1813, at the church of the Purísima Concepción in Álamos.[871] The baptismal record named Jesús Almada and Micaela Zayas as her *padrinos*.

865. Bautismos 1796–1805, June 28, 1801, film 663995, image 155, Registros Parroquiales, Iglesia de La Purísima Concepción, Álamos, Sonora, Mexico (FamilySearch, https://familysearch.org).

866. Bautismos 1796–1805, February 19, 1803, film 663995, image, 191, Registros Parroquiales, Iglesia de La Purísima Concepción, Álamos, Sonora, Mexico (FamilySearch, https://familysearch.org).

867. Bautismos 1796–1805, May 9, 1805, film 663995, images 272–273, Registros Parroquiales, Iglesia de La Purísima Concepción, Álamos, Sonora, Mexico (FamilySearch, https://familysearch.org).

868. Matrimonios 1797–1833, 1846–1868, 1872–1877, June 22, 1831, film 666566, image 343, Registros Parroquiales, Iglesia de La Purísima Concepción, Álamos, Sonora, Mexico (FamilySearch, https://familysearch.org).

869. Bautismos 1791–1796, 1805–1815, September 19, 1809, film 663996, image 343, Registros Parroquiales, Iglesia de La Purísima Concepción, Álamos, Sonora, Mexico (FamilySearch, https://familysearch.org).

870. Bautismos 1791–1796, 1805–1815, July 22, 1811, film 663996, image 440, Registros Parroquiales, Iglesia de La Purísima Concepción, Álamos, Sonora, Mexico (FamilySearch, https://familysearch.org).

871. Bautismos 1791–1796, 1805–1815, May 31, 1813, film 663996, image 457, Registros Parroquiales, Iglesia de La Purísima Concepción, Álamos, Sonora, Mexico (FamilySearch, https://familysearch.org).

vii.   **María Santiaga Esquerra y Rosas** was born in 1815 in Álamos. She was baptized on May 4, 1815, at the church of the Purísima Concepción in Álamos.[872] The baptismal record named Jesús Rosas and Balvanera Ramirez as her *padrinos*.

viii.   **María del Carmen Esquerra y Rosas** was born in 1817 in Álamos. She was baptized on July 20, 1817, at the church of the Purísima Concepción in Álamos.[873] The baptismal record named Antonio Almada and Manuela Zavala as her *padrinos*.

ix.   **Juan José Bautista Esquerra y Rosas** was born in 1818 in Álamos. He was baptized on December 27, 1818, at the church of the Purísima Concepción in Álamos.[874] The baptismal record named Ignacio Almada and Trinidad Salido as his *padrinos*.

139. **José Ygnacio de Jesús González Barreda** (Joseph Fernando Antonio-7, María Raphaela Esquer-6, Francisco Joseph-5, Juan Salvador-4, Salvador-3, Salvador-2, Blas-1) was born in 1789 in Álamos. He was baptized on June 19, 1789, at the church of the Purísima Concepción in Álamos.[875] The baptismal record named José Ygnacio Balderrain and Josefa Balderrain as his *padrinos*.

José Ygnacio de Jesús González Barreda and María Gertrudis Gastélum were married on May 3, 1821, at the church of the Purísima Concepción in Álamos.[876] The matrimonial record stated that the couple were related in the second degree of consanguinity, and therefore required a marriage dispensation. Parents of the bride and groom were named. They received a nuptial blessing on the day of their marriage. José María Valenzuela and Gertrudis de la Paz were named *padrinos*. Francisco Mendoza and Ramón Navarro were named as witnesses to the marriage. The cited marriage information record dated February 23, 1821, outlined the family relationship that required a marriage dispensation. There are no known children of this marriage.

María Gertrudis Gastélum was born about 1788.

140. **Fernando González Barreda** (Joseph Fernando Antonio-7, María Raphaela Esquer-6, Francisco Joseph-5, Juan Salvador-4, Salvador-3, Salvador-2, Blas-1) was born about 1798.

872. Bautismos 1791–1796, 1805–1815, May 4, 1815, film 663996, image 495, Registros Parroquiales, Iglesia de La Purísima Concepción, Álamos, Sonora, Mexico (FamilySearch, https://familysearch.org).
873. Bautismos 1816–1825, 1827–1829, July 20, 1817, film 663997, image 41, Registros Parroquiales, Iglesia de La Purísima Concepción, Álamos, Sonora, Mexico (FamilySearch, https://familysearch.org).
874. Bautismos 1816–1825, 1827–1829, December 27, 1818, film 663997, image 72, Registros Parroquiales, Iglesia de La Purísima Concepción, Álamos, Sonora, Mexico (FamilySearch, https://familysearch.org).
875. Bautismos 1781–1796, June 19, 1789, film 663488, image 298, Registros Parroquiales, Iglesia de La Purísima Concepción, Álamos, Sonora, Mexico (FamilySearch, https://familysearch.org).
876. Matrimonios 1779–1817, May 3, 1820, film 666565, image 250, Registros Parroquiales, Iglesia de La Purísima Concepción, Álamos, Sonora, Mexico (FamilySearch, https://familysearch.org); Información matrimonial 1820–1822, February 23, 1821, film 680058, image 408, Registros Parroquiales, Iglesia de La Asunción, Archivo Diocesano de Hermosillo, Hermosillo, Sonora, Mexico (FamilySearch, https://familysearch.org).

Fernando González Barreda and Josefa Martina Acosta were married on May 9, 1820, at the church of the Purísima Concepción in Álamos.[877] The matrimonial record named Jesús Serrano and Juana Serrano as *padrinos*. Parents of the bride and groom were named. The mother's name was written as "Castelo."

Josefa Martina Acosta, daughter of Bernardo Acosta and Simona Arballo, was born in 1797 in Álamos. She was baptized on November 26, 1797, at the church of the Purísima Concepción in Álamos.[878] The baptismal record named Bernardino Corral and Josefa Corral as her *padrinos*. She was socially identified in the record as a *coyota*.

Fernando González Barreda and Josefa Martina Acosta had the following known children:

    i.   **José Ramón Fermín González Barreda** was born in 1821 in Álamos and was baptized on July 16, 1821.[879] He married María Juliana del Sacramento Esquer after October 2, 1847 in Álamos. The marriage record has not been located.[880]

    ii.   **María Josefa Perfecta González Barreda** was born in 1823 in Álamos. She was baptized on April 27, 1823, at the church of the Purísima Concepción in Álamos.[881] The baptismal record named Aniceto Figueroa and Gabriela Márquez as her *padrinos*.

    iii.   **María Felipa Benicia González Barreda** was born in 1825 in Álamos. She was baptized on September 11, 1825, at the church of the Purísima Concepción in Álamos.[882] The baptismal record named José Soto and María Francisca Acosta as her *padrinos*.

    iv.   **Polonio González Barreda** was born in 1834 in Álamos. He was baptized on March 3, 1834, at the parish of the Purísima Concepción in Álamos.[883] The baptismal record named Juan José Belarde and Ana Ramírez as his *padrinos*. The baptism took place at the chapel of La Aduana.

141. Patricio Alfonso González Barreda (Joseph Patricio Benito-7, María Raphaela Esquer-6, Francisco Joseph-5, Juan Salvador-4, Salvador-3, Salvador-2, Blas-1) was born on January 11, 1783, in Álamos, according to the baptismal record. He was baptized on January 29, 1783, at

877. Matrimonios 1797–1833, 1846–1868, 1872–1877, May 9, 1820, film 666566, image 236, Registros Parroquiales, Iglesia de La Purísima Concepción, Álamos, Sonora, Mexico (FamilySearch, https://familysearch.org).

878. Bautismos 1796–1805, November 26, 1797, film 663995, images 56–57, Registros Parroquiales, Iglesia de La Purísima Concepción, Álamos, Sonora, Mexico (FamilySearch, https://familysearch.org).

879. Bautismos 1816–1825,1827–1829, July 16, 1821, film 663997, image 153, Registros Parroquiales, Iglesia de La Purísima Concepción, Álamos, Sonora, Mexico (FamilySearch, https://familysearch.org).

880. Información matrimonial 1840–1849, September 24, 1847, film 663814, images 333–338, Registros Parroquiales, Iglesia de La Purísima Concepción, Álamos, Sonora, Mexico (FamilySearch, https://familysearch.org).

881. Bautismos 1816–1825, 1827–1829, April 27, 1823, film 663997, image 228, Registros Parroquiales, Iglesia de La Purísima Concepción, Álamos, Sonora, Mexico (FamilySearch, https://familysearch.org).

882. Bautismos 1816–1825, 1827–1829, September 11, 1825, film 663997, image 340, Registros Parroquiales, Iglesia de La Purísima Concepción, Álamos, Sonora, Mexico (FamilySearch, https://familysearch.org).

883. Bautismos 1829–1838, March 3, 1834, film 666560, image 192, Registros Parroquiales, Iglesia de La Purísima Concepción, Álamos, Sonora, Mexico (FamilySearch, https://familysearch.org).

the church of the Purísima Concepción in Álamos.[884] The baptismal record named Juan Miguel Subizar and María de la Luz Barreda as his *padrinos*. He was also known as "Patricio Barreda."

Patricio Alfonso González Barreda and Anastasia Mendívil were married on July 20, 1814, at the church of the Purísima Concepción in Álamos.[885] The matrimonial record named José Mendívil and Lucía Bravo as *padrinos*. Xavier Navarro was named as the witness to the marriage. The couple received a dispensation to marry because they were related in a second with third degree of consanguinity, meaning they were first cousins once removed. Both parents of the groom were named in the record, but only the bride's mother was identified. The couple received a nuptial blessing on the day of their marriage. The cited marriage information record, dated May 2 [?], 1814, is actually the date of the marriage dispensation.[886]

Anastasia Mendívil, daughter of Estéfana Mendívil, was born about 1794.

Patricio Alfonso González Barreda and María del Rosario Rodríguez were married after October 28, 1848, at the parish of the Purísima Concepción in Álamos.[887] The matrimonial record has not been located. The cited marriage information record dated October 18, 1848, provided the ages of the bride and groom. The groom was said to have been the widowed husband of Anastasia Mendívil. The couple were related in the first degree with a second degree of consanguinity. The groom and the bride were uncle and niece. The groom was the brother of the mother of the bride. Parents of the couple were named. A marriage dispensation was granted on October 28, 1848. There are no known children of this marriage.

María del Rosario Rodríguez, daughter of Tomás Rodríguez and María Ignacia González Barreda, was born about 1814.

142. **María Francisca González Barreda** (Joseph Patricio Benito-7, María Raphaela Esquer-6, Francisco Joseph-5, Juan Salvador-4, Salvador-3, Salvador-2, Blas-1) was born on October 10, 1786, in Álamos, according to the baptismal record. She was baptized on November 4, 1786, at the church of the Purísima Concepción in Álamos.[888] The baptismal record named José Antonio Yepes and Dolores Amarillas as her *padrinos*.

María Francisca González Barreda and José Manuel Gil de Lamadrid were married on April 23, 1807, at the church of the Purísima Concepción in Álamos. The matrimonial record did not name witnesses. The groom was said to be the adopted son of his parents who were deceased. The bridal couple received a nuptial blessing on the day of their marriage.

884. Bautismos 1781–1796, July 29, 1783, film 663488, images 93–94, Registros Parroquiales, Iglesia de La Purísima Concepción, Álamos, Sonora, Mexico (FamilySearch, https://familysearch.org).
885. Matrimonios 1779–1817, July 20, 1814, film 666565, image 527, Registros Parroquiales, Iglesia de La Purísima Concepción, Álamos, Sonora, Mexico (FamilySearch, https://familysearch.org).
886. Información matrimonial 1800–1855, July 20,1814, film 663811, images 509–510, Registros Parroquiales, Iglesia de La Purísima Concepción, Álamos, Sonora, Mexico (FamilySearch, https://familysearch.org).
887. Información matrimonial 1840–1849, October 18, 1848, film 663814, images 419–425, Registros Parroquiales, Iglesia de La Purísima Concepción, Álamos, Sonora, Mexico (FamilySearch, https://familysearch.org).
888. Bautismos 1781–1796, November ber 4,1786, film 663488, image 210, Registros Parroquiales, Iglesia de La PurísimaConcepción, Álamos, Sonora, Mexico (FamilySearch, https://familysearch.org).

The baptismal and marriage records for their children identify the parents as María Francisca Barreda and José Manuel Gil.

José Manuel Gil de Lamadrid, son of Antonio Gil de Lamadrid and María Gertrudis Paula Pérez de Tagle, was born about 1784. He died on June 27, 1835, in Álamos. He was buried on June 28, 1835, in Álamos.

José Manuel Gil de Lamadrid and María Francisca González Barreda had the following known children:

i. **Juan José de la Cruz Gil** was born on November 14, 1814, in Álamos and was baptized on December 4, 1814, in Álamos.[889] He married Dolores Verdugo Garcia, about 1845, in Álamos. The marriage record has not been located.

ii. **María Trinidad Gil** was born in 1821 in Álamos. She was baptized on September 12, 1821, at the parish of the Purísima Concepción in Álamos.[890] The baptismal record named Eugenio Gil and Josefa Gil as her *padrinos*. The baptismal ceremony took place in the chapel of La Aduana.

iii. **José Ignacio Gil** was born in 1824 in Álamos. He was baptized on July 31, 1824, at the church of the Purísima Concepción in Álamos.[891] The baptismal record named Antonio Gil and Manuela Tagle as his *padrinos*. The record stated the child's name as "José Ignacio" or José Ignacio Santa Ana." No explanation was provided.

iv. **María de Jesús Gil** was born in 1827 in Álamos and was baptized on October 28, 1827 in Álamos.[892] She married Sebastián Féliz on March 10, 1847, in Álamos.[893]

v. **José Francisco Gil** was born in 1827 in Álamos. He was baptized on October 28, 1827, at the church of the Purísima Concepción in Álamos.[894] The baptismal record named María del Carmen Gil as his *madrina*.

143. **María Ignacia González Barreda** (Joseph Patricio Benito-7, María Raphaela Esquer-6, Francisco Joseph-5, Juan Salvador-4, Salvador-3, Salvador-2, Blas-1) was born about 1788. Her baptismal record was not located. She was also known as "Ignacia Barreda." Her parentage

889. Bautismos 1791–1796, 1805–1815, December 4, 1814, film 663996, image 484, Registros Parroquiales, Iglesia de La Purísima Concepción, Álamos, Sonora, Mexico (FamilySearch, https://familysearch.org).
890. Bautismos 1816–1825, 1827–1829, September 12, 1821, film 663997, image 174, Registros Parroquiales, Iglesia de La Purísima Concepción, Álamos, Sonora, Mexico (FamilySearch, https://familysearch.org).
891. Bautismos 1816–1825, 1827–1829, July 31, 1824, film 663997, image 281, Registros Parroquiales, Iglesia de La Purísima Concepción, Álamos, Sonora, Mexico (FamilySearch, https://familysearch.org).
892. Bautismos 1816–1825, 1827–1829, October 28, 1827, film 663997, image 466, Registros Parroquiales, Iglesia de La Purísima Concepción, Álamos, Sonora, Mexico (FamilySearch, https://familysearch.org).
893. Matrimonios 1797–1833, 1846–1868, 1872–1877, March 10, 1847, film 666566, image 358, Registros Parroquiales, Iglesia de La Purísima Concepción, Álamos, Sonora, Mexico (FamilySearch, https://familysearch. org); Información matrimonial 1846–1849, February 20, 1847, film 666567, images 32–34, Registros Parroquiales, Iglesia de La Purísima Concepción, Álamos, Sonora, Mexico (FamilySearch, https://familysearch. org).
894. Bautismos 1816–1825, 1827–1829, October 28, 1827, film 663997, image 466, Registros Parroquiales, Iglesia de La Purísima Concepción, Álamos, Sonora, Mexico (FamilySearch, https://familysearch.org).

was noted in her marriage record and in the cited marriage information for her daughter María Francisca Rodríguez.[895]

María Ignacia González Barreda and Tomás Rodríguez were married on May 8, 1814, at the parish of the Purísima Concepción in Álamos.[896] The matrimonial record named Patricio Barreda and Guadalupe Amarillas as *padrinos*. The bridal couple received a nuptial blessing on their wedding day. The wedding ceremony took place in the town of Conicari, jurisdiction of Álamos, and the bride was said to be from Cerro Colorado. Parents of the bride and groom were named, and the parents of the groom were said to have been deceased.

Tomás Rodríguez, son of Feliciano Rodríguez and Juana Valenzuela, was born in 1774. He was baptized in January 1774 in Álamos.[897] The baptismal record has not been located.

Tomás Rodríguez and María Ignacia González Barreda had the following known children:

i. **María del Rosario Rodríguez** was born about 1814; she married Patricio Alfonso González Barreda after October 28, 1848, in Álamos. The marriage record has not been located.[898]

ii. **María Francisca Rodríguez** was born about 1823; she married José de Jesús Yepes after June June 22, 1841, in Álamos. The marriage record has not been located.[899]

144. **José Fernando Trinidad Martínez Mendívil** (María Loreto González Barreda-7, María Raphaela Esquer-6, Francisco Joseph-5, Juan Salvador-4, Salvador-3, Salvador-2, Blas-1) was born on May 31, 1791, in Álamos. The cited baptismal record provided his date of birth. He was baptized on June 5, 1791, at the church of the Purísima Concepción in Álamos.[900] The baptismal record named Juan Bautista Esquerra y Rosas and María Lucía Mendívil as his *padrinos*. José Fernando Trinidad died on September 16, 1792, at the age of one in Álamos. He was buried on September 17, 1792, at the church of the Purísima Concepción in Álamos.[901] His funeral service was held with *cruz alta, capa, y caja*. He was interred in a burial site valued at five pesos. The record stated that he was a child (*párvulo*), son of José Mendívil and Loreto Barreda.

---

895. Información matrimonial 1840–1849, June 22, 1841, film 663814, images 83–87, Registros Parroquiales, Iglesia de La Purísima Concepción, Álamos, Sonora, Mexico (FamilySearch, https://familysearch.org).

896. Matrimonios 1797–1833, 1846–1868, 1872–1877, May 8, 1814, film 666566, image 121, Registros Parroquiales, Iglesia de La Purísima Concepción, Álamos, Sonora, Mexico (FamilySearch, https://familysearch.org).

897. Bautismos 1751–1794, matrimonios 1848, defunciones 1735–1752, January 1774, film 666999, image [not located], Registros Parroquiales, Iglesia de La Purísima Concepción, Álamos, Sonora, Mexico (FamilySearch, https:// familysearch.org).

898. Información matrimonial 1840–1849, October 18, 1848, film 663814, images 419–425, Registros Parroquiales, Iglesia de La Purísima Concepción, Álamos, Sonora, Mexico (FamilySearch, https://familysearch.org).

899. Información matrimonial 1840–1849, June 22, 1841, film 663814, images 83–87, Registros Parroquiales, Iglesia de La Purísima Concepción, Álamos, Sonora, Mexico (FamilySearch, https://familysearch.org).

900. Bautismos 1781–1796, June 5, 1791, film 663488, images 377–378, Registros Parroquiales, Iglesia de La Purísima Concepción, Álamos, Sonora, Mexico (FamilySearch, https://familysearch.org).

901. Defunciones 1786–1819, September 17, 1792, film 666996, image 55, Registros Parroquiales, Iglesia de La Purísima Concepción, Álamos, Sonora, Mexico (FamilySearch, https://familysearch.org).

145. **José Fernando Casimiro Martínez Mendívil** (María Loreto González Barreda-7, María Raphaela Esquer-6, Francisco Joseph-5, Juan Salvador-4, Salvador-3, Salvador-2, Blas-1) was born in 1797 in Álamos. He was baptized on March 12, 1797, at the church of the Purísima Concepción in Álamos.[902] The baptismal record named Juan Augustín Rosas and Anna María Mendívil as his *padrinos*.

José Fernando Casimiro Martínez Mendívil and María Isidora Tomasa Gaxiola were married on July 21, 1828, at the church of the Purísima Concepción in Álamos.[903] The matrimonial record named Dionicio Castelo and María de la Luz Castelo as *padrinos*. Ramón Navarro and Ygnacio Malo were named as witnesses to the marriage. Parents of the bridal couple were named in the record, and the groom was said to have originated in La Aduana. The couple received a nuptial blessing on the day of their marriage. The cited marriage information record dated June 10, 1828, revealed no impediments to marriage. [904] Parents of the bride and groom were named in the record. Francisco Esteban Talamantes, José María Corral and José Gabriel Navarrete provided testimony in support of the couple's eligibility to marry. None of the witnesses could sign their names.

María Isidora Tomasa Gaxiola, daughter of Juan Antonio Gaxiola and Francisca Castelo, was born in 1809 in Álamos. She was baptized on January 16, 1809, at the parish of the Purísima Concepción in Álamos.[905] The baptismal record named José María Talamantes and Balvanera Montiel as her *padrinos*. The baptism took place at the chapel of La Aduana.

José Fernando Casimiro Martínez Mendívil and María Isidora Tomasa Gaxiola had one known child:

    i.   **Juan Antonio Martínez Mendívil** was born in 1833 in Álamos. He was baptized on July 14, 1833, at the church of the Purísima Concepción in Álamos.[906] The baptismal record named Josefa Montiel as his *madrina*.

146. **Manuel de Jesús Esteban Martínez Mendívil** (María Loreto González Barreda-7, María Raphaela Esquer-6, Francisco Joseph-5, Juan Salvador-4, Salvador-3, Salvador-2, Blas-1) was born in 1798 in Álamos. He was baptized on December 31, 1798, at the church of the Purísima Concepción in Álamos.[907] The baptismal record named Manuel Anguís and Serafina Barreda as his *padrinos*. He was also known as "Manuel Mendívil."

---

902. Bautismos 1796–1805, March 12, 1797, film 663995, image 34, Registros Parroquiales, Iglesia de La Purísima Concepción, Álamos, Sonora, Mexico (FamilySearch, https://familysearch.org).
903. Matrimonios 1797–1833, 1846–1868, 1872–1877, July 21, 1828, film 666566, images 326–327, Registros Parroquiales, Iglesia de La Purísima Concepción, Álamos, Sonora, Mexico (FamilySearch, https://familysearch.org).
904. Información matrimonial 1800–1855, June 10, 1828, film 663811, images 400–401, Registros Parroquiales, Iglesia de La Purísima Concepción, Álamos, Sonora, Mexico (FamilySearch, https://familysearch.org).
905. Bautismos 1791–1796, 1805–1815, January 16, 1809, film 663996, image 324, Registros Parroquiales, Iglesia de La Purísima Concepción, Álamos, Sonora, Mexico (FamilySearch, https://familysearch.org).
906. Bautismos 1829–1838, July 14, 1833, film 666560, image 161, Registros Parroquiales, Iglesia de La Purísima Concepción, Álamos, Sonora, Mexico (FamilySearch, https://familysearch.org).
907. Bautismos 1796–1805, December 31, 1798, film 663995, image 89, Registros Parroquiales, Iglesia de La Purísima Concepción, Álamos, Sonora, Mexico (FamilySearch, https://familysearch.org).

Manuel de Jesús Esteban Martínez Mendívil and María Encarnación Carrasco were married about 1821.[908] The cited record is a note inserted within a page of a book of marriage investigations. It simply stated that Manuel de Jesús Mendívil and María Encarnación intended to marry. Parents of the candidates for marriage were named. The note contained a partial sentence asking if anyone thought there was any . . . [reason the couple should not be allowed to marry]. The previous page had an inserted note dated 1821 for other marriages. That is the year assumed for this marriage. Although a marriage record has not been located, baptismal records for their children provide evidence that the couple did marry. The marriage likely took place in Álamos, but there is no clear evidence as to the location.

María Encarnación Carrasco, daughter of José María Carrasco and Juana Carrasco, was born about 1800 in Álamos. The cited marriage-related record stated that María Encarnación originated in the Puesto de las Lajas in the jurisdiction of Álamos.

Manuel de Jesús Esteban Martínez Mendívil and María Encarnación Carrasco had the following known children:

i. **María del Carmen Martínez Mendívil** was born in 1825 in Álamos. She was baptized on March 4, 1825, at the church of the Purísima Concepción in Álamos.[909] The baptismal record was not located.

ii. **Juana Salomé Martínez Mendívil** was born in 1827 in Álamos. She was baptized on March 11, 1827, at the church of the Purísima Concepción in Álamos.[910] The baptismal record named José María [illegible] and María Camasco as her *padrinos*.

iii. **José Trinidad Norberto Martínez Mendívil** was born in 1831 in Álamos. He was baptized on June 14, 1831, at the church of the Purísima Concepción in Álamos.[911] The baptismal record named Felipe Rosas and María Josefa Rosas as his *padrinos*.

iv. **María Francisca Martínez Mendívil** was born in 1833 in Álamos. She was baptized on February 8, 1833, in Álamos.[912] The baptismal record named Teodoro Cota and María Guadalupe Carrasco as her *padrinos*.

v. **María del Sacramento Remigio Martínez Mendívil** was born in 1836 in Álamos. He was baptized on October 27, 1836, at the church of the Purísima Concepción in Álamos.[913] The baptismal record named Damasio Pacheco and María Josefa Gil as his *padrinos*.

---

908. Información matrimonial 1800–1855, about 1820, film 663811, image 89, Registros Parroquiales, Iglesia de La Purísima Concepción, Álamos, Sonora, Mexico (FamilySearch, https://familysearch.org).
909. Bautismos 1816–1825, 1827–1829, March 4, 1825, film 663997, image [not located], Registros Parroquiales, Iglesia de La Purísima Concepción, Álamos, Sonora, Mexico (FamilySearch, https://familysearch.org).
910. Bautismos 1816–1825, 1827–1829, March 11, 1827, film 663997, image 439, Registros Parroquiales, Iglesia de La Purísima Concepción, Álamos, Sonora, Mexico (FamilySearch, https://familysearch.org).
911. Bautismos 1829–1838, June 14, 1831, film 666560, image 80, Registros Parroquiales, Iglesia de La Purísima Concepción, Álamos, Sonora, Mexico (FamilySearch, https://familysearch.org).
912. Bautismos 1829–1838, February 8, 1833, film 666560, image 134, Registros Parroquiales, Iglesia de La Purísima Concepción, Álamos, Sonora, Mexico (FamilySearch, https://familysearch.org).
913. Bautismos 1829–1838, October 27, 1836, film 666560, image 371, Registros Parroquiales, Iglesia de La Purísima Concepción, Álamos, Sonora, Mexico (FamilySearch, https://familysearch.org). Source Box Attach to Family TreeTools.

147. **María Gertrudis Catarina Martínez Mendívil** (María Loreto González Barreda-7, María Raphaela Esquer-6, Francisco Joseph-5, Juan Salvador-4, Salvador-3, Salvador-2, Blas-1) was born in 1801 in Álamos. She was baptized on April 30, 1801, at the church of the Purísima Concepción in Álamos.[914] The baptismal record named José Rosas and María Susana Rosas as her *padrinos*.

María Gertrudis Catarina Martínez Mendívil and José Francisco Yepes were married on February 6, 1821, at the church of the Purísima Concepción in Álamos.[915] The matrimonial record named Ygnacio Tena and Gerónima Tena as *padrinos*. Joaquín Espinosa and José María [surname not provided] were named as witnesses to the marriage. Parents of the bride and groom were named in the record. The couple received a nuptial blessing on the day of their marriage.

José Francisco Yepes, son of Ignacio Yepes and Juana Pérez de Tagle, was born on October 4, 1801, in Álamos. The baptismal record provided his date of birth. He was baptized on November 2, 1801, at the church of the Purísima Concepción in Álamos.[916] The baptismal record named Bachiller Felipe Villegas and Valentina Pérez de Tagle as his *padrinos*.

José Francisco Yepes and María Gertrudis Catarina Martínez Mendívil had one known child:

    i.   **José de Jesús Desiderio Yepes** was born in 1830 in Álamos. He was baptized on May 28, 1830, at the church of the Purísima Concepción in Álamos.[917] The baptismal record named Pedro Quirós y Mora and María Josefa Gil as his *padrinos*.

148. **María Dolores de Jesús Josefa Gregoria Anguís** (Serafina González Barreda-7, María Raphaela Esquer-6, Francisco Joseph-5, Juan Salvador-4, Salvador-3, Salvador-2, Blas-1) was born in 1797 in Álamos. She was baptized on November 23, 1797, at the church of the Purísima Concepción in Álamos.[918] The baptismal record named José Mendívil and Loreto Barreda as her *padrinos*.

María Dolores de Jesús Josefa Gregoria Anguís and José Pasqual Prudencio Ygnacio de la Cruz Gómez Lamadrid were married on October 10, 1813, in Álamos.[919] The matrimonial record named Antonio Gómez and María Dolores Pelayo y Tagle as *padrinos*.

914. Bautismos 1796–1805, April 30, 1801, film 663995, image 153, Registros Parroquiales, Iglesia de La Purísima Concepción, Álamos, Sonora, Mexico (FamilySearch, https://familysearch.org).
915. Matrimonios 1797–1833, 1846–1868, 1872–1877, February 6, 1821, film 666566, image 246, Registros Parroquiales, Iglesia de La Purísima Concepción, Álamos, Sonora, Mexico (FamilySearch, https://familysearch.org).
916. Bautismos 1796–1805, November 2, 1801, film 663995, image 161, Registros Parroquiales, Iglesia de La Purísima Concepción, Álamos, Sonora, Mexico (FamilySearch, https://familysearch.org).
917. Bautismos 1829–1838, May 28, 1830, film 666560, image 29, Registros Parroquiales, Iglesia de La Purísima Concepción, Álamos, Sonora, Mexico (FamilySearch, https://familysearch.org).
918. Bautismos 1796–1805, November 23, 1797, film 663995, image 56, Registros Parroquiales, Iglesia de La Purísima Concepción, Álamos, Sonora, Mexico (FamilySearch, https://familysearch.org).
919. Matrimonios 1779–1817, October 10, 1813, film 666565, image 520, Registros Parroquiales, Iglesia de La Purísima Concepción, Álamos, Sonora, Mexico (FamilySearch, https://familysearch.org).

José Pasqual Prudencio Ygnacio de la Cruz Gómez Lamadrid, son of Pasqual Gómez Lamadrid and Anna María de la Luz Velarde, was born on April 28, 1793, in Álamos, according to the baptismal record. He was baptized on May 3, 1793, in Álamos.[920] The baptismal record named Bachiller Juan Villa Sánchez and María Gertrudis Campoy as his *padrinos*.

José Pasqual Prudencio Ygnacio de la Cruz Gómez Lamadrid and María Dolores de Jesús Josefa Gregoria Anguís had one known child:

i.   **Balvanera Gómez Lamadrid** was born on August 8, 1814, in Álamos. She was baptized on August 14, 1814, at the church of the Purísima Concepción in Álamos.[921] The baptismal record named the child's maternal grandparents, Manuel Anguís and Serafina Barreda, and her paternal grandparents, Pascual Gómez and Ana María Velarde as *padrinos*.

149. **María Sixta de la Trinidad Quirós y Mora** (José Miguel-7, Micaela Matilde Esquer-6, Francisco Joseph-5, Juan Salvador-4, Salvador-3, Salvador-2, Blas-1) was born on March 28, 1802, in Cosalá. The cited baptismal record provided her date of birth. She was baptized on May 13, 1802, at the church of Santa Úrsula in Cosalá.[922] The baptismal record named María Montillos as her *madrina*.

María Sixta de la Trinidad Quirós y Mora and Quirino Solís were married on June 30, 1823, at the church of Santa Úrsula in Cosalá.[923] The matrimonial record named Catarino Pardo and María del Carmen Preciado as *padrinos*. Parents of the bride were named and said to be deceased. The groom was said to be the *hijo natural* of Josefa Solís. His father was not named. Bautista Cabanillas and Ygnacio Cabanillas were named as witnesses to the marriage. There are no known children from this marriage.

Quirino Solís was born about 1800 in Culiacán. The cited marriage record provided his place of birth.

150. **Pablo Quirós y Mora** (José Miguel-7, Micaela Matilde Esquer-6, Francisco Joseph-5, Juan Salvador-4, Salvador-3, Salvador-2, Blas-1) was born about 1794 in Culiacán. The cited marriage information record stated that he was twenty-eight years of age at the time of his marriage.

920. Bautismos 1781–1796, October 10, 1813, film 663488, image 590, Registros Parroquiales, Iglesia de La Purísima Concepción, Álamos, Sonora, Mexico (FamilySearch, https://familysearch.org).
921. Bautismos 1791–1796, 1805–1815, August 14, 1814, film 663996, image 477, Registros Parroquiales, Iglesia de La Purísima Concepción, Álamos, Sonora, Mexico (FamilySearch, https://familysearch.org).
922. Bautismos de hijos legítimos 1800–1823, May 13, 1802, film 677442, image 77, Registros Parroquiales, Iglesia de Santa Úrsula, Cosalá, Sinaloa, Mexico (FamilySearch, https://familysearch.org).
923. Matrimonios 1777–1793, 1818–1829, June 30, 1823, film 677469, image 276, Registros Parroquiales, Iglesia de Santa Úrsula, Cosalá, Sinaloa, Mexico (FamilySearch, https://familysearch.org).

Pablo Quirós y Mora and Manuela Ponce were married on May 30, 1822, at the church of the Sagrario de San Miguel in Culiacán.[924] The matrimonial record named Manuel Murguía and Manuel Romero as witnesses to the marriage. The cited marriage investigation record named the parents of the couple and stated that there were no obstacles to marriage. The third and last date the banns of marriage were published was May 26, 1822.

Manuela Ponce, daughter of Juan Ignacio Ponce and Ana López, was born about 1797 in Culiacán.

Pablo Quirós y Mora and Manuela Ponce had the following known children:

    i.   **José Ignacio Quirós y Mora** was buried on April 13, 1826, at the church of the Sagrario de San Miguel in Culiacán.[925] He was identified as a small child. His funeral service was held with a *cruz alta* and he was interred in a burial site valued at three pesos.

    ii.   **Gertrudis Quirós y Mora** was born about 1818 in Culiacán; she married José de Jesús de la Encarnación Fernández Tamayo on August 30, 1838, in Culiacán.

151. **Manuel Eusebio Verdugo** (María Manuela Esquer-7, Francisco Gabriel-6, Francisco Joseph-5, Juan Salvador-4, Salvador-3, Salvador-2, Blas-1) was born on November 14, 1787, in Culiacán. The cited baptismal record stated that the child was born nine days prior to his day of baptism. He was baptized on November 23, 1787, at the church of the Sagrario de San Miguel in Culiacán.[926] The baptismal record named Pedro Verdugo and Faustina Páez as his *padrinos*.

Manuel Eusebio Verdugo and Narcisa Ibarra were married about 1805.[927] The marriage record has not been located. The cited matrimonial record for their daughter María Lorenza Verdugo to José Vicente Zambada claimed that she was the legitimate daughter of Manuel Eusebio Verdugo and Narcisa Ibarra Verdugo.

Narcisa Ibarra was born in 1792 in Culiacán. She was baptized on December 18, 1792, at the church of the Sagrario de San Miguel in Culiacán.[928] The baptismal record named Felipe Sambade and Longina Cardenas as her *padrinos*. She died on October 2, 1833, at the age of 41 in Culiacán. Narcisa was buried on October 3, 1833, at the church of the Sagrario de San Miguel in Culiacán.[929] Her burial service was held with a *cruz baja* and she was laid to rest in a burial site

---

924. Matrimonios 1755–1829, May 30, 1822, film 673378, image 421, Registros Parroquiales, Iglesia Sagrario de San Miguel, Culiacán, Sinaloa, Mexico (FamilySearch, https://familysearch.org); Información matrimonial 1819–1830, May 1822, film 673451, images 83–84, Registros Parroquiales, Iglesia Sagrario de San Miguel, Culiacán, Sinaloa, Mexico (FamilySearch, https://familysearch.org).

925. Defunciones 1746–1833, April 13, 1826, film 674051, image 619, Registros Parroquiales, Iglesia Sagrario de San Miguel, Culiacán, Sinaloa, Mexico (FamilySearch, https://familysearch.org).

926. Bautismos 1755–1789, November 23, 1787, film 665427, image 193, Registros Parroquiales, Iglesia Sagrario de San Miguel, Culiacán, Sinaloa, Mexico (FamilySearch, https://familysearch.org).

927. Matrimonios 1755–1829, July 20, 1824, film 673378, image 453, Registros Parroquiales, Iglesia Sagrario de San Miguel, Culiacán, Sinaloa, Mexico (FamilySearch, https://familysearch.org).

928. Bautismos 1789–1805, December 18, 1792, film 665428, image 52, Registros Parroquiales, Iglesia Sagrario de San Miguel, Culiacán, Sinaloa, Mexico (FamilySearch, https://familysearch.org).

929. Defunciones 1933–1956 [sic], October 3, 1833, film 674052, image 13, Registros Parroquiales, Iglesia Sagrario de San Miguel, Culiacán, Sinaloa, Mexico (FamilySearch, https://familysearch.org).

valued at three pesos. Her husband was named, and the record noted that she died of a fever and that she was survived by eight children.

Manuel Eusebio Verdugo and Narcisa Ibarra had the following children:

i. **José Timoteo Verdugo** was buried on October 30, 1833, at the church of the Sagrario de San Miguel in Culiacán.[930] His burial service was held with a *cruz baja* and he was laid to rest in a burial site valued at three pesos. He was said to have been a single adult. His parents were named in the record. He received the last sacraments of the Catholic Church before death.

ii. **María Lorenza Verdugo** was born about 1806; she married José Vicente Sambade on July 20, 1825, in Culiacán.[931]

iii. **Juan Bautista Timoteo Verdugo** was born on August 29, 1812, in Culiacán, according to the baptismal record. He was baptized on September 12, 1812, at the parish church of the Sagrario de San Miguel in Culiacán.[932] The baptismal record named José María Zazueta (legitimate son of Pedro Zazueta), Manuela Esquer (mother of Serafina Verdugo), and Serafina Verdugo (wife of Antonio Zazueta) as her *padrinos*.

iv. **María Rafaela Verdugo** was born on September 30, 1814, in Culiacán, according to the baptismal record. She was baptized on October 7, 1814, at the church of the Sagrario de San Miguel in Culiacán.[933] The baptismal record named Vicente Castro and Rafaela Esquer as her *padrinos*. The mother of the child was recorded as "María Ibarra."

v. **José Joaquín Julián Verdugo** was born on January 20, 1817, in Culiacán and was baptized on February 10, 1817.[934] He married María Ignacia García on November 9, 1845, in Culiacán.[935]

vi. **Lorenza Verdugo** was born about 1825; she married Joaquín Pomar y Burgos on April 20, 1845, in Culiacán.[936]

---

930. Defunciones 1933–1956 [Family Search labeling error. Should be 1833–1856], October 30, 1833, film 674052, image 14, Registros Parroquiales, Iglesia Sagrario de San Miguel, Culiacán, Sinaloa, Mexico (FamilySearch, https:// familysearch.org).

931. Matrimonios 1755–1829, July 20, 1824, film 673378, image 453, Registros Parroquiales, Iglesia Sagrario de San Miguel, Culiacán, Sinaloa, Mexico (FamilySearch, https://familysearch.org).

932. Bautismos 1796–1818, September 12, 1812, film 665429, image 345, Registros Parroquiales, Iglesia Sagrario de San Miguel, Culiacán, Sinaloa, Mexico (FamilySearch, https://familysearch.org).

933. Bautismos 1796–1818, October 7, 1814, film 665429, image 466, Registros Parroquiales, Iglesia Sagrario de San Miguel, Culiacán, Sinaloa, Mexico (FamilySearch, https://familysearch.org).

934. Bautismos 1796–1818, February 10, 1817, film 665429, image 563, Registros Parroquiales, Iglesia Sagrario de San Miguel, Culiacán, Sinaloa, Mexico (FamilySearch, https://familysearch.org).

935. Matrimonios 1830–1856, November 9, 1845, film 673379, image 348, Registros Parroquiales, Iglesia Sagrario de San Miguel, Culiacán, Sinaloa, Mexico (FamilySearch, https://familysearch.org).

936. Matrimonios 1830–1856, April 20, 1845, film 673379, image 239, Registros Parroquiales, Iglesia Sagrario de San Miguel, Culiacán, Sinaloa, Mexico (FamilySearch, https://familysearch.org); Información matrimonial 1840–1845, April 10, 1845, film 673394, images 73–74, Registros Parroquiales, Iglesia Sagrario de San Miguel, Culiacán, Sinaloa, Mexico (FamilySearch, https://familysearch.org).

vii. **Manuela Verdugo** was born in 1829 in Navolato, Sinaloa; she married Pedro José Sain in December 1850 in Culiacán. The marriage record has not been located.[937]

viii. **Antonio Verdugo** was born about 1831 in Culiacán; he married Petra Ramírez on November 8, 1851, in Culiacán.[938]

ix. **José Clemente Verdugo** was born on November 23, 1832, in Culiacán. The baptism record stated that he was three days old at baptism. He was baptized on November 26, 1832, at the church of the Sagrario de San Miguel in Culiacán.[939] The baptismal record named Cayetano Verdugo and Rafaela Rodríguez de la Rodriguera as his *padrinos*.

152. **Manuela Verdugo** (María Manuela Esquer-7, Francisco Gabriel-6, Francisco Joseph-5, Juan Salvador-4, Salvador-3, Salvador-2, Blas-1) was born about 1794.

Manuela Verdugo and Nicolás Verdugo were married about 1819.[940] The matrimonial record has not been located. The cited marriage information record for their daughter Nicolasa, dated December 1843, provided a genealogical diagram for the couple.

Nicolás Verdugo and Manuela Verdugo had only one known child:

i. **Nicolasa Verdugo** was born about 1820; she married Felipe Ramos on January 8, 1844, in Culiacán.[941]

153. **María Serafina Verdugo** (María Manuela Esquer-7, Francisco Gabriel-6, Francisco Joseph-5, Juan Salvador-4, Salvador-3, Salvador-2, Blas-1) was born in 1789 in Culiacán. She was baptized on September 12, 1789, at the church of the Sagrario de San Miguel in Culiacán.[942] The baptismal record named Francisco Bohorques and María Viviana López as her *padrinos*.

María Serafina Verdugo and Antonio Zazueta were married after October 3, 1806, in Culiacán.[943] The matrimonial record has not been located. The cited marriage information record

---

937. Información matrimonial 1849–1852, December 13, 1850, film 673397, images 217–219, Registros Parroquiales, Iglesia Sagrario de San Miguel, Culiacán, Sinaloa, Mexico (FamilySearch, https://familysearch.org).
938. Matrimonios 1830–1856, November 8, 1851, film 673379, image 497, Registros Parroquiales, Iglesia Sagrario de San Miguel, Culiacán, Sinaloa, Mexico (FamilySearch, https://familysearch.org).
939. Bautismos 1831–1838, November 26, 1832, film 665431, image 93, Registros Parroquiales, Iglesia Sagrario de San Miguel, Culiacán, Sinaloa, Mexico (FamilySearch, https://familysearch.org).
940. Información matrimonial 1840–1845, December 1843, film 673394, images 809–812, 839–840, Registros Parroquiales, Iglesia Sagrario de San Miguel, Culiacán, Sinaloa, Mexico (FamilySearch, https://familysearch.org).
941. Matrimonios 1830–1856, December [illegible], 1843, film 673379, images 297–298, Registros Parroquiales, Iglesia Sagrario de San Miguel, Culiacán, Sinaloa, Mexico (FamilySearch, https://familysearch. org); Información matrimonial 1840–1845, December [various dates] 1843, film 673394, images 809–812, 839–840, Registros Parroquiales, Iglesia Sagrario de San Miguel, Culiacán, Sinaloa, Mexico (FamilySearch, https:// familysearch.org).
942. Bautismos 1755–1792, September 12, 1789, film 674056, image 13, Registros Parroquiales, Iglesia Sagrario de San Miguel, Culiacán, Sinaloa, Mexico (FamilySearch, https://familysearch.org).
943. Información matrimonial 1799–1851, October 3, 1806, film 673454, images 82–83, Registros Parroquiales, Iglesia Sagrario de San Miguel, Culiacán, Sinaloa, Mexico (FamilySearch, https://familysearch.org).

dated October 3, 1806, named the couple's parents. The bride and groom were erroneously said to be second cousins, related in the third degree of consanguinity, and therefore required a marriage dispensation from the bishop. Actually, the couple were related in the second degree of consanguinity, meaning they were first cousins.

María Serafina Verdugo died on May 12, 1836, at the age of forty-seven in Culiacán. She was buried on May 13, 1836, at the church of the Sagrario de San Miguel in Culiacán.[944] Her funeral services were held with *cruz alta y caja*. She was interred in a burial site valued at three pesos. She received the last sacraments of the Catholic Church and was said to have been the wife of Antonio Zazueta. She left no last will and testament and was survived by four children.

Antonio Zazueta, son of Pedro Zazueta and Isabel Policarpia Verdugo, was born about 1787. He appeared in the census of Culiacán in 1804.[945]

Antonio Zazueta and María Serafina Verdugo had the following known children:

i. **Francisco Xavier Zazueta** was born on December 3, 1811, in Culiacán. The baptismal record provided his date of birth. He was baptized in January 1811 at the church of the Sagrario de San Miguel in Culiacán.[946] The baptismal record named the child's *padrinos* as Francisco Rodríguez de la Rodriguera, his wife Josefa Esquer; and Manuela Verdugo, the unwed daughter of Cayetano Verdugo and Juana Verdugo. The actual day the baptism took place is illegible.

ii. **María Antonia Zazueta** was born on January 15, 1814, in Culiacán. She was baptized on February 17, 1814, at the church of the Sagrario de San Miguel in Culiacán.[947] The baptismal record named José María Zazueta and his mother Manuela Esquer as her *padrinos*.

iii. **María Isabel Zazueta** was born on January 5, 1815, in Culiacán, according to the baptismal record. She was baptized on April 25, 1815, at the church of the Sagrario de San Miguel in Culiacán.[948] The baptismal record named María Teresa Esquer, wife of Antonio Valenzuela, as her *madrina*.

iv. **Juan Zazueta** was born about 1818 in Sataya, Sinaloa; he married María Dolores Simona Hernández, after January 25, 1856. The marriage record has not been located.[949]

---

944. Defunciones 1933–1956, May 13, 1836, film 674052, image 63, Registros Parroquiales, Iglesia Sagrario de San Miguel, Culiacán, Sinaloa, Mexico (FamilySearch, https://familysearch.org).

945. Padrones del estado de Sinaloa, Mexico 1778–1804, Archivo Franciscano de la Biblioteca Nacional de México. Padrón de la Villa de Culiacán,1804, item 2, caja 37, exp. 821, pp 1–24v, film 1149545 Item 2, [no image] Culiacán, Sinaloa, Mexico (FamilySearch, https://familysearch.org).

946. Bautismos 1796–1818, January 1811, film 665429, image 329, Registros Parroquiales, Iglesia Sagrario de San Miguel, Culiacán, Sinaloa, Mexico (FamilySearch, https://familysearch.org).

947. Bautismos 1796–1818, February 17, 1814, film 665429, image 435, Registros Parroquiales, Iglesia Sagrario de San Miguel, Culiacán, Sinaloa, Mexico (FamilySearch, https://familysearch.org).

948. Bautismos 1796–1818, April 25, 1815, film 665429, image 488, Registros Parroquiales, Iglesia Sagrario de San Miguel, Culiacán, Sinaloa, Mexico (FamilySearch, https://familysearch.org).

949. Información matrimonial 1855–1856, January 12, 1856, film 673456, images 71–75, Registros Parroquiales, Iglesia Sagrario de San Miguel, Culiacán, Sinaloa, Mexico (FamilySearch, https://familysearch.org).

154. **María Petra Zazueta** (María Manuela Esquer-7, Francisco Gabriel-6, Francisco Joseph-5, Juan Salvador-4, Salvador-3, Salvador-2, Blas-1) was born on May 14, 1797, in Culiacán, according to the baptismal record. She was baptized on May 30, 1797, at the church of the Sagrario de San Miguel in Culiacán.[950] The baptismal record named Thomas Urrea and Felipa Urrea as her *padrinos.*

María Petra Zazueta and Manuel Páez were married on December 3, 1827, in Culiacán.[951] The matrimonial record named Manuel Romero and Miguel Verdugo y Zazueta as witnesses to the marriage. Parents of the bride and groom were named in the record. The couple did not receive a nuptial blessing, *velación*, because the liturgical calendar of the Catholic Church did not allow such blessings during the season of Advent when the marriage took place.

Manuel Páez, son of Pioquinto Páez and Nieves Burgos, was born about 1795.

Manuel Páez and María Petra Zazueta had the following known children:

    i.   **José Lorenzo Páez** was born on August 9, 1828, in Culiacán. The baptismal record stated that he was ten days old on the day he was baptized. He was baptized on August 19, 1828, at the church of the Sagrario de San Miguel in Culiacán.[952] The baptismal record named Esteban Zazueta and Basilia Zazueta as his *padrinos.*

    ii.   **Pedro Páez** was born on May 25, 1832, in Culiacán, according to the baptismal record. He was baptized on May 28, 1832, at the church of the Sagrario de San Miguel in Culiacán.[953] The baptismal record named Rafaela Zazueta as his *madrina.*

    iii.   **María Teresa de Jesús Páez** was born on May 19, 1834, in Culiacán, according to the baptismal record. She was baptized on May 20, 1834, at the church of the Sagrario de San Miguel in Culiacán.[954] The baptismal record named María Zazueta as her *madrina.*

    iv.   **Manuel de Jesús Páez** was born on December 23, 1836, in Culiacán, according to the baptismal record. He was baptized on December 24, 1836, at the church of the Sagrario de San Miguel in Culiacán.[955] The baptismal record named Refugio Verdugo as his *padrino.*

155. **José Esteban Zazueta** (María Manuela Esquer-7, Francisco Gabriel-6, Francisco Joseph-5, Juan Salvador-4, Salvador-3, Salvador-2, Blas-1) was born on August 8, 1799, in Culiacán. The

950. Bautismos 1796–1818, May 30, 1797, film 665429, image 21, Registros Parroquiales, Iglesia Sagrario de San Miguel, Culiacán, Sinaloa, Mexico (FamilySearch, https://familysearch.org).

951. Matrimonios 1755–1829, December 3, 1827, film 673378, image 486, Registros Parroquiales, Iglesia Sagrario de San Miguel, Culiacán, Sinaloa, Mexico (FamilySearch, https://familysearch.org).

952. Bautismos 1820–183, August 19, 1828, film 665430, image 456, Registros Parroquiales, Iglesia Sagrario de San Miguel, Culiacán, Sinaloa, Mexico (FamilySearch, https://familysearch.org).

953. Bautismos 1831–1838, May 28, 1832, film 665431, image 49, Registros Parroquiales, Iglesia Sagrario de San Miguel, Culiacán, Sinaloa, Mexico (FamilySearch, https://familysearch.org).

954. Bautismos 1831–1838, May 20, 1834, film 665431, image 229, Registros Parroquiales, Iglesia Sagrario de San Miguel, Culiacán, Sinaloa, Mexico (FamilySearch, https://familysearch.org).

955. Bautismos 1831–1838, December 24, 1836, film 665431, image 493, Registros Parroquiales, Iglesia Sagrario de San Miguel, Culiacán, Sinaloa, Mexico (FamilySearch, https://familysearch.org).

cited baptismal record for José Esteban Zazueta stated he was born seven days prior to his day of baptism. He was baptized on August 15, 1799, at the church of the Sagrario de San Miguel in Culiacán.[956] The baptismal record named Nicolás Ramos and Gertrudis Saturina Ramos as his *padrinos*.

José Esteban Zazueta and Gertrudis Hernández were married on November 3, 1843, at the church of the Sagrario de San Miguel in Culiacán.[957] The matrimonial record named Pedro Zazueta and Nicolás Vidales as witnesses to the marriage. The couple were related in the third, with fourth degree of consanguinity, meaning they were second cousins once removed. For this reason, they required a dispensation to marry. The couple received a nuptial blessing on the day of their wedding. Parents of the bride and groom were named in the record.

Gertrudis Hernández, daughter of Timoteo Hernández and María Rosa Palazuelos, was born about 1827.

José Esteban Zazueta and Gertrudis Hernández had the following known children:

    i.   **María de Jesús Zazueta** was born on December 18, 1844, in Culiacán and was baptized on December 19, 1844.[958] She married Jesús Aréchiga on June 4, 1868, in Culiacán.[959]

    ii.   **Josefa Zazueta** was born about 1859 in Sataya; she married Belén Verdugo after May 21, 1890, in Culiacán.

156. **Pedro Zazueta** (María Manuela Esquer-7, Francisco Gabriel-6, Francisco Joseph-5, Juan Salvador-4, Salvador-3, Salvador-2, Blas-1) was born about 1803.

Pedro Zazueta and María de Jesús Palazuelos were married on April 4, 1837, at the church of the Sagrario de San Miguel in Culiacán.[960] The matrimonial record named Manuel Bórquez and Francisco Vidales as witnesses to the marriage. The couple were related in the third with a fourth degree in consanguinity, meaning they were second cousins once removed. Parents of the bride and groom were named in the record.

María de Jesús Palazuelos, daughter of José María Palazuelos and María Isabel Castro, was born about 1818.

---

956. Bautismos 1789–1805, August 5, 1799, film 665428, images 235–236, Registros Parroquiales, Iglesia Sagrario de San Miguel, Culiacán, Sinaloa, Mexico (FamilySearch, https://familysearch.org).
957. Matrimonios 1830–1856, November 3, 1843, film 673379, image 294, Registros Parroquiales, Iglesia Sagrario de San Miguel, Culiacán, Sinaloa, Mexico (FamilySearch, https://familysearch.org).
958. Bautismos 1841–1847, December 19, 1844, film 665433, image 355, Registros Parroquiales, Iglesia Sagrario de San Miguel, Culiacán, Sinaloa, Mexico (FamilySearch, https://familysearch.org).
959. Matrimonios 1865–188, June 4, 1868, film 673606, image 68, Registros Parroquiales, Iglesia Sagrario de San Miguel, Culiacán, Sinaloa, Mexico (FamilySearch, https://familysearch.org); Información matrimonial 1871–1873, May 20, 1868, film 673460, images 225–227, Registros Parroquiales, Iglesia Sagrario de San Miguel, Culiacán, Sinaloa, Mexico (FamilySearch, https://familysearch.org
960. Matrimonios 1830–1856, April 4, 1837, film 673379, image 138, Registros Parroquiales, Iglesia Sagrario de San Miguel, Culiacán, Sinaloa, Mexico (FamilySearch, https://familysearch.org).

Pedro Zazueta and María de Jesús Palazuelos had the following known children:

i. **María Rómula del Rosario Zazueta** was born on February 17, 1838, in Culiacán, according to the baptismal record. She was baptized on March 4, 1838, at the church of the Sagrario de San Miguel in Culiacán.[961] The baptismal record named José María Zazueta and María Isabel Castro as her *padrinos.*

ii. **Cosme Damián de Jesús Zazueta** was born on September 27, 1839, in Culiacán and was baptized on September 29, 1839, in Culiacán.[962] He married María de Jesús Cardenas after May 1, 1862, in Culiacán. The marriage record has not been located[963]

iii. **Isidro Zazueta** was born on April 4, 1842, in Culiacán, according to to baptismal record. He was baptized on April 14, 1842, at the church of the Sagrario de San Miguel in Culiacán.[964] The baptismal record named Mariano Palazuelos and María Rosa Palazuelos as his *padrinos.*

iv. **José Seferino de Jesús Zazueta** was born on August 26, 1844, in Culiacán, according to the baptismal record. He was baptized on August 27, 1844, at the church of the Sagrario de San Miguel in Culiacán.[965] The baptismal record named María Loreto Cárdenas as his *madrina.*

157. María Rafaela Zazueta (María Manuela Esquer-7, Francisco Gabriel-6, Francisco Joseph-5, Juan Salvador-4, Salvador-3, Salvador-2, Blas-1) was born on June 12, 1808, in Culiacán. She was baptized on July 3, 1808, at the church of the Sagrario de San Miguel in Culiacán.[966] The baptismal record provided her date of birth and named Raphaela Suárez, wife of Ambrosio Vea, as her *madrina.*

María Rafaela Zazueta and Pedro Juan Tomás Verdugo were married about 1831, at the church of the Sagrario de San Miguel in Culiacán.[967] The cited marriage information record, dated June 30, 1831, stated that the couple were related in the second degree of consanguinity, meaning they were first cousins. The bride's father and the groom's mother were siblings. The matrimonial record has not been located.

961. Bautismos 1838–1841, March 4, 1838, film 665432, image 13, Registros Parroquiales, Iglesia Sagrario de San Miguel, Culiacán, Sinaloa, Mexico (FamilySearch, https://familysearch.org).
962. Bautismos 1838–1841, September 29, 1839, film 665432, image 183, Registros Parroquiales, Iglesia Sagrario de San Miguel, Culiacán, Sinaloa, Mexico (FamilySearch, https://familysearch.org).
963. Información matrimonial 1860–1867, May 1, 1862, film 673459, images 169–171, Registros Parroquiales, Iglesia Sagrario de San Miguel, Culiacán, Sinaloa, Mexico (FamilySearch, https://familysearch.org).
964. Bautismos 1841–184, April 14, 1842, film 665433, images 112–113, Registros Parroquiales, Iglesia Sagrario de San Miguel, Culiacán, Sinaloa, Mexico (FamilySearch, https://familysearch.org).
965. Bautismos 1841–1847, August 27, 1844, images 327–328, Registros Parroquiales, Iglesia Sagrario de San Miguel, Culiacán, Sinaloa, Mexico (FamilySearch, https://familysearch.org).
966. Bautismos 1796–1818, July 3, 1808, film 665429, image 274, Registros Parroquiales, Iglesia Sagrario de San Miguel, Culiacán, Sinaloa, Mexico (FamilySearch, https://familysearch.org).
967. Información matrimonial 1799–1851, about 1831, film 673454, images 186–187, Registros Parroquiales, Iglesia Sagrario de San Miguel, Culiacán, Sinaloa, Mexico (FamilySearch, https://familysearch.org).

María Rafaela died on December 9, 1881, at the age of seventy-three in Culiacán. She was buried on December 10, 1881, at the church of the Sagrario de San Miguel in Culiacán.[968] The burial record stated that she was the widow of Pedro Verdugo. She died of an attack [possibly heart] and received the last rites of the Catholic Church. Her burial service was held with a *cruz alta*.

Pedro Juan Tomás Verdugo, son of Pedro Gregorio Verdugo and María Ignacia Zazueta, was born in December 1787 in Culiacán. The baptismal record stated he had been born one month prior to his date of baptism. He was baptized on January 6, 1788, at the church of the Sagrario de San Miguel in Culiacán.[969] The baptismal record named José Urrea and Gertrudis de Urrea as his *padrinos*. He died on August 3, 1860, at the age of seventy-six in Culiacán. Pedro was buried on August 4, 1860, at the church of the Sagrario de San Miguel in Culiacán.[970] The burial record stated that Pedro Verdugo was seventy-six years of age when he died, and that he had been married to María Rafaela Zasueta. He left two surviving children. Pedro received the last rites of the Catholic Church. His burial service was held with a *cruz alta*.

Pedro Juan Tomás Verdugo and María Rafaela Zazueta had the following known children:

i. **José Gorgonio Verdugo** was born on September 8, 1832, in Culiacán. The baptismal record claimed he was one day old at baptism. He was baptized on September 9, 1832, at the church of the Sagrario de San Miguel in Culiacán.[971] The baptismal record named José Antonio Zazueta and María Zazueta as his *padrinos*.

ii. **Miguel María Verdugo** was born on October 6, 1834, in Culiacán. The cited baptismal record provided his date of birth. He was baptized on October 10, 1834, in Culiacán.[972] The baptismal record named Pedro Zazueta and María Basilia Zazueta as his *padrinos*. He died about October 11, 1834, in Culiacán. Miguel was buried on October 12, 1834, at the church of the Sagrario de San Miguel in Culiacán.[973] The burial record stated that he died at birth. His funeral service was held with *cruz baja, y caja*. He was laid to rest in a burial site valued at three pesos. His parents were named in the record.

iii. **Juan Miguel de la Cruz Verdugo** was born on November 24, 1835, in Culiacán, according to the baptismal record. He was baptized on November 25, 1835, at the

968. Defunciones 1856–1919, December 10, 1881, film 674053, image 296, Registros Parroquiales, Iglesia Sagrario de San Miguel, Culiacán, Sinaloa, Mexico (FamilySearch, https://familysearch.org).
969. Bautismos 1755–1789, January 6, 1788, film 665427, image 197, Registros Parroquiales, Iglesia Sagrario de San Miguel, Culiacán, Sinaloa, Mexico (FamilySearch, https://familysearch.org).
970. Defunciones 1856–1919, August 4 1860, film 674053, image 135, Registros Parroquiales, Iglesia Sagrario de San Miguel, Culiacán, Sinaloa, Mexico (FamilySearch, https://familysearch.org).
971. Bautismos 1831–1838, September 9, 1832, film 665431, image 74, Registros Parroquiales, Iglesia Sagrario de San Miguel, Culiacán, Sinaloa, Mexico (FamilySearch, https://familysearch.org).
972. Bautismos 1831–1838, October 10, 1834, film 665431, image 273, Registros Parroquiales, Iglesia Sagrario de San Miguel, Culiacán, Sinaloa, Mexico (FamilySearch, https://familysearch.org).
973. Defunciones 1933–1956 [sic], October 12, 1834, film 674052, image 33, Registros Parroquiales, Iglesia Sagrario de San Miguel, Culiacán, Sinaloa, Mexico (FamilySearch, https://familysearch.org).

church of the Sagrario de San Miguel in Culiacán.[974] The baptismal record named Cayetano Verdugo and María Isabel Pérez as his *padrinos*.

iv.   **Antonio Verdugo** was born about 1839. The cited record provides proof of his parentage.[975] he married Juana Ramos, about 1859. The marriage record has not been located.

v.   **María Andrea de Jesús Verdugo** was born on February 3, 1841, in Culiacán, according to the baptismal record. She was baptized on February 4, 1841, at the church of the Sagrario de San Miguel in Culiacán.[976] The baptismal record named the priest, Father Ramón Villegas, as his *padrino*. She died on January 8, 1843, in Culiacán. María was buried on January 9, 1843, at the church of the Sagrario de San Miguel in Culiacán.[977] Her funeral service was held with a *cruz baja*. She was interred in a burial site valued at three pesos. The record stated that that she died of a fever. Her parents were named in the record.

vi.   **María de Jesús Verdugo** was born on January 27, 1846, in Culiacán, according to the baptismal record. She was baptized on January 27, 1846, at the church of the Sagrario de San Miguel in Culiacán.[978] The baptismal record named Petra Zazueta as her *madrina*.

vii.   **María de Jesús Verdugo** was born on March 12, 1847, in Culiacán, according to the baptismal record. She was baptized on March 13, 1847, at the church of the Sagrario de San Miguel in Culiacán.[979] The baptismal record named Carlos Verdugo and Carmen Izábal as her *padrinos*. She died on August 27, 1920, at the age of seventy-three in Culiacán. María was buried on August 28, 1920, at the church of the Sagrario de San Miguel in Culiacán.[980] She was said to have died of a fever. She received the last sacraments of the Catholic Church before death. The record named her parents and noted that she had been a widow.

158. Yrene Rodríguez de la Rodriguera (María Josefa Esquer-7, Francisco Gabriel-6, Francisco Joseph-5, Juan Salvador-4, Salvador-3, Salvador-2, Blas-1) was born about 1792.[981] The cited

974. Bautismos 1831–1838, November 25, 1835, image 386, Registros Parroquiales, Iglesia Sagrario de San Miguel, Culiacán, Sinaloa, Mexico (FamilySearch, https://familysearch.org).
975. Información matrimonial 1879–1880, May 4, 1797, film 673401, images 95–97, Registros Parroquiales, Iglesia Sagrario de San Miguel, Culiacán, Sinaloa, Mexico (FamilySearch, https://familysearch.org).
976. Bautismos 1841–1847, February 4, 1841, film 665433, image 9, Registros Parroquiales, Iglesia Sagrario de San Miguel, Culiacán, Sinaloa, Mexico (FamilySearch, https://familysearch.org).
977. Defunciones 1933 [1833]-1956, January 9, 1843, film 674052, image 177, Registros Parroquiales, Iglesia Sagrario de San Miguel, Culiacán, Sinaloa, Mexico (FamilySearch, https://familysearch.org).
978. Bautismos 1841–1847, January 27, 1846, film 665433, image 463, Registros Parroquiales, Iglesia Sagrario de San Miguel, Culiacán, Sinaloa, Mexico (FamilySearch, https://familysearch.org).
979. Bautismos 1841–1847, March 13, 1847, film 665433, image 599, Registros Parroquiales, Iglesia Sagrario de San Miguel, Culiacán, Sinaloa, Mexico (FamilySearch, https://familysearch.org).
980. Defunciones 1920–1949, August 28, 1920, film 674054, image 13, Registros Parroquiales, Iglesia Sagrario de San Miguel, Culiacán, Sinaloa, Mexico (FamilySearch, https://familysearch.org).
981. Información matrimonial 1802–1819, July 14, 1812, film 673450, images 206–208, Registros Parroquiales, Iglesia Sagrario de San Miguel, Culiacán, Sinaloa, Mexico (FamilySearch, https://familysearch.org).

marriage information record claimed that she was twenty years of age at the time she petitioned for marriage.

Yrene Rodríguez de la Rodriguera and Francisco Palma y Mesa were married on July 28, 1812, in Culiacán.[982] The matrimonial record named Manuel Romero and José Pérez as being present at the marriage. *Padrinos* were not named in the record. The couple received a nuptial blessing on the day of their marriage. Parents of the bride and groom were named. The marriage information record dated July 14, 1812, found no impediment to marriage.[983]

Francisco Palma y Mesa, son of Javier Mesa and María Torres, was born about 1774 in Quilá, Sinaloa. The cited marriage information record claimed that the groom was thirty-eight years of age at the time of his petition to marry. It also provided his place of birth.

Francisco Palma y Mesa and Yrene Rodríguez de la Rodriguera had the following known children:

i. **José María Palma y Mesa** was born on October 19, 1813, in Culiacán, according to the baptismal record. He was baptized on October 24, 1813, at the church of the Sagrario de San Miguel in Culiacán.[984] The baptismal record named Francisco Rodríguez de la Rodriguera and Josefa Esquer as his *padrinos*.

ii. **María Josefa Palma y Mesa** was born on November 4, 1815, in Culiacán, according to the baptismal record. She was baptized on November 9, 1815, at the church of the Sagrario de San Miguel in Culiacán.[985] The baptismal record named Luis Rodríguez, husband of Ignacia Cárdenas as her *padrino*. Teresa Rodríguez de la Rodriguera, daughter of Francisco Rodríguez de la Rodriguera and Josefa Esquer, was named as the child's *madrina*.

iii. **María de Jesús Palma y Mesa** was born on November 25, 1817, in Culiacán, according to the baptismal record. She was baptized on December 16, 1817, at the church of the Sagrario de San Miguel in Culiacán.[986] The baptismal record named José María Suarez and Manuela Rodríguez as her *padrinos*.

iv. **Manuela Palma y Mesa** was born on August 5, 1822, in Culiacán and was baptized on August 15, in Culiacán.[987] She married Manuel Antonio de Jesús Andrés Orrantia on November 3, 1843, in Culiacán.[988]

---

982. Matrimonios 1755–1829, July 28, 1812, film 673378, image 304, Registros Parroquiales, Iglesia Sagrario de San Miguel, Culiacán, Sinaloa, Mexico (FamilySearch, https://familysearch.org).

983. Información matrimonial 1802–1819, July 14, 1812, film 673450, images 206–208, Registros Parroquiales, Iglesia Sagrario de San Miguel, Culiacán, Sinaloa, Mexico (FamilySearch, https://familysearch.org).

984. Bautismos 1796–1818, October 24, 1813, film 665429, image 418, Registros Parroquiales, Iglesia Sagrario de San Miguel, Culiacán, Sinaloa, Mexico (FamilySearch, https://familysearch.org).

985. Bautismos 1796–1818, November 9, 1815, film 665429, image 512, Registros Parroquiales, Iglesia Sagrario de San Miguel, Culiacán, Sinaloa, Mexico (FamilySearch, https://familysearch.org).

986. Bautismos 1796–1818, December 16, 1817, film 665429, image 628, Registros Parroquiales, Iglesia Sagrario de San Miguel, Culiacán, Sinaloa, Mexico (FamilySearch, https://familysearch.org).

987. Bautismos 1820–1831, August 15, 1822, film 665430, images 158–159, Registros Parroquiales, Iglesia Sagrario de San Miguel, Culiacán, Sinaloa, Mexico (FamilySearch, https://familysearch.org).

988. Matrimonios 1830–1856, November 3, 1843, film 673379, image 294, Registros Parroquiales, Iglesia Sagrario de San Miguel, Culiacán, Sinaloa, Mexico (FamilySearch, https://familysearch.org).

v.   **Manuel Palma y Mesa** was born about 1839 in Culiacán; he married Gabina
Cárdenas after January 3, 1859, in Mocorito, Sinaloa.[989]

159. María Teresa Cecilia Rodríguez de la Rodriguera (María Josefa Esquer-7, Francisco
Gabriel-6, Francisco Joseph-5, Juan Salvador-4, Salvador-3, Salvador-2, Blas-1) was born on
February 1, 1801, in Culiacán, according to the baptismal record. She was baptized on February
2, 1801, at the church of the Sagrario de San Miguel in Culiacán.[990] The baptismal record named
Antonio Valenzuela and Teresa Esquer as her *padrinos*.

María Teresa Cecilia Rodríguez de la Rodriguera and Pedro Suárez were married after August
20, 1837, at the parish of the Sagrario de San Miguel in Culiacán.[991] The matrimonial record
has not been located. The cited marriage information record dated August 12, 1837, stated that
Pedro Suarez was forty years of age and the widowed husband of María de Jesús Ramos. María
Teresa was noted as single and over twenty-eight years of age. No impediments to the marriage
were found and the banns of marriage were published on August 13, August 18, and August 20,
1837. Marriage must have followed soon after the last bann of marriage was read.

Pedro Suárez was born about 1797.

Pedro Suárez and María Teresa Cecilia Rodríguez de la Rodriguera had one known child:

i.   **María del Pilar Suárez** was born on October 11, 1838, in Culiacán. She was baptized
on October 13, 1838, at the church of the Sagrario de San Miguel in Culiacán.[992]
The baptismal record named Francisco Rodríguez and Josefa Esquer as her *padrinos*.
Her mother's name was noted as "Rodríguez" in the record.

160. María Rafaela Rodríguez de la Rodriguera (María Josefa Esquer-7, Francisco Gabriel-6,
Francisco Joseph-5, Juan Salvador-4, Salvador-3, Salvador-2, Blas-1) was born on March 4,
1807, in Culiacán. The cited baptismal record provided her date of birth. She was baptized on
March 9, 1807, at the church of the Sagrario de San Miguel in Culiacán.[993] The baptismal record
named José Esteban Verdugo and Ana Páez as her *padrinos*.

María Rafaela Rodríguez de la Rodriguera and Claudio Zepeda were married on March 2,
1835, in Culiacán.[994] The matrimonial record stated that the groom was a widower and that

---

989. Información matrimonial 1856–1859, December 16, 1858, film 676728, images 282–283, Registros
Parroquiales, Iglesia de La Purísima Concepción, Mocorito, Sinaloa, Mexico (FamilySearch, https://familysearch.
org).

990. Bautismos 1789–1805, February 2, 1801, film 665428, image 266, Registros Parroquiales, Iglesia Sagrario
de San Miguel, Culiacán, Sinaloa, Mexico (FamilySearch, https://familysearch.org).

991. Información matrimonial 1837–1840, August 12, 1837, film 673393, images 50–52, Registros
Parroquiales, Iglesia Sagrario de San Miguel, Culiacán, Sinaloa, Mexico (FamilySearch, https://familysearch.org).

992. Bautismos 1838–1841, October 13, 1838, film 665432, image 75, Registros Parroquiales, Iglesia Sagrario
de San Miguel, Culiacán, Sinaloa, Mexico (FamilySearch, https://familysearch.org).

993. Bautismos 1796–1818, March 9, 1807, film 665429, image 244, Registros Parroquiales, Iglesia Sagrario de
San Miguel, Culiacán, Sinaloa, Mexico (FamilySearch, https://familysearch.org).

994. Matrimonios 1830–1856, March 2,1835, film 673379, image 106, Registros Parroquiales, Iglesia Sagrario
de San Miguel, Culiacán, Sinaloa, Mexico (FamilySearch, https://familysearch.org).

his first wife was Guadalupe Núñez. Francisco Orrantia and Francisco Vidales were named as witnesses to the marriage. The couple received a nuptial blessing on the day of their marriage. Parents of the bride were named in the record.

Claudio Zepeda was born about 1815.

Claudio Zepeda and María Rafaela Rodríguez de la Rodriguera had the following known children:

i. **Juan Bautista Zepeda** was born on June 24, 1836, in Culiacán. The baptismal record provided his date of birth. He was baptized on June 25, 1836, at the church of the Sagrario de San Miguel in Culiacán.[995] The baptismal record named Francisco Rodríguez and Josefa Esquer as his *padrinos.*

ii. **Luz Zepeda** was born about 1837 in Culiacán; she married Carlos Román Medrano after February 9, 1856. The marriage record has not been located.[996]

iii. **José de la Luz Marcelino Zepeda** was born on June 2, 1838, in Culiacán, according to the baptismal record. He was baptized on June 3, 1838, at the church of the Sagrario de San Miguel in Culiacán.[997] The baptismal record named Tomás Gómez and Ventura Rojo as his *padrinos.*

iv. **María Sóstenes Zepeda** was born on July 21, 1839, in Culiacán, according to the baptismal record. She was baptized on July 21, 1839, at the church of the Sagrario de San Miguel in Culiacán.[998] The baptismal record named José María Izábal and Úrsula Rodríguez as her *padrinos.*

v. **José Francisco Zepeda** was born on April 15, 1843, in Culiacán, according to the baptismal record. He was baptized on April 16, 1843, at the church of the Sagrario de San Miguel in Culiacán.[999] The baptismal record named Manuel Orrantia and Manuela Meza as his *padrinos.*

vi. **María Rafaela Zepeda** was born on January 9, 1845, in Culiacán, according to the baptismal record. She was baptized on January 11, 1845, at the church of the Sagrario de San Miguel in Culiacán.[1000] The baptismal record named Felipe Gómez and his wife María de Jesús Gastélum as the child's *padrinos.*

995. Bautismos 1831–1838, June 25, 1836, film 665431, image 447, Registros Parroquiales, Iglesia Sagrario de San Miguel, Culiacán, Sinaloa, Mexico (FamilySearch, https://familysearch.org).

996. Información matrimonial 1855–1856, January 12, 1856, film 673456, images 65–70, Registros Parroquiales, Iglesia Sagrario de San Miguel, Culiacán, Sinaloa, Mexico (FamilySearch, https://familysearch.org).

997. Bautismos 1838–1841, June 3, 1838, film 665432, image 39, Registros Parroquiales, Iglesia Sagrario de San Miguel, Culiacán, Sinaloa, Mexico (FamilySearch, https://familysearch.org).

998. Bautismos 1838–1841, July 21, 1839, film 665432, image 164, Registros Parroquiales, Iglesia Sagrario de San Miguel, Culiacán, Sinaloa, Mexico (FamilySearch, https://familysearch.org).

999. Bautismos 1841–1847, April 16, 1843, film 665433, image 199, Registros Parroquiales, Iglesia Sagrario de San Miguel, Culiacán, Sinaloa, Mexico (FamilySearch, https://familysearch.org).

1000. Bautismos 1841–1847, January 11, 1845, film 665433, images 363–364, Registros Parroquiales, Iglesia Sagrario de San Miguel, Culiacán, Sinaloa, Mexico (FamilySearch, https://familysearch.org).

161. **Miguel Ygnacio Dolores Antonio de la Luz Esquer** (José Joaquín-7, Pedro Sebastián-6, Francisco Joseph-5, Juan Salvador-4, Salvador-3, Salvador-2, Blas-1) was born on September 29, 1788, in Álamos. The cited baptismal record provided his date of birth. He was baptized on October 7, 1788, at the church of the Purísima Concepción in Álamos.[1001] The baptismal record named Francisco Palomares and Antonia González de Zayas as his *padrinos*. Those present were José Bustillos, *sacristán*; Manuel Anguís, and Ygnacio Gil, among many others. The child received the waters of baptism the day after his birth, out of necessity should he not survive.

Miguel Ygnacio Dolores Antonio de la Luz Esquer and María del Carmen Martínez Mendívil were married on May 11, 1831, at the church of the Purísima Concepción in Álamos.[1002] The matrimonial record named Vicente Esquer and María Dolores Esquer as *padrinos*. Ramón Navarro was present, along with others in the community, as witnesses to the marriage. The couple received a nuptial blessing the day of their marriage. Parents of the bride and groom were named in the record.

María del Carmen Martínez Mendívil, daughter of Luis María Antonio Martínez Mendívil and María Gertrudis de Guadalupe Gerónima de Merced Muñoz, was born about 1811.

Miguel Ygnacio Dolores Antonio de la Luz Esquer and María del Carmen Martínez Mendívil had the following known children:

i. **María Dolores Perfecta Esquer** was born in 1832 in Álamos. She was baptized on April 18, 1832, at the church of the Purísima Concepción in Álamos.[1003] The baptismal record named Vicente Ortiz and María Hortensia Ortiz as her *padrinos*.

ii. **Miguel Antonio Esquer** was born in 1836 in Álamos and was baptized on November 9, 1836, in Álamos.[1004] He married Balvanera Domíngues on February 7, 1859, in Álamos.[1005]

iii. **José de Jesús Victoriano Esquer** was born on September 12, 1838, in El Fuerte. The cited record stated that he was one month and fifteen days old when he was baptized. He was baptized on October 27, 1838, at the church of the Sagrado Corazón in El Fuerte.[1006] The baptismal record named José Martínez Mendívil and Gerónima Muñoz as his *padrinos*.

1001. Bautismos 1781–1796, October 7, 1788, film 663488, image 269, Registros Parroquiales, Iglesia de La Purísima Concepción, Álamos, Sonora, Mexico (FamilySearch, https://familysearch.org).
1002. Matrimonios 1797–1833, 1846–1868, 1872–1877, May 11, 1831, film 666566, image 338, Registros Parroquiales, Iglesia de La Purísima Concepción, Álamos, Sonora, Mexico (FamilySearch, https://familysearch.org).
1003. Bautismos 1829–1838, April 18, 1832, film 666560, image 109, Registros Parroquiales, Iglesia de La Purísima Concepción, Álamos, Sonora, Mexico (FamilySearch, https://familysearch.org).
1004. Bautismos 1829–1838, November 9, 1836, film 666560, image 374, Registros Parroquiales, Iglesia de La Purísima Concepción, Álamos, Sonora, Mexico (FamilySearch, https://familysearch.org).
1005. Información matrimonial 1858–1870, January 14, 1859, film 666572, images 63–68, Registros Parroquiales, Iglesia de La Purísima Concepción, Álamos, Sonora, Mexico (FamilySearch, https://familysearch.org).
1006. Bautismos 1827–1847, October 27, film 678053, image 405, Registros Parroquiales, Iglesia Sagrado Corazón, El Fuerte, Sinaloa, Mexico (FamilySearch, https://familysearch.org).

iv. **Pedro Pascual de Jesús Esquer** was born in 1839 in Álamos and was baptized on December 8, 1839 in Álamos.[1007] He married María Antonia Mendívil on, June 8, 1877, in Álamos.[1008]

v. **José de Jesús Esquer** was born on November 3, 1841, in El Fuerte. The baptismal record stated that he was one month of age when baptized. He was baptized on December 3, 1841, at the church of the Sagrado Corazón in El Fuerte.[1009] The baptismal record named Manuel Murrieta and Dolores Murrieta as his *padrinos.*

vi. **María Concepción Esquer** was born on December 4, 1843, in El Fuerte and was baptized on December 13, 1843, in El Fuerte.[1010] She married Constancio Amadeo Fauvet on January 9, 1876, in Álamos.[1011]

vii. **Loreto Esquer**, was born about 1836 in Álamos; she married José Antonio Rufo Tena on February 6, 1864, in Álamos.[1012]

viii. **María Guadalupe Josefa Esquer** was born about December 1846 in Álamos. She was baptized on January 16, 1847, at the church of the Purísima Concepción in Álamos.[1013]

ix. **María Magdalena Esquer** was born in 1848, in Álamos; she married Luis Acuña on February 15, 1868, in Álamos.[1014]

x. **José Francisco Milano Esquer** was born on October 3, 1852, in Álamos and was baptized on October 5, 1852, in Álamos.[1015] He married Rosenda Rochín on February 20, 1876, in Álamos.[1016]

1007. Bautismos 1838–1871, December 8, 1839, film 667000, image 85, Registros Parroquiales, Iglesia de La Purísima Concepción, Álamos, Sonora, Mexico (FamilySearch, https://familysearch.org).

1008. Matrimonios 1873–1878, 1886–1898, June 8, 1877, film 663804, image 93, Registros Parroquiales, Iglesia de La Purísima Concepción, Álamos, Sonora, Mexico (FamilySearch, https://familysearch.org); Información matrimonial 1871–1882, April 28, 1877, film 666576, images 231–233, Registros Parroquiales, Iglesia de La Purísima Concepción, Álamos, Sonora, Mexico (FamilySearch, https://familysearch.org).

1009. Bautismos 1827–1847, December 3, 1841, film 678053, image 544, Iglesia del Sagrado Corazón, El Fuerte, Sinaloa, Mexico (FamilySearch, https://familysearch.org).

1010. Bautismos 1827–1847, December 13, 1843, film 678053, image 636, Iglesia del Sagrado Corazón, El Fuerte, Sinaloa, Mexico (FamilySearch, https://familysearch.org).

1011. Matrimonios 1873–1878, 1886–1898, January 9, 1876, film 663804, image 66, Registros Parroquiales, Iglesia de La Purísima Concepción, Álamos, Sonora, Mexico (FamilySearch, https://familysearch.org).

1012. Matrimonios 1797–1833, 1846–1868, 1872–1877, February 6, 1864, film 666566, image 470, Registros Parroquiales, Iglesia de La Purísima Concepción, Álamos, Sonora, Mexico (FamilySearch, https://familysearch.org); Información matrimonial 1862–1868, January 16, 1865, film 666573, images 136–138, Registros Parroquiales, Iglesia de La Purísima Concepción, Álamos, Sonora, Mexico (FamilySearch, https://familysearch.org).

1013. Bautismos 1838–1856, January 16, 1847, film 663998, image [not located], Registros Parroquiales, Iglesia de La Purísima Concepción, Álamos, Sonora, Mexico (FamilySearch, https://familysearch.org).

1014. Matrimonios 1867–1899, February 15, 1868, [no film number], images 8– 9, Civil Registrations, Álamos, Sonora, Mexico (FamilySearch, https://familysearch.org).

1015. Bautismos 1838–1856, October 5, 1852, film 663998, image 473, Registros Parroquiales, Iglesia de La Purísima Concepción, Álamos, Sonora, Mexico (FamilySearch, https://familysearch.org).

1016. Matrimonios 1873–1878, 1886–1898, February 20, 1876, film 663804, image 67, Registros Parroquiales, Iglesia de La Purísima Concepción, Álamos, Sonora, Mexico (FamilySearch, https://familysearch.org).

162. **María Josefa Dolores Esquer** (José Joaquín-7, Pedro Sebastián-6, Francisco Joseph-5, Juan Salvador-4, Salvador-3, Salvador-2, Blas-1) was born on July 8, 1790, in El Fuerte. The cited baptismal record provided her date of birth. She was baptized on September 21, 1790, at the church of the Sagrado Corazón in El Fuerte.[1017] The baptismal record named Sebastián Esquer and Anna María Murrieta as her *padrinos*.

María Josefa Dolores Esquer and Juan José Trinidad Francisco Vicente Gervasio Ortíz were married on June 11, 1808, at the parish of the Purísima Concepción in Álamos.[1018] The matrimonial record named Bruno Palacios and María Antonia Palacios as *padrinos*. Ignacio Ortiz was present among many others who witnessed the marriage. The marriage took place at the home of Juan Manuel Ortiz, father of the groom. The following morning the couple received a nuptial blessing. Parents of the bride and groom were named in the record.

María Josefa Dolores Esquer died on November 24, 1868, in Álamos. She was buried on November 25, 1868, in Álamos.[1019] The civil burial record named her parents and stated that she had died of a fever. The record noted in error that she was eighty-four years of age at death. Information was provided by her son Gregorio Ortiz.

Juan José Trinidad Francisco Vicente Gervasio Ortíz, son of Juan Manuel Ortíz and María de los Dolores Manuela Casilda Velarde, was born on June 19, 1787 in Álamos, according to the baptismal record. He was baptized on June 27, 1787, at the church of the Purísima Concepción in Álamos.[1020] The baptismal record named Bartolomé Salido and his wife María Bárbara González de Zayas as his *padrinos*.

Juan José Trinidad Francisco Vicente Gervasio Ortíz and María Josefa Dolores Esquer had the following known children:

i.   **José Vicente Florencio Simón Ortiz** was born in1809 in Álamos and was baptized on October 28, 1809, in Álamos.[1021] He married Rosa María Carlota Retes on November 26, 1846, in Álamos and later married María Policarpia Retes on March 31, 1861, Álamos.[1022]

ii. **María Florentina Josefa del Carmen Ortíz** was born in 1811 in Álamos. She was baptized on October 11, 1811, at the church of the Purísima Concepción in

---

1017. Bautismos 1783–1799, 1806–1829, September 21, 1790, film 678052, image 98, Registros Parroquiales, Iglesia Sagrado Corazón, El Fuerte, Sinaloa, Mexico (FamilySearch, https://familysearch.org).
1018. Matrimonios 1779–1817, June 11, 1808, film 666565, image 482, Registros Parroquiales, Iglesia de La Purísima Concepción, Álamos, Sonora, Mexico (FamilySearch, https://familysearch.org).
1019. Defunciones 1868–1887, November 25, 1868, film [no film number], images 6–7, Registro Civil del Estado de Sonora, Álamos, Sonora, Mexico (FamilySearch, https://familysearch.org).
1020. Bautismos 1781–1796, June 27, 1787, 663488, image 223, Registros Parroquiales, Iglesia de La Purísima Concepción, Álamos, Sonora, Mexico (FamilySearch, https://familysearch.org).
1021. Bautismos 1791–1796, 1805–1815, October 28, 1809, film 663996, image 349, Registros Parroquiales, Iglesia de La Purísima Concepción, Álamos, Sonora, Mexico (FamilySearch, https://familysearch.org).
1022. Matrimonios 1797–1833, 1846–1868, 1872–1877, November 26, 1846, film 666566, image [not located], Registros Parroquiales, Iglesia de La Purísima Concepción, Álamos, Sonora, Mexico (FamilySearch, https://familysearch.org); Nombre del testador: Vicente Ortiz, 1879, Álamos, Sonora, Mexico, Testamentos de Sonora, 1786–1910 (El Colegio de Sonora, http://www.colson.edu.mx:8080/testamentos/principal.aspx).

Álamos.[1023] The baptismal record named Manuel de la Breña and María de la Merced Ortíz as her *padrinos*.

    iii.   **José Gregorio Rodrigo Ortíz** was born on March 12, 1813, in Álamos. He was baptized on March 14, 1813, at the church of the Purísima Concepción in Álamos.[1024] The baptismal record named Jesús Palacios and Merced Ortíz as his *padrinos*.

    iv.   **José Rafael Ortíz** was born in 1814 in Álamos. He was baptized on December 9, 1814, at the church of the Purísima Concepción in Álamos.[1025] The baptismal record named Bachiller Juan José Gómez and Loreto Esquer as his *padrinos*.

    v.   **José Esteban Ortíz** was born in 1819 in Álamos. He was baptized on December 29, 1819, at the church of the Purísima Concepción in Álamos.[1026] The baptismal record named Petra Goycochea as his *madrina*.

163. **Seferina Rojo** (José Miguel-7, María Nicolasa Esquer-6, Francisco Joseph-5, Juan Salvador-4, Salvador-3, Salvador-2, Blas-1) was born in 1800 in Culiacán. The cited marriage information record stated that she was twenty-six years of age in December 1826. Although the marriage records for Serefina Rojo and Rafael Féliz stated that she was the daughter of her father's second marriage to Gertrudis Medina, that is not likely the case because Serefina was already grown when her father remarried.

The cited marriage information record dated December 25, 1826, found no impediment to marriage.[1027] Seferina Rojo and Rafael Féliz were married on January 9, 1827, at the church of the Sagrario de San Miguel in Culiacán.[1028] The matrimonial record named Manuel Romero and Luis Castaños as witnesses to the marriage. The couple received a nuptial blessing on their wedding day. Parents of the bride and groom were named in the record.

Rafael Féliz, son of José María Féliz and Francisca Villarreal, was born in 1798 in Culiacán. The cited marriage information record stated that he was twenty-eight years of age in December 1826. He died on May 15, 1876, in Culiacán.[1029] He died at the Rancho de San Rafael, Culiacán. The death record noted that he was from Tamazula and a *vecino* of Culiacán. The cited matrimonial entry for Rafael Feliz recorded his name as José María Feliz on the left margin.

1023. Bautismos 1791–1796, 1805–1815, October 11, 1811, film 663996, image 419, Registros Parroquiales, Iglesia de La Purísima Concepción, Álamos, Sonora, Mexico (FamilySearch, https://familysearch.org).
1024. Bautismos 1791–1796, 1805–1815, March 14, 1813, film 663996, Image 454, Registros Parroquiales, Iglesia de La Purísima Concepción, Álamos, Sonora, Mexico (FamilySearch, https://familysearch.org).
1025. Bautismos 1791–1796, 1805–1815, December 9, 1814, film 663996, image 485, Registros Parroquiales, Iglesia de La Purísima Concepción, Álamos, Sonora, Mexico (FamilySearch, https://familysearch.org).
1026. Bautismos 1816–1825, 1827–1829, December 29, 1819, film 663997, Registros Parroquiales, Iglesia de La Purísima Concepción, Álamos, Sonora, Mexico (FamilySearch, https://familysearch.org).
1027. Información matrimonial 1790–1794, 1820–1822, 1825–1827, film 673391, images 588–589, Registros Parroquiales, Iglesia Sagrario de San Miguel, Culiacán, Sinaloa, Mexico (FamilySearch, https://familysearch.org).
1028. Matrimonios 1755–1829, January 9, 1827, film 673378, image 471, Registros Parroquiales, Iglesia Sagrario de San Miguel, Culiacán, Sinaloa, Mexico (FamilySearch, https://familysearch.org).
1029. Defunciones 1865 ene–1877 dic, May 15, 1876, [no film number], image 1608, Civil Registrations, Culiacán, Sinaloa, Mexico (FamilySearch, https://familysearch.org).

Rafael Féliz and Seferina Rojo had the following known children:

    i.   **Ramona Féliz** was born in 1830. The cited burial record stated her age to be eighty-five at the time of death. She died on March 25, 1915, in Culiacán. She was buried on March 26, 1915, at the parish of the Sagrario de San Miguel in Culiacán.[1030] The burial record claimed that she had been a widow [husband was not named]. Her parents were named in the record.

    ii.   **María Brígida Féliz** was born on October 8, 1832, in Culiacán, according to the baptismal record. She was baptized on October 20, 1832, at the church of the Sagrario de San Miguel in Culiacán.[1031] The baptismal record named Cleto Sambade as her *padrino*.

    iii.   **Maria Eugenia Féliz** was born on November 15, 1836, in Culiacán. The cited baptismal record noted that she was five days old at the time. She was baptized on November 20, 1836, at the church of the Sagrario de San Miguel in Culiacán.[1032] The baptismal record named José María Aguirre and María Dolores Fraslavina as her *padrinos*.

    iv.   **María Teresa de Jesús Féliz** was born on October 15, 1838, in Culiacán, according to the baptismal record. She was baptized on October 17, 1838, at the church of the Sagrario de San Miguel in Culiacán.[1033] The baptismal record named Anna María Beltrán as her *madrina*.

    v.   **María Isidora Féliz** was born on November 9, 1840, in Culiacán. She was baptized on November 10, 1840, at the church of the Sagrario de San Miguel in Culiacán.[1034] The baptismal record named Dolores Izábal as her *madrina*.

164. José Antonio Rojo (José Miguel-7, María Nicolasa Esquer-6, Francisco Joseph-5, Juan Salvador-4, Salvador-3, Salvador-2, Blas-1) was born before 1804 in Culiacán. He appeared in the census in 1804 in Culiacán.[1035]

José Antonio Rojo and María Guadalupe Rojo were married on October 1, 1828, at the church of the Sagrario de San Miguel in Culiacán.[1036] The matrimonial record named Manuel

1030. Defunciones 1856–1919, film 674053, image 568, Registros Parroquiales, Iglesia Sagrario de San Miguel, Culiacán, Sinaloa, Mexico (FamilySearch, https://familysearch.org).
1031. Bautismos 1831–1838, October 20, 1832, film 665431, image 84, Registros Parroquiales, Iglesia Sagrario de San Miguel, Culiacán, Sinaloa, Mexico (FamilySearch, https://familysearch.org).
1032. Bautismos 1831–1838, November 20, 1836, film 665431, image 485, Registros Parroquiales, Iglesia Sagrario de San Miguel, Culiacán, Sinaloa, Mexico (FamilySearch, https://familysearch.org).
1033. Bautismos 1838–1841, October 17, 1838, film 665432, image 77, Registros Parroquiales, Iglesia Sagrario de San Miguel, Culiacán, Sinaloa, Mexico (FamilySearch, https://familysearch.org).
1034. Bautismos 1838–1841, November 10, 1840, film 665432, image 298, Registros Parroquiales, Iglesia Sagrario de San Miguel, Culiacán, Sinaloa, Mexico (FamilySearch, https://familysearch.org).
1035. Padrones del estado de Sinaloa, Mexico 1778–1804, Archivo Franciscano de la Biblioteca Nacional de México. Padrón de la Villa de Culiacán, 1804, item 2, caja 37, exp. 821, pp 1–24v, film 1149545 Item 2 (FamilySearch, https://familysearch.org).
1036. Matrimonios 1755–1829, October 1, 1828, film 673378, image 521, Registros Parroquiales, Iglesia Sagrario de San Miguel, Culiacán, Sinaloa, Mexico (FamilySearch, https://familysearch.org).

Romero and José Antonio Mendarona as witnesses to the marriage. Parents of the bridal couple were named, and the bride was was identified as the illegitimate daughter of Gertrudis Rojo. The officiating priest stated that there was no impediment to marriage, so the assumption was made that the bride and groom were not related.

There is question regarding the mother of the groom. The matrimonial record claimed that his mother was María Gertrudis Medina, second wife of the groom's father, Miguel José Rojo. The second marriage took place on April 26, 1824, only four years before the marriage of José Antonio's marriage to María Guadalupe. Therefore, the biological mother of the groom must have been Josefa Amarillas. There are no known children from this marriage.

María Guadalupe Rojo was born about 1810 in Culiacán.

165. **José de Jesús Rojo** (José Miguel-7, María Nicolasa Esquer-6, Francisco Joseph-5, Juan Salvador-4, Salvador-3, Salvador-2, Blas-1) was born about 1809.

José de Jesús Rojo and Ana María López were married on October 25, 1837, in Culiacán.[1037] The matrimonial record named Pedro Amarillas and Francisco Vidales as witnesses to the marriage. The couple received a nuptial blessing on the day of their marriage. Parents of the bride and groom were named in the record.

The marriage information record dated October 5, 1837, claimed there were no impediments to marriage.[1038] The groom was said to be twenty-eight years old, and the bride was said to be over eighteen years of age. Parents of the couple were recorded as deceased.

Ana María López, daughter of José Tomás López and María Gertrudis Escobar, was born on January 1, 1822, in Culiacán, according to the baptismal record. She was baptized on January 3, 1822, at the church of the Sagrario de San Miguel in Culiacán.[1039] The baptismal record named Trinidad Quirós as her *madrina*.

166. **María Guadalupe Rojo** (José Miguel-7, María Nicolasa Esquer-6, Francisco Joseph-5, Juan Salvador-4, Salvador-3, Salvador-2, Blas-1) was born about 1816.

María Guadalupe Rojo and Pedro Amarillas were married on July 8, 1830, at the church of the Sagrario de San Miguel in Culiacán.[1040] The matrimonial record named Manuel Romero and Juan Nepomuceno as witnesses to the marriage. The couple received a nuptial blessing on their wedding day. A dispensation for the marriage was necessary because the bride and groom were related in the third degree of consanguinity. They were also related in a second with a third

---

1037. Matrimonios 1830–1856, October 25, 1837, film 673379, images 152–153, Registros Parroquiales, Iglesia Sagrario de San Miguel, Culiacán, Sinaloa, Mexico (FamilySearch, https://familysearch.org).
1038. Información matrimonial 1837–1840, October 5, 1837, film 673393, images 63–64, Registros Parroquiales, Iglesia Sagrario de San Miguel, Culiacán, Sinaloa, Mexico (FamilySearch, https://familysearch.org).
1039. Bautismos 1820–1831, January 3, 1822, film 665430, image 125, Registros Parroquiales, Iglesia Sagrario de San Miguel, Culiacán, Sinaloa, Mexico (FamilySearch, https://familysearch.org).
1040. Matrimonios 1830–1856, July 8, 1830, film 673379, image 13, Registros Parroquiales, Iglesia Sagrario de San Miguel, Culiacán, Sinaloa, Mexico (FamilySearch, https://familysearch.org).

degree of consanguinity. Parents of the bride and groom were named. The father of the groom, and parents of the bride were said to have been deceased.

Pedro Amarillas, son of Andrés Amarillas and María Aguilasocho, was born about 1810.

Pedro Amarillas and María Guadalupe Rojo had the following known children:

i. **José María Amarillas**, was born May 2, 1833, in Culiacán and was baptized on May 2, 1833, in Culiacán.[1041] He married María Rosa Veneranda Amarillas on October 3, 1853, in Culiacán.[1042]

ii. **María Josefa Amarillas** was born on July 26, 1835, in Culiacán, according to the baptismal record. She was baptized on July 27, 1835, at the church of the Sagrario de San Miguel in Culiacán.[1043] The baptismal record named Miguel Amarillas and Nicolasa Rojo as her *padrinos*. She died on May 16, 1907, at the age of seventy-one in Culiacán. María Josefa was buried on May 17, 1907, at the parish of the Sagrario de San Miguel in the municipal cemetery in Culiacán.[1044] She received the last sacraments of the Catholic Church. Her parents were named in the burial record.

iii. **Miguel María Amarillas** was born on February 4, 1838, in Culiacán, according to the baptismal record. He was baptized on February 6, 1838, at the church of the Sagrario de San Miguel in Culiacán.[1045] The baptismal record named Francisca Espinosa as his *madrina*.

iv. **Francisco Amarillas** was born on June 15, 1839, in Culiacán, according to the baptismal record. He was baptized on June 16, 1839, at the church of the Sagrario de San Miguel in Culiacán.[1046] The baptismal record named Lucas Verdugo and Jesús Cárdenas as his *padrinos*.

v. **María Luisa Amarillas** was born on June 22, 1841, in Culiacán, according to the baptismal record. She was baptized on June 23, 1841, at the church of the Sagrario de San Miguel in Culiacán.[1047] The baptismal record named Josefa Espinosa as her *madrina*.

vi. **Pedro Toribio de Jesús Amarillas** was born on April 14, 1846, in Culiacán, according to the baptismal record. He was baptized on April 17, 1846, at the church

1041. Bautismos 1831–1838, May 2, 1833, film 665431, image 134, Registros Parroquiales, Iglesia Sagrario de San Miguel, Culiacán, Sinaloa, Mexico (FamilySearch, https://familysearch.org).
1042. Matrimonios 1830–1856, October 3, 1853, film 673379, image 541, Registros Parroquiales, Iglesia Sagrario de San Miguel, Culiacán, Sinaloa, Mexico (FamilySearch, https://familysearch.org).
1043. Bautismos 1831–1838, July 27, 1835, film 665431, image 358, Registros Parroquiales, Iglesia Sagrario de San Miguel, Culiacán, Sinaloa, Mexico (FamilySearch, https://familysearch.org).
1044. Defunciones 1856–1919, May 17, 1907, film 674053, image 478, Registros Parroquiales, Iglesia Sagrario de San Miguel, Culiacán, Sinaloa, Mexico (FamilySearch, https://familysearch.org).
1045. Bautismos 1831–1838, February 6, 1838, film 665431, image 600, Registros Parroquiales, Iglesia Sagrario de San Miguel, Culiacán, Sinaloa, Mexico (FamilySearch, https://familysearch.org).
1046. Bautismos 1838–184, June 16, 1839, film 665432, image 156, Registros Parroquiales, Iglesia Sagrario de San Miguel, Culiacán, Sinaloa, Mexico (FamilySearch, https://familysearch.org).
1047. Bautismos 1841–1847, June 23, 1841, film 665433, images 46–47, Registros Parroquiales, Iglesia Sagrario de San Miguel, Culiacán, Sinaloa, Mexico (FamilySearch, https://familysearch.org).

of the Sagrario de San Miguel in Culiacán.[1048] The baptismal record named Jorge Casillas and Nicolasa Alcayde as his *padrinos*.

167. **José María Palazuelos** (María Juana Rafaela Rojo-7, María Nicolasa Esquer-6, Francisco Joseph-5, Juan Salvador-4, Salvador-3, Salvador-2, Blas-1) was born about 1791.

José María Palazuelos and María Isabel Castro were married on April 23, 1813, at the church of the Sagrario de San Miguel in Culiacán.[1049] The matrimonial record named Manuel Romero and José Pérez as witnesses to the marriage. Parents of the bride and groom were named in the record. The couple did not receive a nuptial blessing on the day of their marriage due to prohibitions in the liturgical calendar of the Catholic Church.

María Isabel Castro, daughter of Pablo Castro and Balvanera Rocha, was born about 1795.

José María Palazuelos and María Isabel Castro had the following known children:

    i.   **María Eufemia Palazuelos** was born on March 21, 1814, in Culiacán, according to the baptismal record. She was baptized on April 26, 1814, at the church of the Sagrario de San Miguel in Culiacán.[1050] The baptismal record named José Manuel Palazuelos and Rafaela Rojo as her *padrinos*.

    ii.   **Mariano Palazuelos** was born about 1815 in Culiacán; he married María Bruna Cabada on May 14, 1835, in Culiacán.[1051] He later married María Ysabel Castro. The marriage record has not been located.

    iii.   **José Tiburcio Palazuelos** was born on April 14, 1817 in Culiacán. He was baptized on May 8, 1817, at the church of the Sagrario de San Miguel in Culiacán.[1052] The baptismal record named María Rosa Palazuelos as his *madrina*.

    iv.   **María de Jesús Palazuelos** was born about 1818. She married Pedro Zazueta on April 4, 1837, in Culiacán and later married Antonio Castaños on June 19, 1847, in Culiacán.[1053]

    v.   **José Antonio Palazuelos** was born about 1819; he married Francisca Trapero on April 22, 1844, in Culiacán and was buried on October 18, 1846, in Culiacán.[1054]

1048. Bautismos 1841–1847, April 17, 1846, film 665433, image 492, Registros Parroquiales, Iglesia Sagrario de San Miguel, Culiacán, Sinaloa, Mexico (FamilySearch, https://familysearch.org).
1049. Matrimonios 1755–1829, April 23, 1813, film 673378, image 311, Registros Parroquiales, Iglesia Sagrario de San Miguel, Culiacán, Sinaloa, Mexico (FamilySearch, https://familysearch.org).
1050. Bautismos 1796–1818, April 26, 1814, film 665429, image 445, Registros Parroquiales, Iglesia Sagrario de San Miguel, Culiacán, Sinaloa, Mexico (FamilySearch, https://familysearch.org).
1051. Matrimonios 1830–1856, May 14, 1835, film 673379, image 107, Registros Parroquiales, Iglesia Sagrario de San Miguel, Culiacán, Sinaloa, Mexico (FamilySearch, https://familysearch.org).
1052. Bautismos 1796–1818, May 8, 1817, film 665429, image 580, Registros Parroquiales, Iglesia Sagrario de San Miguel, Culiacán, Sinaloa, Mexico (FamilySearch, https://familysearch.org).
1053. Matrimonios 1830–1856, April 4, 1837, film 673379, image 138, Registros Parroquiales, Iglesia Sagrario de San Miguel, Culiacán, Sinaloa, Mexico (FamilySearch, https://familysearch.org); Matrimonios 1830–1856, June 19, 1847, film 673379, image 392, Registros Parroquiales, Iglesia Sagrario de San Miguel, Culiacán, Sinaloa, Mexico (FamilySearch, https://familysearch.org).
1054. Matrimonios 1830–1856, April 22, 1844, film 673379, image 305, Registros Parroquiales, Iglesia Sagrario de San Miguel, Culiacán, Sinaloa, Mexico (FamilySearch, https://familysearch.org); Defunciones 1933–1956, October 18, 1846, film 674052, image 281, Registros Parroquiales, Iglesia Sagrario de San Miguel, Culiacán,

vi.   **Calixta Palazuelos** was born on November 9, 1821, in Culiacán. She was baptized on November 13, 1821, at the church of the Sagrario de San Miguel in Culiacán.[1055] The baptismal record named José María Zazueta and Teresa Castro as her *padrinos*.

vii.   **Teresa Palazuelos** was born about 1827; she married José Gregorio Mariano Cárdenas on October 11, 1845, in Culiacán, and was buried on August 30, 1903, in Culiacán.[1056]

viii.   **José Guadalupe Palazuelos** was born on December 12, 1828, in Culiacán. The baptismal record stated that he was eleven days old at baptism. He was baptized on December 23, 1828, at the church of the Sagrario de San Miguel in Culiacán.[1057] The baptismal record named Casimiro Palazuelos as his *padrino*.

ix.   **Daniel Palazuelos** was born about 1833 in Culiacán; he married Rosalía Sánchez on May 5, 1853, in Culiacán.[1058]

x.   **María del Refugio Palazuelos** was born on January 14, 1839, in Culiacán, according to the baptismal record. She was baptized on January 15, 1839, at the church of the Sagrario de San Miguel in Culiacán.[1059] The baptismal record named Pedro Amarillas and Guadalupe Rojo as her *padrinos*. She died on October 16, 1842, at the age of three in Culiacán. María was buried on October 17, 1842, at the church of the Sagrario de San Miguel in Culiacán.[1060] Her funeral service was held with *cruz baja y caja*. She was described as a child who died of smallpox.

168. José Manuel Palazuelos (María Juana Rafaela Rojo-7, María Nicolasa Esquer-6, Francisco Joseph-5, Juan Salvador-4, Salvador-3, Salvador-2, Blas-1) was born in 1795. The cited marriage information stated that he was twenty-nine years of age at the time of his first marriage. He married three times.

José Manuel Palazuelos and María Loreto Baldenegro were married on September 28, 1824, at the church of the Sagrario de San Miguel in Culiacán.[1061] The matrimonial record named José

Sinaloa, Mexico (FamilySearch, https://familysearch.org).

1055. Bautismos 1820–1831, November 13, 1821, film 665430, image 117, Registros Parroquiales, Iglesia Sagrario de San Miguel, Culiacán, Sinaloa, Mexico (FamilySearch, https://familysearch.org).

1056. Matrimonios 1830–1856, October 11, 1845, film 673379, image 346, Registros Parroquiales, Iglesia Sagrario de San Miguel, Culiacán, Sinaloa, Mexico (FamilySearch, https://familysearch.org); Defunciones 1856–1919, August 30, 1903, film 674053, image 457, Registros Parroquiales, Iglesia Sagrario de San Miguel, Culiacán, Sinaloa, Mexico (FamilySearch, https://familysearch.org).

1057. Bautismos 1820–1831, December 23, 1828, film 665430, image 472, Registros Parroquiales, Iglesia Sagrario de San Miguel, Culiacán, Sinaloa, Mexico (FamilySearch, https://familysearch.org).

1058. Matrimonios 1830–1856, May 5, 1853, film 673379, image 530, Registros Parroquiales, Iglesia Sagrario de San Miguel, Culiacán, Sinaloa, Mexico (FamilySearch, https://familysearch.org); Información matrimonial 1852–1855, March 27, 1853, film 673455, images 93–96, Registros Parroquiales, Iglesia Sagrario de San Miguel, Culiacán, Sinaloa, Mexico (FamilySearch, https://familysearch.org).

1059. Bautismos 1838–1841, January 14, 1839, film 665432, image 114, Registros Parroquiales, Iglesia Sagrario de San Miguel, Culiacán, Sinaloa, Mexico (FamilySearch, https://familysearch.org).

1060. Defunciones 1933–1956, October 17, 1842, film 674052, image 172, Registros Parroquiales, Iglesia Sagrario de San Miguel, Culiacán, Sinaloa, Mexico (FamilySearch, https://familysearch.org).

1061. Matrimonios 1755–1829, September 28, 1824, film 673378, image 440, Registros Parroquiales, Iglesia Sagrario de San Miguel, Culiacán, Sinaloa, Mexico (FamilySearch, https://familysearch.org).

María Castro and Manuel Romero as witnesses to the marriage. Parents of the bride and groom were named in the record.

María Loreto Baldenegro, daughter of José Antonio Baldenegro and Francisca Gracia, was born in 1801. The cited marriage information record stated that María Loreto Baldenegro was twenty-three years of age at the time of her marriage.

José Manuel Palazuelos and María Loreto Baldenegro had one known child:

i. **Ana María Palazuelos** was born between 1824 and 1826 in Culiacán, estimating from the year her parents were married. She died on July 22, 1826, in Culiacán. She was buried on July 23, 1826, at the church of the Sagrario de San Miguel in Culiacán.[1062] The burial was for a small child (*párvula*). Her funeral service was held with a *cruz baja* and she was laid to rest in a burial site valued at three pesos.

José Manuel Palazuelos and María Josefa Isideria Páez were married on November 17, 1831, at the church of the Sagrario de San Miguel in Culiacán.[1063] The matrimonial record named Manuel Rodríguez and Manuel Romero as witnesses to marriage. The record stated that the groom was the widowed husband of his first wife, Loreto Baldenegro. The bride was said to have been the natural daughter of María Teresa Páez. The couple received a dispensation to marry because they were in the fourth degree of consanguinity, meaning they were third cousins.[1064]

María Josefa Isideria Páez, daughter of María Teresa Páez, was born on February 11, 1809. The cited baptismal record stated that she had been born twenty days before her baptism. She was baptized on March 3, 1809, at the church of the Sagrario de San Miguel in Culiacán.[1065] The baptismal record stated that she was the natural child of Teresa Páez. Luis Rodríguez de la Rodriguera and Josefa Esquer were named as her *padrinos*. José Manuel Palazuelos and María Josefa Isideria Páez had the following known children:

i. **María Isabel Palazuelos** was born on November 8, 1832, in Culiacán and was baptized on November 9, 1832, in Culiacán.[1066] She married married Juan Camaron on April 29, 1852, in Culiacán.[1067] She later married Tomás Paredes on October 25, 1859, in Culiacán.[1068]

1062. Defunciones 1746–1833, July 23, 1826, film 674051, image 625, Registros Parroquiales, Iglesia Sagrario de San Miguel, Culiacán, Sinaloa, Mexico (FamilySearch, https://familysearch.org).
1063. Matrimonios 1830–1856, November 17, 1831, film 673379, images 40–41, Registros Parroquiales, Iglesia Sagrario de San Miguel, Culiacán, Sinaloa, Mexico (FamilySearch, https://familysearch.org).
1064. Información matrimonial 1819–1830, November 17, 1831, film 673451, images 190–191, Registros Parroquiales, Iglesia Sagrario de San Miguel, Culiacán, Sinaloa, Mexico (FamilySearch, https://familysearch.org).
1065. Bautismos 1796-1818, March 3, 1809 film 665429, images 282–283, Registros Parroquiales, Iglesia Sagrado Corazón, Culiacán, Sinaloa, Mexico (FamilySearch, https://familysearch.org).
1066. Bautismos 1831–1838, November 9, 1832, film 665431, image 88, Registros Parroquiales, Iglesia Sagrario de San Miguel, Culiacán, Sinaloa, Mexico (FamilySearch, https://familysearch.org).
1067. Matrimonios 1830–1856, April 29, 1852, film 673379, image 508, Registros Parroquiales, Iglesia Sagrario de San Miguel, Culiacán, Sinaloa, Mexico (FamilySearch, https://familysearch.org); Información matrimonial 1852–185, April 27, 1852, film 673455, images 44–49, Registros Parroquiales, Iglesia Sagrario de San Miguel, Culiacán, Sinaloa, Mexico (FamilySearch, https://familysearch.org).
1068. Matrimonios 1856–1865, October 25, 1859, film 673380, images 146–147, Registros Parroquiales, Iglesia Sagrario de San Miguel, Culiacán, Sinaloa, Mexico (FamilySearch, https://familysearch.org); Información matrimonial 1857–186, August 13, 1859, film 673458, images 560–564, Registros Parroquiales, Iglesia Sagrario de San Miguel, Culiacán, Sinaloa, Mexico (FamilySearch, https://familysearch.org).

ii.   **María Guadalupe Anastasia de Jesús Palazuelos** was born on January 22, 1835, in Culiacán and she was baptized on January 31, 1835, in Culiacán.[1069] She married Juan Russell on July 17, 1854, in Culiacán.[1070]

iii.   **María Josefa de Jesús Palazuelos** was born on April 6, 1837, Culiacán and she was baptized on June 1, 1837, in Culiacán.[1071] She married Juan Russell after December 3, 1858, Culiacán.[1072]

José Manuel Palazuelos and María Gertrudis Rodríguez de la Rodriguera were married on March 7, 1840, at the church of the Sagrario de San Miguel in Culiacán.[1073] The matrimonial record named Pedro Amarillas and Francisco Vidales as witnesses to the marriage. The record stated that the groom was the widowed husband of his second wife, Josefa Páez. The couple received a dispensation to marry because they were related in the fourth degree of consanguinity, meaning they were third cousins. They were also related in the second degree of affinity because the second and third wives were first cousins. Parents of the bride were named in the record

María Gertrudis Rodríguez de la Rodriguera, daughter of Sebastián Rodríguez de la Rodriguera and María Francisca Páez, was born on July 4, 1813, in Culiacán, according to the baptismal record. She was baptized on August 16, 1813, at the church of the Sagrario de San Miguel in Culiacán.[1074] The baptismal record named Manuel López and his wife María Pérez as her *padrinos*.

José Manuel Palazuelos and María Gertrudis Rodríguez de la Rodriguera had the following known children:

i.   **José Víctor Palazuelos** was born on March 22, 1841, in Culiacán and was baptized on April 7, 1841.[1075] He married María Eugenia Palazuelos on August 25, 1864, in Culiacán.[1076]

ii.   **María Úrsula Palazuelos** was born on October 21, 1852, in Culiacán, according to the baptismal record. She was baptized on December 6, 1852, at the church of the Sagrario de San Miguel in Culiacán.[1077] The baptismal record named Francisco Sambade and María Estanislao González as her *padrinos*.

1069. Bautismos 1831–1838, January 31, 1835, image 305, Registros Parroquiales, Iglesia Sagrario de San Miguel, Culiacán, Sinaloa, Mexico (FamilySearch, https://familysearch.org).

1070. Matrimonios 1830–1856, July 17, 1854, film 673379, image 558, Registros Parroquiales, Iglesia Sagrario de San Miguel, Culiacán, Sinaloa, Mexico (FamilySearch, https://familysearch.org).

1071. Bautismos 1831–1838, June 1, 1837, film 665431, images 535–535, Registros Parroquiales, Iglesia Sagrario de San Miguel, Culiacán, Sinaloa, Mexico (FamilySearch, https://familysearch.org).

1072. Información matrimonial 1857–1860, November 23, 1858, film 673458, images 411–415, Registros Parroquiales, Iglesia Sagrario de San Miguel, Culiacán, Sinaloa, Mexico (FamilySearch, https://familysearch.org).

1073. Matrimonios 1830–1856, March 7, 1840, film 673379, images 221–222, Registros Parroquiales, Iglesia Sagrario de San Miguel, Culiacán, Sinaloa, Mexico (FamilySearch, https://familysearch.org).

1074. Bautismos 1796–1818, July 4, 1813, film 665429, image 404, Registros Parroquiales, Iglesia Sagrario de San Miguel, Culiacán, Sinaloa, Mexico (FamilySearch, https://familysearch.org).

1075. Bautismos 1841–1847, April 7, 1841, film 665433, image 26, Registros Parroquiales, Iglesia Sagrario de San Miguel, Culiacán, Sinaloa, Mexico (FamilySearch, https://familysearch.org).

1076. Matrimonios 1856–1865, August 25, 1864, film 673380, image 296, Registros Parroquiales, Iglesia Sagrario de San Miguel, Culiacán, Sinaloa, Mexico (FamilySearch, https://familysearch.org).

1077. Bautismos 1850–1854, December 6, 1852, film 666172, image 298, Registros Parroquiales, Iglesia Sagrario de San Miguel, Culiacán, Sinaloa, Mexico (FamilySearch, https://familysearch.org).

169. **José Laureano Palazuelos** (María Juana Rafaela Rojo-7, María Nicolasa Esquer-6, Francisco Joseph-5, Juan Salvador-4, Salvador-3, Salvador-2, Blas-1) was born on June 4, 1800, in Culiacán. The cited baptismal record provided his date of birth. He was baptized on July 8, 1800, at the church of the Sagrario de San Miguel in Culiacán.[1078] The baptismal record named Manuel Verdugo, legitimate son of Cayetano Verdugo and Brígida de Ibarra, as his *padrinos*. The child had previously received the waters of baptism by a priest as a precaution, should he not survive. On his baptismal day he was anointed with the holy oil and sacred chrism of baptism.

José Laureano Palazuelos and Concepción Murrieta were married on April 28, 1829, at the church of the Sagrario de San Miguel in Culiacán.[1079] The matrimonial record named Manuel Romero and Nepomuceno Valenzuela as witnesses to the act of matrimony. Parents of the bride and groom were named, and the father of the groom was said to have been deceased.

Concepción Murrieta, daughter of Joaquín Murrieta and Josefa Madero, was born about 1811.

José Laureano Palazuelos and Concepción Murrieta had the following known children:

i. **Antonio Palazuelos** was born about 1831; he married María del Carmen Palazuelos on September 13, 1856, in Culiacán.[1080]

ii. **Ana María Palazuelos** was born on April 16, 1834, in Culiacán, according to the baptismal record. She was baptized on May 30, 1834, at the church of the Sagrario de San Miguel in Culiacán.[1081] The baptismal record named José Antonio Zazueta as her *padrino*.

iii. **María Filomena Palazuelos** was born on July 5, 1836, in Culiacán, according to the baptismal record. She was baptized on August 15, 1836, at the church of the Sagrario de San Miguel in Culiacán.[1082] The baptismal record named María Josefa Páez as her *madrina*.

iv. **José de Jesús Palazuelos** was born on August 8, 1838, in Culiacán, according to the baptismal record. He was baptized on September 8, 1838, at the church of the Sagrario de San Miguel in Culiacán.[1083] The baptismal record named Vicente Sanz as his *padrino*.

v. **María Guadalupe Palazuelos** was born on December 5, 1840, in Culiacán, according to the baptismal record. She was baptized on January 13, 1841, at the church of the

---

1078. Bautismos 1796–1818, July 8, 1800, film 665429, image 90, Registros Parroquiales, Iglesia Sagrario de San Miguel, Culiacán, Sinaloa, Mexico (FamilySearch, https://familysearch.org).
1079. Matrimonios 1755–1829, April 28,1829, film 673378, image 513, Registros Parroquiales, Iglesia Sagrado Corazón, Culiacán, Sinaloa, Mexico (FamilySearch, https://familysearch.org).
1080. Matrimonios 1830–1856, September 13, 1856, film 673379, image 657, Registros Parroquiales, Iglesia Sagrario de San Miguel, Culiacán, Sinaloa, Mexico (FamilySearch, https://familysearch.org); Información matrimonial 1855–1856, August 20, 1856, film 673456, images 334–337, Registros Parroquiales, Iglesia Sagrario de San Miguel, Culiacán, Sinaloa, Mexico (FamilySearch, https://familysearch.org).
1081. Bautismos 1831–1838, May 30, 1834, film 665431, image 232, Registros Parroquiales, Iglesia Sagrario de San Miguel, Culiacán, Sinaloa, Mexico (FamilySearch, https://familysearch.org).
1082. Bautismos 1831–1838, August 15, 1836, film 665431, images 457–458, Registros Parroquiales, Iglesia Sagrario de San Miguel, Culiacán, Sinaloa, Mexico (FamilySearch, https://familysearch.org).
1083. Bautismos 1838–1841, September 8, 1838, film 665432, image 63, Registros Parroquiales, Iglesia Sagrario de San Miguel, Culiacán, Sinaloa, Mexico (FamilySearch, https://familysearch.org).

Sagrario de San Miguel in Culiacán.[1084] The baptismal record named José Manuel Palazuelos and María Trinidad Rodríguez as her *padrinos*. The parents were said to be *vecinos* of Iraguato, Sinaloa.

vi. **José Lucio Palazuelos** was born on January 4, 1843, in Sataya, Sinaloa and was baptized on February 1,1843 in Culiacán.[1085] He married María Apolonia de Jesús Sanz on December 14, 1866, in Culiacán.[1086] He later married María Josefa Anastasia de Jesús Sanz after June 29, 1871.[1087]

vii. **Sebastián Esteban Palazuelos** was born on January 31, 1846, in Culiacán, according to the baptismal record. He was baptized on January 31, 1846, at the church of the Sagrario de San Miguel in Culiacán.[1088] The baptismal record named Nicolás Rodriguera and María Sacramento Pérez as his *padrinos*.

170. **María Rosa Palazuelos** (María Juana Rafaela Rojo-7, María Nicolasa Esquer-6, Francisco Joseph-5, Juan Salvador-4, Salvador-3, Salvador-2, Blas-1) was born about 1801. She was also known as "Rosa María Palazuelos."

María Rosa Palazuelos and Timoteo Hernández were married on July 2, 1826, at the church of the Sagrario de San Miguel in Culiacán.[1089] The matrimonial record named Manuel Romero and Francisco Rodríguez as witnesses to the marriage. Parents of the bride and groom were named in the record.

Timoteo Hernández, son of José María Hernández and Manuela López, was born about 1806.

Timoteo Hernández and María Rosa Palazuelos had the following known children:

i. **Gertrudis Hernández** was born about 1827; she married José Esteban Zazueta on November 3, 1843, in Culiacán.[1090]

ii. **María Cándida Hernández** was born on December 4, 1831, in Culiacán, according to the baptismal record. She was baptized on February 9, 1832, at the church of the

1084. Bautismos 1838–1841, January 13, 1841, film 665432, images 312–313, Registros Parroquiales, Iglesia Sagrario de San Miguel, Culiacán, Sinaloa, Mexico (FamilySearch, https://familysearch.org).
1085. Bautismos 1841–1847, February 1, 1843, film 665433, image 185, Registros Parroquiales, Iglesia Sagrario de San Miguel, Culiacán, Sinaloa, Mexico (FamilySearch, https://familysearch.org).
1086. Matrimonios 1865–1883, December 14, 1866, film 673606, image 37, Registros Parroquiales, Iglesia Sagrario de San Miguel, Culiacán, Sinaloa, Mexico (FamilySearch, https://familysearch.org); Información matrimonial 1860–1867, November 1, 1866, film 673459, images 455–457, Registros Parroquiales, Iglesia Sagrario de San Miguel, Culiacán, Sinaloa, Mexico (FamilySearch, https://familysearch.org).
1087. Información matrimonial 1871–1873, June 29, 1871, film 673460, images 841–843, Registros Parroquiales, Iglesia Sagrario de San Miguel, Culiacán, Sinaloa, Mexico (FamilySearch, https://familysearch.org).
1088. Bautismos 1841–1847, January 31, 1846, film 665433, image 464, Registros Parroquiales, Iglesia Sagrario de San Miguel, Culiacán, Sinaloa, Mexico (FamilySearch, https://familysearch.org).
1089. Matrimonios 1755–1829, July 2, 1826, film 673378, image 465, Registros Parroquiales, Iglesia Sagrario de San Miguel, Culiacán, Sinaloa, Mexico (FamilySearch, https://familysearch.org).
1090. Matrimonios 1830–1856, November 3, 1843, film 673379, image 294, Registros Parroquiales, Iglesia Sagrario de San Miguel, Culiacán, Sinaloa, Mexico (FamilySearch, https://familysearch.org).

Sagrario de San Miguel in Culiacán.[1091] The baptismal record named Manuela López as her *madrina*.

iii. **María Juana Hernández** was born on November 17, 1833, in Culiacán, according to the baptismal record. She was baptized on February 17, 1834, at the church of the Sagrario de San Miguel in Culiacán.[1092] The baptismal record named Ramón Bojórquez and María Antonia Hernández as her *padrinos*.

iv. **María Rafaela Hernández** was born on February 1, 1835, in Culiacán. She was baptized on March 6, 1835, at the church of the Sagrario de San Miguel in Culiacán.[1093] The baptismal record named María de Jesús Castro as her *madrina*.

v. **María Dolores Simona Hernández** was born on February 18, 1838, in Sataya, Sinaloa and she was baptized on April 5, 1838.[1094] She married Juan Zazueta after January 25, 1856, in Culiacán. The marriage record has not been located.[1095]

vi. **José Antonio de Jesús Hernández** was born on December 5, 1841, in Culiacán. He was baptized on January 16, 1842, at the church of the Sagrario de San Miguel in Culiacán.[1096] The baptismal record named José Manuel Palazuelos and Micaela Rojo as his *padrinos*.

vii. **María Ventura Hernández** was born about 1826 in Culiacán; she married Francisco Clemente Rodríguez de la Rodriguera on May 20, 1848, in Culiacán.[1097]

171. **María Antonia Palazuelos** (María Juana Rafaela Rojo-7, María Nicolasa Esquer-6, Francisco Joseph-5, Juan Salvador-4, Salvador-3, Salvador-2, Blas-1) was born on May 6, 1803, in Culiacán, according to the baptismal record. She was baptized on May 18, 1803, at the church of the Sagrario de San Miguel in Culiacán.[1098] The baptismal record named Manuel Rojo and Nicolasa Esquer, his wife, as her *padrinos*.

María Antonia Palazuelos and Pedro José Páez were married on November 3, 1824, at the church of the Sagrario de San Miguel in Culiacán.[1099] The matrimonial record named José María

1091. Bautismos 1831–1838, February 9, 1831, film 665431, image 17, Registros Parroquiales, Iglesia Sagrario de San Miguel, Culiacán, Sinaloa, Mexico (FamilySearch, https://familysearch.org).
1092. Bautismos 1831–1838, February 17, 1833, film 665431, image 206, Registros Parroquiales, Iglesia Sagrario de San Miguel, Culiacán, Sinaloa, Mexico (FamilySearch, https://familysearch.org).
1093. Bautismos 1831–1838, March 6, 1835, film 665431, images 324–325, Registros Parroquiales, Iglesia Sagrario de San Miguel, Culiacán, Sinaloa, Mexico (FamilySearch, https://familysearch.org).
1094. Bautismos 1838–1841, April 5, 1838, film 665432, image 25, Registros Parroquiales, Iglesia Sagrario de San Miguel, Culiacán, Sinaloa, Mexico (FamilySearch, https://familysearch.org).
1095. Información matrimonial 1855–1856, January 12, 1856, film 673456, images 71–75, Registros Parroquiales, Iglesia Sagrario de San Miguel, Culiacán, Sinaloa, Mexico (FamilySearch, https://familysearch.org).
1096. Bautismos 1841–1847, January 16, 1842, film 665433, image 88, Registros Parroquiales, Iglesia Sagrario de San Miguel, Culiacán, Sinaloa, Mexico (FamilySearch, https://familysearch.org).
1097. Matrimonios 1830–1856, May 20, 1848, film 673379, image 406, Registros Parroquiales, Iglesia Sagrario de San Miguel, Culiacán, Sinaloa, Mexico (FamilySearch, https://familysearch.org).
1098. Bautismos 1796–1818, May 18, 1803, film 665429, image 160, Registros Parroquiales, Iglesia Sagrario de San Miguel, Culiacán, Sinaloa, Mexico (FamilySearch, https://familysearch.org).
1099. Matrimonios 1755–1829, November 3, 1824, film 673378, image 442, Registros Parroquiales, Iglesia Sagrario de San Miguel, Culiacán, Sinaloa, Mexico (FamilySearch, https://familysearch.org).

Palazuelos and Manuel Romero as witnesses to the marriage. The couple received a nuptial blessing on their wedding day. Parents of the bride and groom were named in the record. The couple were related in the third degree (second cousins), and also in the third degree with a fourth degree of consanguinity (second cousins once removed).

Pedro José Páez, son of Pedro Lino Páez and María Teresa López, was born on January 3, 1800, in Culiacán. The cited baptismal record provided his date of birth. He was baptized on January 13, 1800, at the church of the Sagrario de San Miguel in Culiacán.[1100] The baptismal record named Timoteo Trapero and his wife, Ana Verdugo, as his *padrinos*.

Pedro José Páez and María Antonia Palazuelos had the following known children:

    i.   **Ramón Páez** was born about 1823 on Sataya and was; he married María Silvestre Taylor on May 20, 1848, in Culiacán.[1101]

    ii.   **Basilio Páez** was born on June 14, 1829, in Culiacán and was baptized on July 20, 1829 in Culiacán.[1102] He married Bruna López on December 11, 1865, in Culiacán.[1103]

    iii.   **José Severiano Páez** was born on February 22, 1832, in Culiacán, according to the baptismal record. He was baptized on April 13, 1832, at the church of the Sagrario de San Miguel in Culiacán.[1104] The baptismal record named María del Loreto Rodríguez as his *madrina*.

    iv.   **María Ignacia Emeteria Páez** was born on April 4, 1835, in Culiacán, according to the baptismal record. She was baptized on April 18, 1835, at the church of the Sagrario de San Miguel in Culiacán.[1105] The baptismal record named Luis Rodríguez de la Rodriguera and María Ignacia Cárdenas as her *padrinos*.

    v.   **José del Carmen de Jesús Páez** was born on February 11, 1838, in Culiacán, according to the baptismal record. He was baptized on March 17, 1838, at the church of the Sagrario de San Miguel in Culiacán.[1106] The baptismal record named Onofre Sain as his *padrino*.

1100. Bautismos 1796–1818, January 13, 1800, film 665429, image 77, Registros Parroquiales, Iglesia Sagrario de San Miguel, Culiacán, Sinaloa, Mexico (FamilySearch, https://familysearch.org).

1101. Matrimonios 1830–1856, May 20, 1848, film 673379 image 406, Registros Parroquiales, Iglesia Sagrario de San Miguel, Culiacán, Sinaloa, Mexico (FamilySearch, https://familysearch.org); Información matrimonial 1847–1849, April 24, 1848, film 673396, images 87–89, Registros Parroquiales, Iglesia Sagrario de San Miguel, Culiacán, Sinaloa, Mexico (FamilySearch, https://familysearch.org).

1102. Bautismos 1820–1831, July 20, 1829, film 665430, image 531, Registros Parroquiales, Iglesia Sagrario de San Miguel, Culiacán, Sinaloa, Mexico (FamilySearch, https://familysearch.org).

1103. Matrimonios 1865–1883, December 11, 1865, film 673606, image 13, Registros Parroquiales, Iglesia Sagrario de San Miguel, Culiacán, Sinaloa, Mexico (FamilySearch, https://familysearch.org).

1104. Bautismos 1831–1838, April 13, 1832, film 665431, image 37, Registros Parroquiales, Iglesia Sagrario de San Miguel, Culiacán, Sinaloa, Mexico (FamilySearch, https://familysearch.org).

1105. Bautismos 1831–183, April 18, 1835, film 665431, image 333, Registros Parroquiales, Iglesia Sagrario de San Miguel, Culiacán, Sinaloa, Mexico (FamilySearch, https://familysearch.org).

1106. Bautismos 1838–1841, March 17, 1838, film 665432, image 17, Registros Parroquiales, Iglesia Sagrario de San Miguel, Culiacán, Sinaloa, Mexico (FamilySearch, https://familysearch.org).

vi.   **Antonio Páez** was born about 1841 in Sataya; he married Luisa Hernández on April 10, 1875, in Culiacán.[1107]

vii.   **José Anastasio Páez** was born on January 22, 1841, in Culiacán, according to the baptismal record. He was baptized on April 10, 1841, at the church of the Sagrario de San Miguel in Culiacán.[1108] The baptismal record named José Manuel Palazuelos and María Juana Rojo as his *padrinos*.

172. Justo Palazuelos (María Juana Rafaela Rojo-7, María Nicolasa Esquer-6, Francisco Joseph-5, Juan Salvador-4, Salvador-3, Salvador-2, Blas-1) was born about 1810.

Justo Palazuelos and María de Jesús Castro were married on November 15, 1832, at the church of the Sagrario de San Miguel in Culiacán.[1109] The matrimonial record named José María Palazuelos and Manuel Avilés as witnesses to the marriage. The couple received a nuptial blessing on their wedding day. Parents of the bride and groom were named in the record.

María de Jesús Castro, daughter of Julián Castro and Josefa Montoya, was born about 1812 in Mocorito, Sinaloa. The cited marriage record noted that she had originated in Mocorito.

Justo Palazuelos and María de Jesús Castro had the following known children:

i.   **María Tomasa Gertrudis Palazuelos** was born on September 18, 1835, in Culiacán. The baptismal record stated that she was thirty-three days old when baptized. She was baptized on October 21, 1835, at the church of the Sagrario de San Miguel in Culiacán.[1110] The baptismal record named José Rafael Castro and Josefa Montoya as her *padrinos*.

ii.   **María del Carmen Palazuelos** was born on January 25, 1838, in Aguaruto, Sinaloa and was baptized on February 5, 1838, in Culiacán.[1111] She married Antonio Palazuelos on September 13, 1856, in Culiacán. [1112] She later married Luis Inzunza after January 24, 1863, in Culiacán.[1113]

1107. Matrimonios 1865–1883, April 10, 1875, film 673606, images 186–187, Registros Parroquiales, Iglesia Sagrario de San Miguel, Culiacán, Sinaloa, Mexico (FamilySearch, https://familysearch.org); Información matrimonial 1871–1873, April 6, 1875, film 673460, images 867–869, Registros Parroquiales, Iglesia Sagrario de San Miguel, Culiacán, Sinaloa, Mexico (FamilySearch, https://familysearch.org).
1108. Bautismos 1841–1847, April 10, 1841, film 665433, images 26–27, Registros Parroquiales, Iglesia Sagrario de San Miguel, Culiacán, Sinaloa, Mexico (FamilySearch, https://familysearch.org).
1109. Matrimonios 1830–1856, November 15, 1832, film 673379, image 61, Registros Parroquiales, Iglesia Sagrario de San Miguel, Culiacán, Sinaloa, Mexico (FamilySearch, https://familysearch.org).
1110. Bautismos 1831–1838, October 21, 1835, film 665431, image 376, Registros Parroquiales, Iglesia Sagrario de San Miguel, Culiacán, Sinaloa, Mexico (FamilySearch, https://familysearch.org).
1111. Bautismos 1831–1838, February 5, 1838, film 665431, image 600, Registros Parroquiales, Iglesia Sagrario de San Miguel, Culiacán, Sinaloa, Mexico (FamilySearch, https://familysearch.org).
1112. Matrimonios 1830–1856, September 13, 1856, film 673379, image 657, Registros Parroquiales, Iglesia Sagrario de San Miguel, Culiacán, Sinaloa, Mexico (FamilySearch, https://familysearch.org); Información matrimonial 1855–1856, August 20, 1856, film 673456, images 334–337, Registros Parroquiales, Iglesia Sagrario de San Miguel, Culiacán, Sinaloa, Mexico (FamilySearch, https://familysearch.org).
1113. Información matrimonial 1860–1867, January 23, 1863, film 673459, images 215–219, Registros Parroquiales, Iglesia Sagrario de San Miguel, Culiacán, Sinaloa, Mexico (FamilySearch, https://familysearch.org).

iii.   **Esteban de Jesús Palazuelos** was born on December 23, 1842, in Culiacán, according
to the baptismal record. He was baptized on January 3, 1843, at the church of the
Sagrario de San Miguel in Culiacán.[1114] The baptismal record named Manuel Palazuelos
and María Gertrudis Rodríguez as his *padrinos.*

iv.   **María Eugenia Palazuelos** was born on November 15, 1843, in San Pedro de Quilá,
Sinaloa and was baptized on November 27, 1843.[1115] She married José Víctor Palazuelos
on August 25, 1864, in Culiacán.[1116]

v.   **José Manuel Palazuelos** was born on March 6, 1846, in Sataya; he married María
Concepción Cabada on October 10, 1870, in Culiacán.[1117]

vi.   **María Mauricia Palazuelos** was born about 1851 in Culiacán; she married Manuel
Cardenas on February 4, 1871, in Culiacán.[1118]

vii.   **María Felipa Palazuelos** was born on February 5, 1851, in Culiacán, according to
the baptismal record. She was baptized on February 15, 1851, in Culiacán.[1119] The
baptismal record named Ysabel Castro as her *madrina.*

viii.   **María del Rosario Palazuelos** was born about 1856; she married Miguel Palazuelos
on November 15, 1876, in Culiacán.[1120]

173. **Casimiro Palazuelos** (María Juana Rafaela Rojo-7, María Nicolasa Esquer-6, Francisco
Joseph-5, Juan Salvador-4, Salvador-3, Salvador-2, Blas-1) was born about 1812.

Casimiro Palazuelos and María Josefa Niebla were married on August 31, 1842, at the church
of the Sagrario de San Miguel in Culiacán.[1121] The matrimonial record named Jesús Rojo and
Nicolás Vidales as witnesses to the marriage. Parents of the bride and groom were named in the
record. The couple received a nuptial blessing on the day they were married.

1114. Bautismos 1841–1847, January 3, 1843, film 665433, image 179, Registros Parroquiales, Iglesia Sagrario de
San Miguel, Culiacán, Sinaloa, Mexico (FamilySearch, https://familysearch.org).
1115. Bautismos 1841–1847, November 27, 1843, film 665433, image 251, Registros Parroquiales, Iglesia
Sagrario de San Miguel, Culiacán, Sinaloa, Mexico (FamilySearch, https://familysearch.org).
1116. Matrimonios 1856–1865, August 25, 1864, film 673380, image 296, Registros Parroquiales, Iglesia Sagrario
de San Miguel, Culiacán, Sinaloa, Mexico (FamilySearch, https://familysearch.org).
1117. Matrimonios 1865–1883, October 10, 1870, film 673606, image 110, Registros Parroquiales, Iglesia
Sagrario de San Miguel, Culiacán, Sinaloa, Mexico (FamilySearch, https://familysearch.org).
1118. Matrimonios 1865–1883, February 4, 1871, film 673606, image 113, Registros Parroquiales, Iglesia
Sagrario de San Miguel, Culiacán, Sinaloa, Mexico (FamilySearch, https://familysearch.org); Información
matrimonial 1871–1873, January 12, 1871, film 673460, images 810–812, Registros Parroquiales, Iglesia Sagrario
de San Miguel, Culiacán, Sinaloa, Mexico (FamilySearch, https://familysearch.org).
1119. Bautismos 1850–1854, February 15, 1851, film 666172, image 135, Registros Parroquiales, Iglesia Sagrario
de San Miguel, Culiacán, Sinaloa, Mexico (FamilySearch, https://familysearch.org).
1120. Matrimonios 1865–1883, November 15, 1876, film 673606, image 215, Registros Parroquiales, Iglesia
Sagrario de San Miguel, Culiacán, Sinaloa, Mexico (FamilySearch, https://familysearch.org); Información
matrimonial 1874–1876, October 15, 1876, film 673462, images 249–251, Registros Parroquiales, Iglesia Sagrario
de San Miguel, Culiacán, Sinaloa, Mexico (FamilySearch, https://familysearch.org).
1121. Matrimonios 1830–1856, August 31, 1842, film 673379, image 266, Registros Parroquiales, Iglesia Sagrario
de San Miguel, Culiacán, Sinaloa, Mexico (FamilySearch, https://familysearch.org).

María Josefa Niebla, daughter of Francisco Niebla and Juliana Murrieta, was born about 1824.

Casimiro Palazuelos and María Josefa Niebla had the following known children:

i. **Rafaela Palazuelos** was born on April 1, 1848, in Sataya, Sinaloa, and she was baptized on April 8, 1848.[1122] She married Carlos Borges on October 6, 1868, in Culiacán.[1123]

ii. **José Rafael Palazuelos** was born on October 24, 1852, in Culiacán and was baptized on December 12, 1852.[1124] He married Damiana Verdugo, about 1870. The marriage record has not been located.[1125] He later married Refugio Niebla on January 11, 1881, in Sinaloa.[1126]

iii. **Marcelino Palazuelos** was born on July 10, 1860, in Culiacán, according to the baptismal record. He was baptized on July 25, 1860, at the church of the Sagrario de San Miguel in Culiacán.[1127] The baptismal record named Justo Palazuelos as his *padrino*.

174. José Ignacio Dionisio Peñúñuri (María Balvanera Mallén de Navarrete-7, Gabriel-6, Vicente-5, Agustina Salvadora Esquer-4, Salvador-3, Salvador-2, Blas-1) was born in 1803 in Álamos. He was baptized on May 28, 1803, at the parish of the Purísima Concepción in Álamos.[1128] The baptismal record named Bachiller Felipe Villegas and Xaviera Padilla as his *padrinos*. The baptism took place at the chapel of La Aduana.

José Ignacio Dionisio Peñúñuri and Josefa Noriega had one known child:

i. **Florencio Peñúñuri** was born about 1845 in Batuc, Sonora; he married Ramona Yañes, about 1870. The marriage record has not been located. He died on December 10, 1910, in Batuc, Sonora.[1129]

1122. Bautismos 1847–1850, April 8, 1848, film 665434, image 111, Registros Parroquiales, Iglesia Sagrario de San Miguel, Culiacán, Sinaloa, Mexico (FamilySearch, https://familysearch.org).

1123. Información matrimonial 1871–1873, September 19, 1868, film 673460, images 160–162, Registros Parroquiales, Iglesia Sagrario de San Miguel, Culiacán, Sinaloa, Mexico (FamilySearch, https://familysearch.org); Matrimonios 1865–1883, October 6, 1868, film 673606, image 80, Registros Parroquiales, Iglesia Sagrario de San Miguel, Culiacán, Sinaloa, Mexico (FamilySearch, https://familysearch.org).

1124. Bautismos 1850–1854, December 12, 1852, film 666172, image 299, Registros Parroquiales, Iglesia Sagrario de San Miguel, Culiacán, Sinaloa, Mexico (FamilySearch, https://familysearch.org).

1125. Información matrimonial 1894, December 28, 1894, film 673467, images 380–382, Registros Parroquiales, Iglesia Sagrario de San Miguel, Culiacán, Sinaloa, Mexico (FamilySearch, https://familysearch.org).

1126. Matrimonios 1874–1905, January 11, 1881, film 676776, image 62, Registros Parroquiales, Iglesia de San Felipe y Santiago, Sinaloa, Sinaloa, Mexico (FamilySearch, https://familysearch.org).

1127. Bautismos 1858–1861, July 25, 1860, film 665497, image 344, Registros Parroquiales, Iglesia Sagrario de San Miguel, Culiacán, Sinaloa, Mexico (FamilySearch, https://familysearch.org).

1128. Bautismos 1796–1805, May 28, 1803, film 663995, image 199, Registros Parroquiales, Iglesia de La Purísima Concepción, Álamos, Sonora, Mexico (FamilySearch, https://familysearch.org).

1129. Deaths, 1862–1987, Civil Registration, December 10, 1910, [indexed subscription database online], images 164–165, Batuc, Sonora, Mexico (Ancestry, https://www.ancestry.com).

175. **Catharina María Loreto Josepha Ygnacia Gertrudis Ymaz Camacho** (Joseph María Ygnacio Pedro Mathias Severino-7, Joseph Mateo Miguel-6, Juan Miguel Gordiano-5, Salvadora Manuela Silvestra Esquer-4, Salvador-3, Salvador-2, Blas-1) was born on November 25, 1788, in Mexico City, according to the baptismal record. She was baptized on November 26, 1788, at the parish church of San Miguel Arcángel in Mexico City.[1130] The baptismal record named her grandparents, Escribano Publico Cirilo Joseph Camacho de Almonarriz and María Manuela Velasco y Negrín as her *padrinos.*

Catharina María Loreto Josepha Ygnacia Gertrudis Ymaz Camacho and José Francisco Pérez de León Aguiar y Seixas were married on February 19, 1807, at the parish of San Sebastián Mártir in Mexico City.[1131] The matrimonial record did not name *padrinos.* José Antonio Pérez de León, Petronila López, and José Prieto among other present were identified as witnesses to the marriage. The banns of marriage were waived by special dispensation. The wedding took place at the Casa de Santa Ynés at seven in the evening. The couple received a nuptial blessing on September 27, 1807.

José Francisco Pérez de León Aguiar y Seixas, son of Miguel Pérez de León and Micaela Aguiar, was born about 1787 in Santa María Guadalupe Tecalitlán, Diocese of Guadaljara. The cited baptismal record for his son provided José Francisco's place of birth.

José Francisco Pérez de León Aguiar y Seixas and Catharina María Loreto Josepha Ygnacia Gertrudis Ymaz Camacho had one known child:

    i.   **José Francisco María Julio Pérez de León Aguiar y Seixas** was born on December 20, 1807, in Mexico City, according to the baptismal record. He was baptized on December 21, 1807, at the parish church of the Asunción Sagrario Metropolitano in Mexico City.[1132] The baptismal record named Francisco Prieto as his *padrino.* The child's father was said to be from Santa María Guadalupe Tecalitlán, Diocese of Guadalajara. Capitán Miguel Pérez de León and Micaela Aguiar were named as paternal grandparents. José María Ymaz and Margarita Camacho were said to be the child's maternal grandparents.

176. **José María Antonio Francisco de Paula Juan Nepomuceno Luis Gonzaga Ymaz** (Manuel Joseph María Ygnacio-7, Pedro Martín Joseph Manuel-6, Juan Miguel Gordiano-5, Salvadora Manuela Silvestra Esquer-4, Salvador-3, Salvador-2, Blas-1) was born on February 15, 1799, in Mexico City. The cited baptismal record provided his date of birth. He was baptized on February 16, 1799, at the parish church of the Asunción Sagrario Metropolitano in Mexico City.[1133] The baptismal record named Lucas Arenas del Valle and María de Loreto de la Peña, his maternal grandparents, as his *padrinos.* Paternal grandparents were also named in the record.

1130. Bautismos de españoles 1782–1794, November 26, 1788, film 205944, image 362, Registros Parroquíales, Iglesia San Miguel Arcángel, Mexico City, Mexico (FamilySearch, https://familysearch.org).

1131. Matrimonios de españoles 1772–1809, February 19, 1807, film 37425, image 541, Registros Parroquíales, Iglesia San Sebastián Mártir, Mexico City, Mexico (FamilySearch, https://familysearch.org).

1132. Bautismos de españoles 1809–1813, December 21, 1807, film 35196, image 541, Registros Parroquiales, Iglesia Asunción Sagrario Metropolitano, Mexico City, Mexico (FamilySearch, https://familysearch.org).

1133. Bautismos de españoles 1799–1803, February 16, 1799, film 35194, image 120, Registros Parroquiales, Iglesia Asunción Sagrario Metropolitano, Mexico City, Mexico (FamilySearch, https://familysearch.org).

José María Antonio Francisco de Paula Juan Nepomuceno Luis Gonzaga Ymaz and María del Carmen Pérez Anca were married on September 20, 1820, at the parish church of Santa Veracruz in Mexico City.[1134] The matrimonial record named Manuel Ymaz and Ana María Ymaz as *padrinos*. Juan [illegible] and Francisco Visueto were named as witnesses to the marriage. The bride and groom were said to be twenty-two and twenty-one years of age, respectively. Parents of the bride and groom were named and the mother of the groom was said to have been deceased. The couple received a nuptial blessing on their wedding day. The cited marriage information record dated September 3, 1820, found no impediment to marriage for the couple. [1135] The fathers of the bride and groom both gave their permission for the couple to marry.

José María Antonio Francisco de Paula Juan Nepomuceno Luis Gonzaga Ymaz died on April 8, 1864, at the age of sixty-five in Mexico City. José was buried on April 9, 1864, at the church of Santa Veracruz in Mexico City.[1136] He received the last sacraments of the Catholic Church and was laid to rest at the Camposanto de Santa Paula. He was said to have been the widowed husband of Carmen Pérez.

José María Antonio Francisco de Paula Juan Nepomuceno Luis Gonzaga Ymaz and María del Carmen Pérez Anca had the following known children:

i. **Manuel José María Anastasio Francisco Nicolás de Santa Rita Ymaz** was born on April 15, 1821, in Mexico City, according to the baptismal record. He was baptized on April 16, 1821, at the parish church of Santa Veracruz in Mexico City.[1137] The baptismal record named the child's grandfather, José Manuel Ymaz, and Ana María Ymaz as his *padrinos*. Paternal and maternal grandparents were named. The child's mother was identified as "María de la Encarnación" in the record.

ii. **María Dominga Ana Josefa Severiana Francisca Nicolasa Ymaz** was born on February 21, 1823, in Mexico City, according to the baptismal record. She was baptized on February 21, 1823, at the parish church of Santa Veracruz in Mexico City.[1138] The baptismal record named Mariano Noreña and María Isabel Ymaz as her *padrinos*. Paternal and maternal grandparents were named in the record.

iii. **Mariano de la Concepción José Nicolás Domingo Francisco Juan Nepomuceno Benito Ymaz** was born on December 8, 1824, in Mexico City, according to the baptismal record. He was baptized on December 9, 1824, at the parish church of Santa Veracruz in Mexico City.[1139] The baptismal record named Manuel Ymaz

1134. Matrimonios de españoles 1760–1823, September 20, 1820, film 35851, image 859, Registros Parroquiales, Iglesia Santa Veracruz, Mexico City, Mexico (FamilySearch, https://familysearch.org).
1135. Información matrimonial 1818–1820, September 3, 1820, film 35879, images 850–852, Registros Parroquiales, Iglesia Santa Veracruz, Mexico City, Mexico (FamilySearch, https://familysearch.org).
1136. Defunciones y entierros 1848–1917, April 9, 1864, film 35961, image 773, Registros Parroquiales, Iglesia Santa Veracruz, Mexico City, Mexico (FamilySearch, https://familysearch.org).
1137. Bautismos de españoles 1804–1826, April 16, 1821, film 35826, image 665, Registros Parroquiales, Iglesia Veracruz, Mexico City, Mexico (FamilySearch, https://familysearch.org).
1138. Bautismos de españoles 1804–1826, February 21, 1823, film 35826, image 745, Registros Parroquiales, Iglesia Santa Veracruz, Mexico City, Mexico (FamilySearch, https://familysearch.org).
1139. Bautismos de españoles 1804–1826, December 9, 1824, film 35826, image 863, Registros Parroquiales, Iglesia Santa Veracruz, Mexico City, Mexico (FamilySearch, https://familysearch.org).

Cabanillas and María Isabel Ymaz del Valle as his *padrinos*. Paternal and maternal grandparents were named in the record.

iv.   **Manuel José Domingo Susano Francisco Nicolás Ymaz** was born on May 23, 1826, in Mexico City, according to the baptismal record. He was baptized on May 24, 1826, at the parish church of Santa Veracruz in Mexico City.[1140] The baptismal record named Manuel Ymaz and Dolores Ymaz as his *padrinos*. Paternal and maternal grandparents were named in the record.

v.   **José María Domingo Nicolás Mauricio Ymaz** was born on September 23, 1828, in Mexico City. The baptismal record provided his date of birth. He was baptized on September 23, 1828, at the church of San José de Carmelitas Descalzos in Mexico City.[1141] The baptismal record named Francisco Torres and Guadalupe Yglesias as his *padrinos*. Paternal and maternal grandparents were named in the record.

vi.   **María Josefa Dominga Lorenza Antonia Brígida Juana Nepomucena Ymaz** was born on August 10, 1831, in Mexico City, according to the baptismal record. She was baptized on August 11, 1831, at the parish church of Santa Veracruz in Mexico City.[1142] The baptismal record named Francisco Torres and María Dolores Ymaz as her *padrinos*. Paternal and maternal grandparents were named in the record.

vii. **María Dolores Petra Josefa Dominga Ymaz** was born on January 29, 1834, in Mexico City, according to the baptismal record. She was baptized on January 31, 1834, at the parish church of Santa Veracruz in Mexico City.[1143] The baptismal record named Francisco Cervantes and María Ymaz as her *padrinos*. Paternal and maternal grandparents were named in the record.

177. José María Nicolás Francisco Ymaz (Manuel Joseph María Ygnacio-7, Pedro Martín Joseph Manuel-6, Juan Miguel Gordiano-5, Salvadora Manuela Silvestra Esquer-4, Salvador-3, Salva-dor-2, Blas-1) was born on December 22, 1808, in Mexico City, according to the baptismal record. He was baptized on December 23, 1808, at the parish church of Santa Veracruz in Mexico City.[1144] The baptismal record named María Rita de Castro as his *madrina*. Paternal and maternal grandparents were named in the record.

José María Nicolás Francisco Ymaz and Nicolasa Urquiaga were married on June 28, 1854, at the parish church of Santa Veracruz in Mexico City.[1145] The matrimonial record named Francisco

---

1140. Bautismos de españoles 1804–1826, May 24, 1826, film 35826, images 992–993, Registros Parroquiales, Iglesia Santa Veracruz, Mexico City, Mexico (FamilySearch, https://familysearch.org).
1141. Bautismos de españoles 1826–1833, September 23, 1828, film 35827, image 282, Registros Parroquiales, Iglesia Santa Veracruz, Mexico City, Mexico (FamilySearch, https://familysearch.org).
1142. Bautismos de españoles 1826–1833, August 11, 1831, film 35827, image 672, Registros Parroquiales, Iglesia Santa Veracruz, Mexico City, Mexico (FamilySearch, https://familysearch.org).
1143. Bautismos de españoles 1833–1844, January 31, 1834, film 35828, image 26, Registros Parroquiales, Iglesia Santa Veracruz, Mexico City, Mexico (FamilySearch, https://familysearch.org).
1144. Bautismos de españoles 1804–1826, December 23, 1808, film 35826, image 197, Registros Parroquíales, Iglesia de Santa Veracruz, Mexico City, Mexico (FamilySearch, https://familysearch.org).
1145. Matrimonios 1824–1878, June 28, 1854, film 35852, image 756, Registros Parroquíales, Iglesia de Santa Veracruz, Mexico City, Mexico (FamilySearch, https://familysearch.org).

Cervantes and Jesús Hoara as *padrinos*. Manuel Torres and Fermín Fernández were named as witnesses to the marriage. Parents of the bride and groom were named, and all were said to have been deceased. The mother of the groom was identified as "María Zeferina" rather than "María Josefa." Her full name was likely "María Josefa Zeferina Arenas del Valle."

The marriage information record, dated June 13, 1854, claimed there was no impediment to marriage.[1146] The record stated that the couple had lived together for many years as though married, and that announcing the public banns of marriage would cause scandal to their children and to the community. The groom was said to be ill and that he desired to right his wrong of having lived out of wedlock. For that reason, the banns of marriage were dispensed.

Nicolasa Urquiaga, daughter of José Urquiaga and María de la Paz Gutiérrez, was born in 1812 in Mexico City.

José María Nicolás Francisco Ymaz and Nicolasa Urquiaga had the following known children:

i. **José Miguel Ymaz** was born on July 16, 1837, in Mexico City, according to the baptismal record. He was baptized on July 17, 1837, at the parish church of the Asunción Sagrario Metropolitano in Mexico City.[1147] The baptismal record named Francisco Cervantes and María del Carmen Pérez as his *padrinos*.

ii. **Juan José Joaquín Domingo Nicolás Francisco de Paula Ymaz** was born on March 30, 1842, in Mexico City, according to the baptismal record. He was baptized on April 2, 1842, at the parish church of Santa Veracruz in Mexico City.[1148] The baptismal record named José María Ymaz and Ana María Ymaz as his *padrinos*.

iii. **José María Joaquín Valentín Francisco de Paula Ymaz** was born on February 14, 1845, in Mexico City, according to the baptismal record. He was baptized on February 15, 1845, at the parish church of Santa Veracruz in Mexico City.[1149] The baptismal record named Francisco Cervantes and Ana María Ymaz as his *padrinos*.

178. José Trinidad Feliciano Quirós y Mora (María Ygnacia Campoy-7, María Manuela Esquer-6, Pedro Fernando-5, Miguel Fernando Simón-4, Salvador-3, Salvador-2, Blas-1) was born in 1794 in San Pedro de Quilá, Sinaloa. The cited matrimonial record provided her place of birth. He was baptized on November 19, 1794, at the church of Santa María de Quilá in San Pedro de Quilá, Sinaloa.[1150] The baptismal record named Francisco Anselmo Verdugo y Chávez as his *padrino*. The cited matrimonial record provided his place of birth.

1146. Información matrimonial 1853–1854, June 13, 1854, film 35891, images 496–499, Registros Parroquíales, Iglesia de Santa Veracruz, Mexico City, Mexico (FamilySearch, https://familysearch.org).
1147. Bautismos de españoles 1837–1839, July 17, 1837, film 35204, image 159, Registros Parroquiales, Iglesia Asunción Sagrario Metropolitano, Mexico City, Mexico (FamilySearch, https://familysearch.org).
1148. Bautismos de españoles 1833–1844, April 2, 1842, film 35828, image 998, Registros Parroquíales, Iglesia de Santa Veracruz, Mexico City, Mexico (FamilySearch, https://familysearch.org).
1149. Bautismos de españoles 1844–1853, February 15, 1845, film 35829, images 73–74, Registros Parroquíales, Iglesia de Santa Veracruz, Mexico City, Mexico (FamilySearch, https://familysearch.org).
1150. Bautismos 1786–1815, November 19, 1794, film 674060, image 60, Registros Parroquiales, Iglesia Santa María de Quilá, Quilá, Sinaloa, Mexico (FamilySearch, https://familysearch.org).

José Trinidad Feliciano Quirós y Mora and María Francisca Gil Samaniego were married on November 19, 1822, at the parish of the Purísima Concepción in Álamos.[1151] The matrimonial record named Pascual Gómez and Dolores Anguís as *padrinos*. José María Quirós, Joaquín Gil, Juan Padilla, among others present were named as witnesses to the marriage. The couple received a nuptial blessing the the day of their marriage. Parents of the bride and groom were named. The marriage ceremony took place at the home of the bride.

María Francisca Gil Samaniego, daughter of José Gil Samaniego and Josefa Anguís, was born about 1804 in Álamos.

179. María Isabel Quirós y Mora (María Ygnacia Campoy-7, María Manuela Esquer-6, Pedro Fernando-5, Miguel Fernando Simón-4, Salvador-3, Salvador-2, Blas-1) was born about 1795.

María Isabel Quirós y Mora and José María Almada were married on April 18, 1813, at the church of the Purísima Concepción in Álamos.[1152] The matrimonial record named José Jesús Almada and Isabel Quirós as *padrinos*. Antonio Almada, Pedro Quirós, among others present, were witnesses to the marriage. Parents were named in the record, and the parents of the groom were said to be deceased.

José María Almada, son of Antonio Almada y Reyes and María de la Luz Alvarado, was born about 1793. He died on September 29, 1866, at the age of 73 in Mazatlán, Sinaloa. He was buried on September 30, 1866, at the Santa Iglesia Cathedral in Mazatlán, Sinaloa.[1153] The burial record noted that he was originally from Álamos.

José María Almada and María Isabel Quirós y Mora had the following known children:

    i.   **Maria Rafaela Florentina Almada** was born on February 4, 1814, in Álamos, according to the baptismal record. She was baptized on February 26, 1814, at the church of the Purísima Concepción in Álamos.[1154] The baptismal record named José María Quirós [y Mora] and María Ygnacia Campoy, as her *padrinos*. Paternal and maternal grandparents where also named as the child's *padrinos*. She died on May 16, 1826, at the age of twelve in Álamos. Maria was buried on May 17, 1826, at the church of the Purísima Concepción in Álamos.[1155] Her burial service was held with *cruz alta, capa, incensario, cajón y tres mesas*. She was interred in a burial site valued at fifty pesos, having received the last sacraments of the Catholic Church before death.

1151. Matrimonios 1797–1833, 1846–1868, 1872–1877, November 19, 1822, film 666566, images 268–269, Registros Parroquiales, Iglesia de La Purísima Concepción, Álamos, Sonora, Mexico (FamilySearch, https://familysearch.org).

1152. Matrimonios 1779–1817, April 18, 1813, film 666565, image 528, Registros Parroquiales, Iglesia de La Purísima Concepción, Álamos, Sonora, Mexico (FamilySearch, https://familysearch.org).

1153. Defunciones 1849–1920, September 30, 1866, film [none], image 276, Registros Parroquiales, Santa Iglesia Catedral, Mazatlán, Sinaloa, Mexico (FamilySearch, https://familysearch.org). .

1154. Bautismos 1791–1796, 1805–1815, February 26, 1814, film 663996, image 470, Registros Parroquiales, Iglesia de La Purísima Concepción, Álamos, Sonora, Mexico (FamilySearch, https://familysearch.org).

1155. Defunciones 1809–1842, May 17, 1826, film 666997, image 116, Registros Parroquiales, Iglesia de La Purísima Concepción, Álamos, Sonora, Mexico (FamilySearch, https://familysearch.org).

ii.   **José Antonio Anselmo Almada** was born on January 17, 1815, in Álamos, acccording to the baptismal record. He was baptized on January 18, 1815, at the church of the Purísima Concepción in Álamos.[1156] The baptismal record named Jesús Almada y Reyes and María Trinidad Salido as his *padrinos.*

iii.   **Antonio Anselmo Demetrio Almada** was born on December 20, 1817, in Álamos, according to the baptismal record. He was baptized on December 25, 1817, at the church of the Purísima Concepción in Álamos.[1157] The baptismal record named Antonio Almada y Reyes and Manuela Zavala as his *padrinos.* Paternal and maternal grandparents were named in the record.

iv.   **María Guadalupe Paula Almada** was born on March 2, 1819, in Álamos, according to the baptismal record. She was baptized on March 14, 1819, at the church of the Purísima Concepción in Álamos.[1158] The baptismal record named Ygnacio Almada and María Rafaela Zayas as her *padrinos.*

v.   **Francisco Anselmo Almada**, was born on February 24, 1820, in Álamos and was baptized on February 26, 1820.[1159] He married María Damiana Josefa Manuela Almada after October 20, 1840, in Álamos. The marriage record has not been located.[1160]

vi.   **Jorge Marcelino Almada** was born on April 23, 1821, in Álamos and was baptized on April 26, 1821, in Álamos.[1161] He married María Dolores Eduviges Petra Almada after October 21, 1840, Álamos. The marriage record has not been located.[1162]

vii.   **José María Anselmo Damaso Almada** was born on December 11, 1822, in Álamos, according to the baptismal record. He was baptized on December 14, 1822, at the church of the Purísima Concepción in Álamos.[1163] The baptismal record named María Manuela Esquer as his *madrina.*

1156. Bautismos 1791–1796, 1805–1815, January 18, 1815, film 663996, image 489, Registros Parroquiales, Iglesia de La Purísima Concepción, Álamos, Sonora, Mexico (FamilySearch, https://familysearch.org).

1157. Bautismos 1816–1825, 1827–1829, December 25, 1817, film 663997, image 52, Registros Parroquiales, Iglesia de La Purísima Concepción, Álamos, Sonora, Mexico (FamilySearch, https://familysearch.org).

1158. Bautismos 1816–1825, 1827–1829, March 14, 1819, film 663997, image 78, Registros Parroquiales, Iglesia de La Purísima Concepción, Álamos, Sonora, Mexico (FamilySearch, https://familysearch.org).

1159. Bautismos 1816–1825, 1827–1829, February 26, 1820, film 663997, image 104, Registros Parroquiales, Iglesia de La Purísima Concepción, Álamos, Sonora, Mexico (FamilySearch, https://familysearch.org).

1160. Información matrimonial 1840–1849, October 20, 1840, film 663814, images 92–98, Registros Parroquiales, Iglesia de La Purísima Concepción, Álamos, Sonora, Mexico (FamilySearch, https://familysearch.org).

1161. Bautismos 1816–1825, 1827–1829, April 26, 1821, film 663997, image 146, Registros Parroquiales, Iglesia de La Purísima Concepción, Álamos, Sonora, Mexico (FamilySearch, https://familysearch.org).

1162. Información matrimonial 1840–1849, October 21, 1840, film 663814, images 29–33, Registros Parroquiales, Iglesia de La Purísima Concepción, Álamos, Sonora, Mexico (FamilySearch, https://familysearch.org).

1163. Bautismos 1816–1825, 1827–1829, December 14, 1822, film 663997, images 209–210, Registros Parroquiales, Iglesia de La Purísima Concepción, Álamos, Sonora, Mexico (FamilySearch, https://familysearch.org).

viii.   **Manuel Antonio Almada** was born in 1824 in Álamos. He was baptized on January 13, 1824, at the church of the Purísima Concepción in Álamos.[1164] The baptismal record named Manuel de la Breña and Josefa Palacios as his *padrinos.*

ix.   **Carlos Isidro Almada** was born in 1825 in Álamos. He was baptized on May 25, 1825, at the church of the Purísima Concepción in Álamos.[1165] The baptismal record named Carlos Espinosa de los Monteros and Rafaela Almada as his *padrinos.*

x.   **José María Tranquilino Almada** was born about 1826 in Álamos; he married Rufina Ibarra on July 18, 1853, in Álamos.[1166]

xi.   **Cosme Damián Almada** was born in 1828 in Álamos. He was baptized on September 27, 1828, at the church of the Purísima Concepción in Álamos.[1167] The baptismal record named Pedro Serrano and María Rafaela Almada as his *padrinos.*

xii.   **Rafael Almada** was born about 1828 in Álamos; he married María Trinidad Almada on July 14, 1853, in Álamos.[1168] He died on January 28, 1899, in Álamos.[1169]

xiii.   **María Cornelia Tomasa Almada** was born in 1829 and was baptized on January 18, 1829, in Álamos.[1170] She married Jesús Pioquinto Almada about 1847 in Álamos and died on died January 4, 1910, in Álamos.[1171]

xiv.   **José Diego Almada** was born in 1830 in Álamos and was baptized on November 12, 1830.[1172] He married Luz Quirós y Mora on February 16, 1855, in Álamos.[1173]

1164. Bautismos 1816–1825, 1827–1829, January 13, 1824, film 663997, image 254, Registros Parroquiales, Iglesia de La Purísima Concepción, Álamos, Sonora, Mexico (FamilySearch, https://familysearch.org).

1165. Bautismos 1816–1825, 1827–1829, May 25, 1825, film 663997, images 321–322, Registros Parroquiales, Iglesia de La Purísima Concepción, Álamos, Sonora, Mexico (FamilySearch, https://familysearch.org).

1166. 1797–1833, 1846–1868, 1872–1877, July 18, 1853, film 666566, image 372, Registros Parroquiales, Iglesia de La Purísima Concepción, Álamos, Sonora, Mexico (FamilySearch, https://familysearch.org).

1167. Bautismos 1816–1825, 1827–1829, September 27, 1828, film 663997, image 517, Registros Parroquiales, Iglesia de La Purísima Concepción, Álamos, Sonora, Mexico (FamilySearch, https://familysearch.org).

1168. Matrimonios 1797–1833, 1846–1868, 1872–1877, July 14, 1853, film 666566, image 372, Registros Parroquiales, Iglesia de La Purísima Concepción, Álamos, Sonora, Mexico (FamilySearch, https://familysearch.org).

1169. Nombre del testador: Rafael Almada, 1899, Álamos, Sonora, Mexico, Testamentos de Sonora, 1786–1910 (El Colegio de Sonora, http://www.colson.edu.mx:8080/testamentos.

1170. Bautismos 1816–1825, 1827–1829, September 18, 1829, film 663997, image 554, Registros Parroquiales, Iglesia de La Purísima Concepción, Álamos, Sonora, Mexico (FamilySearch, https://familysearch.org).

1171. Nombre del testador: Almada Viuda de Almada Cornelia, 1901, Álamos, Sonora, Mexico, Testamentos de Sonora, 1786–1910 (El Colegio de Sonora, http://www.colson.edu.mx:8080/testamentos/principal.aspx).

1172. Bautismos 1829–1838, November 12, 1830, film 666560, image 47, Registros Parroquiales, Iglesia de La Purísima Concepción, Álamos, Sonora, Mexico (FamilySearch, https://familysearch.org).

1173. Matrimonios 1797–1833, 1846–1868, 1872–1877, February 16, 1855, film 666566, image 389, Registros Parroquiales, Iglesia de La Purísima Concepción, Álamos, Sonora, Mexico (FamilySearch, https://familysearch.org).

xv. **Isidoro Vicente Almada**, was born in 1832 in Álamos and was baptized on April 2, 1832 in Álamos.[1174] He married María Dolores Goyeneche on February 16, 1855, in Álamos.[1175]

xvi. **María Isabel Almada** was born on June 5, 1833, in Álamos. She was baptized on June 5, 1833, at the church of the Purísima Concepción in Álamos.[1176] The baptismal record named Antonio Benigno Almada and Guadalupe Almada as her *padrinos*.

xvii. **María Ascención Teodora Almada** was born in 1835 in Álamos. She was baptized on May 29, 1835, at the church of the Purísima Concepción in Álamos.[1177] The baptismal record named Guadalupe Almada as her *madrina*. She died on December 10, 1909, at the age of seventy-four in Álamos.[1178] Her last will and testament stated that she died of cardiac paralysis at the age of seventy-five, rather than seventy-four as calculated from her baptismal record.

xviii. **María Balvanera Josefa Almada** was born in 1836 in Álamos. She was baptized on November 26, 1836, at the church of the Purísima Concepción in Álamos.[1179] The baptismal record named José María Almada and Carmen Almada as her *padrinos*.

xix. **Pomposo Almada** was born in 1838 in Álamos; he married María Josefa Reteguini on October 26, 1858, in Álamos.[1180]

180. **José Manuel Tiburcio Quirós y Mora** (María Ygnacia Campoy-7, María Manuela Esquer-6, Pedro Fernando-5, Miguel Fernando Simón-4, Salvador-3, Salvador-2, Blas-1) was born about 1800 in Culiacán. The cited marriage record provided his place of birth.

José Manuel Tiburcio Quirós y Mora and María Petra Fox were married on May 7, 1823, at the church of the Purísima Concepción in Álamos.[1181] The matrimonial record named José María Almada and Ysabel Quirós y Mora as *padrinos* to the marriage. Ygnacio Fox and Pedro Quirós y Mora, among others, were said to have been present at the ceremony. The couple received a nuptial blessing on the day of their marriage. Parents of the bride and groom were named in the record, and the father of the bride was said to have been deceased at the time. The couple

1174. Bautismos 1829–1838, April 2, 1832, film 666560, image 107, Registros Parroquiales, Iglesia de La Purísima Concepción, Álamos, Sonora, Mexico (FamilySearch, https://familysearch.org).
1175. Matrimonios 1797–1833, 1846–1868, 1872–1877, February 16, 1855, film 666566, image 389, Registros Parroquiales, Iglesia de La Purísima Concepción, Álamos, Sonora, Mexico (FamilySearch, https://familysearch.org).
1176. Bautismos 1829–1838, June 5, 1833, film 666560, image 157, Registros Parroquiales, Iglesia de La Purísima Concepción, Álamos, Sonora, Mexico (FamilySearch, https://familysearch.org).
1177. Bautismos 1829--1838, May 29, 1835, film 666560, image 303, Registros Parroquiales, Iglesia de La Purísima Concepción, Álamos, Sonora, Mexico (FamilySearch, https://familysearch.org).
1178. Nombre del testador: Almada Ascención, 1896, Álamos, Sonora, Mexico, Testamentos de Sonora, 1786–1910 (El Colegio de Sonora, http://www.colson.edu.mx:8080/testamentos/principal.aspx).
1179. Bautismos 1829–1838, November 26, 1836, film 666560, image 375, Registros Parroquiales, Iglesia de La Purísima Concepción, Álamos, Sonora, Mexico (FamilySearch, https://familysearch.org).
1180. Matrimonios 1797–1833, 1846–1868, 1872–1877, October 26, 1858, film 666566, image 426, Registros Parroquiales, Iglesia de La Purísima Concepción, Álamos, Sonora, Mexico (FamilySearch, https://familysearch.org).
1181. Matrimonios 1797–1833, 1846–1868, 1872–1877, May 7, 1823, film 666566, images 276–277, Registros Parroquiales, Iglesia de La Purísima Concepción, Álamos, Sonora, Mexico (FamilySearch, https://familysearch.org).

received a marriage dispensation for having been related in the fourth degree of consanguinity, meaning they were third cousins.

José Manuel Tiburcio Quirós y Mora died before December 26, 1868. The cited matrimonial record for his son Domingo stated that his father was deceased on the date of his marriage. His name appeared as "José Manuel Quirós" in most of his children's baptismal records. "José Manuel Tiburcio Quirós" was used in the baptismal record of his daughter Bernarda.

María Petra Fox, daughter of Luis Juan Joseph Raphael Fox and María Gertrudis Esquer, was born in 1797 in Álamos. She was baptized on July 8, 1797, at the church of the Purísima Concepción in Álamos.[1182] The baptismal record named Juan Fox and María Loreto Anguís as her *padrinos*. She died before December 3, 1868.[1183] The cited matrimonial record for her son Domingo stated that his mother was deceased on the date of his marriage, December 3, 1868.

José Manuel Tiburcio Quirós y Mora and María Petra Fox had the following known children:

i. **José Pascual Bernardino de Jesús Quirós y Mora** was born in 1824 in Álamos. He was baptized on May 20, 1824, at the church of the Purísima Concepción in Álamos.[1184] The baptismal record named José María Quirós and María Ignacia Campoy as his *padrinos*.

ii. **Juan José Secundino Quirós y Mora** was born in 1827 in Álamos. He was baptized on July 5, 1827, at the church of the Purísima Concepción in Álamos.[1185] The baptismal record named José María Almada and María Isabel Quirós as his *padrinos*.

iii. **María Josefa Quirós y Mora** was born in 1829 in Álamos. She was baptized on March 29, 1829, at the parish of the Purísima Concepción in Álamos.[1186] The baptismal record named Ygnacio Fox and María Gertrudis Esquer as her *padrinos*. The baptism took place at the chapel of La Aduana.

iv. **Bernarda María del Carmen Quirós y Mora** was born in 1832 in Álamos. She was baptized on August 20, 1832, at the church of the Purísima Concepción in Álamos.[1187] The baptismal record named the officiating priest, Father Nicolás Quirós, and Isabel Quirós as her *padrinos*.

v. **Francisco María de Candelaria Quirós y Mora** was born on January 29, 1835, in Álamos, according to the baptismal record. He was baptized on February 2, 1835, at

---

1182. Bautismos 1796–1805, July 8, 1797, film 663995, image 47, Registros Parroquiales, Iglesia de La Purísima Concepción, Álamos, Sonora, Mexico (FamilySearch, https://familysearch.org).
1183. Matrimonios 1851–1909, 1911–1917, December 3, 1868, film 687240, image 153, Registros Parroquiales, Iglesia de Nuestra Señora de Guadalupe, Altar, Sonora, Mexico (FamilySearch, https://familysearch.org).
1184. Bautismos 1816–1825, 1827–1829, May 20, 1824, film 663997, image 272, Registros Parroquiales, Iglesia de La Purísima Concepción, Álamos, Sonora, Mexico (FamilySearch, https://familysearch.org).
1185. Bautismos 1816–1825, 1827–1829, July 5, 1827, film 663997, image 454, Registros Parroquiales, Iglesia de La Purísima Concepción, Álamos, Sonora, Mexico (FamilySearch, https://familysearch.org).
1186. Bautismos 1816–1825, 1827–1829, March 29, 1829, film 663997, image 542, Registros Parroquiales, Iglesia de La Purísima Concepción, Álamos, Sonora, Mexico (FamilySearch, https://familysearch.org).
1187. Bautismos 1829–1838, August 20, 1832, film 666560, image 123, Registros Parroquiales, Iglesia de La Purísima Concepción, Álamos, Sonora, Mexico (FamilySearch, https://familysearch.org).

the church of the Purísima Concepción in Álamos.[1188] The baptismal record named
José María Almada and María Isabel Quirós as his *padrinos*.

    vi.   **Domingo Quirós y Mora** was born about 1840 in Álamos; he married María de
Jesús Carmelo on December 3, 1868, in Altar, Sonora.[1189]

181. **Pedro Francisco Quirós y Mora** (María Ygnacia Campoy-7, María Manuela Esquer-6,
Pedro Fernando-5, Miguel Fernando Simón-4, Salvador-3, Salvador-2, Blas-1) was born on
August 4, 1804, in Álamos, according to the baptismal record. He was baptized on August 5,
1804, at the church of the Purísima Concepción in Álamos.[1190] The baptismal record named
Elías González y Zayas and his sister, Agueda González y Zayas as his *padrinos*.

Pedro Francisco Quirós y Mora and María Balvanera de Lamadrid were married about
1824.[1191] The matrimonial record has not been located. Proof of marriage was provided in the
civil marriage record of his son Emigdio Quiros and Dolores Zayas dated June 8, 1876.

Pedro Francisco Quirós y Mora and María Balvanera de Lamadrid had the following known
children:

    i.   **Luz Quirós y Mora** was born about 1832; she married José Diego Almada on
February 16, 1855, in Álamos.[1192]

    ii.   **José Clemente Quirós y Mora** was born on November 23, 1836, in Álamos,
according to the baptismal record. He was baptized on November 25, 1836, at the
church of the Purísima Concepción in Álamos.[1193] The baptismal record named José
de los Reyes Gil y Tagle and Manuela Tagle as his *padrinos*.

    iii.   **Lauro Liberato Quirós y Mora** was born in 1838 in Álamos; he married Martina
Almada on June 22, 1860, in Álamos.[1194]

1188. Bautismos 1829–1838, February 2, 1835, film **666560**, image 261, Registros Parroquiales, Iglesia de La
Purísima Concepción, Álamos, Sonora, Mexico (FamilySearch, https://familysearch.org).
1189. Matrimonios 1851–1909, 1911–1917, December 3, 1868, film **687240**, image 153, Registros
Parroquiales, Iglesia de Nuestra Señora de Guadalupe, Altar, Sonora, Mexico (FamilySearch, https://
familysearch.org).
1190. Bautismos 1796–1805, August 5, 1804, film **663995**, image 246, Registros Parroquiales, Iglesia de La
Purísima Concepción, Álamos, Sonora, Mexico (FamilySearch, https://familysearch.org).
1191. Marriages 1870–1914, Civil Registration, June 8, 1876, [indexed subscription database online], image
266, Álamos, Sonora, Mexico (Ancestry, https://www.ancestry.com).
1192. Matrimonios 1797–1833, 1846–1868, 1872–1877, February 16, 1855, film **666566**, image 389,
Registros Parroquiales, Iglesia de La Purísima Concepción, Álamos, Sonora, Mexico (FamilySearch, https://
familysearch.org).
1193. Bautismos 1829–1838, November 25, 1836, film **666560**, image 375, Registros Parroquiales, Iglesia de La
Purísima Concepción, Álamos, Sonora, Mexico (FamilySearch, https://familysearch.org).
1194. Matrimonios 1797–1833, 1846–1868, 1872–1877, June 22, 1860, film **666566**. images 445–446,
Registros Parroquiales, Iglesia de La Purísima Concepción, Álamos, Sonora, Mexico (FamilySearch, https://
familysearch.org).

iv.   **Emigdio María de Jesús Quirós y Mora** was born on August 5, 1843, in Álamos and was baptized on August 7, 1843.[1195] He married Dolores Zayas on August 4, 1876, in Álamos.[1196]

v.   **José Manuel de Jesús María y José Quirós y Mora** was born on June 3, 1847, in Álamos, according to the baptismal record. He was baptized on June 3, 1847, at the church of the Purísima Concepción in Álamos.[1197] The baptismal record named Francisco Torrez and his wife María Dolores de Lamadrid as his *padrinos.*

vi.   **José de Jesús Quirós y Mora** was born in 1851 in Álamos. He was baptized on June 3, 1851, at the church of the Purísima Concepción in Álamos.[1198] The baptismal record named Bárbara Ceballos as his *madrina.*

vii.   **María Guadalupe Quirós y Mora** was born on August 18, 1854, in Álamos, according to the baptismal report. She was baptized on August 21, 1854, at the church of the Purísima Concepción in Álamos.[1199] The baptismal record named Lauro Quirós and María Luz Quirós as her *padrinos.*

viii.   **Aureo Antonio Quirós y Mora** was baptized on August 26, 1856, at the church of the Purísima Concepción in Álamos.[1200] The baptismal record named Diego [illegible] and Luz Quirós as his *padrinos.* He was born on August 23, 1856, in Álamos, according the the baptismal record.

ix.   **María Isabel Quirós y Mora** was born in 1857 in Álamos. She was baptized on August 9, 1857, at the church of the Purísima Concepción in Álamos.[1201] The baptismal record named Emigdio Quirós and Paula Quirós as her *padrinos.*

x.   **Balvarena Quirós y Mora** was born in 1859 in Álamos. She was baptized on February 24, 1859, at the church of the Purísima Concepción in Álamos.[1202] The baptismal record was not located.

1195. Bautismos 1838–1871, August 7, 1843, film 667000, image 275, Registros Parroquiales, Iglesia de La Purísima Concepción, Álamos, Sonora, Mexico (FamilySearch, https://familysearch.org).
1196. Nacimientos, matrimonios, defunciones 1870–1914, August 4, 1876, film [none], image 577, Civil Registrations, Álamos, Sonora, Mexico (FamilySearch, https://familysearch.org); Marriages 1870–1914, Civil Registration, June 8, 1876, [indexed subscription database online], image 266, Álamos, Mexico (Ancestry, https://www.ancestry.com).
1197. Bautismos 1838–1856, June 3, 1847, film 667000, image 323, Registros Parroquiales, Iglesia de La Purísima Concepción, Álamos, Sonora, Mexico (FamilySearch, https://familysearch.org).
1198. Bautismos 1838–1856, June 3, 1851, film 663998, image 435, Registros Parroquiales, Iglesia de La Purísima Concepción, Álamos, Sonora, Mexico (FamilySearch, https://familysearch.org).
1199. Bautismos 1854–1861, August 21, 1854, film 663999, image 18, Registros Parroquiales, Iglesia de La Purísima Concepción, Álamos, Sonora, Mexico (FamilySearch, https://familysearch.org).
1200. Bautismos 1854–1861, August 26, 1856, film 663999, image 129, Registros Parroquiales, Iglesia de La Purísima Concepción, Álamos, Sonora, Mexico (FamilySearch, https://familysearch.org).
1201. Bautismos 1854–1861, August 9, 1857, film 663999, image 194, Registros Parroquiales, Iglesia de La Purísima Concepción, Álamos, Sonora, Mexico (FamilySearch, https://familysearch.org).
1202. Bautismos 1854–1861, February 24, 1859, film 663999, image [not located], Registros Parroquiales, Iglesia de La Purísima Concepción, Álamos, Sonora, Mexico (FamilySearch, https://familysearch.org).

xi. **Angel Fabian Quirós y Mora** was born on January 20, 1863, in Álamos, according to the baptismal record. He was baptized on January 24, 1863, at the church of the Purísima Concepción in Álamos.[1203] The baptismal record named Lauro Quirós and Martina Aranda as his *padrinos*.

xii. **Paula Quirós y Mora** was born in 1846 in Álamos; she married Quinino Corbala on October 23, 1863, in Álamos.[1204]

182. **Juan Hipólito de Jesús Quirós y Mora** (María Ygnacia Campoy-7, María Manuela Esquer-6, Pedro Fernando-5, Miguel Fernando Simón-4, Salvador-3, Salvador-2, Blas-1) was born on August 13, 1817, according to the baptismal record. He was baptized on August 19, 1817, at the church of the Purísima Concepción in Álamos.[1205] The baptismal record named José Almada y Reyes and Isabel Quirós y Mora as his *padrinos*. He had previously received the waters of baptism out of necessity should he not survive. Grandparents were named in the record.

Juan Hipólito de Jesús Quirós y Mora and María Josefa Torres Gil were married after June 19, 1847, at the church of the Purísima Concepción in Álamos.[1206] The matrimonial record has not been located. The cited marriage investigation dated June 19, 1847, provided evidence of marriage.

1203. Bautismos 1861–1863, January 24, 1863, film 663499, image 162, Registros Parroquiales, Iglesia de La Purísima Concepción, Álamos, Sonora, Mexico (FamilySearch, https://familysearch.org).
1204. Matrimonios 1797–1833, 1846–1868, 1872–1877, October 23, 1863, film 666566, image 467, Registros Parroquiales, Iglesia de La Purísima Concepción, Álamos, Sonora, Mexico (FamilySearch, https://familysearch. org).
1205. Bautismos 1816–1825, 1827–1829, August 19, 1817, film 663997, image 43, Registros Parroquiales, Iglesia de La Purísima Concepción, Álamos, Sonora, Mexico (FamilySearch, https://familysearch.org).
1206. Información matrimonial 1840–1849, June 19, 1847, film 663814, images 347–352, Registros Parroquiales, Iglesia de La Purísima Concepción, Álamos, Sonora, Mexico (FamilySearch, https://familysearch. org).

Index

9 781653 379910